DYNAMIC MANAGEMENT AND LEADERSHIP IN EDUCATION

This book presents a new integrated theory of dynamic management and leadership in one comprehensive approach. It offers a new way of looking at the field, drawing on a wide body of research and practice in the fields of leadership and management, across all sectors in education and more broadly.

The book focuses on management against a backdrop of leadership theory. Including examples of practice and application in schools, colleges and universities, it uses a range of historical leadership approaches to scaffold different management techniques that are known to work in effective organisations. It explores the overlap between management and leadership as dynamic theoretical and practical activities, merging the two together into a holistic model that can be applied by managers working in educational settings. Its twenty-six chapters also consider the praxis of educational leadership and management from political, economic and ethical perspectives in relation to issues such as equity and widening participation, and outline how 'managership' impacts on student achievement.

Offering a unique balance of theory and practice, across school, college and university sectors, the book will be of great interest to researchers, academics, graduate students and practitioners in the field of educational leadership and management, and will be important reading for all stakeholders in the area of educational effectiveness and improvement.

Anthony Kelly is Professor of Education and formerly Head of Department at the University of Southampton. He researches in the areas of educational effectiveness and improvement, policy and leadership.

DYNAMIC MANAGEMENT AND LEADERSHIP IN EDUCATION

High Reliability Techniques for Schools and Universities

Anthony Kelly

Routledge
Taylor & Francis Group

LONDON AND NEW YORK

First published 2022
by Routledge
2 Park Square, Milton Park, Abingdon, Oxon OX14 4RN

and by Routledge
605 Third Avenue, New York, NY 10158

Routledge is an imprint of the Taylor & Francis Group, an informa business

British Library Cataloguing-in-Publication Data
A catalogue record for this book is available from the British Library

Library of Congress Cataloging-in-Publication Data
A catalog record has been requested for this book

ISBN: 978-1-032-10821-6 (hbk)
ISBN: 978-1-032-10822-3 (pbk)
ISBN: 978-1-003-21722-0 (ebk)

DOI: 10.4324/9781003217220

Typeset in Bembo
by SPi Technologies India Pvt Ltd (Straive)

In memory of
Dr Patricia Elliott-Kelly, MD
1921–2016

CONTENTS

FIGURES

TABLES

1

INTRODUCTION

Leadership is the great modern narrative, like religion in the 19th century, and managers the new priestly class. Although its effect is probably overestimated in the short term and underestimated in the long term, it is convenient for education policy-makers to assert that good leadership makes for good schools. This assumption offers a cost-effective route to system-wide improvement: simply recruit enough good leaders, put one in every school, college and university department, and the problem of underperformance is solved. It was the premise upon which the UK's National College for School Leadership (NCSL), as it was then called, was founded in the 1990s.[1] It adopted a pragmatic approach: leaders were not born with certain desirable traits, as some theorists would have us believe; rather, leadership was an activity for which candidates could be trained, so that it just required a suitably qualified cohort of headteachers to be let loose on the education system, and society would see a transformation in the fortunes of schools. Amid the euphoria that followed (and survived) the election of the New Labour government in May 1997, these approaches dovetailed well with the growing dominance of management consultants and "Third-Way" public-private initiatives in the state sector. In keeping with this political creed, the National College introduced a qualification for those being prepared to transform schooling in Britain – the National Professional Qualification for Headship (NPQH) – without which advancement to the top jobs in schools became virtually impossible. Alongside many established practitioners, some academics were recruited by the national college to deliver NPQH in bite-size modules, while others stayed put in universities to ride shotgun on the venture. The college was a prolific funder of research into why what it was doing was right, and those who played ball prospered under the regime. With several notable exceptions, there was a paucity of criticism. It was hard to dismount the tiger!

DOI: 10.4324/9781003217220-1

Outside the college, euphemisms like "entrepreneurship" kept pace with the proliferation of acronyms, as commonplace concepts dating back to Shakespearean times were reborn in the public sector as divine revelation and made to sound pensive. Slogans such as "catch a colleague doing something good today" were as common in business leadership lectures as they were on London Underground posters. But the lifespan of an acronym in education is short, and in 2013 NCSL was merged with the Teaching Agency (TA) to become the National College for Teaching and Leadership (NCTL) with an expanded remit to include "senior children's services leaders and more generic professional leadership development". The closure of NCSL had been considered by some policy-makers within the new Conservative government because they thought it had failed to deliver what had been promised for it: UK schools had *not* been "transformed"; educational attainment in England had *not* improved dramatically in international comparison tests; recruitment to the teaching profession had *not* increased in quality or quantity; and the recruitment and retention of headteachers had plummeted across the system.

In fairness, most of the staff at NCSL – those who sought experience as well as those best qualified to bestow it – were excellent and delivered good courses in a very flexible and pedagogically blended way, and the professionals who underwent NPQH generally found the course informative. So what went wrong? Well, in theory, NCSL (or any equivalent form of national structure) and a national qualification for headship are sensible ideas, but the ideology that gave birth to them was by its nature bureaucracy-intensifying and de-professionalising to an extent that recruits to the profession, and those already in it, found overwhelming, intrusive and in some cases downright offensive. This was also the case in the UK with medical professionals in the National Health Service, with legal professionals in the justice system and, in fact, with all public sector occupations. The only profession left standing after two decades of "reform" was that of management consultant, whose firms had grown fat on overspending government initiatives and finding public problems for every private sector solution. The NCSL/NCTL was not badly run – not by any stretch of the imagination – but it became flawed in its implementation when the heavy hand of government was simultaneously undermining the integrity of the very profession it was attempting to create.

The second problem was that the idea of a national college for the profession of educational leadership ran out of political capital. It had been a New Labour initiative which perfectly reflected the zeitgeist of that era, but the new Conservative government that saw Michael Gove enjoying himself as Secretary of State for Education regarded the institution as part of what he called 'The Blob' (Garner, 2014): an army of cultural terrorists, left-wing pilgrims and haughty academics whose purpose was to thwart the bijou 'progressive' radicalism that meant so much to Notting Hill Tories. The Blob was to Michael Gove and advisor Dominic Cummings an oligopolistic cabal of 1960s hippy self-interest, which had come together to stop Britain from having a world-class education service. Was he wrong? Michael Gove was an intelligent and diligent education minister, although blessed with more self-confidence than was strictly necessary for his minor role in government. He certainly overstated the conspiracy, as Department for Education (DfE) insiders like his former Permanent Secretary Sir David Bell pointed out at the time, but it was perfectly predictable that as general factotum in David Cameron's kitchen cabinet, Minister Gove would dismantle the comfortable consensus that pervaded the education academy at that time. The fact that in 2013 some 100 academics signed a letter to *The Independent* newspaper expressing fears that Gove's new national curriculum would disadvantage students with its insistence on rigour and would "threaten creativity in the classroom", while representing the views of most in the research community, served only to justify Gove and his supporters in their view that his ideological reformation was being opposed by an equally ideological counter-reformation. In any event, it became impossible during this period to offer any intelligent critique of either side, as anecdote was substituted for evidence, and actual evidence was ignored in the struggle to be righteous. The arguments on both sides did not vary much except in the allegorical garb of their discourse. Certain nouns had to have verbal adjectives and gerunds assigned: "paradigms" had to be "shifting"; "stakeholder views" needed to be "captured"; the only "comprehensives" were "bog-standard" ones; and the "suburbs" where the middle classes horded their cultural capital were invariably "leafy".

The reality is that few if any children come home from school enthusing about the government's Academy programme or worrying about The Blob's paradigm wars. Nor are they distracted by how "distributed" leadership is at the school. Their world is the world of the classroom. What child has *not* come home to complain about having been assigned certain teachers for certain subjects or ranting at the unfairness of subject choices and the impossibility of their timetables? In short, it is *management* and not *leadership* that circumscribes the realm of students and their educational attainment.

Leadership versus management

The differences and overlaps between management and leadership are in part cultural and in part a question of definition. For decades, leadership has assumed a pre-eminence and superiority over management. There was never a "national college" for school *management*. To many politicians and policy-makers, but not to academics or practitioners, a leader is a Churchillian figure who knows what others do not: a seer that alone can navigate the unpredictable; a pilot in times of crisis, which in education, is every day! In contrast, a manager is seen as a mere functionary: an employee operationalising the policies that others higher up the food chain have determined; a lesser professional. An "administrator", outside the US at least, is even lower on the totem pole: a bureaucrat; a secretary. Peter Drucker famously (but somewhat fatuously) promoted this view when he quipped that "management was about doing things right; leadership was about doing the right things". For him the role of management was to improve operational performance, maximise income, minimise costs and increase productivity, whereas the purpose of leadership was to establish an organisation's priorities, set and sell its vision, and allocate resources to achieve that vision. In education, we could rescue the Drucker dictum somewhat by adding a *philosophical* layer that leadership is about doing the right things *for the right reasons*, meaning that it demands proper motivation and must stand for something; for example, the belief that all children irrespective of socio-economic background should benefit from formal schooling. And we could then add a *moral* layer on top of that by saying that leadership is about doing the right things for the right reasons *and in the right way*, meaning that leaders should acknowledge ethical boundaries; for example, that it is not 'good leadership' to better the lot of poor students by stealing money or by cooking the books to get extra staff.[2]

Setting aside the differences between management and leadership, most policy-makers, practitioners and academics agree on certain things: that leadership is both a responsibility and a power; that management is important; and that the two are inextricably linked in some hard-to-define way that we could call "managership". This book explores the overlap between the two: between *management* as a dynamic theoretical activity – the act of creating order and structure that would not otherwise exist – and *leadership* as a practical exercise. We call this "dynamic" in the sense that it reverses the usual polarity. It sees management not as practice but as theory, and leadership not as theory but as practice, and the constant toggling of the two is a dynamism that creates high reliability in the effective oversight of educational institutions. Let us take a moment to discuss each of these terms in turn.

Praxis, theoria and poiesis

Aristotle held that there were three basic human activities: *praxis* (doing), *theoria* (thinking) and *poiesis* (creating something that did not previously exist). Praxis is the process by which a theory is actualised. It is a skill enacted and refers to the act of applying or practising ideas. In Ancient Greek, the word "praxis" referred to an activity willingly pursued by *free* people, and we see that reflected today in education in the fact that schools, colleges and universities are staffed by *unencumbered* professionals. The Polish philosopher August Cieszkowski used the term to mean "action oriented *towards changing* society" (McLellan, 1970, my emphasis), and his contemporary Karl Marx used the term to refer to the "free and creative activity through which man *creates and changes his world* and himself" (Petrovic, 1991, my emphasis). Both have obvious links to transformational leadership theory as it relates to managing change, which is discussed in Chapters 23–25.

Corresponding to these three Aristotelian activities are three types of knowledge: *practical*, whose objective is action; *theoretical*, whose objective is truth; and *poietical*, whose objective is production. This book presents dynamic leadership as a combination of all three. Traditionally, it is assumed that leadership is the theoria and management the praxis, but we reject this dichotomy as false. Both leadership and management have "thinking" and "doing" facets, and between them dynamically is the job of running an organisation and poietically bringing something into being – order, structure and a culture of high expectation – that would not otherwise exist.

This last point is discussed in detail in Chapter 8 because one of the historical biases in leadership theory has been the presumption that schools are inherently orderly and stable places, and that the job of leader is therefore to keep disorder at bay, rather than inherently *dis*orderly *un*stable places, where the job is to *create* (poiesis) order.

Defining dynamic leadership

The adjective "dynamic", when applied to a process or system, refers to constant change or activity. When applied to a person, it denotes someone who is positive in attitude and full of energy and new ideas. In the scientific sense, it is the branch of physics concerned with the study of forces and movement. It is used intentionally in this book in all three senses to define a combinatory form of management and leadership. Dynamic leadership refers to the practice of switching from reflective practice as a leader – planning, deciding, inspiring and motivating – to high reliability implementation as a manager – auditing, overseeing, remediating, changing, monitoring and rewarding. It assumes reciprocal effects: not only does leadership affect management, but it is in turn affected by it.

Dynamic leadership also refers to *context*: that schools, colleges and universities are situated in their own dynamic market, and they are dynamically disordered and chaotic organisations. Chaos itself is a dynamic system, transitive and evolving in nature, with random and unpredictable behaviour within. It is sensitive to initial conditions – the so-called "butterfly effect" – which means that each point in the system is closely approximated by other points with significantly different future trajectories, so that an arbitrarily small disturbance to a current situation can lead to a significantly different chain of future events.

This is not to suggest that traditional leadership theory is devoid of "dynamism". It is not. More than 70 years ago, Lewin (1948) used applied action research to study *group dynamics* and their relationship to organisational development. Belbin followed later by developing his famous team-role descriptors in order to understand *team dynamics*, and Porter's Competitive Analysis model provided an insight into the *dynamics* of markets. In the 1990s, Peter Senge, who developed the notion of a learning organisation in his book *The Fifth Discipline,* conceptualised organisations as *dynamic* systems in various states of continuous adaptation. What is different about dynamic leadership is the belief that the chaos – and this is not a pejorative term – inherent in schools, colleges and universities means that the slightest adjustment to its boundary conditions can result in a totally different scenario to manage, and therefore that scenario planning has limited application. Of course, it helps educational organisations to understand and plan for the most likely unknown, but the dynamic leader accepts that the exact trajectory of educational change is unknowable, is prepared for an (as yet) unrecognisable future and is happy to limit long-term decision-making, which is counter-intuitive in a culture that values foresight as a characteristic of leadership. Dynamic leadership accepts the complexity that arises when cause and effect are separated in time and space in such a way as to make consequences unknowable.

Dynamic leadership of learning organisations (as schools, colleges and universities must be) relies on restless learning and networks that allow dispersed individuals (as teachers, lecturers and researchers must be) to connect together flexibly to solve problems and respond to opportunities. Charisma or "presence" – that inner clarity which is unhindered by doubt or anxiety – plays a part in this dynamism. This is not to dismiss traditional behavioural, contingency or transformational approaches, but dynamic leadership sees leadership and management as coupled together, like the role of leader and follower; not necessarily interchangeable, but co-dependent and mutually influencing. This is not to reject management (or leadership) as driven by technique. Tools and routines are essential for enabling action, and they are presented aplenty in this book: scorecards and dashboards (see Chapter 14), matrices and grids (see Chapter 18), ways of measuring responsibility (see Chapter 20) and metrics for evaluating jobs (see Chapter 21). They are part of the poiesis (knowledge whose aim is production of the new) and part of the general praxis (know-how that is practical). They are not just menial accessories, as traditional theory would have us believe. Tools and routines shape, enable and constrain the dynamic practice of leadership and, in their regular patterns and repetitions, are known to be positively correlated with leader effectiveness (Bass, 1990; Yukl, 2006).

Dynamic leadership *is* management. They are not two opposing forces: one theoretical and aspirational, the other practical and menial. Drucker's dichotomy is false and unhelpful. Leadership and management are constituent parts of the same dynamic binary. Effective managers know this and embrace it, although it increases uncertainty and chaos as well as the size of the skill set required to do the job. Dynamic leadership both creates and depends upon high reliability management. It is in the nature of high reliability organisations and their leaders that they seek to produce and reproduce reliability, constantly trying to improve and intervening both to prevent errors and failures and to cope and recover quickly when errors and failures do occur. That is what dynamic management and leadership is about.

Defining the education context

National training colleges and qualifications for leaders failed to transform schooling and educational outcomes, not just in the UK but in many developed countries, because they trained leaders for a *static* role that does not exist, ignoring the unpredictable, the uncomfortable and the immeasurable. Dynamic leadership need not fall into this trap, but it does acknowledge the relevance of the education *setting*. What differentiates education and similar professional settings from commercial and production ones? Firstly, staff in schools, colleges and universities are equally qualified *as professionals*. That is not to say that all teachers, tutors, lecturers, professors and researchers have the same qualification, but they all pass the same threshold for admission into the profession. One headteacher might have a BA and another an MSc, while a third might have a PhD, but they are all equally qualified *as headteachers*. Qualifications over and above the threshold are superfluous. When these three headteachers come together at a conference, they have parity *as headteachers*.

Similarly, in universities, some professors have doctorates, others have additional advanced doctorates like a DSc; yet more do not have doctorates at all. However they all have parity *as professors* in (say) their eligibility for fellowships of learned societies and academies.

This situation is not unique to education. In the legal profession, some barristers have higher university degrees; others have none. What qualifies them as barristers is the fact that (in England) they have been "called to the bar" as a member of one of the four Inns of Court. When they appear before a judge, they all have parity *as barristers*. It is a binary condition: someone is either qualified or not. This affects how managership is enacted in education. It is a situation that belongs to a certain category of professional settings. It is *not* about the size of the organisation. Universities, for example, are usually among the biggest employers in any given location and have some of the biggest real estate too. It is about the nature and parity of those being led, an idea that has a long tradition in politics. The Whig tract of 1709, *Vox Populi, Vox Dei*,[3] asserts that there is no form of leadership that would see:

> one person rather than another have the sovereign administration of affairs, or have power over many, *who are by nature all equal, being of the same rank*.
>
> (My emphasis)

Secondly, the educational setting differs in its complexity and moral imperative. Schools, colleges and universities – but particularly schools – deliver a service that uniquely, is also a human right. (Justice is a human right too, although arguably barristers deliver legal advice through the court system, not justice.) Teachers deliver education in a way that is unique. It is more than the egregious quantities of commemorative tat found in ancient schools and universities: plaques, busts and memorabilia with carved exhortations to remember "Mr Chips" and "Colley Minor" who "fell in the Great War". It is more than the anachronisms and brutalities sold by long-established fee-paying private schools. It is about the moral imperative of leading the delivery of a basic human entitlement without which civilisation itself disappears.

Defining high reliability

High reliability organisations are organisations that succeed in avoiding catastrophes despite the fact that they operate in unforgiving contexts where the risk of failure is high and operations are complex. They need to work error-free, "first time, every time". High Reliability Organisation Theory emerged from Normal Accident Theory (Roberts, 1989; Rochlin, 1996) and from some important case studies:

- The 1977 Air Traffic Control (ATC) disaster at Tenerife airport in Spain when two large passenger jets collided on the runway resulting in 583 fatalities, is the deadliest accident to date in aviation history. Flights had been diverted to Tenerife airport from the larger Gran Canaria airport because of a terrorist threat, and the airport had become congested. The accident was caused largely by misunderstandings in radio communications between the aircraft and ATC, which had a lasting influence on the industry, precipitating the introduction of standardised phraseology in all ATC radio communications worldwide.

- The Three Mile Island nuclear accident, which involved the meltdown in 1979 of a reactor at the Three Mile Island nuclear generating station in Pennsylvania, USA, remains to this day the most significant accident ever in a US commercial nuclear power plant.
- The 1984 Bhopal disaster in India, caused by a gas leak at the Union Carbide pesticide plant, is still considered one of the world's worst industrial disasters. Over 500,000 people were exposed to a highly toxic gas, from which nearly 4,000 died.

Normal Accident Theory (NAT) and High Reliability Organisation Theory (HROT) agree that interactive complexity and tight-coupling can lead to cascading failure, but the two theories hold different views on whether or not those malfunctions are inevitable and the extent to which they are manageable. Serious shortcomings in high-risk operations can be prevented through a combination of organisational design, culture and the management of risk and choice. NAT sees human interaction with the system as the *cause* of accidents, which are regarded as inevitable and impossible to foresee or prevent. In contrast, HROT sees human interaction with systems as a way to *prevent* accidents, and holds that high-risk organisations *can* function very well despite their complexity. Within HROT, one view (e.g. Rochlin, 1993) is that such organisations are reliability-*seeking* rather than reliability-*achieving*, so they are distinguished not by a zero malfunction rate, but rather by their effective management of risk through 'organisational control of both hazard and probability'. Both NAT and HROT accept that high reliability organisations are characterised by their efforts to increase attentiveness across the organisation and by encouraging 'collective mindfulness' (Weick & Sutcliffe, 2001; Weick et al., 1999).

Sam Stringfield, David Reynolds and Gene Schaffer (2008) applied HROT to education, making Air Traffic Control their preferred exemplar of a complex organisation where society simply does not accept failure, even when counterbalanced by many years of earlier successes. They added several characteristics of high reliability organisations to the already established list (Roberts & Rousseau, 1989). We further expand that list here, bearing in mind that while many 'ordinary' effective organisations, including schools, display some of these high reliability characteristics, high reliability organisations display them all simultaneously.

- High reliability organisations are hyper-complex organisations with a great variety of 'moving parts' and many critical outcomes happen simultaneously.
- They come into being when both society and the professionals involved believe that failure to achieve their objectives would be disastrous, and they institute inspection regimes to achieve their aims *every time*.

- They have an organisation-wide sense of vulnerability, a widely distributed sense of responsibility and accountability and an abiding concern for misunderstandings, and they are very precautionary.
- High reliability organisations are very sensitive to unexpected changes, so situational awareness is extremely important to these organisations and to their managers.
- They have clear and limited goals, shared at all levels of the organisation. High reliability requires focus. It is not possible to be highly reliable when the number of tasks and aims is huge and distracting.
- They are alert to emerging failures or lapses in performance. "Small failures in key systems are monitored closely because they can cascade into major problems". For this reason they have access to large datasets, which are goal-relevant, triangulated, available in real time and regularly accessed and cross-checked.
- High reliability organisations are preoccupied with failure. They treat anomalies as symptoms of a problem, so errors are reported promptly. Organisational weaknesses that contribute to small errors also contribute to larger problems.
- They standardise formal decision-making processes and working practices; that is, they turn repeated tasks into Standard Operating Procedures to spread best practices throughout the organisation.
- They have many decision-makers in a network that is characterised by systems "redundancy"; that is, having at least one backup. Redundancy removes single points of failure. It eliminates dependence on a single process or person by providing multiple options in the event of failure.
- They have a level of accountability that does not exist in other organisations. Substandard performance or deviations from standard procedures are not tolerated.
- There is immediate feedback about decisions, and all staff are encouraged to identify flaws in Standard Operating Procedures. High reliability organisations *reward* those who find flaws and who help remedy them, in the manner of Genba Kaizen, which we discuss in Chapter 9. High reliability organisations are reluctant to simplify interpretations but take deliberate steps to understand *thoroughly* the work environment. They know that the operating environment is very complex, so they look across work boundaries to identify and solve problems, and (in the best tradition of Genba Kaizen) welcome diversity of experience and opinion.
- The severity and scale of any possible failure precludes learning through experimentation, so high reliability organisations ensure regular targeted professional development and compulsory training for everyone. They make extensive use of peer observation and peer communication.
- They have rigorous performance and job evaluation, which we discuss in Chapters 20 and 21. Monitoring is not perceived by staff as surveillance, and there is no perceived loss of professional autonomy. Experience and necessity have taught everyone that reliability depends on good feedback and the frank exchange of professional views in a constructive manner.

- High reliability organisations are hierarchies with multiple levels, each with its own control and regulating mechanisms, but during times of crisis, they defer to the person with the expertise on the frontline, regardless of hierarchical rank. During a crisis, decisions are made on the front line, and authority devolves to the person who can solve the problem, very much in the tradition of follow-ership discussed in Chapter 5. In military organisations, this doctrine is called "mission command": the belief that the leader in the field is always right and acts in accordance with the situation on the ground, and is therefore allowed maximum discretion.
- They forestall and contain errors and crises, and require leaders and staff to shape the social infrastructure of the organisation to establish a culture of safety. This is essentially about creating a "mindful" organisation where individuals interact continuously to develop a shared understanding of processes, crisis situations and the ability to react.
- High reliability organisations recover from errors. Errors will happen, but high reliability organisations are not paralysed by them.
- Time factors are compressed in high reliability organisations; that is, cycles of significant activity occur frequently and are tightly coupled with no slack. There is reciprocal interdependence across many units and levels, as a result of which these organisations prioritise reliability over efficiency.

Most pertinently for the purposes of this book, the Stringfield et al. (2008) project found that the part played by a school leader is critical in high reliability organisations in education. When a headteacher is focused on high reliability goals but open-minded as to their specifics and dynamic as to how they are achieved, significant gains can be made. Dynamic leadership, using the management techniques described in this book, ensures that the high reliability characteristics just listed obtain in the school, college or university. As Stringfield et al. (2008: 9) themselves say, high reliability organisations and their characteristics are not stable but are "dynamic and regularly evolving".

A brief morphology of leadership theory

This is a book about management set against the backdrop of different leadership theories and practices. It is not an academic review. It is a book for practitioners, using a panoptic view of historical leadership approaches to scaffold a range of management techniques that are known to work in effective organisations. It assumes only that effective schools, colleges and universities need good management as well as good leadership, and that the two are so entwined and co-dependent that they should be discussed alongside each other. Taken together, they can create high reliability organisations in education.

No single book (or series of books) could possibly capture the extraordinary range of theory in the fields of management and leadership; so from necessity, the theoretical scaffolding used in the book is simple. We identify four basic families of theory, although these are not always grouped together in this way in the literature. They are not exhaustive, and there are inevitable overlaps. In order of historical development, the typology consists of trait theories, behavioural theories, situational or contingency theories, and transformational theories. They fall largely into the *theoria* (thinking) category of Aristotle's scheme, but not completely. Moral leadership and cultural leadership, for example, both discussed in Chapter 17, slot better into the *praxis* (doing) category that Marx called "ethical" or "self-creative". Within these four broad family types lurk many individual theories: democratic, distributed, strategic, transactional, charismatic, populist, networked, virtual, purposeful, invisible, trans-national and so on. Some suffer from hasty generalisation and are based on insufficient evidence. Others cherry-pick data on the basis of predetermined conclusions and suffer from the so-called Texas Sharpshooter fallacy.[4] Still more are not theories at all, but rather aspirations. Some parts of the field have suffered from truisms and *de trop* assertions – people who own carts are more likely to own horses – and inserted adjectives that simply define leadership in terms that favour that particular theory. For example, distributed theory, which views leadership as a democratic process with leaders and followers working together on tasks, defines leadership *a priori* as "a set of activities that are *designed by organisational members* to influence the knowledge or practices of other organisational members". It is clear that the democratic element is already built into the definition. If this is the definition of leadership, it *must* be distributed!

In a similar way, trait theory defines leadership as "the exercise of formal authority by someone with the exceptional gifts to affect the motivation and practice of subordinates". Well, if this is the definition of leadership, it *must* be linked to having certain traits! And so on for moral, authentic, behavioural and transformational types. Sometimes, then, leadership becomes its own definition, and by definition, then, there is no shortage of evidence to support it. This is not to dismiss these theories or theorists. The author is not in search of heresy. Some of the finest and most original minds in academia, especially in educational research, have ploughed the fields of leadership, school improvement and educational effectiveness. Spillane's (2006) distributed theory is a case in point. It is widely and properly respected as one of the best in the field. However, running alongside these genuine academic efforts to hypothesise, theorise and test is a parallel universe of consultants and commentators who squeeze obscurity into these theories like toothpaste from a tube. Their whimsy is fortunately not accorded much importance in education, but they torture the field with neologisms and platitudes and *obfuscate* what is a critical component of effectiveness in schools and universities. Educational managership is important. It is not a commercial product: a washing powder that washes whiter than white; a golf club that brings your game to the next level; a watch that is already a family heirloom. Demands on it are changing all the time, as we have seen during the Covid-19 pandemic, and if we do not perceive its true nature clearly through the obfuscation, we cannot respond to its demands.

The second problem with a distinct morphology for educational leadership and management is that most theories are interrelated anyway and the contrast between competing approaches is not as distinct as one might suppose. It is what Freud called "*der Narzissmus der kleinen Differenzen*" (the narcissism of small differences). The development of the field has never been linear; it has been cyclical, with many eddies! In the 1950s, Maslow made case studies of what he called "the master race of people": the great and the good of his day, like Einstein, Kuhn, Thoreau and Eleanor Roosevelt. He wrote that "the study of crippled, stunted, immature, and unhealthy specimens can yield only a cripple psychology and a cripple philosophy" (Maslow, 1954: 236) and when he studied the student population, he studied the healthiest 1% (Mittelman, 1991). Maslow held that people who have become self-actualised share certain *traits*, so although his work gave rise to behavioural theory, it retained elements of the trait theory it replaced. Similarly, Fiedler's (1964, 1966, 1967) contingency theory was based on his decade-long work on leadership traits and group effectiveness (Fiedler, 1958), and Yukl's (2006) participative leadership was linked *ab initio* to Fiedler's model. Hunt's work in the 1970s on functional leadership, a subset of situational leadership, also leaned towards trait theory. All this is not as surprising as it might seem because most of the theorists were themselves linked! Douglas McGregor, the founder of modern democratic management and a leading theorist in the behavioural camp, considered Warren Bennis his protégé, although Bennis himself places his work in both transformational and contingency camps. Both served as professors at the MIT Sloan School of Management. Peter Senge, another professor at MIT, closes this circle with his transformational approach in which leadership is about modern 'traits' like being passionate, having an inner voice and a sense of destiny, instilling faith and offering hope. And Spears (2010) took a similar view in his work on servant leadership. Even at the managerial end of the spectrum, where it is easier to be distinctive because the literature is more technical, we see for example the focus on task in the Blake and Mouton behavioural-theory grid survive as a defining feature of what later became distributed leadership, which in turn drew on Mintzberg's (1989, 1992) organisational framework model.

The point here is that the development of leadership and management theory as a field is not a linear progression and the term 'evolution', often applied to it, is slightly misleading. There are cycles of reinforcement, replacement and reinvention between the four main families used to scaffold this book, and there are many eddy currents of disturbance within each. It is a pattern of motifs within a ring-cycle of four larger leitmotifs. This is not unique to the leadership and management field – it can be seen in many disciplines, from the hard sciences to mathematics and historiography – and it is not problematic *per se*, but it just makes it difficult to construct a clearly differentiated morphology.

The layout of the book

This book concentrates on management and leadership in the belief that both are essential to the core purpose of overseeing the effective delivery of formal education. It is a book for managers and practitioners, which uses a simple four-way typology of historical leadership approaches to present a range of management techniques.

Where appropriate, those leadership approaches are critiqued, but the purpose is not to diminish previous contributions to the field or to dismiss certain types of research. Theory is the distillation of practitioner experience, and both leadership and management experience are as critical in the education sector as they are in the commercial world; perhaps more so. To debate and decide the right things to do, and to have a rationale for doing them, is essential in schools, colleges and universities. Educational leadership has a moral dimension in establishing priorities in relation to issues such as equity and widening participation that go to the heart of what organisations like schools and universities are all about, and its effectiveness is the extent to which the manager or leader achieves the output required of such a role. A leader's main job, like that of a manager, is to be effective.

This book is laid out in 26 chapters. The remaining chapters cover the following:

2. Trait leadership theory
3. Charismatic leadership and the Core Quadrants
4. Participative leadership and De Bono's Six Thinking Hats
5. Behavioural theories: dynamic leadership, followership and style
6. Behavioural theories: motivational, authentic and transactional leadership
7. Situational and contingency theories of leadership and management
8. Keeping dysfunction at bay, or creating order?
9. Genba Kaizen
10. Managing innovation and change
11. Approaches to intellectual capital
12. Dynamic leadership and intellectual capital
13. Process improvement
14. Scorecards and dashboards
15. Structures and systems
16. Three levels of leadership and self-mastery
17. Moral leadership and cultural leadership
18. Matrices and grids
19. Pay and reward
20. Measuring responsibility
21. A profile guide chart method for job evaluation
22. Measuring competition and competitiveness
23. Transformational theory: team and network leadership
24. Transformational theory and change: the dynamic leadership of risk and choice
25. Transformational theory and vision leadership
26. Distributed, instructional and virtual leadership

And finally ...

It is difficult to measure effectiveness in organisations like schools, colleges and universities because the correlations between inputs and educational outcomes are uncertain. Most of the criteria currently used to gauge it are subjective: the extent to which staff are involved in decision-making; the appropriateness of the leadership shown by senior managers; student satisfaction surveys like the UK's National Student Survey (NSS);[5] peer assessment of research productivity like the UK's Research Excellence Framework (REF)[6]; and so on. They all have one thing in common: the belief that good management and good leadership are necessary for success. This book seeks to merge both in an education setting; to bring together the *why*, *how* and *wherefore* of doing things right, because that is what matters to students and what links effectiveness directly to staff performance and student achievement. The focus is on combining leadership and management to form one holistic 'dynamic' model that can be used by those working in schools, colleges and universities. Hopefully the reader will see it as a *new* formulation rather than a *re*-formulation, and will accept the author's apologies for adding yet another leadership adjective to the long list.

Notes

1 The National College for School Leadership was an executive agency of the UK's Department for Education (DfE). On 1 April 2013, it was merged with the Teaching Agency (TA) to become the National College for Teaching and Leadership (NCTL). The college offers headteachers, principals, middle leaders and senior children's services personnel opportunities for professional leadership development.

2 The 2004 embezzlement scandal in the Roslyn School District in New York is discussed in Chapter 19.

3 This was expanded the following year as *The Judgment of Whole Kingdoms and Nations*, written (probably) by Robert Ferguson.

4 The person who fires a gun at a barn door and then paints a target around the closest cluster of bullet holes as evidence of expert marksmanship!

5 The National Student Survey is a high-profile annual survey of half a million students across the UK. It gathers opinions from all final-year undergraduate degree students about their experience in further and higher education, asking them to provide feedback on their courses at college and university. The survey is conducted by Ipsos MORI on behalf of the Office for Students. It was launched for universities in 2005 with Further Education colleges joining in 2008. At the time of writing, the questionnaire has a core set of 27 attitude questions assessing aspects of the student learning experience, supplemented by open-ended questions to capture any particular positive or negative aspects that the students wish to highlight.

6 The Research Excellence Framework (REF) in the UK is an assessment undertaken every six or seven years on behalf of the UK government to gauge the quality of research in British universities.

2

TRAIT LEADERSHIP THEORY

Trait theories suggest that leadership can be attributed to the possession of various extraordinary qualities, like energy, courage, foresight and persuasiveness. Therefore, one only needs to define these leadership qualities for one to be able to identify those leaders who were born (or raised) to do the job. The theory holds that any system, whether military, educational or commercial, should pinpoint these individuals so that they can immediately – perhaps after a short period of induction – be given the reins of office. Trait theory sees leadership as an integrated pattern of personal characteristics that foster effective practice across a variety of group and organisational situations (Zaccaro, 2007; Zaccaro et al., 2004). It is a modern take on Carlyle's 'Great Man' theory,[1] according to which great leaders are born with the necessary characteristics that make them naturally suited to leadership roles: charisma, confidence, superior intelligence, heroic courage and social intelligence. It assumes that leadership is innate – nature rather than nurture – and that great leaders are born to (or destined for) their roles. Leadership is seen as unique only to a select number of individuals who possess certain immutable traits that cannot be developed (Galton, 1869). Although its provenance can be traced to an even earlier era,[2] the popularity of the Great Man theory can be attributed to the pre-eminence of the 19th-century historian Thomas Carlyle (1795–1881), reflecting his view that the 'history of the world was the biography of great men' (Carlyle, 1841). This view of history[3] was strongly endorsed by philosophers such as Hegel (whose subtle view was that the great leader uncovers an *inevitable* future rather than creates one), Kierkegaard and Max Weber, the inventor of bureaucratic management.

DOI: 10.4324/9781003217220-2

History of trait leadership theory

Early research on leadership looked at people who were successful leaders – mostly those who had achieved their position through birth and inherited wealth – and found some credence in the theory; although unsurprisingly, people from poor backgrounds, who had few (if any) opportunities to lead, were in short supply. This led sociologist Herbert Spencer (1820–1903) to suggest, as an alternative interpretation, that leaders were not 'born', but were the product of their social state. In *The Study of Sociology*, he wrote that before a person can remake society, society must make the person (Spencer, 1873: 35). Spencer, inventor of Social Darwinism and coiner of the phrase 'survival of the fittest', believed that attributing historical events to great individuals was unscientific. Others supported him by making a logical, rather than a sociological, criticism; namely, if leadership were simply a set of innate characteristics, then all those who had the traits should eventually find themselves in leadership positions, and this is simply not the case.

In fairness to Carlyle, his Great Man theory does not claim that *all other* factors are unimportant and inconsequential in determining events; just that great leaders are *the* decisive factor because of their unique talents and that those in authority are there because of destiny and necessity. William James (1842–1910), the influential US philosopher, educator and one of the founders of American psychology, defended this view and refuted Spencer's criticism. James saw the unique physiological and psychological nature of leaders as the deciding factor in making them great, and they in turn were the deciding factor in changing their environment, although the extent of the change depended on the receptiveness of the environment to the leader's stimulus. The 'unique genetic anomalies' in the brains of great leaders, 'the personal tone' of their minds and their 'spontaneous variations of genius, which are independent of social environment' and 'not present in lesser mortals', made this so, according to James – although it is difficult to think of a less appropriate explanation for efficacious leadership in schools and universities than this!

Francis Galton in *Hereditary Genius* (1869) solidified Carlyle's Great Man theory by asserting that the traits that leaders possess were immutable and could not be developed. But over the course of the early 20th century, there was a subtle shift away from the Carlyle–Galton view in that there was a growing dilution of the assumption that leadership traits resided only in a select number of people (Judge et al., 2002). This post-Galton version of trait leadership was widely accepted by the early 1950s, when the need for more leaders in the business of post-war reconstruction encouraged the view that personality traits were insufficient *in themselves* in predicating leader effectiveness (Mann, 1959; Stogdill, 1948) and that leadership was something that could be developed in military academies like West Point and in university business schools. Stogdill (1948), perhaps inadvertently, sounded the death knell for trait theory when he stated explicitly that persons who are effective leaders in one situation were not necessarily effective leaders in other situations, a fact that has often been borne out in education with the appointment of experienced school principals and university vice-chancellors. Other scholars extended Stogdill's assertion by suggesting that the effect of a trait on leadership *behaviour*, rather than solely on leadership *effectiveness*, also depended on the situation (Hughes et al., 1996; Yukl & Van Fleet, 1992), and analysis of behaviour and situation gained primacy over analysis of traits in the field of leadership research (Bass, 1990). This eventually led to Fiedler's (1967) contingency model, Blake and Mouton's (1964) managerial grid, and Hersey and Blanchard's (1969a) situational leadership model, which are discussed in Chapters 5 and 7 respectively.

In practical terms, trait theory was made redundant during World War II when the US armed forces needed to 'discover' more leaders than birth alone could reasonably provide. Hundreds of studies were conducted to establish the efficacy of the theory, but they proved inconclusive. Many studies looked at the top leaders in industry and commerce to try to establish common features, but the only conclusion drawn with any certainty was that leaders were likely to be taller than average, which of course could be attributed to diet and therefore (generationally) to social class. Despite this, a guarded mutation of trait theory is re-emerging today, some 75 years later, in the study of business organisations, but with more sophisticated traits such as 'high energy levels', 'tolerance of stress', 'self-confidence' and 'emotional maturity'. In some ways, it was kept alive in the field of political biography, many of which show strong evidence of trait theory. For example, in the UK, Sir Bernard Ingham, Margaret Thatcher's press secretary throughout her time as Prime Minister (1979–1990), attributed the following leadership characteristics to her: ideological security; moral courage; constancy; iron will; and a low need for love (Ingham, 2019). Some of these were *perceived* to be present, rather than present *per se*, by manipulating her media presence – the colour of her clothes (dark blues and sombre shades) and the tone of her voice (deliberately lowered and slowed) – so the question is really whether leadership traits need to be present or just need to be *perceived* to be present. Trait theory is an attractive simplification that enables easy comparisons, particularly in political biography. It is amusing to note, for example, that while Margaret Thatcher had a low need for love but a high need to be respected, Tony Blair, arguably a more successful Prime Minister, exhibited the converse; namely, a high for love and a low need for respect. So it cannot be that certain traits are necessary or sufficient for successful leadership. Sometimes they are present; sometimes they are absent but are perceived to be present; sometimes the same traits are absent without any deleterious effect; at other times, the opposing traits are present, again without affecting the quality of the leadership exercised.

One trait that is often referred to by biographers – mostly in hindsight, and mostly by followers – is 'presence'. The best leaders usually have – or are perceived to have – something beyond their behaviour; something distinctive that commands attention, wins the trust of colleagues and subordinates, which enables leaders to be successful (Scouller, 2011). However, that 'special something' – leadership presence – seems to vary from person to person and has proved virtually impossible to define in terms of personality traits, so even if true, trait theory neither captures its elusive nature nor indicates how it might be gauged or developed.

It is a similar problem with another original plank of trait theory; the assertion that leadership traits are genetic as evidenced by the fact that leadership seems to run in families – the Kennedy, Churchill and Bush families immediately spring to mind – and that therefore, there must be an innate component. The flaw with this argument is that these are people, and the children of people, who were raised and encouraged to seek out positions of authority, and who had the social and financial capital to indulge their pursuit of power. Students of history will have no difficulty noting that there are more exceptions to the genetic component theory than examples of it, so that in isolation, trait theory looks like a type of astrology in the firmament of leadership theories – an amusing anecdotal distraction that can tell people what they want to hear, if they are needy enough – except for the fact that a growing body of modern evidence supports *some* link between leadership traits and leadership effectiveness (de Vries, 2012) since the tech revolution of the 1980s and the end of the Cold War. Proponents of trait theory (Kenny & Zaccaro, 1983; Lord et al., 1986) point out that some research cited as evidence *against* the theory do in fact contain some evidence supporting it; and that certain individual traits can be shown to be reasonably good predictors of leader effectiveness (Judge et al., 2002; Judge et al., 2004). Scholars have also been busy extending the theory by looking at 'malleable' traits (i.e. those susceptible to development) in addition to the traditional 'dispositional' ones (Hoffman et al., 2011; Kenny & Zaccaro, 1983) and this has gained considerable traction in the 21st century as the emphasis in western economies has shifted from industrial production to high-tech services, artificial intelligence and machine learning. For example, a 'gift for innovation' or 'being liberated from the tyranny of knowing things' is now heralded as a core trait among business leaders in the modern 'gig' economy (see Chapter 23), replacing those traditional traits that were more in evidence in stable environments requiring less creativity.

Categorising leadership traits

There are two main ways in which leadership traits are categorised:

- *Demographic, task competence or interpersonal.* Derue et al. (2011) claims that most leadership traits can be organised into three categories: demographic; task competence; and interpersonal. In the demographic category, gender has received the most attention in terms of leadership, but most research has found that male and female leaders are equally effective. Task competence relates to how individuals approach the execution and performance of tasks (Bass & Bass, 2008). Hoffman et al. (2011) grouped intelligence, conscientiousness, openness to experience, and emotional stability in this category. Lastly, interpersonal attributes are related to how a leader approaches social interactions. Being extroverted and agreeable lie in this category.
- *Distal (trait-like) or proximal (state-like).*[4] Distal traits are internal and dispositional, the individual characteristics that influence behaviour and actions, such as personality traits, temperament and genetics. Distal traits cannot be developed. In contrast, proximal traits such as knowledge and skills are malleable (Hoffman et al., 2011). They are not stable through the life-course and *can* be

developed. Hoffman et al. (2011) examined the effect of distal versus proximal traits on leader effectiveness, finding that *distal* traits of achievement motivation, energy, flexibility, dominance, honesty, integrity, self-confidence, creativity and charisma are strongly correlated with leadership effectiveness, as are the *proximal* traits of interpersonal skills, oral and written communication skills, management skills, problem-solving skills and decision-making. These results suggest that distal and proximal traits have a broadly similar relationship with effective leadership (Hoffman et al., 2011).

A modern trait leadership model

Zaccaro et al. (2004) created a model based on the second categorisation described in the previous section – distal as opposed to proximal characteristics – to help understand leadership traits and their influence on leader effectiveness. It is based on two basic premises:

- Leadership emerges from the combined influence of multiple traits, and effective leadership is derived from an integrated set of cognitive abilities, social capabilities and dispositional tendencies. Each set of traits adds to the influence of the other.
- Traits differ in their proximal influence on leadership.

The model is a multistage one in which certain distal dispositional attributes, cognitive abilities, motives and values serve as precursors for the development of proximal personal characteristics like sociability, problem-solving skills and expert knowledge. Adopting this categorisation, and based on several comprehensive meta-analyses of trait leadership (Derue et al., 2011; Hoffman et al., 2011; Judge et al., 2009; Zaccaro, 2007), it is possible to compile a list of leadership traits and their known correlations to leader efficacy. These are shown in Table 2.1.

One trait not included in Table 2.1 is 'presence'. The best leaders usually have, or are perceived to have, something beyond their behaviour; something distinctive that commands attention, wins the trust of colleagues and subordinates and enables leaders to be successful. However, that 'special something', leadership presence, varies from person to person, and research has shown it is impossible to define in terms of personality traits, so trait theory does not capture its elusive nature or indicate how it can be developed. It is discussed in greater detail in Chapter 16.

Several other trait models have emerged in recent times to capture the relationship between leadership traits and leader effectiveness. They try to reconcile the conflict between traits and other situational factors such as context (Derue et al., 2011; Judge et al., 2009; Zaccaro, 2007). The 'Leader Trait Emergence Effectiveness' model (Judge et al., 2009) and the 'Integrated Model of Leader Traits, Behaviours and Effectiveness' (Derue et al., 2011) are two such examples. The former combines the behavioural genetics and evolutionary psychology theories of how personality traits are developed into a model that explains the emergence of leaders

TABLE 2.1 Leadership traits and their correlations to leader efficacy

Being extroverted (Distal–Dispositional)	The tendency to be sociable and assertive, to have good social skills, to like mixing with others and to have energy and social zeal. This is significantly positively related ($r = +0.31$) to leadership (Judge et al., 2002).
Being agreeable (Distal–Dispositional)	The tendency to be agreeable refers to the tendency to be 'clubbable', trusting, compliant, caring and not aggressive. The relationship between being agreeable and leadership is ambiguous. Being agreeableness is positively related, but not significantly so ($r = +0.08$), to leadership (Judge et al., 2002).
Being conscientious (Distal–Dispositional)	The tendency to be conscientious refers to achievement and dependability. Being conscientious is significantly positively related ($r = +0.28$) to leadership (Judge et al., 2002).
Openness (Distal–Dispositional)	Openness is the disposition to be imaginative, nonconforming, unconventional and autonomous. It is significantly positively related ($r = +0.24$) to leadership (Judge et al., 2002).
Neuroticism (Distal–Dispositional)	Neuroticism is the tendency to exhibit poor emotional adjustment and negative affects like anxiety, insecurity and hostility. Neuroticism is significantly negatively correlated ($r = -0.24$) to leadership (Judge et al., 2002).
Honesty and integrity (Distal–Dispositional)	Honesty and integrity is about being truthful and not being deceitful. Honesty and integrity is significantly positively related ($r = +0.29$) to leadership (Judge et al., 2002).
Charisma (Distal–Dispositional)	Charisma is the ability to influence followers by articulating a compelling vision, inspiring commitment and a sense of self-efficacy among followers. It is significantly positively related ($r = +0.57$) to leadership (Judge et al., 2002).
Intelligence (Distal–Cognitive abilities)	Intelligence is the most important trait in psychology, and it has been identified as one of the critical traits that must be possessed by all leaders (Judge et al., 2004).
Creativity (Distal–Cognitive abilities)	Hoffman and others (2011) found a significant positive relationship between creativity and leader effectiveness ($r = +0.31$).
Achievement motivation (Distal–Motive-value)	The motivation to achieve has been shown to have a significant positive relationship with leadership effectiveness ($r = +0.23$) (Judge et al., 2002).
Need for power (Distal–Motive-value)	The need for power is characterised by the satisfaction leaders derive from exerting influence over others. The need for power has a positive relationship with leader effectiveness (McClelland & Boyatzis, 1982).
Oral and written communication skills (Proximal–Social skills)	Oral and written communication skills have been found to have a significant positive relationship with leader effectiveness (Hoffman et al., 2011).
Interpersonal skills (Proximal–Social skills)	Interpersonal skills have a significant positive correlation with leader effectiveness (Hoffman et al., 2011). These include skills associated with understanding human behaviour and the group dynamic (Locke, 1991; Yukl, 2006).

(Continued)

TABLE 2.1 *Continued*

Problem-solving skills (Proximal–Problem-solving)	Problem-solving skills are strongly correlated with leader effectiveness (Hoffman et al., 2011).
Decision-making skills (Proximal–Problem-solving)	Decision-making skills are strongly correlated with leader effectiveness (Hoffman et al., 2011).
Technical knowledge (Proximal–Expert knowledge)	Technical knowledge and know-how includes the methods and processes of management (Yukl, 2006). It has been proved to be positively correlated with leader effectiveness (Bass, 1990).
Management skills (Proximal–Expertise knowledge)	Management skills, including coordinating the work of colleagues and subordinates, are crucial to leadership effectiveness. This positive relationship has been proved significant (Hoffman et al., 2011).

and their effectiveness. It is a flexible model that separates objective and subjective leader effectiveness into different criteria. The Integrated Model of Leader Traits, Behaviours and Effectiveness combines traits and behaviours in predicating leader effectiveness and takes account of the mediating effect of leader behaviour on the relationship between traits and effectiveness. The model holds that some types of leader behaviour mediate the effect between traits and effectiveness.

Criticisms of trait leadership theories

Trait leadership theory has been criticised as being too simplistic (Conger & Kanungo, 1998) and 'futile' (House & Aditya, 1997), mainly for its focus on how leader effectiveness is *perceived* by followers (Lord et al., 1986) rather than on the leader's *actual* effectiveness (Judge et al., 2009). Generally, personality traits have low explanatory and predictive power with regard to job effectiveness and in that sense cannot help organisations select leaders on the basis of who will turn out to be effective (Morgeson & Ilies, 2007). Derue et al. (2011) have found that leader *behaviour* is a better predictor of effectiveness than leadership traits. Trait theory also ignores, in addition to leader behaviour, the influence of situation and context (Ng et al., 2008), despite the early finding (Stogdill, 1948) that persons who are good leaders in one situation and context may not be good leaders in a different situation and context. As early as 1941, Murphy asserted that leadership did not reside in the person of the leader and that one needs to look at the whole setting. In light of these shortcomings, it is no surprise that trait theory has been supplanted by transformational leadership theory, and by transactional, charismatic and authentic theories (Schaubroeck et al., 2007). Even within its own paradigm, trait theory has failed to uncover a definitive list of traits that differentiate leaders from followers (Kenny & Zaccaro, 1983), and researchers cannot agree on a common list of those traits that have been recognised, which undermines the idea that a leader's effectiveness can be traced back to unique and specific character qualities. The theory's focus on a small set of personality traits to the neglect of more malleable traits such as social and problem-solving skills remains a shortcoming, as does its failure to consider the integration of multiple traits when studying leader effectiveness.

Notwithstanding the recent increase in evidence and support for trait theory (Ng et al., 2008), and even if trait theorists *could* agree a list of necessary traits, the theory does not help to *develop* leaders. In the theory's defence, it could be argued that leadership development is not the intention of the theory in the first place, and in any case, (it is thought that) innate personality distal traits are relatively immune to development, although the proximal traits of later trait models *are* susceptible to leadership development programs to stretch existing capabilities of leaders. Ng et al. (2008) have suggested using personality traits as selection tools for identifying emerging leaders, using the list of individual traits that predict leader effectiveness as well as those that are detrimental. But this does not get over the fundamental problem that leader selection and any judgement about subsequent effectiveness *is one of perception* in the absence of agreed objective metrics. We really cannot go further than Derue et al. (2011) in saying that individuals who are conscientious, extroverted[5] and agreeable are more likely to be *perceived* as successful leaders, and that individuals who are narcissistic are more likely to be perceived as unsuccessful.

Paradoxically, trait theory fell victim to its own appeal. Generally, research intended or designed to support it found evidence in its favour, but in order to survive as a legitimate approach, it needed to graft on the acknowledgement that the extent to which leader traits were causally linked to leader effectiveness *depended on behaviour, situation and context*, and that leadership was a behaviour that needed sometimes to balance conflicting traits. In that sense, it was the end of innocence for trait leadership theory and led to new approaches – behavioural and situational theories – that replaced it. Before we leave trait theory behind, however, the next chapter will look at one management technique that is predicated on it – Ofman's (2001a, 2004) Core Quadrants model, which enables people to diagnose their own core leadership traits – and a new theory that is partly trait-based: 'charismatic leadership'.

Notes

1 The gendered title reflects the fact that in the 19th century, one of the traits deemed necessary for leadership, especially military leadership, was being male!

2 For example, Blaise Pascal (1623–1662), by way of his parable of the shipwrecked castaway (who is mistaken for a king by the inhabitants) in his *Three Discourses on the Condition of the Great*, promotes the legitimacy of great men who, because of the accident of birth, are in the right place with the right traits to lead.

3 The alternative view is 'history from below', which emphasises the life of ordinary people and the mass of smaller events, in addition to the effect of the leader, as a generating force of history.

4 'Proximal' means near the core or the point of origin. 'Distal' means away from the core or the point of origin.

5 People, perhaps unconsciously, favour the traits of extroverts and suppress those of introverts (Cain, 2013). While both extrovert and introvert leaders can be effective, the public has a general proclivity towards extroverted traits, which, when evaluating trait leadership, can skew the perception of what is important.

3

CHARISMATIC LEADERSHIP AND THE CORE QUADRANTS

Charismatic leadership was originally developed by the German sociologist Max Weber. It is a type of leadership where authority derives from the charisma of the leader as opposed to legal or coercive authority. 'Charisma' is a Greek term that referred originally to a God-given 'gift'. Weber generalised it into a quality of an individual's personality that sets some persons apart from the ordinary. In common parlance, it refers to a compelling attractiveness or charm that can inspire follower-ship in others, although it has more recently come to describe self-assured zealots who assuage their own gnawing self-doubt with the certainty that others are wrong. According to Weber, authority is the legitimate power that a leader or manager exercises over others. Legitimacy is the means by which authority is distinguished from the more general concept of power, which can be exerted by the use of force or violence. Unlike power, authority depends on the acceptance by subordinates of the right of their leaders to give them orders. Charismatic authority is the most lasting because the leader is seen as the possessor of exceptional personal qualities, insight and accomplishment, and any rebellion against that authority is seen as an 'offence' against the natural order. Charismatic leaders typically develop a cult of personality, but usually this is not of their own doing.

Charismatic leadership,[1] more than other forms of authority, depends strongly on perceived legitimacy. Should the strength of followers' belief fade, the power of the charismatic leader fades quickly alongside it, which makes this form of leader-ship unstable. Although charisma is seen as the main character trait of this type of leadership, Weber did not see it entirely as such, but rather as a relationship between the leader and his followers. For Weber, 'the validity of charismatic leadership lies in its recognition by followers' (*Anhänger*, in German).

Charismatic leadership challenges the boundaries set by coercive and legal authority. It can be seen as challenging to authority and is often seen as revolutionary

DOI: 10.4324/9781003217220-3

in its early stages, but it typically ends up being incorporated or 'routinised' into the organisation when the challenge it once perceived to present subsides. At this stage, it is succeeded by a bureaucracy controlled by legal or coercive authority, or by a combination of both.

The problem of succession

Charismatic leaders are often found in autocratic organisations established by personality cult, and a predictable problem arises when such a leader leaves an organisation. The departure of the charismatic leader – one day a rooster; the next, a feather duster! – means the destruction of the organisation's management structure unless prior arrangements were made to routinise fully the charismatic authority. The organisation must then decide on either another form of leadership – Weber holds that charismatic leadership will eventually give way to institutionalisation anyway – or to look for another charismatic leader as a replacement. Adapting Weber's view to an education setting, the usual ways in which schools, colleges and universities maintain charisma in their leadership are by 'executive search', 'revelation' following a fair selection process, 'ordination' by the original leader, 'acclaim' by qualified staff or 'consecration'.

- *Executive search*
  The search for a replacement charismatic leader typically proceeds on the basis of the qualities that will best equip the person for the job. It is an example of the way in which charismatic leaders 'live on' through their successors. Headhunting firms are typically given exact briefs as to the qualities required, an approach common in the appointment of vice-chancellors in the university sector.[2]
- *Revelation following a fair selection process*
  In this scenario, the legitimacy of the new leader is dependent on the legitimacy of the selection process. The choice of successor is imbued with the charismatic authority that comes from official 'endorsement' of a fair and robust recruitment procedure. This is common across the whole public sector, but it is not enough that the selection process is fair and robust; it must be *perceived* as fair and robust.
- *Ordination by the original leader*
  In this form, the original charismatic authority figure passes authority to his or her successor. It is a 'laying on of hands', as it were. This occurs occasionally in the secondary school sector when an internal candidate succeeds to the post of headteacher.
- *Acclaim by qualified staff*
  This is not an election, nor is it something determined by majority vote, although unanimity is often required in the final acclaim. An example of this form of succession is the choosing of a new pope by the College of Cardinals. The cardinals taking part in the conclave are considered 'charismatically

qualified' by the Roman Catholic congregations they represent, and therefore their choice of pope is imbued with charismatic authority. The approach is common in some universities where a Head of Department is chosen every four or five years by acclaim, feelers having been put out and without election, a candidate emerges as the most suitable to fill the role.

- *Consecration*
  This is where charisma is transmitted by ritual from one leader to a successor. It is done by dissociating charisma from a particular individual and making it an objective, transferable entity. Priestly consecration is an example in the religious sphere; priests inherit their charisma and are subsequently perceived by their congregations as having the charismatic authority that comes with priesthood. The installation of a chancellor at an ancient university like Oxford is another example.

Charismatic leaders are unpredictable. They are not bound by tradition or rules, and they are typically not subject to normal accountability measures. By definition, they acquire unquestioning personal allegiance and devotion not by imposition, demand or diktat, but because followers – 'disciples' might be a better term – want to give it. That is the charisma. They encourage dependency without wishing it, but charismatic leaders exhibit some traits of narcissism and volatility. They display extraordinary energy and dynamism, and an inner clarity that is unhindered by doubt or anxiety. Ultimately, their continued leadership position is legitimised by the success they bring to the school, college or university community. The problem is what happens when they leave the institution: employees tend to lose motivation in the absence of devotion; their dependency may have endured for too long; they miss the dynamism and the clarity of vision; and they tend to become concerned for their own continued well-being and career success. The only hope is that the institution's processes were codified in its institutional memory before the leader's departure.

Core Quadrants management

Charismatic leadership can be seen as a type of trait leadership, depending on whether or not a 'trait' is defined solely as an innate physical characteristic. This begs the question of how such traits are measured and managed, and that is where the Core Quadrants management model can help.

There are two interesting dichotomies in trait theory: one is the tension between leaders *actually having* certain traits and the *perception* that they have them; the other is the dichotomy between observers and biographers asserting that leaders possess certain characteristics and the reality that a leader's true self might be entirely different, entirely void of the desirable traits that others claim on their behalf. The two dichotomies are related. In terms of the first – the tension between reality and perception – it could reasonably be claimed that Winston Churchill and John F. Kennedy (to take two obvious examples) were inspirational leaders simply because of their 'ability to inspire', a trait rightly judged *by others*, whether or not the incumbents themselves agree. However, when we claim that Margaret Thatcher had 'a low need for love', this is a trait that we need to know objectively whether it existed or not in her. The perception that the trait exists is not enough for it to have the desired effect. Her true self might have had an overpowering need for love, but not show it. For some traits, the mere belief that they are present is enough; for others – and charisma fits into this second category – we need to know whether the trait is present or absent. The is obviously the single most important question in trait theory, but just as obviously, regarding the second dichotomy, it is a question that cannot be answered except by the person! Ofman (2001a, 2004) designed the Core Quadrants model to help people diagnose their own core traits and answer what we might call 'trait questions'. It tries to overcome the danger inherent in trying to label oneself or others without having a firm basis for it. Of course, it cannot overcome the danger completely, but it does at a minimum generate self-awareness. The more insight one has into one's own core qualities and those of others, the easier it is to integrate different leadership styles into one's own personality, taking account of the traits that are present, or perceived by others to be present, and those that are not.

Every leader has certain special core qualities that describe the 'self' and which generate followership. They are attributes that form part of a leader's essence and vary from person to person. People are steeped in these qualities; they are the traits that immediately come to mind when we think of the person. Examples include determination, consideration for others, precision, courage, orderliness, empathy, flexibility and so on. Core qualities manifest themselves through the person's actions, values, feelings, words and deeds. Other, less prominent traits are infused with the core traits, which cannot be switched on and off at will, although they can be concealed. The main distinction between core traits and skills is that the former (which can be developed) come from inside and the latter (which can be learned) are acquired from outside. Core traits describe 'the real you', but they can cause friction between colleagues.

Ofman (2001b: 1) made it clear that for the Core Quadrants model, asking the right questions is as important as finding the right answers; perhaps more so:

> Some cultures consider it more of an art to ask the right questions than to find the right answers, and these cultures particularly respect people for the quality of their questions. The answers are considered less important, because it is recognized that there are no unequivocal answers. This has to do with leadership 'from inside' … with management from the core.

The Core Quadrants model is a two-by-two matrix (see Figure 3.1) designed to understand relationships and to explain the frictions caused when core qualities clash. A 'core quality' (top-left quadrant) is someone's natural positive quality; a strong point of a personality that can become a weakness if taken too far (a 'pitfall', top-right quadrant), like being compulsively tidy or obsessively punctual.

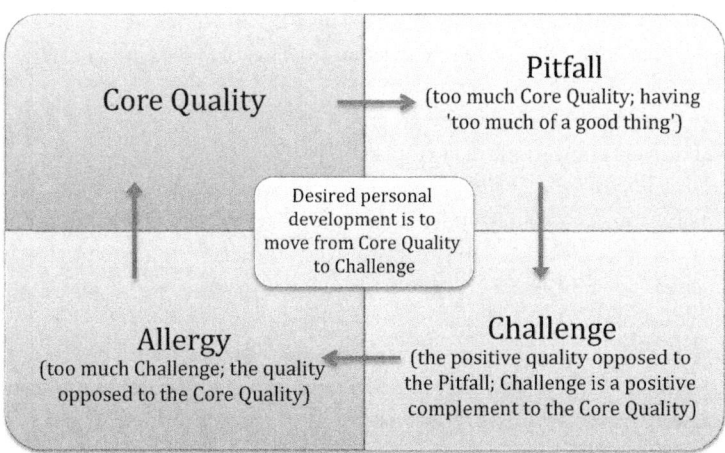

FIGURE 3.1 The Core Quadrants model.

A pitfall is a distortion of its core quality. It is a label the person is often given by others. For example, a person whose core quality is decisiveness can be described by others as pushy. Whether or not this perception is correct, the pitfall and the core quality are inextricably bound. They go together, but one is not the opposite of the other in the way 'strong' is the opposite of 'weak'. A pitfall is instead an *over-developed* core quality. Ofman (2001b) calls it 'having too much of a good thing'. When a core quality becomes a pitfall, the trait has a negative effect on the environment and becomes an obstacle for others. Mulder (2012) gives some examples of core qualities and their pitfalls:

- Core Quality = perfectionist; Pitfall = fault-finder
- Core Quality = helper; Pitfall = meddler
- Core Quality = leader; Pitfall = dictator
- Core Quality = mediator; Pitfall = busy-body
- Core Quality = flexibility; Pitfall = inconsistency

Just as a pitfall derives from a core quality, we can trace *back* to the core quality *from* the pitfall, although this is usually more difficult. Sometimes it is hard to imagine anything positive (core quality) behind the negative (pitfall). Managers are often confronted with employee pitfalls, so learning to spot the positive aforepresent core qualities behind them is a very useful skill, separating the 'sin' (the pitfall behaviour) from the 'sinner' (the person with the core quality). It is a necessary skill for school principals and senior managers in universities (deans and vice-chancellors) where the educative context is so person-centred and success so personnel-dependent that it pays to see the good teacher behind the overly strict practitioner, or the original researcher behind the harsh academic critic.

A negative pitfall can become a positive supplement to the core quality when it becomes a 'challenge' (bottom-right quadrant). The challenge provides more of a balance; for example, not tidying up after people and learning to accept trivial lateness by colleagues. The challenge is the positive quality diametrically opposed to the pitfall. For example, the pitfall of pushiness may offer 'patience' as a challenge. The core quality and the challenge are complementary qualities. Striking the right balance between decisiveness and patience is what matters. Too much decisiveness can turn into pushiness, and to prevent the pitfall, it is advisable to develop the challenge. Creating balance means thinking in terms of 'and–and' instead of 'either–or' (Ofman, 2001b). The secret is to be *simultaneously* decisive and patient. It is not a matter of becoming less decisive for fear of being pushy, but to develop a patient decisiveness. The problem is usually trying to see how the two qualities can be combined; the tendency is usually to consider these qualities as opposites when really they are complementary.

When a challenge goes too far, it becomes an 'allergy'. An allergy is directly opposite of its core quality; it's where a person finds the core quality difficult. Formulating the allergy completes the core quadrant. To complete Ofman's (2001b) example:

- Core Quality = decisiveness
- Pitfall = pushiness
- Challenge = patience
- Allergy = becoming passive oneself.

Potential conflicts can often be deduced from a person's core qualities. The average person is 'allergic' to an excess of his or her challenge, particularly if personified in someone else. For example, decisive people are allergic to (and will be in conflict with) passivity in another because passivity is an excess of their challenge (patience), and they often do not know how to handle it.

The more Person A confronts Person B with B's own allergy, the greater B's chance of falling into her or his pitfall. If the core quality is decisiveness, B runs the risk of becoming even pushier, while reproaching A for being passive. This can become a vicious circle, with A and B reinforcing each other in a hopeless conflict. Ofman (2001b: 13) advises to:

> look out for your pitfall when you spot your allergy in another. It is not their pitfall, but their allergy, that makes people most vulnerable, because this is what drives them into their pitfall.

What happens if two similar characters meet? Two decisive persons or two very pushy types will not have an easy time together, and the risk is high that their meetings will turn confrontational. The difference in confrontations between similar characters and contrasting characters is that, although decisive people may have problems with others who are *similar*, they will respect the other. This is not the case for *opposites*. If a 'decisive' person encounters a 'patient' person, the opposite, he or she will soon label the patient person as 'passive' in a pejorative sense. As Ofman (2001b: 13) puts it:

> Disdain is characteristic of situations in which people are confronted with their allergies'. Looking down on someone makes you vulnerable, because before you know it you will have fallen into your pitfall and cease to be effective.

Likewise, orderly people will find it difficult to appreciate flexibility in someone else, because they will immediately want to label it as inconsistency or chaotic. Something to which Person A is allergic in someone else is probably an excess of the quality Person A needs most (ibid.: 14)

Ofman's Core Quadrant model provides information about other people's actions and about one's own actions. It is about 'me-versus-you-thinking' and not experiencing oneself (or one's own organisation) as separate from other colleagues (or other organisations). As such, applying the model creates sympathy for others, and by using self-insight, people discover that a core quality can sometimes go too far and irritate others. The model finds out where strengths and weaknesses, pitfalls, challenges and allergies lie, creating self-awareness as well as a feeling of empathy for others. Van den Berg and Pietersma (2016) pose the following guiding questions for managers:

- What is your major pitfall, where you have too much of your core quality?
- What is your biggest challenge; that is, what is the opposite of your pitfall?
- What is your allergy in terms of core qualities in others; that is, the opposite of your core quality and too much of a challenge?

The power of Ofman's model lies in the fact that it provides four different perspectives on a core quality, but any given core quality can have slightly different pitfalls, challenges and allergies, so it is important to specify the four quadrants in detail for each person. Ofman (2001a) suggests three additional perspectives, slightly tweaked to suit each quadrant, in each of the four quadrants (see Figure 3.2). For example:

1. Something that *you* would say or feel (like or dislike) *about yourself*. For example, what do I play down in myself?
2. Something that *you* would say or feel (like or dislike) *about others*. For example, what do I expect from others?
3. Something that *others* would say or feel (like or dislike) *about you*. For example, what do others appreciate in me?

Too much of a good thing

- What I play down in myself
- What others appreciate in me
- What I expect from others

Core Quality +

Pitfall −

- What I try to justify in myself
- What others blame me for
- What I will forgive in others

Allergy −

Challenge +

- What I would hate in myself
- What others tell to relate
- What I despie in others

- What I miss in myself
- What others miss in me
- What I admire in others

Too much of a good thing

FIGURE 3.2 Core Quadrants with three additional perspectives.

These three additional perspectives with variations superimposed on the four underlying quadrants can be a revealing management technique. Inconsistencies between the three additional perspectives indicate that you are not who/what/how you want to be. You are 'trying to hide your true feelings, avoid your pitfalls and curb your dislike of your allergy. In other words, you are acting' (Van den Berg & Pietersma, 2016).

Notes

1 Here we include '*neo*-charismatic' leadership, which in turn includes servant leadership, ethical leadership, spiritual leadership and visionary leadership.
2 Weber gave as an example the search for a new Dalai Lama: 'the search for a child with characteristics which are interpreted to mean that he is a reincarnation of the Buddha'.

4

PARTICIPATIVE LEADERSHIP AND DE BONO'S SIX THINKING HATS

Participative or democratic leadership is an approach that invites input from staff on all (or almost all) decisions. Typically, colleagues are given all the relevant information, and a majority vote determines the eventual course of action for the organisation. The theory holds that effective leadership requires the input of others, and leaders should encourage the participation of followers to help them feel ownership of the decision-making process, although usually the leader remains the gatekeeper.

Participative leadership is most successful in educational organisations like schools and universities where management is more light-touch, where organisations are flatter than in the commercial sector, and where there is a high degree of independent working for teachers and researchers. In educational institutions, the participative approach is essentially a sequence of steps: the issue is discussed as a group, which the leader facilitates; the leader shares all relevant information to enable the group to make a decision; ideas emerge and are shared about how to address the issue at hand; the leader summarises both the information and the emergent ideas for the group; the group then makes the best decision it can, based on the information and ideas presented; and finally, that decision is implemented across the organisation.

There are three types[1] of participative leadership: consensus, collective and democratic.

- *Consensus participative leadership.* Here, the leader does not have additional power over other members of the group but works exclusively as a facilitator. To reach a decision in this type of participative leadership, *all* participant-followers must agree, so sometimes goals or decisions need to be modified until everyone can agree on one course of action.

DOI: 10.4324/9781003217220-4

- *Collective participative leadership.* Here, responsibility falls equally on the group. The leader will facilitate, but all participants are responsible for the process and for the outcome. To reach a decision, *the majority of* participants must agree.
- *Democratic participative leadership.* Here, the leader has more power than the collective group. Ideas and suggestions are provided by the group and voting may occur on the outcome, but the leader has the final say on what action to take.

Participative leadership has several advantages for an educational organisation, its leader and the staff. Firstly, it boosts morale. Staff feel they are part of a team; part of something greater than themselves. Participative leadership provides a deeper feeling of community throughout the organisation. Secondly, staff feel empowered when they participate in decision-making and as a consequence are more likely to implement the decisions made to the best of their ability. Thirdly, for the leader, by having input from 'the many' rather than from 'the few', decisions are likely to be more creative and inventive, and problems can be resolved in unanticipated ways. Next, the organisation benefits because good employees are more likely to stay with such an organisation. They feel loyalty and feel more valued when their ideas are sought and heeded, which in turn leads to higher productivity. Finally, because colleagues are active in the decision-making process, when it comes time to implementing decisions, they require less managerial oversight. They already know what needs to be done and how to do it.

However, participative leadership also has its disadvantages. It can be costly, slow and take a long time to communicate and implement decisions, especially if the group is large. Secondly, participation can be contrived, with some colleagues feeling pressure to conform to the desires of the majority or the leader. Next, participative leadership is not an efficient system for gathering opinions and ideas. Not everyone in the organisation has the background, skills or training necessary to participate productively in particular decision-making groups. This can affect the group's ability to reach consensus and, indeed, to reach good decisions.

Participative leadership and motivation

Participative leadership is really a management theory, defined by the designed (if sometimes contrived) involvement and doings of different participants. As such, it depends on a strong motivational element. The theory actually dates back to the Hawthorne experiments of the 1920s. These investigations, conducted at the Hawthorne plant of the Western Electric Company in Illinois, USA, were designed initially to find ways to improve productivity, but the findings as they emerged related more to motivation. The studies were conducted by Mayo and Roethlisberger as part of refocusing managerial strategy to incorporate the socio-psychological aspects of human behaviour in organisations. They discovered that workers were highly responsive to additional attention from their managers and the feeling that their managers actually *cared* about their work (Greenwood et al., 1983; Jones, 1992; Mayo, 1949; Parsons, 1974). The studies gave rise *post facto* to what became known as the Hawthorne Effect (Landsberger, 1958): the fact that individuals modify their behaviour in response to an awareness of being observed because of the motivational effect of having interest shown in them.

Kurt Lewin's research in the 1930s, described at greater length in the next chapter, also found that different levels of participation impacted on follower motivation – his so-called democratic leadership style lies clearly within the participatory leadership paradigm – but the major basis for participative leadership is Maslow's theory of human motivation, introduced in 1943 and discussed in detail in Chapter 6. According to Maslow, needs must be met starting with the basic, inborn needs and moving upwards through his famous hierarchy. Participative leadership focuses on both basic (or 'deficiency'[2]) needs and high-level (or 'growth') needs. Growth motivation occurs when basic needs have been fulfilled. They include a person's need to improve and grow, achieve goals, have greater autonomy and excel in self-actualisation (discussed in dynamic leadership terms as 'self-mastery' in Chapter 16). Participative leadership in schools and universities holds to the idea that participation satisfies the higher-level needs of teachers, academics and researchers. If they are growth-motivated, then professionalism is the driving force.

In the mid-1960s, Rensis Likert, the famous American social psychologist who developed the scale that bears his name, identified a fourfold model for leadership based on three decades of research. He called his fourth leadership style 'participative', in contrast to 'authoritative' and 'consultative'. Likert (1967) found that participative leadership improved teamwork, communication and efficacy, and was the best in terms of long-term benefits to organisations. It was also the most satisfying leadership style for lower-level employees (Hall, 1972) and featured:

- Decision-making, where responsibility and values are spread across all tiers
- Confidence and trust in all subordinates
- Decisions that are formed through group participation and consultation
- Communication where managers actively try to really understand issues
- Employees that are cooperative and openly accountable
- Motivation through involvement in goal-setting
- Teamwork, satisfaction and high productivity.

Yukl (1971) found similarly while also discussing the link between participative leadership and Fiedler's contingency model, discussed in Chapter 7. But in the modern era, the focus of the theory has shifted from *leadership* style to the *decision-making* style of the leader. Essentially, different decision-making styles constitute a spectrum from zero participation (where subordinates are listened to but the decisions are made by the leader alone) to high participation (a collective, where the decisions are fully delegated to subordinates). In the middle of the spectrum, subordinates supply ideas and suggestions, and the leader makes the final decision, justifies it to followers and resolves any subsequent objections. There are many variations on the theme of participative leadership, but they all have the essential feature of input from *both* leader and follower.

The six dimensions of participative leadership

John Cotton and others (1988) identified six dimensions of participative leadership:

- *Participation in decisions*
  Here, subordinates/followers are only included in work decisions. Their participation is partly consultative. The style is a 'formal participatory structure', and the leader retains full control of important aspects.
- *Consultative participation*
  This is a deeper participation by subordinates. The final decision remains with the leader, but subordinates are able to give their opinions *before* the decision is made so that they can influence it, although there is no guarantee that this will happen. Again, it is a formal participatory structure. After the leader consults and makes the decision, the leader reports back to subordinates on the rationale behind the decision. In some versions, subordinates are able to respond again to the decision before it is rolled out across the organisation.
- *Short-term participation*
  Some organisations can have participative leadership but only for the short term; that is, subordinates are included in the decision-making process on a temporary basis, usually for the duration of a time-limited project. Researchers in universities will be familiar with this scenario. It sounds a bit insincere – to tick some publicity boxes, perhaps – but ironically, in this situation participation often has a higher impact on outcomes. It is a formal structure with a more active role in decision-making, despite not being long-lived.
- *Informal participation*
  This is participative leadership on an informal basis. There is no formal structure – no rules or procedures or pre-planning – for subordinate participation in the decision-making process. Everything is *ad hoc* and discursive.
- *Role-dependent ownership*
  Here, subordinates participate in some decision-making, depending on the positional role of the individual. Staff in low positions, like post-docs in universities or teaching assistants in schools, have few if any opportunities to participate, or they do so only occasionally and on less important issues. The participation framework is formal, and usually only involves senior staff on important issues.
- *Tiered participation*
  Here, participation is on three levels: the leader; representatives; and the general staff body. Representatives have consultative power and can influence decision-making. They represent the employee in the manner of a trade union, but in practice the layer usually consists of middle managers. They act as mediators between the leader and the general staff body. This is a formal arrangement, with middle-manager representatives acting as messengers between the higher and lower levels. Before a decision is made, representatives unofficially consult the lower general staff body and then participate in

decision-making alongside the leader. This middle tier can be very political, with the middle tier of representatives coalescing the views of subordinates into their own and claiming to speak for the entire community in order to gain advantage for themselves.

The qualities of a participative leader

Participative leadership has different requirements from those of most other leadership styles because involving others in decision-making adds work and stress for managers. The main focus is on communication and managing knowledge. Participative leaders must be approachable and empathetic yet have a natural 'leadership presence' (see Chapter 16), be extroverted but unaffected, be a good listener with time for junior colleagues, have the ability to hoard information, be realistic but optimistic, not be afraid to be honest in appraisal, be fair, be an excellent communicator of ideas and issues, be able to get to the root of problems, be thoughtful and kind, be open-minded in listening to ideas from (usually) less experienced colleagues, able to look at alternatives in an unbiased manner, be confident about relinquishing power, and be able to work outside their comfort zones. Participative leaders should not be prone to jealousy or overly political and careerist, because the job is about empowering and giving credit to others and ensuring that subordinates have opportunities to develop themselves.

Participative leadership starts with an understanding of the objectives and ethics of the school or university. Ultimately, the leader is charged with achieving organisational goals, albeit through the participation of subordinates. Participative leaders must explain what they understand about organisational objectives and then open up discussions with staff about ways to achieve them. Participative leaders must learn how to relinquish control and not to micro-manage. They must acquire all the necessary information to pass to colleagues, while protecting some commercial and person-sensitive information, so that everyone's contribution is properly informed. Otherwise, the decisions reached will be flawed. A big part of communicating with subordinates is explaining decisions and the rationale behind the choices that *have* been made. Participative leadership slows the decision-making process, especially when reaching a consensus is necessary, so good preparatory work is essential.

De Bono's Six Thinking Hats

Participative leadership has the effect of flattening an organisation, yet ironically it is easier to implement when the organisation is already flat! It is difficult to justify the claim made for it that it 'democratises the workplace' because participative leadership is sometimes mere consultation, and when it is more deeply participative, it can be contrived to those who don't want to be involved or who do not have the experience or the social skills. It is also unclear how this type of leadership plays out in cultures where there is no expectation of democracy in the wider society, but irrespective of cultural context, it depends totally on teamwork and the ability of colleagues to think through issues together. In management terms, this is difficult to achieve in practice without definite techniques. Edward de Bono (1971, 1985) developed one such approach: his model of six so-called 'thinking hats' and his associated idea of 'parallel thinking'. The model enables groups to think together more effectively, to be more productive, focused and mindfully involved.

Six Thinking Hats was originally designed for group brainstorming exercises, allowing staff to develop tactics for thinking about particular issues. The premise is that the human brain thinks in six distinct ways, in each of which the brain will identify and make apparent certain aspects of issues being considered. None of these directions is a completely natural way of thinking, but rather how some people already represent the results of their thinking. It is an approach that works well in schools, colleges and universities since participants are well educated and in most cases, trained to think critically.

Each of the six ways of thinking or 'hats' has its own colour to correspond to the way people think and the input they make. Using the process of wearing different-coloured hats in team discussions, participants are tasked with playing different roles according to the hats they wear. Everyone wears the same colour hat at any given time. The hats do not represent natural modes of thinking, but they are metaphors for ways of thinking. Switching ways of thinking is symbolised by the act of putting on a different-coloured hat, allowing for ways of thinking to be segregated.

In brainstorming sessions, everyone gets a coloured hat plus an assignment in which to participate and think about from a specific perspective. De Bono believed that people develop thinking habits much like learning styles and that this limits the way they think. By defining the various orientations and approaches to thinking, people can become more participative and productive by thinking outside their own box; that is, by thinking from the perspective of wearing a different-coloured hat. By trying on different hats, collaboration can become more effective and efficient, and more fun. The model forces people out of their comfort zones; shifting them away from their normal way of thinking. This helps to overcome the shortcoming of participative leadership situations where followers feel pressured into contrived collaboration. It also helps everyone to understand the complexity of issues in education, the difficulties and nuances of making decisions and the opportunities for innovation, and it encourages creativity and lateral thinking, which in university-research and school-pedagogy settings is a great benefit. The model can work very well alongside Belbin's idea of Apollo Teams (discussed in Chapter 23) in that de Bono's model encourages complementarity and the avoidance of one-type-dominance in team situations.

The Six Thinking Hats are:

- *Blue hat*: This is the 'process control hat' worn by the chairperson of the meeting or workshop; typically, the headteacher, principal, dean, head of department or a deputy vice-chancellor. It is the hat that manages the thinking process.

The blue hat's job is to organise all the other hats, intervening in the process and telling everyone when to change hats. As such, the focus is on managing communications and summarising progress. The relevant questions for the chairperson are: What are the salient points so far? What conclusions can be drawn? How can the meeting best proceed?

- *White hat*: This is the 'factual hat', where the focus is on data, facts and figures, analysis and the interpretation of data. The relevant questions for the white hat-wearer are: What data are missing? What information might be wrong? What additional information is needed, and where can it be obtained?
- *Red hat*: This is the 'emotional hat', where the focus is on feelings. Problems are examined intuitively and emotionally. The relevant questions for red hat-wearers are: how would other people respond emotionally to this problem; how do I feel and how does that differ from how others feel; how can I understand the different emotional responses of others to the same problem; what does my intuition tell me and do I recognise my own intuition?
- *Yellow hat*: This is the 'optimistic hat', where the focus is on thinking positively and optimistically. The relevant questions for the yellow hat-wearer are: What are the benefits of the decision? What are the opportunities? What are the advantages;? How does the hat-wearer give colleagues hope?
- *Black hat*: This is the 'critical hat' where the focus is on the bad points, dangers and pitfalls of a decision, and why it will not work or has not worked. The relevant questions for black hat-wearers are: What are the weak points? What are the risks? What are the difficulties? What are the problems? What are the unintended consequences, and what are the potential mistakes? This is the opposite of the yellow hat. When wearing the black hat, wearers play devil's advocate.
- *Green hat*: This is the 'innovative hat', where the focus is on thinking creatively. Creativity and artistry thrive on curiosity, embracing chaos and trial-and-error and bending the rules. The relevant questions for green hat-wearers are: What creative solutions exist to the problem? How can I think innovatively? How can I challenge the prevailing wisdom?

The Six Thinking Hats model encourages different ways of thinking and considers problems from new perspectives. De Bono suggests that the best way of using the model in practice is to choose a particular focus during the discussion that suits the needs of a particular hat: use one colour to (say) develop organisational strategy; use another colour hat to (say) collect data on student feedback. This way, all colleagues will be focused on the same problem at the same time, and will be more collaborative in trying to find a solution under participative leadership.

In development sessions, each hat should be used for a limited time only, because some teachers and academics will feel that using the hats is uncomfortable, childish or counterproductive. Having identified the six modes of thinking that can be accessed, distinct programmes can be created in school and university settings (see Table 4.1 for a selection of examples). These are sequences of hats – they may need

TABLE 4.1 A selection of distinct programmes in an education setting

Activity	Hat Sequence
Initial ideas	Blue, White, Green, Blue
Choosing between alternatives	Blue, White, (Green), Yellow, Black, Red, Blue
Identifying solutions	Blue, White, Black, Green, Blue
Quick feedback	Blue, Black, Green, Blue
Strategic planning	Blue, Yellow, Black, White, Blue, Green, Blue
Process improvement	Blue, White, White (other people's views), Yellow, Black, Green, Red, Blue
Solving problems	Blue, White, Green, Red, Yellow, Black, Green, Blue
Performance review of research or teaching	Blue, Red, White, Yellow, Black, Green, Blue

to be tweaked – that structure the thinking process toward a goal. Sometimes these sequences or programmes are emergent, meaning that the group must plan the first few hats, and then the manager decides on the best way forward following that initial sub-sequence.

Sequences always begin and end with the blue hat. The group agrees how they will think, then they think, then they evaluate the outcomes and what they should do next. Sequences (and hats) can be used by individuals or by sub-groups. Each hat is typically used for, say, two minutes at a time, although at the start of the process an extended white hat session is common to get everyone on the same page. The red hat is recommended for use for only a short period of time to get a visceral gut reaction, sometimes by a show of hands or a quick vote.

De Bono believed that the key to the successful use of the Six Thinking Hats methodology is the deliberate focusing of the discussion on a particular approach during the meeting or session; for example, calling a meeting to review a particular problem and to find a solution to it. The method is used first to explore the problem, then to develop possible solutions and, finally, to choose one solution through the critical examination of all possible solutions. Typically, the meeting starts with everyone assuming a *blue* hat to discuss how the meeting should be conducted and to develop and agree the goals and objectives. The discussion then moves to *red* hat thinking in order to collect opinions and gut reactions to the problem. This phase can also be used to develop constraints for the actual solution, such as who will be affected. Next, the discussion moves to the *yellow* hat and then to the *green* hat in order to generate ideas and solutions. The discussion then moves between *white* hat thinking, as part of developing information, and *black* hat thinking, to critique the set of possible solutions. Since everyone is focused on one particular approach (colour) at any one time, the group tends to be more participative than if one person were thinking emotionally (in a red hat) while another person was being critical (in a black hat).

The Six Thinking Hats framework helps staff in schools, colleges and universities think more expansively while ensuring that critical ideas, concepts and approaches in pedagogy and research are not overlooked. As the blue hat-wearer, the job of the leader is to sum up, crystallise the key points and eventually put them into action. It is a model so suited to participative leadership that it is difficult to imagine how (or why) such a leadership style would not use de Bono's approach as a core management technique, or, indeed, how de Bono's framework could work effectively without a participative leader.

Notes

1 The literature mentions a fourth type, 'autocratic participative leadership', but this is a contradiction in terms, and we omit it here.
2 So-called because a deficiency in any of these needs would result in issues with mental well-being.

5

BEHAVIOURAL THEORIES

Dynamic leadership, followership and style

The growth in behavioural leadership theories coincided with the success of American military leadership during and after World War II. The emergence of these theories was a matter of necessity rather than any Pauline conversion to widening social access; the US Army simply could not supply in its traditional manner a sufficient quantity of officers from (what was then) the existing 'officer class'. The focus shifted from 'the *traits* that identify natural-born *leaders*' to 'the *behaviours* that identify good *leadership*'. In practice, this shift in philosophy meant that if leadership was a behavioural rather than a genetic predisposition, leadership was simply a matter of training. Thus was the MBA[1] industry born in business schools across the world, and a new field of leadership studies opened up across the public sector to which generations of talented academics made their contribution. These academics can be grouped in two sets. The first set is led by Kurt Lewin, who influenced Robert Tannenbaum and Richard Schmidt (who created their own leadership approach, contingency theory). These in turn influenced Robert Blake and Jane Mouton in developing their concept of 'leadership orientation' and its measurement. The second set is led by Douglas McGregor, Abraham Maslow and Frederick Hertzberg, and we will discuss their work in the next chapter.

Kurt Lewin (1890–1947) was a German-born US psychologist who is regarded as one of the pioneers of social and organisational psychology. A survey published in 2002 ranked him as the most cited psychologist of the 20th century (Haggbloom et al., 2002). He specialised in analysis using applied and action research and was one of the first to study group dynamics and their relationship to organisational development (Lewin, 1948).

Lewin (1936) came up with his now-famous equation:

$$B = f(P,E)$$

DOI: 10.4324/9781003217220-5

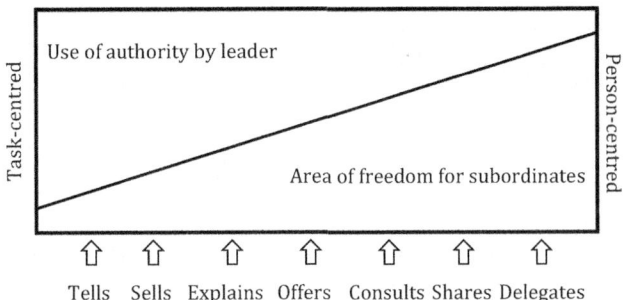

FIGURE 5.1   The Tannenbaum and Schmidt continuum model.

asserting that behaviour (*B*) is a function of personality (*P*) and environment (*E*). He suggested that leaders need to display a level of autocratic authority while at the same time having a willingness to adopt a more participative democratic approach, involving others in the decision-making process. This idea was extended and conceptualised in an article in the *Harvard Business Review* by Tannenbaum and Schmidt (1958) as a continuum from (at one end) *manager-centred* behaviour to (at the other end) *subordinate-centred* behaviour (see Figure 5.1).

The Tannenbaum and Schmidt continuum of behaviour, from left to right, describes seven different approaches, ranging from a style that uses a lot of authority to one that minimises the use of authority in favour of giving subordinates a lot of freedom and input. It is worth noting that the diagonal in Figure 5.1 does not go into the corners, implying that the total use of authority at the left-hand end of the spectrum is not leadership at all, but dictatorship; and giving total freedom to subordinates at the right-hand end is not leadership but represents the complete abrogation of responsibility. Reading from right to left:

1. The first point (Delegates) on the spectrum is where the leader or manager allows subordinates to function within limits defined by the leader, who conducts only an occasional check on progress.
2. The second point (Shares) is where the leader defines the limits within which a group of subordinates work, allowing the group to decide how to undertake the necessary tasks.
3. The next point (Consults) is where the leader or manager defines the problem to be solved, asks subordinates for suggestions and then decides on the best way forward.
4. 'Offers' is where the leader makes an initial decision without prior discussion regarding options, but the leader's decision is subject to change.
5. 'Explains' is where the leader presents ideas and strategies, and simply invites questions.

6. The sixth point (Sells) is where the leader makes decisions without prior discussion and sells those decisions to subordinates.

7. The last point (Tells) is where the leader makes a decision and subordinates are simply expected to enact it.

According to the Tannenbaum and Schmidt model, as leaders become more relationship-oriented, they become less task-oriented, and this brings us to the managerial grid model developed by Robert Blake and Jane Mouton in 1964. For them, leadership is a *style* based on five different leadership approaches reflecting the relative importance (to the leader) of concern for people and concern for task. Although this grid theory dates from the 1960s, it has continued to evolve to the present day with more leadership styles and a new element added, 'resilience', but we will focus here on the original version. The model was developed when Blake and Mouton from the University of Texas were hired as consultants by the oil giant Exxon. It is essentially a grid with *concern for task* on the horizontal axis and *concern for people* on the vertical axis. The axes range from a low of 1 to a high of 9 (see Figure 5.2), and the resulting five leadership styles thus defined are as follows:

- (1,1). This 'indifferent' or 'impoverished' style is characterised by 'evade and elude'. Here, leaders and managers have low concern for both people and task. They use it to preserve their seniority and are essentially just avoiding trouble and avoiding being held responsible for mistakes. Decisions are consequently very risk-averse and passive, and leaders exert only minimum effort to sustain organisational membership. Minimum attention is paid to both task and

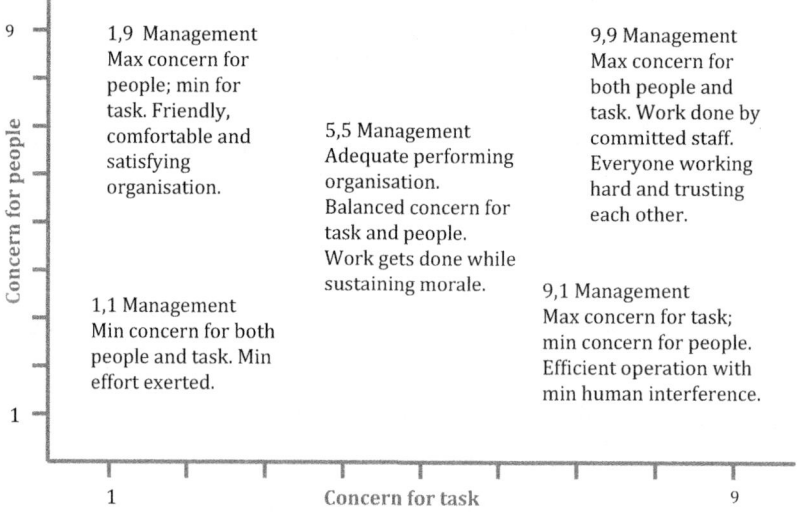

FIGURE 5.2 The Blake and Mouton managerial grid.

relationships, and in practical terms, there is partly an abrogation of leadership and responsibility. The style can be seen in failing schools and underperforming university departments where good staff leave because they are professionally dissatisfied and because they *can* leave. Those who remain are happy to work in a failing endeavour as long as they get paid.

- (1,9). The 'accommodating' or 'country club' style is characterised by 'yield and comply'. This style has a high concern for people and a low concern for task. Leaders here attach great importance to the well-being of subordinates, perhaps in the belief that happy employees work better. The resulting organisational atmosphere is friendly without being very productive and is typical of coasting schools and well-established fee-paying, socially selective private schools. In this mode, the primary concern for leaders and managers is the needs of people, and there is a focus on satisfying relationships. In practical terms, this approach leads to a comfortable low-tempo work environment where results may be sacrificed for the sake of harmonious working conditions.

- (9,1). This 'dictatorial' or 'produce-or-perish' style is characterised by 'do this or else'. Leaders using this style pressurise their subordinates through rules and punishments to achieve goals set by the leader. This style is predicated on McGregor's Theory X view of human endeavour, discussed in detail in the next chapter: the belief that workers will do nothing (or very little) unless forced to, and that they are inherently lazy. This style is commonly used in schools, universities and sports teams that are, or are perceived to be, on the brink of failure. It is essentially 'crisis management' and is common in failing schools and in universities with a 'publish-or-perish' approach to academic work. In this mode, the primary concern of leaders and managers is task completion, and they arrange working conditions so that the human element is kept to a minimum. In practical terms, the leader typically dictates to staff what should be done and how to do it because to do otherwise would be to 'trust' subordinates who, the leader assumes, are innately disinterested.

- (5,5). This 'status quo' or 'middle-of-the-road' style is characterised by 'compromise'. Leaders try to balance organisational goals against the needs of employees. By giving moderate concern to both people and task, managers hope to achieve a suitable balance between productivity and human resource management. In schools and universities where this is seen to fail, it is usually because giving equal concern to both means that neither is properly satisfied. In this mode, the primary concern of leaders is to maintain *adequate* performance by balancing the needs of task with the need to maintain staff morale. In practical terms, the style manifests itself as quite a political approach that maintains, rather than challenges, the status quo.

- (9,9). This 'sound' or 'team' style is characterised by 'commit and contribute'. High concern is paid to both person and task, with leaders and managers encouraging teamwork and commitment among subordinates. It is predicated on McGregor's Theory Y view of human endeavour – the belief that workers naturally *want* to do their best for the organisation, and *will* do their best if enabled – and relies heavily on making subordinates feel co-ownership of the organisation and its goals. Education leaders in this category have a sense of missionary zeal about them, but they run high-pressure work environments where nobody wants to 'let the side down', and these environments typically have a high incidence of stress-related staff turnover. The style can be found mostly in academically selective schools[2] and their 'wannabe' public sector equivalents. Leaders put a strong emphasis on both task and relationships, and objectives are accomplished by committed people. In practical terms, there is a sense of interdependence because everyone feels a common stake in the enterprise, leading to relationships of trust and mutual respect. The school or university department is then both task-centred and person-centred, but overall it is goal-focused and seeks progress through the involvement and participation of all staff. Blake and Mouton linked this style with 750 of the most successful managers in the business sector.

A later revised version of the Managerial Grid (Blake & Mouton, 1985) added two more styles:

- The 'opportunistic' style, which is characterised by 'exploit and manipulate', where managers adopt whichever behaviour offers the greatest personal benefit to them. It does not have a fixed location on the matrix.
- The 'paternalistic' style, which is characterised by 'prescribe and guide'. It is said to alternate between the (1,9) and (9,1) locations on the grid with managers using it to praise and support, but in such a way as to discourage challenges to their own thinking.

Some of the usefulness of the Blake and Mouton grid is lost by its failure to recognise that some situations benefit from being (9,1) and not (9,9), and that the latter is not always the ideal. There is also an element of the False Dilemma fallacy about the model, as it (wrongly) presents complex issues in terms of two inherently opposed and mutually exclusive sides. Although the grid's focus-on-task survived as a defining feature of what later became 'distributed leadership' (see Chapter 26), albeit not exactly as the term was used earlier, the recognition that leadership is a subtle activity and contingent on circumstance led ultimately to another category, situational or contingency theory, which we will discuss in Chapter 7.

Followership

Followership is the intentional practice on the part of a subordinate to enhance the interchange with the leader. It is more than simply 'being led'. Followership has been called the 'mirror image' of leadership because the actions of followers determine the success of a leader, so the term is used in this book when there is an expectation that 'subordinates' are active and intentional and seek synergy with their leaders in the praxis of leadership.

Followership has developed along the lines of leadership, but it is at an early stage of theorisation and the literature concentrates on 'traits' in the same way that leadership theory did in *its* infancy, albeit without the 'Great Man' element. It is said that good followers have courage, a good work ethic, discretion, loyalty and honesty. In terms of behaviour, they have good judgement, are competent in the exercise of their duties and self-manage their egos. Unfortunately, the same could be said of a burglar or a mass murderer! The canvas is so wide and generic that virtually every-thing and everyone could fit into it.

Actually, despite followership's apparent recent provenance, it is reminiscent of the old-fashioned concept of the perfect manservant epitomised by the Winchester College 'Trusty Servant': an emblematic figure displayed in a mural at the famous English private school. Painted in 1579, it sets out the desirable traits of domestic servants in pictorial form (see Figure 5.3). It is a human figure in outline, standing upright, but with a boar's head, a stag's feet and a donkey's ears. It has a padlock on its mouth and assorted symbols in its hands. The painting is accompanied by an allegorical poem, in Latin as befits the proud intellectual tradition of the place, which associates the servant's various animal parts with those virtues that students of the College were taught to value and expect: the padlock shows that the good

FIGURE 5.3 The Trusty Servant at Winchester College.

servant will not disclose his employer's secrets; the donkey ears show that he will be a good listener to his master; the boar's head that he will not be a fussy eater; the stag's feet that he will be swift in doing errands; his open hand that he will be honest and faithful; the sword that he will be loyal and protective; the well-tailored coat that he will be neat and competent; and so on. The ideal follower, in fact … from the 16th century!

Today, followership, while still the actions of a subordinate, is seen as a specific set of skills that complement leadership and as a formally defined role within the hierarchy of the organisation. Like the Trusty Servant, it is a social construct, but today it is seen as integral to the leadership process, especially popular in the military as a better means to achieve objectives. It is intentional and synergistic and has skills and competencies that it shares with leadership. The two do not exist on one single spectrum like task-centred versus person-centred behaviour, but they are separate dimensions. Leadership can be exercised by followers, and followership by leaders (Baker, 2007; Riggio, 2014). Followers might not create the strategic vision for an organisation, but they do make the vision a reality. It is claimed, as a way of legitimising the concept, that Aristotle suggested that follow-ership was a necessary precursor to leadership, but this is not what Aristotle had in mind or what the current theory claims for itself. Nor should followership be confused with empowerment or a more 'inclusive' democratisation of organisa-tions. It is a practical utilitarian approach to meeting objectives which shares the burden of achievement between those being led and those doing the leading (and its take-up in military organisations reflects those limitations). Unsurprisingly, Warren Bennis was a supporter (see Chapter 24). He saw leadership as being like beauty: hard to define, but you know it when you see it! And that was his view of followership too.

Robert Kelley was one of the early movers in the field of followership. In his 1988 *Harvard Business Review* article and in his subsequent (1992) book *The Power of Followership*, he lists a set of four 'essential qualities' of followership and went on to make three critical points:

- Firstly, he introduced a two-by-two matrix with on the vertical axis, criti-cal v. uncritical thinking (the former representing independence and the lat-ter dependence) on the vertical axis; and active v. passive on the horizontal axis. The four quadrants thus inscribed show 'sheep' (dependent and passive followers), 'yes-people' (dependent but active followers), 'alienated' followers (independent and passive), and 'effective' or 'star' followers (independent and active).[3] 'Sheep are individuals that require external motivation and constant supervision. 'Yes people' are conformists committed to the leader (and to the collective) and to the task, and will defend their leader when faced with oppo-sition. They do not question the leader. The 'Alienated' are negative and often attempt to bring the group down by constantly questioning the decisions and actions of the leader. 'Star' followers are positive, active and independent thinkers. They do not blindly accept the decisions or actions of a leader until they have evaluated them completely, but they can be trusted to get the job done.

- Secondly, Kelley raised the issue of follower self-management. The key to being an effective follower is the ability to think for oneself, to exercise independence and to work without supervision. Good followers are subordinates 'to whom a leader can safely delegate responsibility'.
- And thirdly, Kelley highlighted the paradox of followers being 'more apt to openly and unapologetically disagree with leadership and less likely to be intimidated by hierarchy and organisational structure'. For Kelley, effective followers see themselves 'except in terms of line responsibility, as the equals of the leaders they follow' (Kelley, 1988).

Followership in the military, where the theory has found considerable traction, is a role-based followership with a focus on technical and tactical proficiency, setting an example for others, understanding and finishing tasks, compliance with orders and taking appropriate and timely action in the absence of superior officers. The doctrine is called 'mission command': the belief that the 'leader in the field' is always right and acts with maximum discretion in accordance with the situation on the ground. Followership has also had some traction in education (Hurwitz & Hurwitz, 2015; Kouzes & Posner, 2012), but in that context it is not as utilitarian in its approach or in its application. For one thing, it is obvious in the military, being such a perfect bureaucratic pyramid, who the follower is and who the leader is, particularly in the absence of conscription or compulsory service. Schools, colleges and universities are by their nature flatter organisations, and the follower 'class' is sometimes conceptualised as the student body. This is problematic for education because it confuses an employee with a consumer of the service that is schooling or higher education. There is an argument to be made that education is a human right and not a 'good' or a 'service', but this is to ignore the reality of decades of marketisation. Nor is it clear, in universities at least, whether followership is the best preparation for (say) post-doc graduate students wanting to move into tenured academic careers. In a military structure, a superior officer *must* be followed irrespective of worthiness – that is the definition of Weber's bureaucracy (Waters & Waters, 2015) – but not every educational leader is 'worthy' of being, or needs to be, followed. If we include *student* followership turning into leadership in curriculum matters, then that needs to be taken into account in formal assessment procedures, and that has not yet been done. Kleiner (2008) went some way towards addressing similar issues in college admission; specifically that student followership needs to place greater emphasis on its contribution to classroom learning. If teachers encourage followership, Kleiner says, they should find ways of using it to improve the quality of their pedagogy and enable their students to practise effective leadership.

Chaleff (2009) developed a model called 'courageous followership'. While general followership is aligned with distributed leadership (to be discussed in Chapter

26), courageous followership is aligned with moral leadership (see Chapter 17). The Chaleff model proposes four dimensions in which followers operate within a group, and a fifth dimension in which they operate either within or outside a group depending on the response of the leader:

- *Assume responsibility.* Courageous followers assume responsibility for themselves and for the organisation. They do not expect the leader or the organisation to provide for their growth, nor do they need permission to act. Courageous followers discover and create opportunities to fulfil their potential and maximise their utility value to the organisation. They initiate values-based action to improve the organisation's activities and processes.
- *To serve.* Courageous followers are not afraid of hard work. They assume new responsibilities, stay alert for areas in which their strengths can complement those of the leader, and assert themselves in these areas. They stand up for their leader and the tough decisions the leader must take.
- *To challenge.* Courageous followers say what they think when they have a disagreement or when the organisation acts improperly. They are willing to risk rejection and not to shy away from conflict when that is necessary. They value harmony, but not at the expense of integrity.
- *To participate in transformational leadership.* Courageous followers champion the need for change, and they examine their own need for improvement.
- *To take moral action.* Courageous followers know when it is time to take a stand opposing the leader. The same exists in the military when refusing to obey a direct order on moral grounds. It is not done lightly. Moral action involves personal professional risk (Chaleff, 2009).

A more realistic take on followership is the Leader–Member Exchange (LMX) theory. It focuses on how leaders and followers engage together to generate effective working relationships. LMX theory acknowledges followership as part of this process, but the theory is more leadership than followership in that it privileges the leader as the driver of the process (Uhl-Bien et al., 2000), although it is suggested by promoters of implicit followership theory that a leader's belief in followership has an impact on its efficacy. Higher expectations for followership make followers more effective. Sadly, this is not quite the great revelation that it appears, since effective followership is itself defined by its synergy with responsive leadership, and vice versa.

Notes

1 A master's degree in business administration.
2 For example, public sector grammar schools and elite fee-paying private schools in England.
3 In the middle of the matrix, an average mixture of all four quadrants are 'survivors'. These individuals are not trailblazers. They wait until the majority has expressed its support before they express theirs, and prefer to stay in the background.

6

BEHAVIOURAL THEORIES

Motivational, authentic and transactional leadership

The second set of writers in the behavioural theory field is led by Douglas McGregor, Abraham Maslow and Frederick Hertzberg. Douglas McGregor (1906–1964) was a professor of management at the MIT Sloan School of Management and president of Antioch College, Ohio, from 1948 to 1954. His 1960 book *The Human Side of Enterprise* had a profound influence on education. He contributed much to the development of management and motivational theory and is best known for his Theory X and Theory Y assumptions about human nature and behaviour, and how these contrasting views (should) determine how leaders manage their employees. The Theory X managerial approach creates an environment within which employees are motivated by authoritative direction and control. The Theory Y approach creates an environment within which employees are motivated by integration and *self*-control (Kopelman et al., 2008). Essentially, Theory X represents an autocratic approach, and Theory Y represents a softer and more democratic approach. They represent two extremes, of course, and as such are more theoretical than practical, but it can be said that Theory Y underpins the participative, person-centred approach described by Blake and Mouton, and Theory X the other.

A Theory X manager believes that:

- People have a natural dislike of work and will avoid it if possible. Therefore, it is necessary for effective managers to use a 'carrot and stick' approach to motivation; for example, incentive schemes coupled with a performativity approach.
- Since people innately dislike work, it is necessary for effective managers to command and control, and if necessary to threaten with dismissal, in order to ensure that organisational goals are met.
- People's dislike of work also means that they will avoid responsibility and will *want* to be commanded and controlled, and will gladly trade any illusion of independence for job security.

DOI: 10.4324/9781003217220-6

In contrast, a Theory Y manager believes that:

- Work is a natural endeavour for humans, and employees do not need to be threatened to get them to do their best and to achieve an organisation's goals.
- People can and will direct *themselves* in their work.
- Commitment is a function of the rewards offered for achievement, particularly if those rewards speak to a person's ego.
- The average subordinate not only accepts responsibility but will naturally seek it out.
- The ability to be imaginative, creative and problem-solving is innate in people, not just in an elite few, and modern organisational structures should enable people to contribute to the maximum extent possible.

McGregor was working on a Theory Z at time of his death in 1964, which attempted to synthesise organisational and individual imperatives. His Theory X and Theory Y are very much of their time and reflect a Fordist production economy. In the real world, most leaders and managers flirt with Theory Y approaches and then retreat to Theory X for fear of losing control, particularly in schools and colleges where the applicability of Theory X is questionable and culturally inappropriate with managers and subordinates being equally qualified *as job-holders*. McGregor was commonly thought to be a proponent of Theory Y, but as Edgar Schein says in his introduction to McGregor's posthumous book *The Professional Manager*:

> In my own contacts with Doug, I often found him to be discouraged by the degree to which Theory Y had become as monolithic a set of principles as those of Theory X, the over-generalization which Doug was fighting. ... Yet few readers were willing to acknowledge that the content of Doug's book made such a neutral point or that Doug's own presentation of his point of view was that coldly scientific.
>
> (McGregor et al., 1970)

Cleverley in *Managers & Magic* (1971) comments that McGregor:

> coined the two terms Theory X and Theory Y and used them to label two sets of beliefs a manager might hold about the origins of human behaviour. ... [He] hoped that his book would lead managers to investigate the two sets of beliefs, invent others, test out the assumptions underlying them, and develop managerial strategies that made sense in terms of those tested views of reality. But that isn't what happened. Instead McGregor was interpreted as advocating Theory Y as a new and superior ethic – a set of moral values that ought to replace the values managers usually accept.
>
> (Cleverley, 1971)

The Human Side of Enterprise was voted the fourth most influential management book of the 20th century in a poll of Fellows of the Academy of Management (Bedeian & Wren, 2001).

McGregor was close to Abraham Maslow (1908–1970), the famous American psychologist who is today best known for creating his 'hierarchy of needs' (although he didn't use that term exactly). Maslow's hierarchy is a theory of psychological well-being based on fulfilling innate human needs in order of priority, culminating in what he called 'self-actualisation' (Maslow, 1954). He stressed the importance of focusing on the positive qualities in people – negative people have a problem for every solution! – as opposed to treating them as a 'bag of symptoms' (Hoffman, 1999: 109). His mentor was Alfred Adler, one of Sigmund Freud's early colleagues, but Maslow's view is based on the concept of free will, which contrasts with (and opposes) Freud's theory of biological determinism.

Just as the replacement of trait leadership theory by behavioural theory emerged from the experience of World War II, so too did Maslow's ground-breaking studies into self-actualisation. Maslow urged people to acknowledge their basic needs before addressing higher ones and ultimately self-actualisation, where individuals are in harmony with themselves and with their surroundings. Maslow believed that leadership should be non-interventionist, and he rejected the idea that organisations should have formal 'leaders' at all. His thinking was that to be mentally healthy, individuals should take personal responsibility for their actions, both good and bad, and that every person is inherently worthy despite occasionally doing the wrong thing. Only through constant self-improvement and self-understanding can an individual ever be truly happy, a view that aligns with McGregor's Theory Y view of humanity.

Maslow's hierarchy (see Figure 6.1) is applicable in many fields: economics, criminology, business, education and leadership studies. Its relevance to leadership and management studies lies in the fact that those who subscribe to it hold that practical structures should reflect this 'reality' of human motivation. The theory describes human needs as being ordered in a hierarchy. A pressing need must be (mostly, if not fully) satisfied before someone gives their attention to the next-highest need. As far as this author can ascertain, none of Maslow's own published works included a visual representation of the hierarchy: the well-known pyramid diagram illustrating the hierarchy was probably created subsequently by a textbook publisher. Unfortunately, the pyramid suggests a fixed, rigid progression from one need to another, even though Maslow always said that human needs were relatively fluid and simultaneously present in any person at any given time. Notwithstanding, Maslow's theory *does* claim that when a person ascends the levels of the hierarchy having fulfilled the lower needs in the hierarchy, the person probably arrives at the top self-actualisation level, although that is not necessarily automatic.

- At the bottom of the hierarchy are the 'Basic' physiological needs: food, shelter, water, sleep, sex, and so forth.
- The next level has 'Safety' needs: security, order and stability. These bottom two steps are important to the physical survival of a person. Once individuals have basic nutrition, shelter and safety, they attempt to accomplish more.
- The third level has 'Love and Belonging' needs, which are psychological rather than physiological. When individuals have taken care of themselves physically, they are ready to share themselves with family and friends.

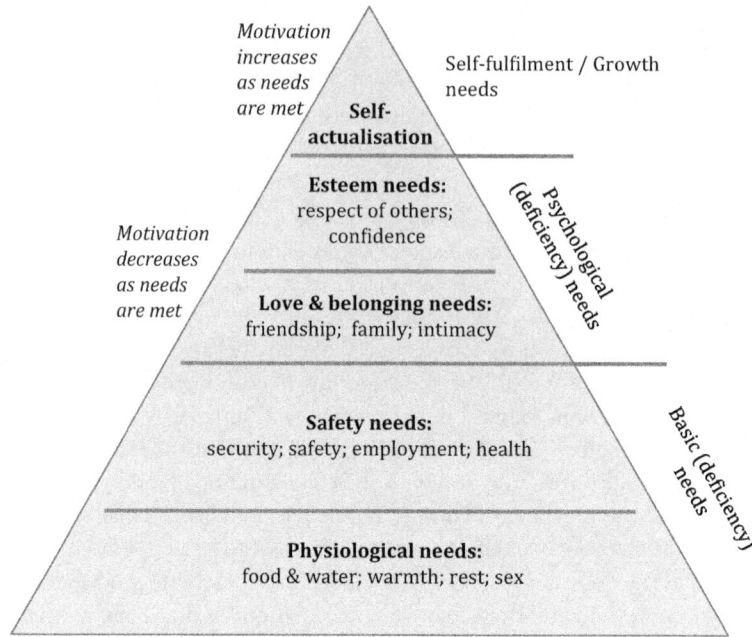

FIGURE 6.1 Maslow's hierarchy of needs.

- The fourth level is the 'Esteem' level, the need to be competent and recognized through status and level of success. It is achieved when individuals feel comfortable with what they have accomplished.
- Fifth is the 'Cognitive' level, where individuals intellectually stimulate themselves and explore.
- The next level is the 'Aesthetic' level, which is the need for, and appreciation of, harmony and beauty.
- Finally, at the apex of the pyramid is the need for 'Self-actualisation'. It occurs when individuals reach a state of self-understanding and self-confidence as a result of achieving their full potential. At this level people focus on themselves and on building their own image.

The first four levels are known as 'Deficiency' or 'D' needs. If a person does not have enough of one of these four needs, the person will be driven to get it. Maslow proposed that certain conditions must be fulfilled for basic needs to be satisfied – for example, freedom of speech and freedom to express oneself – but the most relevant part of Maslow's theory of motivation as it pertains to leadership is the self-actualisation tier. Self-actualisation means achieving the fullest use of one's talents and interests. It is the need to become 'everything that one is capable of becoming' (Hagerty, 1999). Self-actualisation is very individualistic and reflects Maslow's view that people are 'sovereign and inviolable' with their own tastes, opinions and values. Some writers have characterised self-actualisation as 'healthy narcissism' (Pauchant & Dumas, 1991), which is also a familiar refrain in leadership studies. According to Maslow, who made case studies of the great and the good of his day – Einstein, Kuhn and Thoreau, amongst others – people who have self-actualised share certain characteristics in the fashion of trait theory, so in this respect Maslow reminds us of behavioural theory's provenance in the earlier trait approach. Outstanding practitioners in their fields, like Einstein, Kuhn and Thoreau, are characterised (according to Maslow) by their focus on reality, their meaningful relationships with other people and with the larger world and their ability to treat life's challenges as problems to be solved. They are comfortable with being alone but have healthy personal relationships, typically with a few close friends and family rather than with a large circle of acquaintances. They are focused on problems outside themselves, have a clear sense of what is true and what is false, have a clear moral compass, are creative and spontaneous (sometimes even slightly impulsive), are not bound too strictly by social conventions, are accepting of who they are themselves and accepting of the world as it is, are very independent and private, and are finishers.

Self-actualised people are driven by innate forces beyond their basic needs – what Maslow called 'meta-motivation' – but it is not clear from his theory why more people do not self-actualise when their basic needs are met. Attempting to answer this conundrum, this author's own research and experience in the education sector suggests that leaders in schools and universities who are in pursuit of self-actualisation but have not yet achieved it are characterised by self-promotion and the management of self-image, rather than by the desire to solve problems, their work driven by the need to 'fail upwards': to get promoted to the next unsatisfying level of their own incompetence. They have a focus on quantity rather than quality of work, and an absence of *meaningful* relationships with other people beyond those who can advance their careers. Although they have a large cocktail party of reference-givers, they lack the critical component of self-actualisation in their own leadership: they lack something bigger than themselves. Their need is to be bigger than others: to be bigger than the school, the college or the research team they manage. They wrongly see personal success and the acclaim that follows it as evidence of their efficacy, but truly self-actualised leaders seek primarily to advance the institution; they don't need the applause.

The third leading light in the behavioural theory field is Frederick Hertzberg (1923–2000). Herzberg was a US psychologist famous for developing his Motivator-Hygiene theory of job satisfaction. His 1968 publication *One More Time, How Do You Motivate Employees?* remains one of the most requested articles from the *Harvard Business Review*. Herzberg conducted his research on organisations in the 1950s at the University of Utah and acted as consultant to many governments and commercial companies. According to his theory, also known as the Two-Factor or Dual-Factor theory, people are influenced by two sets of factors: one set causes job *satisfaction* while another causes job *dissatisfaction*. Both sets of factors act independently of each other, but they both relate to Maslow's theory of motivation. According to

Herzberg, employees are not content with the satisfaction of lower-order needs at work: minimum salary levels, pleasant working conditions, etc. Instead, they seek the gratification of higher-level psychological needs: achievement, recognition, responsibility, advancement and the nature of the work itself. The factors that lead to satisfaction (achievement, intrinsic interest in the work, responsibility, and advancement) are mostly 'unipolar'; that is, they contribute very little to job *dis*satisfaction. Conversely, the factors that lead to dissatisfaction (organisational policy, administrative practices, supervision, interpersonal relationships, working conditions, and salary) contribute very little to job satisfaction.

Herzberg's extension of Maslow's theory lies in the fact that he proposed a two-factor model of motivation, based on the notion that the presence of one set of job characteristics or incentives leads to employee *satisfaction*, while another separate set of job characteristics leads to employee *dissatisfaction*. The two (satisfaction and dissatisfaction) are two ends of a continuum, with one increasing as the other decreases, but they are independent of each other. Herzberg found that job characteristics related to what an employee *does* – that is, to the nature of the work the employee performs – can gratify needs like achievement, status, personal worth and self-actualisation, thus making the employee happy and satisfied. However, the *absence* of these self-actualising job characteristics does *not* lead to unhappiness and dissatisfaction. Instead, dissatisfaction results from unfavourable job-related factors like organisational policies, poor supervision, technical problems, low salary, poor interpersonal relations on the job and bad working conditions. The implication for managers is that they must look after both sets of characteristics and not assume that an increase in satisfaction automatically leads to decrease in dissatisfaction. If managers want to increase satisfaction on the job, they must be concerned with the *nature* of the work itself, with the opportunities the work presents for gaining status and responsibility, for the challenge and meaningfulness of the work, for achievement and recognition, for involvement in decision-making and a sense of importance to the organisation, and for achieving self-actualisation (Herzberg, 1968). Simultaneously, managers wanting to reduce dissatisfaction should focus on the workplace *environment*; having sensible policies, fair procedures, good supervision, fringe benefits, good pensions, adequate vacation time and good working conditions. These factors do not give positive satisfaction or lead to higher motivation, but dissatisfaction results from their absence (Bassett-Jones & Lloyd, 2005).

Herzberg called the first set of factors that increase satisfaction 'motivators' and the second set that reduce dissatisfaction he called 'hygiene' or 'maintenance' factors'. Hygiene factors (or 'dissatisfaction-avoidance') are extrinsic to the work itself, meaning that the factor refers to doing something because it leads to a distinct outcome, something external that the employee expects to receive, rather than doing something because it is inherently interesting or enjoyable, an internal reward. Herzberg often referred to them as 'KITA' ('kick-in-the-ass') factors providing incentives or the threat of punishment. There are several ways for managers to decrease dissatisfaction via negating or removing hygiene factors: pay reasonable wages, ensure job security and create a positive culture in the work-place.[1] Herzberg thought it was important to eliminate job dissatisfaction before going on to creating conditions for job satisfaction because they would work against each other.[2]

According to Herzberg's Motivator-Hygiene theory, there are four possible combinations laid out in a Blake and Mouton–style two-by-two matrix:

- (High Hygiene, High Motivation). This is the ideal situation where employees are highly motivated and have few complaints.
- (High Hygiene, Low Motivation). Employees have few complaints but are not highly motivated. The job is viewed merely as a source of income.
- (Low Hygiene, High Motivation). Employees are motivated but have a lot of complaints. This is a situation where the job is exciting and challenging, but salaries and work conditions are poor and do not reflect the work done.
- (Low Hygiene, Low Motivation). This is the worst of the four situations where employees are not motivated *and* have many complaints.

The Seven Colour Motivation model

Another motivation approach is the Seven Colour Motivation model. Graves (1970) and Beck and Cowan (1996) categorised behaviour according to personality type and identified seven different motivations, each represented by a colour, like de Bono's six colour thinking hats discussed in Chapter 4. The theory is that each person has developed a unique combination of these seven motivations.

- The *purple* personality type is motivated by 'stability'. It is characterised by respect for tradition and rituals and is common to Ivy League universities and elite English public schools. It is also characterised by the avoidance of situations that are perceived as dangerous or risky, acceding to the wishes of superiors, and the primacy of the majority over 'self'. Strengths include the ability to bring people together as a team, to understand social relationships and sustain traditional organisational values. Weaknesses include a difficulty in adapting to change and a tendency to sacrifice self too easily.
- The *red* personality type is motivated by 'power' and is characterised by a slight impulsiveness and an inclination to rush to action, a tendency to enjoy long-lasting friendships and the belief that leadership respect has to be earned. This type is common among deputy heads and vice-principals, particularly when the headteacher or principal is younger or less experienced. Strengths include the ability to make decisions and take action, to protect junior colleagues and to have good experiential instinct. Weaknesses include a tendency to distrust and over-react, and to take the view that others are either friend or foe.
- The *blue* personality type is motivated by 'structure'. This type is characterised by faith in rules and regulations, in hierarchy, in there being one right way to do a job, and in doing things 'one step at a time'. Strengths include reliability, loyalty, the ability to set a good example for others, and predictability. Weaknesses

include an inability to multi-task, unconditional loyalty and having too much faith in the old ways of doing things.

- The *orange* personality type is motivated by 'results' and characterised by an emphasis on effectiveness, strategy, finding solutions, optimism and a belief that those who take risks should be rewarded. Strengths include the smart use of resources, and self-awareness about own position and that of the competition. Weaknesses include an over-emphasis on competition when cooperation might be a better option, a tendency to break the rules to make the most of opportunities as they arise, and a tendency to hoard success.
- The *green* personality type is motivated by 'people-mindedness'. This type is characterised by sensitivity to the feelings of others, consensus-building, collegiality, collective responsibility, and a belief in the fair distribution of reward. Strengths include the ability to create harmonious relations, build teams and encourage teamwork, and develop a salutogenetic view within the organisation. (We discuss this last point in Chapter 8.) Weaknesses include a tendency to put good relations above everything else, being too person-centred at the expense of task, difficulty making decisions and taking action, and having a problem with authority.
- The *yellow* personality type is motivated by 'innovation'. It is characterised by flexibility and the freedom to think outside the box, the belief that competence is more important than seniority or hierarchy, and creating a shared understanding and vision. Strengths include the ability to manage complexity, embrace change, deal with uncertainty and multi-task. Weaknesses include a tendency to theorise and create models that lack a focus on practicality, and a slightly chaotic approach to managing.
- The *turquoise* personality type is motivated by a holistic view. This final type is characterised by connectedness, intuitiveness and a belief that the environment is a single entity with a collective consciousness. Strengths include the ability to think quickly in complex situations, to be open to different approaches, to make good use of information and to not be egocentric. Weaknesses include a tendency to take on board too many points of view and to lack focus.

A questionnaire based on the Seven Colour model asks questions about how a person would react to hypothetical situations, and a profile is then drafted as an indicator of likely behaviour. The benefit of such tests is that they reveal the extent to which people are susceptible to the negative weaknesses within each motivator type (colour) so that certain behaviours and tensions can be avoided. The tests also show how likely people are to have the positive strengths associated with each colour, and to calculate and map the balance between the positives and the negatives for each colour. These motivational insights are useful in schools and university departments when colleagues are coming together in teams and getting to know each other. The model can also be used to get to know oneself (Van den Berg & Pietersma, 2016), but the danger of bias is difficult to overcome.

Authentic leadership

Authentic leadership is a leadership model that advocates building a leader's legitimacy through honest genuine relationships with followers, stressing the importance of ethical foundations in how leaders motivate followers (and self). Authentic leadership is open, trusting and generally person-centred. It is a precondition for 'ethical leadership'. It generates enthusiastic followership, and it puts great value on team-working, although its theoretical and research underpinning has been questioned recently for its tautological conceptualisation and 'poor research practice' (Alvesson & Einola, 2019; Retraction Watch, 2014a, 2014b, 2014c; Sidani & Rowe, 2018).[3]

The concept of authenticity claims a long provenance. 'Know thy own measure' was the first of three maxims inscribed in the forecourt of the Temple of Apollo at Delphi, and Aeschylus used the phrase in his play *Prometheus Bound*. The phrase was also common in Latin texts (*nosce te ipsum*), and it features in *The Art of War*, the ancient (5th century BC) Chinese text attributed to Sun Tzu. However, in these usages, authenticity was meant to convey the importance of being in control of one's own life, and to ignore the opinion and flattery of others. In that sense, it is not strictly speaking the progenitor of authentic leadership, as is claimed, although there is an obvious link. Authentic leadership is about how leaders define their own roles within an organisation, being true to their moral values and (coming across as) being true to followers and stakeholders. It is particularly important when schools and universities are dealing with students and parents.

There are many different definitions of authentic leadership and some subtle differences in approach, but most of them, if not all, assert that it includes being self-aware, 'knowing thyself', being a reflective practitioner, being open and sharing thoughts and beliefs, getting different opinions and giving everyone a respectful hearing, and having a firm personal moral and ethical foundation that can stand up to the seemingly endless pressure in education for greater efficiency and performativity. Some commentators have disputed the need to include the moral component, suggesting that a leader can be 'true' to a corrupt value system or be motivated by selfishness and still be authentic, and that merely *pretending* to have certain moral standpoints should *not* be a bar to authenticity (Shamir & Eilam, 2005). Konrad Adenauer, Chancellor of Germany and chief architect of its political reconstruction after World War II, said in an interview[4] in 1946:

> Any fool … can be a man of conviction. In fact, fanatics are sincere, all too sincere. What I am interested in are values, permanent values.
>
> (Prittie, 1972: 315)

Authentic leadership can also be understood as a pattern of behaviours rather than as a set of values, beliefs, motivations or traits. As such, the focus is on the leader's conduct being such that followers and stakeholders view the leader as authentic, and the challenge becomes one of identifying those factors that contribute to the most effective way of working. Authentic leaders must be clear about their own values and how to present them in order to be *perceived* as 'authentic' by followers, and they have to demonstrate consistency between those values and their own conduct. Jensen and Luthans (2006) found that truly authentic leaders behave with optimism and resilience: they set and explain goals effectively to create a more hopeful environment for followers; they are resilient in supporting their followers in a changing world; and followers are more easily motivated by their optimism. Authentic leaders also promote the belief among followers in the ability of the collective – the school, college, university department or team – to succeed. This is known as 'team potency', and it improves performance (Lester et al., 2002; Rego et al., 2013). Authentic leadership also encourages what in universities is commonly called 'good citizenship': the willingness of staff to accept largely unpaid roles within the collective, for the common good and because 'it's their turn'.

Authentic leadership metrics

Measuring levels of authentic leadership is difficult, but a number of scales and questionnaires have been proposed. They are more a testament to the field's desire to measure than they are reliable scientific instruments.

- The Leader Authenticity Scale: This is a 32-item scale, developed for use in schools, which measures a leader's tendency to behave genuinely ('salience') regardless of formal job titles ('role'). It also measures a leader's willingness to acknowledge mistakes and avoid being manipulative (Gardner et al., 2011; Henderson & Hoy, 1983).
- Authentic Leadership Questionnaire: This is a survey completed *by followers* to capture the extent of authentic leadership behaviour exhibited by their leaders. The metric comprises 16 items grouped into four categories: self-awareness; transparency; morality; and balanced processing. It uses a qualitative subjective approach.
- Authentic Leadership Inventory: The Authentic Leadership Inventory (ALI) is another survey completed by followers about their leaders. It is based on the same theoretical research as the aforementioned Authentic Leadership Questionnaire, but more rigorous and better tested.

Leaders become 'authentic' as a result of their personal experiences and how these experiences collectively create, or reinforce, a leader's morality. How leaders interpret their own biographies creates their identities and ethical development. Authentic leadership is about being true to oneself and one's ideals of leadership, bought by a lifetime of experiential capital; so while leaders must change their behaviour to the situation at hand, this must occur within their personal ethical bounds, rather than adapt their ethics to the behaviour. They must remain true *in what they do* to the set of values they have already 'advertised' to followers. In that sense, authentic leadership is transactional (see the next section), but in another sense it is transformational in the charismatic tradition, motivating followers by acting (or seeming to act) ethically and to high standards.

Transactional leadership

Transactional leadership focuses on remediation and performance. It is a style where leaders promote compliance and motivation among followers using a system of reward and punishment. Unlike transformational leadership, transactional leaders do not seek change. They don't want to 'create their own future' (see Chapters 23–25): they look to keep things the same, but correct faults and increase efficiency. Transactional leadership is useful in crisis situations or when an important project (say) must be finished urgently. It is task-centred and as such is closely aligned to coaching with its focus on task, reward and punishment.

Transactional leaders reward followers – sometimes with salary increases and sometimes with recognition – when they meet the goals set for them. They also maintain a constant watch on subordinates to evaluate performance and 'punish' poor work. Transactional leadership works at the basic level of need-satisfaction in Maslow's hierarchy, focusing on lower-level needs and stressing task-performance-specific, in contrast to transformational leadership, which focuses on higher-level needs. It is primarily concerned with *processes now* rather than *ideas in the future*. Transactional leadership has three dimensions:

- *Contingent rewards.* These are made when goals are accomplished on schedule or to keep subordinates working at a good pace. They reward desired behaviour.
- *Active management-by-exception.* This means that the leader continually monitors performance and takes immediate corrective action when something looks like it's going wrong.
- *Passive management-by-exception.* This is about waiting until completion before taking corrective action.

Unlike transformational leaders, transactional leaders are not concerned specifically with the well-being of subordinates. They accept the culture of an organisation as it is, and they are willing to work within existing systems. They are directive and action-oriented. Unlike transformational leaders, they don't think outside the box and are more passive in their leadership, but it is practical and directive with explicit and simple measures for success, reward and punishment. Transactional leadership is good for situations where everyone needs to be aligned in a large organisation, and as such it is not really suitable for schools, colleges and university departments. In addition, transactional leadership is not long-term, does not work well in flexible work environments and does not reward individuals who take the initiative, all of which are requirements for, and features of, working in an education setting. Transactional leadership is associated with McGregor's Theory X, where managers assume that staff, being inherently lazy, will do the minimum unless rewarded and punished, and in that sense transactional leadership highlights, by holding up a mirror to it, the inadequacies of the Theory X approach *in education*. It also affords us an easy contrast with transformational leadership, which is more closely aligned with McGregor's Theory Y and which assumes that staff are inherently self-motivated to do their best and just need to be 'enabled' with the necessary resources for success, suggesting that the transformational model is better suited, with some limitations, to school and university management.

Notes

1 Herzberg considered the following hygiene factors from highest to lowest importance: organisational policies; modes of supervision; employee relationships with the manager; working conditions; salary; and relationships with other employees.
2 Herzberg classified actions and how and why employees do them; for example, a work-related task that employees *must do* is defined as a 'movement', but if employees perform a work-related task because they *want to*, then it is classed as a 'motivation'.
3 For example, *The Leadership Quarterly*, a management journal published by Elsevier, retracted seven papers by one American academic in 2014.
4 Recorded in a personal memorandum by US journalist James O'Donnell.

7
SITUATIONAL–CONTINGENCY THEORIES OF LEADERSHIP AND MANAGEMENT

Situational or contingency theory flows fairly seamlessly from behaviour theory; indeed, some of the writers mentioned already in relation to behaviour theory could easily be accommodated in the contingency camp as their work developed over the years. The difference between the two is relatively simple. Behaviour theory suggests that leaders should always follow a certain style: democratic, autocratic or a mixture of the two, depending on personality. Contingency theorists, on the other hand, say it depends on circumstances or situation, not on personality. In a crisis, for example, there may be a greater need for an autocratic style, whether the context is a failing school or a university facing bankruptcy. There are many examples from the political sphere: Churchill's leadership during World War II followed by his emphatic election defeat in 1945 when the British electorate wanted a different type of leadership for peacetime; and, staying in the UK, the cabinet revolt against Thatcher in 1990 when her political and economic revolution was no longer popular with her own Conservative Party.

Formative writers in this field include Paul Hersey and Ken Blanchard, who developed it in the late 1960s while working on their book *Management of Organisational Behavior* (Hersey & Blanchard, 1969a, 1977). The theory was introduced as the 'life cycle theory of leadership' (Hersey & Blanchard, 1969b) and renamed 'situational' leadership theory by Hersey in the 1970s. But the approach can be traced to earlier work by Frederick Fiedler (1964, 1966, 1967) who by then had been working and publishing on leadership characteristics and group effectiveness for a decade (e.g. Fiedler, 1958).

DOI: 10.4324/9781003217220-7

Fiedler's contingency model

The Fiedler contingency model was created in the mid-1960s. The model holds that there is no single best style of leadership, but that a leader's effectiveness is dependent or 'contingent' on the situation. Leader efficacy is then the product of two factors: the leader's natural style and situation 'control'. The former needs to be matched to the latter, but identifying leadership style is the first step in using the model. Fiedler believed leadership style to be fixed and measurable using a bipolar Likert scale called the Least Preferred Co-worker (LPC) scale (see Table 7.1). The LPC scale asks the subject to remember another person[1] with whom they have worked and to rate that person on each of the scale items. If the total score is high, the subject is likely to be a person-centred, relationship-oriented leader because, according to Fiedler's theory, relationship-oriented leaders usually view their LPCs more positively and as a result score higher. If the total score is low, the subject is likely to be task-centred because task-oriented leaders usually view their LPCs negatively, producing a lower score.

Fiedler introduced the dichotomy 'task-oriented' versus 'relationship-oriented'. He called task-oriented leaders 'Low LPC leaders'. They are very effective at completing tasks and good at organising teams to get tasks done. They are directive- and achievement-oriented (House & Mitchell, 1974) rather than instrumental (Kerr & Jermier, 1978). Relationships and people are low priorities. In contrast, relationship-oriented leaders ('High-LPC leaders') focus more on personal relationships and managing conflict. They are good at making complex decisions and multi-tasking, are supportive and participative (House & Mitchell, 1974), and have a focus on maintenance rather than performance (Misumi, 1985).

TABLE 7.1 Fiedler's Least-Preferred Co-worker (LPC) scale

Unfriendly	1	2	3	4	5	6	7	8	Friendly
Unpleasant	1	2	3	4	5	6	7	8	Pleasant
Rejecting	1	2	3	4	5	6	7	8	Accepting
Boring	1	2	3	4	5	6	7	8	Interesting
Uncooperative	1	2	3	4	5	6	7	8	Cooperative
Untrustworthy	1	2	3	4	5	6	7	8	Trustworthy
Unkind	1	2	3	4	5	6	7	8	Kind
Tense	1	2	3	4	5	6	7	8	Relaxed
False	1	2	3	4	5	6	7	8	Sincere
Reserved	1	2	3	4	5	6	7	8	Open
Gloomy	1	2	3	4	5	6	7	8	Cheerful
Unsupportive	1	2	3	4	5	6	7	8	Supportive
Boring	1	2	3	4	5	6	7	8	Interesting
Disloyal	1	2	3	4	5	6	7	8	Loyal
Cold-hearted	1	2	3	4	5	6	7	8	Warm-hearted
Trouble-maker	1	2	3	4	5	6	7	8	Harmonious

Identifying the situation and control of it (or 'favourableness') is the second step in using the model. According to Fiedler, this depends on three factors:

- *Leader-staff relations*. This is the level of trust and confidence that a team has in the leader. A leader who is more trusted and has greater influence among staff is in a more favourable situation – i.e. has a higher 'favourableness' score – than a leader who is not trusted. In assessing this part of the favourableness of a situation, the question to ask is whether leader-staff relations are good or bad.
- *Task structure*. This refers to the type of task being done: whether it is clear and structured, or unclear and unstructured. An unstructured task is one where the team and the leader have little knowledge of how to achieve the objective and are therefore in a less favourable situation (i.e. have a lower 'favourableness' score). In assessing this part of the favourableness of a situation, the question to ask is whether the task being done is structured or unstructured, and whether the team has know-how and experience from solving similar problems.
- *The leader's positional authority*. This is the amount of power the leader has to direct staff, to give out (or retain) rewards and to impose sanctions. The more authority the leader has (i.e. 'stronger power'), the more favourable the situation. In assessing this part of the favourableness of a situation, the question to ask is whether the leader has strong or weak power over the team.

Having identified leadership style in the first step and having identified situation-favourableness in the second, the third and final step is to determine the most effective leadership style for the given scenario. For example, a newly appointed headteacher replacing a successful predecessor who was popular in the staff room and in the community will be a more effective leader as a High LPC (person-centred) leader who focuses initially and primarily on building relationships. There is no established trust base yet, the tasks being done by the new head and the teaching staff are usually structured and well-defined, and the head's position of power is high because she or he has the authority to reward and sanction. In contrast, a task-focused leadership style is more effective in urgent situations like when a school is failing or seriously underperforming, and the head is already leading a team with established trust and good staff relations, and the tasks are less structured and require greater creativity.

The Fiedler contingency model holds that once leaders understand their own 'natural' style, they can match it to situations in which that style is most effective. However, the model does not allow much flexibility – it is not very nuanced because Fiedler believed that a leader's natural style is fixed – and LPC scores might not be very accurate as a snapshot of a leader's style,[2] especially if the scores fall near the middle of the range so that the style is unclear. The problem with the model's lack of flexibility is that if leaders are in situations to which their fixed natural styles are unsuited, the only logical solution would be to replace them because they cannot 'find' a different style. This is impractical and just plain silly in the context of educational leadership, where hugely different situations, challenges and crises occur on a weekly or monthly basis.

Collectively, situational leadership theories emerged in short steps as a related group of two-factor theories, many of which originated in research done at Ohio State University in the 1960s. They all hold that leadership is a combination of, or tension between, task-centred behaviour and person-centred behaviour. The relationship to earlier leadership models like the Managerial Grid of Blake and Mouton is obvious (see Chapter 5) and as a consequence it led eventually to diagnostic models like Reddin's 3D Leadership Model, which we will now consider.

Reddin's 3D Leadership model

Reddin's 3D Leadership model (1983, 1989) is a framework for using different leadership styles in different situations to maximise leader effectiveness. A British academic and management behaviouralist who studied and worked at MIT, Reddin developed key theories relating to situational leadership styles and their impact on organisational effectiveness. The four basic leadership styles identified by Reddin are represented on a two-by-two matrix with task-oriented behaviour (concern for task) on the horizontal axis and relationship-oriented behaviour (concern for those performing the task) on the vertical axis (see Figure 7.1).

The central matrix in Figure 7.1 represents Reddin's initial model, showing the four major leadership styles:

- *Related.* Related leaders enjoy cooperative working. They do not focus on directing staff by fiat, and they allow freedom and responsibility to junior colleagues. This is common in middle-leadership in schools.
- *Integrated.* Integrated leaders maintain group cooperation and emphasise the effectiveness of communication to build strong teams capable of completing tasks to the best of everyone's potential. This is common in university faculties

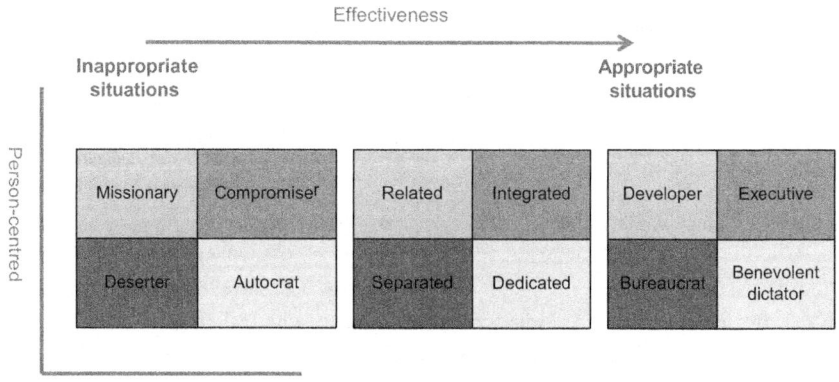

FIGURE 7.1 Reddin's 3D Leadership model.

where teams usually coalesce around certain pressing issues such as preparing a submission for a research assessment or an external Health and Safety Audit, say.

- *Dedicated*. Dedicated leaders are concerned only with task. They focus on improving the system and its processes, keeping power and responsibility to themselves. They dictate roles and instructions to others, as heads and principals do when their schools or colleges are failing.
- *Separated*. Separated leaders focus on correcting mistakes and deviations. They formulate policies and rules and impose them on others, but do not take a direct, commanding role themselves. This is common at the most senior levels within universities where policies and regulations are made and then passed down the food chain to deans and then to department heads.

When Reddin expanded his theory, he added 'effectiveness' as a third dimension, thus the '3D' in the title. Effectiveness is defined by the appropriateness (or inappropriateness) of a particular leadership style to a given situation. It increases from left to right on the diagram so the most effective styles when applied to situations are on the right-hand side ('appropriate situations') – 'Developer', 'Executive', 'Benevolent dictator' and 'Bureaucrat' – and the least effective styles – 'Missionary', 'Compromiser', 'Autocrat' and 'Deserter' – are on the left-hand side ('inappropriate situations'). The notion of introducing an effectiveness dimension is particularly relevant in education settings, although the nomenclature would be problematic in schools and colleges where even 'bureaucrat' has a taint to it, never mind 'benevolent dictator'! On a more serious note, it is interesting that the 'least acceptable' titles for education settings – ('*benevolent dictator*' is high concern for task and low concern for staff, in appropriate situations; '*bureaucrat*' is low concern for task and low concern for staff, also in appropriate situations; '*autocrat*' is high concern for task and low concern for staff, in *in*appropriate situations; '*deserter*' is low concern for task and low concern for staff, also in *in*appropriate situations) – all represent low concern for people. This may be significant, but we must be careful about assigning too much importance to a nomenclature that itself may be biased.

According to Reddin, the strength of an effective leader is knowing when to use each of the basic leadership styles and apply them to appropriate situations, but there are two other ingredients to effectiveness: how flexible or rigid the leader's style is in various scenarios; and experience. Task-oriented approaches are generally most effective in urgent situations like failing schools, or when resources are scarce (for example, cutbacks in university funding), or when staff are inexperienced or unskilled for the task in hand, as happens when senior staff leave university departments or retire and are replaced by younger academics. However, it is important to remember that the urgency of a problem – and most problems in education *are* urgent – cannot of itself summon a solution into being. Relationship-oriented approaches are more effective with tasks that require greater creativity, when the leader needs the opportunity to develop staff skills or, for structural reasons, needs to devolve greater responsibility as part of a faculty reorganisation, say, or when the leader already has an experienced and skilled team.

The Hersey and Blanchard Situational Leadership model

In the late 1970s and early 1980s, Paul Hersey and Ken Blanchard developed their own slightly divergent versions of situational leadership theory: Hersey's (1985) Situational Leadership model; and Blanchard's Situational Leadership II model (Blanchard et al., 1985). Blanchard was a populist and an academic, as is so often the case in the US leadership field. His *One-Minute Manager* (1983) series of books, which he co-authored with Spencer Johnson, are very conversational, but they sold 9 million copies in 25 languages and had a huge impact on management studies. Blanchard also invented the *Leader Behaviour Analysis Questionnaire*.

In *Management of Organisational Behaviour: Utilizing Human Resources* (1969a), Blanchard and Hersey suggested that a manager or leader is most successful when matching style to situation and that (as Reddin later said repeatedly) there is no single best style of leadership. The most effective leaders are those who adapt their style to the performance readiness (ability plus willingness) of their followers. Effective leadership varies with employee and with task.

The Situational Leadership model has two fundamental elements: leadership style; and the performance-readiness or 'maturity' of employees in any given circumstance. Maturity is the sum of ability plus willingness: the capacity of followers or employees or a team to set high but achievable goals, their willingness and ability to take responsibility, and having the skills, know-how and experience necessary to complete the task. The theory is based on research that suggests that leadership is not static or fixed, but flexible and task-specific, and adapts to the situation or context in which it is exercised, and to followers. In their situational model, Hersey and Blanchard differentiate between the task-centred and the person-centred leader, finding that effective leaders can switch between the two styles. When employees are capable of completing a task successfully – that is, when the staff group is mature – effective leaders should avoid being task-centred. Mature employees need less hands-on task leadership. Conversely, the person-centredness of a leader should match the willingness and commitment of followers. Less motivated employees need more motivational leadership and less task-centredness. When followers are already very willing, effective leadership should also avoid too much person-centredness because employees do not need motivation or monitoring.

Leadership style, then, is a mixture of task-centred and person-centred behaviours. The leader will have a natural inclination, of course, and that natural preference can be determined by completing a leadership questionnaire that can identify both a 'dominant' and a 'supporting' style, and the extent to which the leader currently uses these to best effect. Blanchard and Hersey identified four key leadership styles:

- *Telling*. Employees lack the specific skills required for the task but are willing to do it. They are not experienced, but they are enthusiastic.
- *Selling*. Employees are more capable of doing the task than in the 'telling' category, but they are demotivated or unwilling to do it. This often arises in schools from professional cynicism, which comes from seeing decades of useless

innovations come and go without any meaningful or lasting effect beyond wasting time.

- *Participating*. Employees are experienced and capable of doing the task, but lack the confidence or willingness to take on the responsibility.
- *Delegating*. Employees are experienced and confident in their ability to complete the job. They are able to do it and willing to take responsibility for doing so. This is the desired state for most new heads of department in universities, for example, but there can be an inclination growing out of that desire to assume that the right conditions already exist; that the staff to whom the head *has already delegated* tasks are skilled, confident and experienced enough to do them. This is not leadership; it's roulette!

The appropriate style of leadership depends on three factors:

- *The characteristics of the leader*. How does the leader or manager perceive employees generally and in terms of their competence? Does the leader trust the employees? Does the leader hold a Theory X or a Theory Y point of view?
- *The characteristics of employees*. What styles of leadership are employees used to? How do employees rate their own competence? How confident are they, how much ambiguity can they tolerate and for how long?
- *The situation*. How urgent is the situation? Is the situation existential for the organisation? In the case of a school, is it failing? How immediately do mistakes impact on the goals of the organisation? How minor or major is the immediate task?

Blanchard and Hersey went on to define four *styles* based on the amount of leader task behaviour and leader relationship behaviour. Hersey and Blanchard characterised leadership style in four behaviour categories, which they labelled S1 to S4.

- Style S1: *Directive* (telling) style. This is characterised by a lot of direction to subordinates, and very little support. Subordinates are expected to accept orders without question. This is a style recommended for short-timeframe work of a simple nature, especially where staff are also new to the job. The manager says: 'Here is the task. Go do it!'
- Style S2: *Coaching* (selling) style. This is characterised by both high direction and high support. The manager says: 'Here is the task and here is how I want you to do it. If you need help, I am here for you'.
- Style S3: *Supporting* (participatory) style. This is characterised by high support and low direction and is a style recommended for situations where experienced managers are working together, trusted by the manager, who says: 'Here is the task. I trust you to get on with it'.
- Style S4: *Delegating* style. This is characterised by both low support and low direction. Managers trust subordinates who have a high degree of expertise and experience. The manager says: 'Here is the task. You are experienced and as senior people, you are paid to take on this responsibility and take decisions'. This is common within research teams where, from necessity, the principal

investigator (PI) as leader assigns elements within the project to various junior research assistants and associates. It is usually the case that the more experienced the research assistant, the less 'delegating' is the approach used by the PI.

There is a sequence through these four styles, and a leader can 'progress' through them as followers mature (see Figure 7.2). No single style is considered optimal for all leaders all the time. Effective leaders should be flexible and adapt themselves to

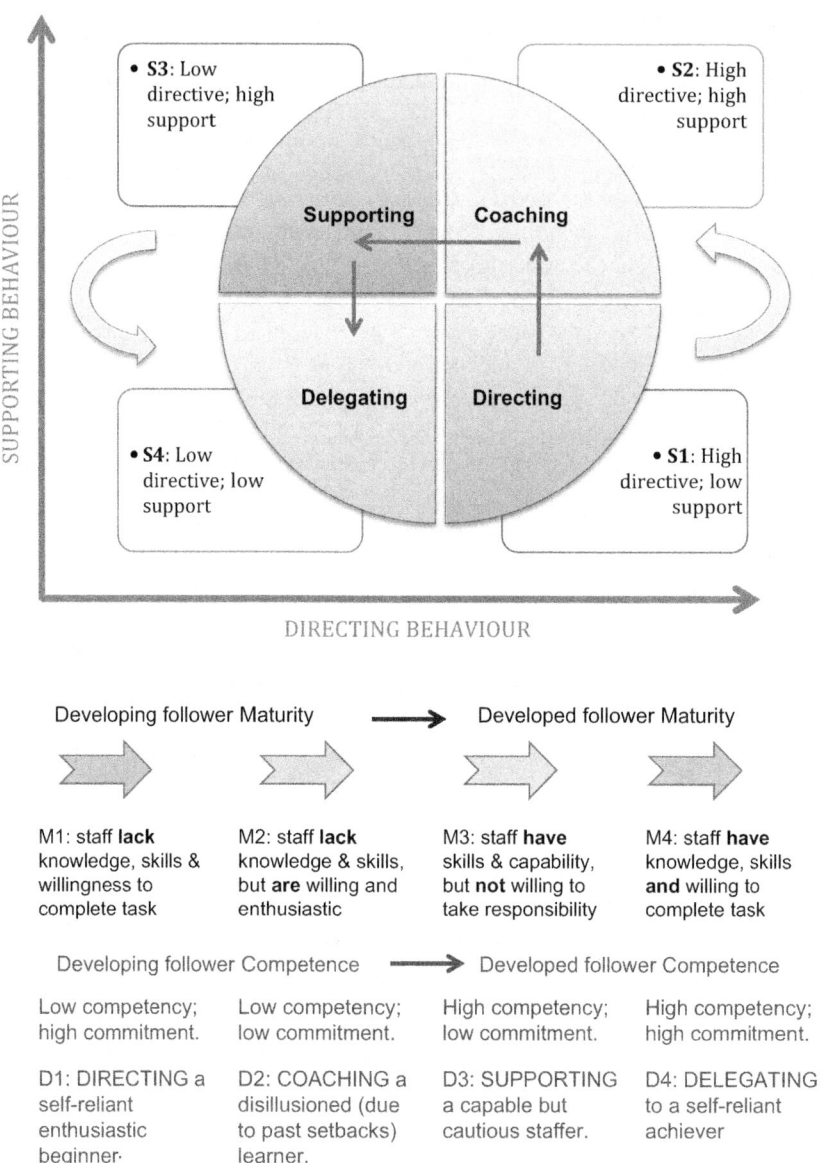

FIGURE 7.2 Progression through the four styles as subordinates mature.

the situation. Hersey (1985) later added that a leader's high expectation can cause high performance in employees; and a leader's low expectations can lead to low performance, something that is known to apply to teachers and their students.

Hersey and Blanchard also identified four levels of maturity, M1 through M4:

- M1 has low maturity value. Staff lack the specific skills required for the job in hand, and are unwilling to work at the task. They are novices.
- M2 has moderate maturity value. Employees lack experience and ability to do the task, but have the willingness to take on the job.
- M3 also has moderate maturity value. Employees are better able to do the task than M2, but they are demotivated for the job or unwilling to take responsibility.
- M4 has high maturity value. Employees are experienced at the task and comfortable with their own ability to do it well. They are highly skilled and willing not only to do the task, but to take responsibility for it.

Maturity levels are task-specific in education. A schoolteacher or university researcher might be skilled, confident and motivated in one job – a specific pedagogy or research methodology, say – but might have a maturity level M1 when asked to perform a different job requiring skills they do not possess. The Hersey–Blanchard Situational Leadership model depends on being able to assess this 'situation' in context; at a minimum, to be able to assess the motivation (commitment) and maturity (ability/capability) of staff. This is particularly true in research-intensive universities, and in colleges and schools, where most employees are expected to multi-task on a broad range of activities on an almost daily basis, and this range of tasks varies in terms of the commitment and ability required to complete them. As a consequence, effective leadership in education requires huge flexibility and a constant awareness of 'context' and followership.

Blanchard's Situational Leadership II model

Hersey and Blanchard continued with their original theory until 1977 when they split to run their respective companies. Blanchard founded *Blanchard Training & Development Inc.* in 1979, and in 1985 introduced Situational Leadership II in his book *A Situational Approach to Managing People* (Blanchard et al., 1985). Situational Leadership II made changes to the original concept of 'maturity levels' M1 to M4, re-labelling them as 'development levels' D1 to D4. The model uses the term 'competence' to describe ability, knowledge and skill, and the term 'commitment' for confidence and motivation, so that four combinations of competence and commitment make up the development levels D1 to D4 (see Figure 7.2 again):

- D1 represents low competence with high commitment.
- D2 represents low competence with low commitment.
- D3 represents high competence with low commitment.
- D4 represents high competence with high commitment.

Blanchard's Situational Leadership II model views development as an evolutionary progression. When individuals approach a new task for the first time, they start out with little or no knowledge, ability or skills, but have high enthusiasm, motivation and commitment. The individual employee then moves from develop*ing* to develop*ed*, but the leader's role is still to diagnose development level and use an appropriate leadership style. As employees gain experience, and if they are appropriately managed, they reach D2 and gain some competence; but their commitment may drop off because the task may be more complex than was originally thought. With the appropriate leadership, employees can then move to D3 where competence fluctuates between moderate and high, and commitment is variable as the individual member of staff continues to seek mastery of task. Finally, the individual moves to D4, where competence and commitment are high.

The Situational Leadership II model is in part backed by research in an education setting. To determine the validity of the Hersey and Blanchard approach, Vecchio (1987) conducted a study of more than 300 high school teachers and their principals. He found that newly hired teachers were more satisfied and performed better under principals who had highly structured leadership styles, but the performance of more experienced and mature teachers was unrelated to the style of the leader. In essence, Vecchio found that in terms of situational leadership, it is appropriate to match a highly structured S1 style of leadership to immature subordinates, but it is not clear whether it is appropriate to match S2, S3 or S4 with mature followers. In a replica study using university employees, Fernandez and Vecchio (1997) found similar results (Thompson & Vecchio, 2009).

Situational leadership and coaching

Blanchard subsequently became an advocate of the leader-as-coach approach and in association with Don Shula, football coach for the Miami Dolphins for 25 years, wrote *Everyone's a Coach* (Blanchard & Shula, 1995), which had a big impact at the time. Keeping the link to situational leadership, Blanchard and Shula produced five core practices for coaching:

- *Conviction driven.* Effective leaders stand for something. They do the right things for the right reasons. The leader sharing beliefs and convictions not only sets goals and sets directions, but also sets boundaries. This is almost axiomatic in the secondary/high school sector, but not so much in universities, which allow themselves a more utilitarian world view. Nevertheless, it is a hugely valuable approach to the leadership of a university department.
- *Overlearning.* Effective leaders help their followers and teams achieve what Shula calls 'practice-perfection'. Good coaching is about the mastery of detail and the continuous analysis of results on an ongoing basis, as can be seen with top-level football managers like Jurgen Klopp and Pep Guardiola. Continuous improvement is the goal here.

- *Audible-ready*. Effective leaders are ready to change their 'game plans' when the situation demands it. This is about being adaptable, but also about being well-informed and prepared. Planning that is fixed and intended to remain unchanged even when it is failing is unacceptable. Sometimes the educative context limits 'audible readiness': in schools and university undergraduate programmes, much of the pedagogic delivery is fixed in terms of staffing and schedule, with very limited scope for adjustment, but there is some wriggle room if something is not working and that should be preserved. University research is not as tightly coupled; it is common for project managers to change methodologies or avenues for exploration as and when required.
- *Consistency*. Effective leaders are predictable and behave in the same way under the same circumstances. Effective leaders do not respond randomly or moodily. Inconsistency is a fundamentally destructive flaw. It's intolerable, to the point of madness, if followers don't know what to expect from (say) reporting a flaw in procedures or an outcomes failure, and if similar incidences produce wildly different reactions from the manager, depending on the time of day or sugar levels.
- *Honesty-based*. Effective leaders have integrity and are straightforward in their dealings. Subordinates want their leaders to 'be straight with them'. In schools and universities, this will need to be coupled with follower security about levels of confidentiality. If, for example, a lecturer is not producing research of sufficient quality or quantity, or a schoolteacher is not maintaining proper order in the classroom, this needs to be addressed early (but not prematurely) and frankly (but not aggressively). In most cases, this is appreciated (if a little upsetting at the time), but only if the shortcoming and its suggested remedy are not widely broadcast. Leaders also need to trust that their frank advice is not misconstrued outside the meeting, just as the employee needs to trust that certain elements of the discussion will remain confidential.

Functional and action-centred leadership

Other writers in the contingency field include John Adair, Professor of Leadership Studies at Surrey University in the UK, who wrote *Effective Leadership* (1983), *Effective Motivation* (1987a) and *Great Leaders* (1989), and who developed the theory of functional leadership (Hackman & Walton, 1986; McGrath, 1962). Functional leadership addresses specific leadership behaviours expected to contribute to organisational effectiveness. It argues that a leader's main job is to see that whatever is necessary for staff is provided, and leaders can be said to be effective when they have contributed to group effectiveness and team cohesion (Hackman & Walton, 1986; McGrath, 1962). In the functional model, leadership rests not with one person but on a set of behaviours across the group. Any member of the group can perform these behaviours, so any member can participate in leadership. The theory places greater emphasis on how an organisation or task is being led rather than on who has been formally assigned to the leadership role.

One of the best-known and most influential functional theories is John Adair's Three-Circle Action-Centred leadership model (1973, 1988a, 1988b). Adair is a behaviourist in the sense that he believes that leadership is a behaviour that can be taught, that it does not depend on a person's innate traits and that it is a transferable skill. His ideas are practical and relevant to managers irrespective of their working environment so they can easily be applied to education settings, although sometimes his assertions seem like they are merely stating the obvious. Adair was another contributor who drew a clear distinction between leadership and management: the latter was about mechanics, control and systems; the former – particularly his own Action-Centred leadership model – was about the overlapping, interdependent aspects of task, team and individual. The Action-Centred leadership model describes what leaders have to do and the actions they must take in order to be effective: complete the task; build and maintain teams and develop the synergy of their work; and develop individuals who respond to individual physical and psychological needs. In Adair's model, task, team and individual overlap. Achieving the task builds the team and satisfies individuals. If team needs are not met or if the team lacks cohesiveness, then task performance is impaired and individual job satisfaction is diminished. If individual needs are not met, the team will lack cohesiveness and task performance is again impaired.

Adair's theory is that leadership exists at three different levels:

- Team leadership, typically of between 5 and 20 people.
- Operational leadership, where a number of team leaders report to the main leader.
- Strategic leadership of the whole organisation, with overall accountability for all lower levels of leadership.

At whatever level leadership is being exercised, task, team and individual needs must always be considered independently of situation, sector and organisational culture, and to fulfil these three facets of leadership (task, team and individual need) and to achieve success, the following eight functions must be performed and developed by the functional leader:

- *Defining the task.* Individuals and teams need to have tasks set out as clear objectives, which are specific, measurable, achievable, realistic and time-constrained (SMART). The second of these elements – measurability – can be problematic in education as many of the desirable elements of education are affective, social and long term.
- *Planning.* This is essentially horizon-scanning for alternatives and is best done with others in an open, positive and creative way. Contingencies should be planned, and plans and hypotheses tested.

- *Briefing.* Team briefing is a basic leadership function that creates a good atmosphere, promotes and rewards teamwork, and motivates individuals.
- *Controlling.* Good leaders get maximum results with the minimum of effort and resources, which is just as well in education since resources are always scarce! To do this, leaders need self-control, good systems, effective delegation and good monitoring of progress.
- *Evaluating.* Leaders need to be good at assessing consequences, evaluating team and individual performance, appraising and training individuals, and gauging follower effectiveness.
- *Motivating.* Adair distinguishes eight principles for managers in motivating others:
  - Be motivated yourself.
  - Select people who are highly motivated.
  - Treat each person as an individual.
  - Set realistic but challenging targets.
  - Remember that progress motivates.
  - Create a motivating environment.
  - Provide fair rewards.
  - Give recognition.
- *Organising.* Good leaders organise themselves, their teams, their structures and their processes. Leading change requires a clear purpose and effective organisation to achieve results.
- *Setting an example.* Good leaders set an example to individuals and to teams. This is easier if the head of a university research department (say) is herself or himself a competent researcher; or if the school principal has credibility as a classroom teacher.

Adair's ideas about motivation are in line with those of Maslow, McGregor and Hertzberg, discussed in the previous chapter. At the heart of Adair's approach is his variation on the theme of the Pareto principle, sometimes called 'the ratio of the vital few and the trivial many'. Adair's variation is his 'fifty-fifty rule', which he described in his book *Effective Motivation* (1987a). It states that 50% of motivation comes from within a person and 50% from the person's environment, including the leadership the person experiences. As we have seen in previous chapters, people are motivated by a complex mix of different factors, and in Adair's functional model, strength of motivation is affected by the expectations of certain outcomes from certain actions, strengthened by other factors such as an individual's working conditions, desires and fears (Adair, 1987a, 1987b).

Like Peter Drucker, Adair's theory stresses the importance of time management and argues for the need to manage time before anything else. Adair was one of the first management thinkers to emphasise its critical importance, its central role in focusing action and in helping leaders to achieve goals. Time management is not simply about being organised or efficient or completing tasks promptly. It is about managing time with a focus on achievement, in a goal-driven and results-oriented way. A leader's success in time management is measured by the *quantity* of work produced, the *quality* of that work and the extent to which the employee is maintaining a work-life balance. Policy-makers in education would do well to follow Adair's advice. Ever-increasing school and curriculum 'innovation' and the publish-or-perish culture in universities resulting from research assessment exercises, have diminished, if not destroyed, the work-life balance in education. The point is not an ethical or even a social one, but a question of effectiveness diminishing inversely with the huge increased input of time.

Adair (1990) proposed ten principles of time management:

- Develop a personal sense of time, which is the most important principle.
- Identify long-term goals.
- Make medium-term plans.
- Plan the day.
- Make best use of time.
- Organise office work.
- Manage meetings.
- Delegate effectively.
- Make use of committed time.
- Manage own health and well-being.

One major criticism of Adair's Three-Circle Action-Centred leadership is that it takes little account of the flat structures that have always been common in education, and are increasingly common and widely advocated in the commercial sector as being optimal for today's business environment. The model is also criticised for being too simplistic and too authoritarian. It works well in a rigid and formal environment, but less so in the modern workplace where leadership is about driving change, managing knowledge and fostering innovation.

Another influential writer in this field, but with a less techno-structural emphasis, is John Hunt, Professor of Organisational Behaviour at London Business School, who in the late 1970s wrote *Managing People at Work* (1992, 3rd edition). His work leans towards trait theory and takes the somewhat philosophical view that employees are more than mere 'cogs in a machine'. His view is that organisations need to recognise the importance of emotion and 'gut feeling' and not rely too much on structure (Hunt & Larson, 1974). He was an early advocate of 360-degree appraisal where managers are appraised by subordinates, peers *and* superiors.

The role of societal culture in organisations is an important element in Hunt's work and in situational leadership generally. This is true in the commercial sector – for example, Hunt's research showed that British organisations are more individualistic than their European counterparts, perhaps explaining why they are better at inventing things and establishing rather than running businesses – but it is also true in education settings. In education management at the system level, systems like China (more accurately, Shanghai) and Singapore have been singled out for praise for their high attainment in mathematics without acknowledging that China is a totalitarian state on the verge of ecological meltdown whose citizens are subject to political repression, and Singaporeans live without many of the liberal democratic rights that citizens in Western countries enjoy (Kelly, 2020). The criterion for educational success in these terms is clearly driven by *economic* imperatives, which is what China and Singapore have in common. But education is about more than the training of compliant units of production, and therefore there are normative reasons why educational leadership should involve value judgements regarding democratic entitlement and moral purpose. For Western nations, it may be that the price of political freedom is a 'less efficient' education system, but a system that produces vigilant citizens capable of selecting and de-selecting their own governments (Kelly, 2020), and, in line with Hunt's view, this should be reflected in how management and leadership are actualised within schools, colleges and universities.

Notes

1 It assumes that the former colleague remembered was not too much of a freakish outlier!
2 Mitchell et al. (1970) suggest that the LPC scale only has a 50% reliable variance.

8

KEEPING DYSFUNCTION AT BAY OR CREATING ORDER?

As we have seen in Chapter 3, Ofman (2001b) described a paradigm in which organisations are treated as 'living organisms' that have both internal and external tasks to fulfil; tasks that require 'an organic and respectful approach aimed at healthy growth and healing'. He used this paradigm to warrant his Core Quadrants model.

> Healthy organisms are characterised by rhythm and balance, and have room for expansion and contraction, for exhaling and inhaling. Healthy organisms are vital and aligned. Vitality ensues from attention and care for primary work processes. Within the organisation this manifests itself in working on relations and connections between people, departments and levels; externally, it entails maintaining the relationship between the company and the client. Alignment occurs when people behave as parts of an integrated whole and combine their energy.
>
> (Ofman, 2001b: 4)

Ofman rightly sees this as affecting the purpose and aims of management:

> According to [this] paradigm, managers are responsible for their own motivation and inspiration. The more a manager discovers about himself, the better he will be able to ... perform his role as coach or 'facilitator'. His main responsibility is to take care of his own development [and knowing] his strengths and core qualities. Besides awareness of his positive qualities, he should also have some insight into the distortions of his positive qualities.
>
> (Ofman, 2001b: 9)

DOI: 10.4324/9781003217220-8

The fundamental question is whether the idea of an organisation as a living organism – be it a healthy or an unhealthy one – has implications for leadership. If leadership assumes that organisations are inherently 'healthy' and orderly places, then the job of the leader is to keep ill health and disorder at bay. If, on the other hand, organisations are thought to be inherently 'unhealthy' and disorderly places, then the job of leadership is to *create* health and order within. The dominant, almost universal, view in educational management is the former – that organisations like schools are inherently 'healthy' and orderly places – so the theory and practice of leadership and management today has unconsciously assumed that the core function of the job is to keep out ill health and disorder. Researchers in the field, having unknowingly made the same assumption, have investigated what works in the battle *to keep this disorder at bay*, instead of looking at what works in the struggle *to create health and order* internally in the midst of inherent disorder. Yet, anyone who has ever worked in a school would to a person acknowledge that educational institutions are dynamically disordered – even chaotic – places; brilliantly so, and all the more exciting and interesting for it, but chaotic places nevertheless.

This chapter discusses the dichotomy between disorder-avoidance and order-creation and flows from the discussion in Chapter 1 on Aristotle's notion of *poiesis* or bringing something into being that did not previously (or would not otherwise) exist; in this case, order, structure and a supportive culture. It introduces and explores the concept of 'salutogenesis' as a way of interpreting educational leadership in two significant areas: its effect on student outcomes; and the motivation of incumbent managers.[1]

In its original setting, salutogenesis describes an approach that focuses on health, rather than on disease, but regards both as points on the same continuum. 'Pathogenesis' is the opposite, more traditional view. The two make very different *ab initio* assumptions: pathogenesis starts by regarding illness (or disorder in the case of organisations) as a departure from the natural state and something to be 'cured'; salutogenesis regards illness or disorder as the natural condition, and health or order as something to be created. In the context of adapting these concepts to educational settings, where 'illness' can be read as 'dysfunction' or 'disorder', the salutogenetic approach would take the view that schools, colleges and universities are inherently chaotic places, and that the aim of leadership is therefore to *create* (rather than *protect*) a functional state. The traditional pathogenic approach, on the other hand, assumes that the natural state is inherently stable, so that the purpose of leadership is simply to ward off malfunction (Kelly, 2015).

As we discussed in Chapter 1, the concept of 'leadership-as-panacea', popular among policy-makers for three decades, is an aspiration driven more by convenience than science. The anecdotal evidence suggests that good leadership on its own is a necessary but not a sufficient condition for the effective delivery of education, and that not all good leaders can be snatched from one institution and parachuted into another with the desired impact over the long term. Generally, the field has either been in pursuit of the effect on student outcomes (the search for effect) or looking at the motivation of incumbents[2] (the search for meaning). This chapter sifts through a sample of empirical research in these two areas – the search for effect and the search for meaning – in order to examine to what extent a salutogenic perspective can act as a theoretical bridge between method and interpretation. The aim is to offer an introduction to, and to problematise, the notion of salutogenesis in the interpretation of educational leadership.

Salutogenesis[3] (Antonovsky, 1979; Becker et al., 2010) focuses on health, rather than on disease; on factors that support well-being, rather than on factors that cause disease. It rejects the traditional dichotomy separating health and illness, instead regarding the two as values of a continuous variable; what Antonovsky called the 'health-ease versus dis-ease continuum'. Antonovsky developed the approach from his research on how people manage stress, noting that although stress was everywhere, not everyone had negative health outcomes as a result of exposure to it; and considerable evidence has been collected in recent decades in support of his view (Eriksson, 2007). In salutogenesis, people continually battle hardship forces ('resource deficits'), countering which there are 'resistance resources' – the things that help people manage stress – which include wealth, self-confidence, a good attitude, family and other support networks and various forms of social capital. Resource deficits cause resistance resources to fail when one's 'sense of coherence' is not robust enough, and this causes illness. Sense of coherence is the extent to which one feels confident that the stimuli deriving from one's environment are predictable and explicable ('comprehensibility'), that adequate resources are available to control stress ('manageability'), and most importantly, that the demands made on one by stress forces are worth fighting and may even be satisfying to overcome ('meaningfulness').

Adapting these notions to education, a salutogenic approach would take the view that schools and universities will wind down to their natural state of dysfunction if left to their own devices, and that the aim of leadership is therefore to *create* a more desirable 'healthy' functional state. The pathogenic approach, in contrast, assumes that the natural state is inherently functional and stable, and that the purpose of leadership is therefore merely to ward off dysfunction. If the salutogenic assumption is accepted, purposive leadership can be re-theorised as 'management working towards an unstable healthy state', and this purposiveness can be seen as the driving force in the search for meaning or '*logos*'. It can also help us re-think issues like leader turnover as natural *and desirable* consequences of that unstable-but-healthy state (Kelly, 2015).

Antonovsky's notion of 'comprehensibility' within his 'sense of coherence' construct (i.e. that the stimuli deriving from one's environment are predictable and explicable) can be linked to chaos theory[4] and the behaviour of dynamic systems – thus, the title of this book – which are so sensitive to initial conditions that small boundary differences produce very different outcomes and make long-term prediction virtually impossible.

Salutogenesis and the search for effect

The underpinnings of educational leadership have been analysed and queried on a number of occasions; in particular, the desirability in theory, but the difficulty in practice, of conducting robust research on its efficacy. The insightful Hallinger and

Heck (1996a, 1996b) review looked at 15 years (1980–1995)[5] of empirical research on the role and impact of principalship within the educational effectiveness paradigm, focusing on the conceptual underpinnings of various theoretical models.

- *The simple versus the complex.*
  Hallinger and Heck grouped research studies into those that used simple bivariate designs (with or without controls) and those that used sophisticated theoretical models, stronger research designs or more powerful statistical methods. One-third of studies were in the latter category and showed a clear effort to build longitudinally on the conceptual and methodological work of others. All were theoretically informed and could define and defend their constructs, but only one-third were theoretically 'sophisticated'. In terms of research design, almost all the studies used a non-experimental cross-sectional correlational design with survey or interview research instruments, the fact of which alone would make it difficult to understand the causal relationships regarding impact. Hallinger and Heck concluded that research on educational leadership would make better conceptual progress if greater use were made of more comprehensive, more complex models that placed the leader within the context of the educational institution and its environment.

  In terms of interpretation, Hallinger and Heck found that the research methods used affected findings. Those that used simple bivariate designs made weak or conflicting claims and were suspect in terms of validity. Those that used more sophisticated theoretical models, with stronger research designs or more powerful statistical approaches, yielded more positive findings more often. This is unexpected in the sense that more rigorous methods in educational effectiveness research usually make it *more* difficult to make definitive claims. It may be that sophisticated methodologies lead to more frequent and more positive findings not because of their sophistication *per se* but because they take account of process and context in a salutogenic manner. The real dichotomy, therefore, may be not between simple and complex methodologies, but between the underpinning presumptions of pathogenesis (with its problem-solving, reactive outlook) and salutogenesis (with its process-improvement, proactive outlook). The fact that the Hallinger and Heck review also found that an institution's socio-economic environment influences the type of leadership exercised, and that the type of leadership that makes the greatest difference is the one aimed at influencing internal teaching and learning *processes*, would support this view.

  An explanation for the small *size* of the leadership effect found in these reviews is offered by Leithwood (2001), who distinguishes generic leadership practices intended to be useful *in most situations* from those suited *to a particular context*. According to Leithwood, the quantitative studies reviewed by Hallinger and Heck measured only those leadership practices *common across all contexts* and not the additional practices used by leaders as a means of dealing with their unique circumstances. For this reason, Leithwood suggests, empirical research underestimates the effect of leadership on student outcomes.

- *The experimental versus the non-experimental.*

  From the 1950s to the start of the period reviewed by Hallinger and Heck (1980), logical positivism and the 'theory movement' framed leadership, but during the Hallinger and Heck review period, researchers in the field tended to criticise traditional conceptualisations and develop new ways of thinking about knowledge-construction. The challenge today is to *integrate* findings from these different philosophical perspectives and methodologies. It is relatively easy to summarise research approaches and findings; what is needed is a theoretical approach that will *reconcile* them and enable us to respond to criticisms, like those of Thomas (2007), Pan and Chen (2011) and others who assert that educational leadership has failed to keep pace with, for example, business-leadership and leadership-psychology on both theoretical and methodological levels. The concern is that, theoretically, educational leadership has become a compendium of low-reliability folk wisdom and that, methodologically, survey-by-questionnaire dominates to such an extent that there are problems with the identification of matching sample populations and the equivalency of scales. Levačić (2005) has produced a review in this area; specifically, on the methodological problems of trying to establish a causal effect of leadership on student outcomes. She reminds us that any attempt to test such a causal relationship must be able to take account of other factors affecting student outcomes, but that this cannot be replicated in natural settings like it can in a laboratory, and that the counterfactual cannot be directly observed. The easiest way around this would be to mimic experimental conditions using the random assignment of cases into 'control' and 'treatment' groups, but while this Randomised Controlled Trial (RCT) approach is the preferred design if the objective is to obtain unbiased estimates of the size of the effect, it is a minority pursuit in education (cf. Hutchison & Styles, 2010; Gove, 2013) and is regarded by some as unsuitable, even in medicine where it has been most frequently and most successfully applied (e.g. Garbutt & Davies, 2011).

  The next-best alternative would seem to be quasi-experimentation, which has many similarities with both traditional experimental design and RCT but lacks the element of random assignment to treatment and control groups so that there are concerns about internal validity. Levačić (2005) points out that research on the effects of educational leadership on student outcomes has not employed either of these two research designs to any significant extent because leadership is not regarded as a 'treatment' to be applied or not. If it is accepted that leadership *has* a significant effect on student outcomes, it is difficult to conceive of leadership studies that could use RCT as a methodology and still remain ethical, so that studies in the field have traditionally used data generated from natural settings. Levačić suggests a three-way typology: a Direct Effects model; a Mediated Effects model; and a Reciprocal Effects model (Kelly, 2015). In the first, student outcome (adjusted for prior attainment) is the dependent variable, and the model can include antecedent variables that directly affect both student outcomes and leadership. In the Mediated Effects model, leadership is regarded as having an indirect effect on student outcomes in that it affects intervening variables such as school culture and classroom practice. The Reciprocal Effects model is a dynamic model which assumes a two-way causality: not only does leadership affect mediating variables, but it is in turn affected by them. Research by Gu et al. (2008), which found that leadership has a significant effect on student outcomes in schools with low attainment and low value-added, is an example of the counterfactual approach favoured by Levačić. They found that while some schools had significant and sustained improvement *with no change of principal*, changing the principal could contribute to the rapid improvement of schools with an initial low-attainment profile. The underpinning assumption here is clearly pathogenic, as it is with most RCT and quasi-experimental approaches: that leadership can correct an unnatural state of dysfunction and underachievement. The alternative is not considered; namely, that leadership is not necessarily about maintaining a naturally functional state of achievement but may be about maintaining an *unnatural* functional state against an entropic pull-back to chaos and dysfunction. RCT and experimental paradigms assume in the manner of traditional medical treatment that leadership is the cure for an ailment, whether directly or indirectly, in what would otherwise be a healthy organisational body, accepting that there might be reciprocal effects of the 'leadership treatment' much like the unintended side effects of a drug on the mediating organs of a patient. The salutogenic view is that educational leadership is not about impacting (directly or indirectly) on the problem of dysfunction, but about constructing a desirable state of effectiveness *from a natural state of chaos* and working towards it creatively (Kelly, 2015).

Salutogenesis and the search for meaning

Most investigation in the field of educational leadership, when not in search of its effect on student outcomes, is about the search for meaning or '*logos*' (Frankl, 2006). This is an existential perspective: a 'will to meaning' perspective, after Kierkegaard, as opposed to the 'will to power' perspective of Adler and Nietzsche or the 'will to pleasure' perspective of Freud. The desire to find meaning is a common feature of academic life, but in the sense in which it is adapted here for use in education, it is the belief that the act of striving to find *professional* meaning is the primary motivating force in educational leadership, which has (and needs) meaning no matter what the size of its effect on student attainment or the nature of the educational institution.

* *Salutogenesis, agency and supply*
  The hypothesised link with salutogenesis is that the act of striving to find professional meaning is more likely to be associated with a successful *logos*, strong values and a dedication to clearly envisioned goals; and that both *logos* and salutogenesis are likely to be linked antecedently to developmental maturity, which

we define as the extent to which there is an understanding of the 'intentional-ity' of educational leadership. (We discussed developmental maturity as part of the Situational Leadership model.) The search for meaning, and the extent to which that need is met, is by definition linked to retention and recruitment. In fact, recruitment can be seen as a proxy measure for *logos*, and the turnover of leaders in education has been a focus of attention in developed systems because of the large number of leaders approaching retirement age and because the role is perceived as becoming more unpleasantly managerialist and bureaucratic. In the pathogenic paradigm, leader turnover is theorised as being acutely prob-lematic because it diminishes an organisation's sense of purpose and makes it difficult to maintain a favourable trajectory. In the salutogenic paradigm, leader turnover is regarded as an inevitable but desirable fact of life; a consequence of the chaotic nature of educational institutions. The acknowledgement that leader turnover is a *desirable* thing is mostly absent from the literature, so that the question of how to maximise the opportunities presented by it and how to use it to leverage improvement has sometimes gone unanswered empiri-cally because of the prevailing pathogenic paradigm. For example, in Canada, Mascall and Leithwood (2010) found that where there is high leader turnover, taking a coordinated approach to the distribution of leadership can mitigate its negative effects; quite a pathogenic view.

On the supply side, Barty et al. (2005) examined the declining number of applications for educational leadership positions in Australia, finding that loca-tion, the size of the organisation, the presence of an incumbent and local politics were key issues. Increased bureaucratic burden was explicitly ignored by Barty et al. but *was* considered by Kwan (2011) when researching the recruitment of leaders in Hong Kong. Somewhat unusually, Kwan analysed the criteria used to assess applicants as a proxy for the traits that school governors believe result in success. Like other research (e.g. in Israel by Addi-Raccah, 2006), Kwan acknowledged the importance of context, finding that governor-recruiters treated *active religious affiliation* as the most useful proxy indicator – more use-ful than criteria like 'experience' and 'communication skills' – in judging the value-orientation of potential recruits. This suggests that the notion of *logos* extends beyond incumbents and recruits *to those doing the recruiting*, in the sense that those with an appropriate 'active religious affiliation' were assumed to have a matching 'search-for-meaning' ethic (Kelly, 2015).

• *Salutogenesis and efficacy*

Catano and Stronge (2007) examined the evaluation of professional standards for principals juggling to satisfy the competing demands of various stakehold-ers. Catano and Stronge conceptualised this tension as being between 'external' and 'internal' stakeholders, and in their content analysis of job descriptions and evaluation instruments, they suggest that performance appraisal for prin-cipals should be based on what they are expected to do, and evaluation instru-ments should match these expectations. Torres et al. (2008), Tuytens and Devos (2010) and others have analysed principal perceptions of school improvement policies, recognising that principals are under pressure to run their schools *and* implement national (state) and local initiatives which have over time caused the job to shift from resource-management to accountability. They suggest that while aggressive educational improvement policies can have positive outcomes, they also have unintended consequences – low staff morale, loss of confidence and reduced commitment – that represent an absence of *logos*.

One interpretation of findings like these is that the complexity of educational leadership stems from the initial conditions set by external agencies, and that these conditions are at the boundary of what is known to be the effect of an action. This is where leaders spend most of their time, which makes formal assessment of leaders a daunting task, especially when the expectations of incumbents are so often grounded (from their training and induction) in pathogenic conceptualisations of leadership, which compete with the day-to-day salutogenic functions of running a school, college or university (Kelly, 2015).

The impact of educational leadership is complex and not easily made subject to empirical verification. Research suggests that it is best conceived as a web of contextual, personal and professional relationships, which combine with other factors to influence educational outcomes. Salutogenesis suggests that the natural state for educational institutions is one of dysfunction rather than function, and if this assumption is made, leadership and the search for meaning within it can be re-theorised as management working towards an unstable healthy state. The theoretical construct of *logos* within salutogenesis can also help re-conceptualise issues like leader turnover by treating it as a *desirable* consequence of dysfunction, and justify the need for *intentional* training as a way of addressing it in a practical way.

Notes

1 An earlier version of this appeared in the *International Journal of Leadership in Education* (Kelly, 2015).
2 In which we include recruitment to the leadership profession and the retention of incumbents.
3 Literally, 'the origin of health'.
4 More precisely, chaos is defined as a dynamic system that is sensitive to initial conditions. Sensitivity to initial conditions – the butterfly effect – means that each point in the system is closely approximated by other points with significantly different future trajectories, so that a small disturbance to a current trajectory can lead to a significantly different chain of future events. In practice, if we have only a finite amount of information about a system, then beyond a certain point, the system is no longer predictable.
5 By the 1980s, accountability had become *the* major driving force in the allocation of resources to education, with diverse pro- and anti-privatisation reforms emerging, particularly in the US. Within a decade, the evaluation of principals had gone from being mandatory in 9 of the 50 US states to being mandatory in 40.

9

GENBA KAIZEN

Genba Kaizen is the Japanese concept of continuous improvement to enhance internal processes and increase efficiency. It is about developing a lean organisation with little waste. 'Genba' (sometimes, 'gemba') refers to the 'actual place' where value is created: the factory floor; the scene of an accident; a building site; a meeting place (Imai, 1986, 1997). The idea behind it is that the best ideas for how to improve an organisation come from 'going to the Genba' and being customer-focused; that is, the organisation must go its customers' actual place. This 'Genba walk' is really management-by-walking-about: senior staff going to the front line to look-and-learn and to identify opportunities to enact practical improvements (Womack, 2013). In education, it might be a college principal going to the staff room or teaching some classes. Managers go to the Genba (genchi gembutsu) to understand better their organisation's problems, to see how problems impact on delivery of services, to gather data and to question employees on site in an open, unscripted manner. Some organisations have a Genba teacher or coach (sensei) who accompanies managers on their walks and helps in the struggle to develop a fitter and leaner organisation. The Genba walk was developed at Toyota (Ohno & Bodek, 1988) in order to understand the value stream and its problems and learn from them, rather than just reviewing results and outcomes from afar. At its most basic, it is similar to the old-fashioned time-and-motion studies[1] of Frederick Taylor (1911), the world's first management consultant and founder of scientific management.

The accompanying concept of 'kaizen' (kai meaning 'change'; zen meaning 'to become good') means continuous improvement. It aims to eliminate waste and inefficiency (muda), and make an organisation leaner. Although it became known as 'the Toyota way', it was actually an American idea introduced to Japan as part of reconstruction after World War II. The US Army charged experts with rebuilding Japanese industry and developing a management training program that taught statistical control methods. One particular group, the Economic and Scientific

DOI: 10.4324/9781003217220-9

Section, was additionally charged with improving Japanese management skills. The programme it developed was called 'Improvement in Four Steps' (Kaizen eno Yon Dankai) and introduced kaizen to Japan.

There are several kaizen approaches:

- *Point Kaizen* is the most common type. It usually happens *ad hoc*, without much planning. As soon as something is malfunctioning or found to be inadequate, immediate action is taken to correct things. The measures are usually small, incremental and easy to implement, but they solve the problem.
- *Systemic Kaizen* is an organised approach devised to address system-level problems in the organisation. It requires senior-level strategic planning and several planned kaizen events over a period of time. Unlike Point Kaizen, the measures are usually large and take longer to implement.
- *Linear Kaizen* is a structured approach applied to two processes: a 'point' upstream and a downstream process, between which is the line that gives the type its name. The planning is usually upstream and the kaizen is performed at one or more points downstream, thus forming a line.
- *Plane Kaizen* is a higher level of line kaizen where several lines are connected together. As such, it is a value stream where instead of traditional departments, the organisation is structured into product lines and value streams. Improvements made to one line are implemented across multiple other lines and processes.
- *Cube Kaizen* is where all the points of the planes are connected to each other and no point is unconnected. The organisation is already lean and improvements are made throughout the organisation, both upstream and downstream.

Kaizen is a continuous process. It 'humanises' the workplace by nurturing people and teaches everyone how to be critically reflective of their own work using objective data. In this respect, it is particularly suited to education settings. Successful implementation of kaizen requires everyone's participation at all levels of an organisation, as well as external stakeholders. It is about focusing on quality, making the effort, being willing to change and having good communications. It is usually associated with manufacturing sectors, but it can be (and has been) used in non-manufacturing organisations. In Japan, it is usually local to a small group improving their own environment and performance. These small groups are usually guided through the kaizen process by a sensei-supervisor. In the Toyota Production System kaizen, all line personnel are expected to stop production in the event of a malfunction and, with their sensei-supervisor, suggest an improvement to resolve the problem, which may in turn initiate a kaizen across the whole organisation or a section of it.

Kaizen usually delivers small improvements to small groups, but the culture of continuous incremental improvement and its standardisation across a whole organisation can yield large returns in terms of *overall* productivity. It is the opposite philosophy to the command-and-control approach to improvement prevalent in traditional Western organisations. Unlike the command-and-control approach,

FIGURE 9.1 The Genba Kaizen house.

kaizen is about making changes, monitoring results, and then learning and adjusting. Pre-planning and large-scale projects are replaced by smaller experiments, which are quickly adapted as newer improvements are suggested and come on-stream. It is a way to help organisations re-structure and re-focus their processes, structures and effort, sometimes as simply as looking at particular issues in a kaizen 'blitz'.[2]

Putting kaizen and Genba together creates 'Genba Kaizen', which is sometimes shown diagrammatically as a Genba House (see Figure 9.1). In an education setting, the basement of the house has five fundamental elements: teamwork; self-discipline; high morale; quality control cycles; and suggestions for whole-school and subject-specific improvement. The focus of Genba Kaizen is on the elimination of waste, which is the next floor up in the 'house'. Types of waste in an education setting include: poor-quality teaching and lecturing; oversupply of courses, which is the worst type of waste because too large a portfolio of services obfuscates problems; too much work-in-progress that is costing money without making a significant return; time wasted by tutors and researchers waiting for resources to be allocated, waiting for legal services to get contracts signed, course coordinators waiting for marketing to roll out and so on; and wasting too much time on over-inputting/over-processing unnecessary admin, typical of intrusively bureaucratic organisations like universities.

The next floor up in the Genba house is the 'good housekeeping' floor. It comprises the Five 'S's (Van den Berg & Pietersma, 2016):

- *Seiri*, or tidiness. Separating what is necessary from what is not, in order to tidy up work processes.
- *Seiton*, or orderliness. Increasing efficiency by making decisions in an orderly manner.
- *Seiso*, or cleanliness. Keeping things clean, organised and neat.
- *Seiketsu*, or clean-up. Standardising tidiness across the school or university and keeping everything organised.

- *Shitsuke*, or self-discipline. Taking personal responsibility for the other four Ss. Shitsuke is similar to the last strand ('shared values') of the '7-S Framework', which will be discussed in Chapter 15, and to Senge's 'Fifth Discipline', to be discussed in Chapter 25. It is the unifying element at the centre of the 'good housekeeping' floor.

The fourth and top floor in the Genba House is the standardisation of good practices and embedding the Five 'S's to encourage and support continuous improvement. In an education setting, this is embedded in the concept of High Reliability Schools (HRS) discussed in Chapters 1 and 13. Like Genba Kaizen, High Reliability Schools have a widely distributed sense of responsibility, have shared goals at all levels of the school or university, are alert to emerging failures in performance, and have access to and use relevant data like student satisfaction rates and staff achievement. And, like the top floor in the Genba House, HRS standardise effective decision-making processes and practices, turning repeated tasks into Standard Operating Procedures to spread best practice throughout the organisation. The standardisation of work is particularly important for new recruits so that they can imbibe the kaizen culture (Imai, 2012). Staff are encourage to identify flaws in Standard Operating Procedures and are rewarded when they help remedy them. For this to work in an education setting, there must be regular and issue-specific professional development, and scheduled use of peer observation in teaching.

Dynamic leadership ensures that Genba Kaizen is used throughout the school or university, but will supplement it with some high-reliability approaches. For example, there is no specific mention in Genba Kaizen of systems redundancy as an objective, but it should be a prominent feature of HRS because of the necessity to remove single points of failure from a critical service-focused enterprise like teaching.

Notes

1 A time-and-motion study is a business efficiency technique for improving and upgrading work practices. The original one combined Taylor's time-study work with the motion-study work of Frank and Lillian Gilbreth, but the two techniques became integrated and refined.
2 A person who makes a large contribution to the successful implementation of kaizen during a blitz is awarded the title of *Zenkai*.

10

MANAGING INNOVATION AND CHANGE

For educational institutions, the purpose of managing and assessing risk is to support innovation and improvement, as we discussed in the previous chapter. One such model is the Bass Diffusion model (Bass, 1969). It forecasts the extent to which a market will adopt a new product or service like a new degree course or a new qualification. This 'market adoption rate' is traditionally represented by a skewed bell-shaped curve with 'time' on the horizontal axis and the 'number of people' who adopt the new service on the vertical axis. Mathematically, the curve is based on a simple differential equation – more specifically, a Riccati equation with constant coefficients – that describes the process of how current and potential adopters interact. The basic premise is that adopters can be classified as either 'innovators' or 'imitators', and the speed and timing of adoption depends on their degree of 'innovativeness' and 'imitation'.

Decisions can shift the Bass curve in time, but its shape remains the same. The most common depiction is the Generalised version developed by Bass et al. (1994), depicted in Figure 10.1.

The Bass model has been very influential and has recently been used as a means of estimating the size and growth rate of online social networks. It is one of the most cited works in marketing management, but there are alternatives in the field of innovation. One is the Disruptive Innovation model (Bowyer & Christensen, 1995). A 'disruptive innovation' is one that leads to a product or service aimed at a *new* set of customers which changes the entire market; as opposed to a 'sustaining innovation', which is simply an innovation in a new technology or its application. The Disruptive Innovation model can help organisations avoid displacement caused by radical change. Emerging disruptive innovations are usually unprofitable initially, and because their development requires significant resources initially, they are unpopular with established organisations. Newer universities – and organisations

DOI: 10.4324/9781003217220-10

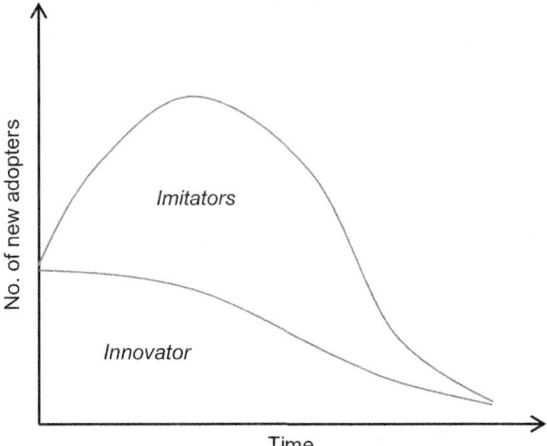

FIGURE 10.1 The Generalised Bass Diffusion model.

like tech start-ups – are not as hindered in this respect because they do not have existing high-prestige services to maintain simultaneously.

There are two types of disruptive innovation: 'low-end disruption', and 'new market disruption'.

- *Low-end disruption* targets the low end of the market; that is, the part of the market that is not willing (or able) to pay premium rates. This is a good place to start for a disruptive innovation to try to grow market presence because it is not of interest to established market leaders since it has such a low profit margin. Further development enables the innovation to move upmarket in due course and enter the more profitable segment of the market where the customer *is* willing to pay more, and the disruptor organisation starts to compete (and outperform) established market-leaders (Van den Berg & Pietersma, 2016).
- *New market disruption* targets customers who have needs that are not being met by existing services on the assumption that the market is waiting for, and wants, the new service, and that the market will adopt the innovation if it outperforms current services.

Disruptive innovation management is similar to the management of research and development. An organisation like a university identifies what type of course innovation is being developed and whether it is disruptive or not, and if it *is* disruptive, whether it is 'low-end' or 'new market'. The organisation should know the strategic importance of the innovation and, according to Van den Berg and Pietersma (2016: 214), should 'keep the disruptive innovation independent' and not integrate it 'into mainstream business activities as this tends to lower its disruptive power'.

'MOOCs' are an example of disruptive innovation in the field of education. A MOOC is a 'massive open online course' aimed at unlimited participation and open access via the web. In addition to traditional course materials, such as videoed lectures and home reading, MOOCs provide interaction with user forums and social media discussion groups to support peer learning and provide feedback on assignments. They emphasise individual self-paced lessons. MOOCs were first introduced in the 'noughties' following decades of distance learning through correspondence courses and television programmes like those provided by the Open University in the UK. Early MOOCs (cMOOCs) promoted open access and open licensing of content to encourage the use and reuse of online materials. Later MOOCs (xMOOCs) use closed licenses for their course material but have open access to it.

The first cMOOCs emerged from the MIT OpenCourseWare project and were motivated by the discovery that class size in universities did not determine learning outcomes. cMOOCs emphasised a connectivist pedagogy, connecting learners to each other to answer questions or collaborate on assignments. They constitute a low-end disruptive innovation. Material was not pre-selected but was remixed and reused. cMOOCs were good at supporting collaboration and knowledge-building, and were typically more creative and dynamic that their modern counterpart, xMOOCs, which more closely resemble traditional courses extended to the general public and present a clearly specified syllabus of recorded lectures and self-test assignments. Most xMOOCs are subscription services resembling television shows or digital textbooks, and they constitute a high-end disruptive innovation. They are essentially branded IT platforms that offer content distribution partnerships to institutions. Student interactions are usually limited to seeking guidance.

MOOCs have followed a 'Hype Cycle' where expectations undergo wild swings and as a consequence some MOOCs have morphed into MOODs, massive online open degrees, usually master's degrees.

The Hype Cycle

Disruptive theory is most easily applied to information technology industries – machine learning, artificial intelligence, software design, computer hardware manufacture and so on – alongside guides like Moore's Law,[1] but it could be adapted to the education sector regarding the introduction of new degree courses like MOOCs and new educational qualifications like MOODs. A more graphical (and less mathematical) representation of the adoption and application of innovations than Moore's Law is the so-called Hype Cycle[2] developed in the US by Gartner, the IT global research and advisory firm (Fenn & Raskino, 2008). It provides a conceptual representation of the maturity of innovation through five life cycle phases (see Figure 10.2):

1. *Trigger.* A potential innovation, like an idea for a new MOOC or a new platform, starts the cycle (point 'A' on the graph). There is early take-up when it goes to market (point 'B' on the graph), and expectations continue to grow. Media interest triggers significant publicity (point 'C' on the graph) but commercial viability has yet to be proved.

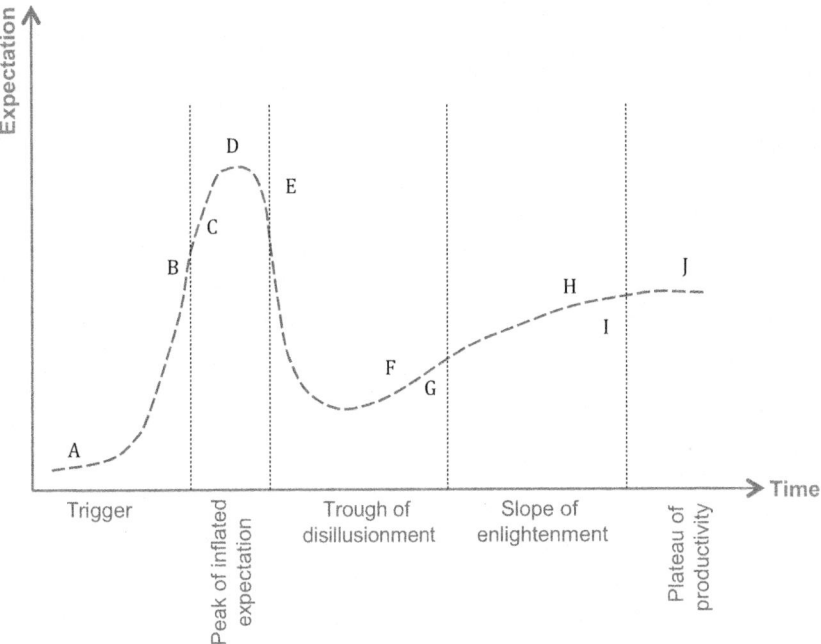

A= R&D
B= first generation comes online and early adopters look at it
C= publicity hype begins
D= activityspreads beyond early adopters
E= negative hype begins
F= only a small % of the market has adopted the innovation
G= second generation comes online
H= best practice developing
I= third generation comes online
J= a growing % of the market adoptsthe innovation

FIGURE 10.2   The Hype Cycle.

2. *Peak of Inflated Expectation.* Early publicity produces a number of success stories and activity spreads beyond early adopters (point 'D' on the graph).
3. *Trough of Disillusionment.* Interest wanes as implementation and early hopes fail to deliver. Some negative publicity emerges (point 'E' on the graph). Many MOOCs and similar innovations fail at this point and are withdrawn from the market. Investment continues only if the survivors prove and improve their services to the satisfaction of early adopters, but at this stage only a small percentage of the market has adopted the innovation (point 'F' on the graph). More benefits of the new course come to light or are better understood, and second-generation versions appear with new funding (point 'G' on the graph).

4. *Slope of Enlightenment.* As good practice in delivering the new MOOC (or whatever the innovation happens to be) becomes embedded (point 'H' on the graph), mainstream adoption starts to take off, and criteria for assessing its viability become better defined.
5. *Plateau of Productivity.* A third generation emerges (point 'I' on the graph), it starts to pay off and the market for it grows (point 'J' on the graph).

Media hype, from which the model takes its name, plays a large part in the adoption of innovations and it has a long provenance in fields like clinical pharmacology and new drug development (Henton & Held, 2013). However, critics point out that the model is not really a 'cycle', that it is not scientific and that there is no data that justifies it theoretically. Nor does it capture the *speed* at which innovation or change develops. It assumes that performance is tied to this shape of curve, but this is not proven, and in any case the model does not describe the *actions* that move things from one phase to the next.

The Innovation Life Circle

An alternative model that *is* genuinely a cycle is the Innovation Circle, which is a model for analysing and managing the life cycle of a new product or service (see Figure 10.3). The model identifies the important phases in a clockwise life cycle.

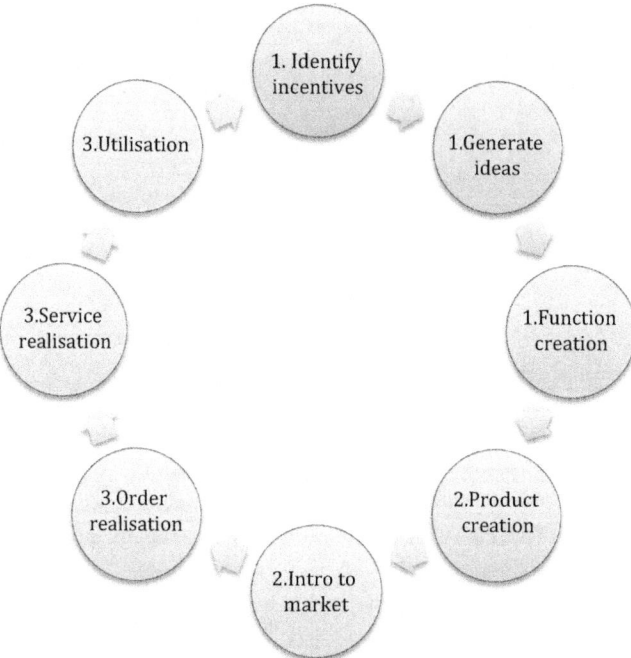

FIGURE 10.3 The Innovation Circle.

There are three main phases, each with sub-phases: creation, implementation and capitalisation.

1. The *creation phase* is shown from 12 o'clock to 3 o'clock on Figure 10.3. It is the phase where ideas for new services are generated and get organised. In the creation phase, the search for new ideas is dominant and the focus is on managing creativity (Van den Berg & Pietersma, 2016). The goals are not clearly delineated. There is a lot of exploration and many potential innovations. This iterative process ends when the best and most suitable ones are agreed. The phase comprises three sub-phases:
    a. The external incentives that initiated the innovation are identified; for example, the reputation of the school had been declining, or research income in the university had been falling.
    b. The generation of new ideas is stimulated by a creative culture within the school, college or university. The best new ideas survive filtering and get adopted, focusing on student need, on a return on investment in new staff, on the risks involved for reputation and on the resources required to deliver the new offering.
    c. In the function-creation process, ideas are transformed into clear functions. From necessity, given the daily pressures under which they operate, schools traditionally have a tendency to devalue left-field thinking in favour of a conservative here-and-now approach. Given the necessity to think originally about research problems, universities have traditionally valued creative thinking more than schools but lack focus when it comes to implementing innovations. In the function-creation process in education, there must be clarity about roles and responsibilities.
2. The *implementation phase* is shown from 4 o'clock to 6 o'clock. In this phase, the new degree course, service or research innovation (e.g. a new research centre) is further developed and the market for it analysed. The implementation phase is managed more tightly than the creation phase, and in universities this is particularly important. This is essentially a 'project management' phase where the goals are clear from the outset, as are the different functions of the new service and the required resources. The phase comprises two sub-phases:
    a. The *product-creation process* is where the new service is developed and tested using prototypes or trial runs or in the case of a new degree course, enrolling a *small* first cohort.
    b. The *market-introduction phase* is where preparation for the new full-on phase is done.
3. *The capitalisation phase* is shown from 7 o'clock to 11 o'clock. This is where the commercialisation of the new service takes place, building the business case and modelling income streams. In this phase, the innovation is integrated into the existing operation. It comprises three sub-phases:

a. The *order-realisation process* is where the service is delivered logistically: Who is teaching the new course? Who is leading the new research centre?

b. *Service realisation* is where the delivery of the new service is integrated into existing processes in the school or university.

c. The *utilisation* sub-phase is where the new service revenues are managed with an eye to synergies, economies of scale and efficiency. This sub-phase will continue until the service is superseded or supplemented, when the cycle begins all over again.

The Phase-Gate model for filtering innovations

The idea of the Innovation Circle model just described is that it allows attention to be paid at the right phase to the right aspect of the innovation. It is basically an analytical tool for managing the process of bringing an innovation, like a new university degree or a new college qualification, to market. It is a continuous cyclical process because the search for innovation does not stop at the end of the utilisation sub-phase. The Phase-Gate model is similar to the Innovation Circle model in that they both provide an approach to managing the different stages of an innovation, although the Phase-Gate model does not focus so much on the capitalisation phase. It divides the complex process of taking an innovation from inception to market into stages, separated by gates where evaluations and 'go/kill' decisions are made to continue or discontinue the process (see Figure 10.4).

The Phase-Gate model originated in the chemical industry in the mid-1990s (Cooper et al., 2002). It is a solution to the problem of having too many projects in the pipeline at any one time, when limited resources are available. Clear stages and gates at which a weak project can be 'killed off' enables an organisation to filter and prune the development portfolio and avoid gridlock. They are essentially quality control checkpoints to remind everyone why the innovation is being undertaken,

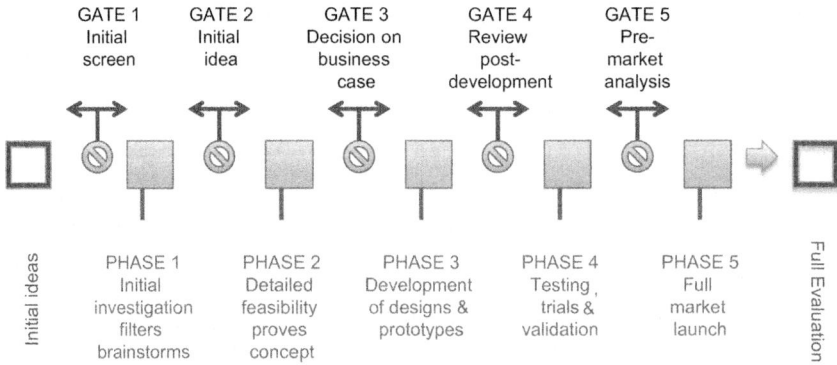

FIGURE 10.4 The Phase–Gate model: the 'go-kill' cure for having too many projects.

why it is important going forward and how resources need to be allocated. The Phase-Gate model has five 'gates' that open into five subsequent 'phases':

1. The first gate filters the original brainstorming ideas based on their synergistic fit within the school or university and with existing courses, services and research interests. Getting through the first gate means that an idea becomes a project, defined and planned, with a focus on how it will benefit staff, students and other stakeholders.
2. The second gate starts the process of building the business case, the potential market and its customer base, and potential applications and benefits. The emphasis is on what gives a particular innovation the edge over innovations from competitors. It is about proving concept and doing feasibility studies.
3. The third gate gives access to the development phase where detailed course specifications are reviewed and prototypes are trialled, including the design of future delivery plans.
4. The fourth gate starts the testing and validation phase where the proofs-of-concept developed in embryonic form in the second phase are reviewed alongside the prototype courses, and detailed delivery plans developed in the third phase. Trials in the marketplace and surveys of student opinion, for example, are conducted to validate the proposed plans.
5. The fifth and final gate starts the launch phase. The new product or service is commercialised, and preparation and marketing ramps up to full scale. This phase also includes an evaluation (a 'post-implementation review') of the previous gates and phases so that the school or university can learn from the experience.

The great benefit of the Phase-Gate model is its ability to 'pull the plug' early on projects that sounded great as initial ideas – usually advocated convincingly by a few zealous promoters – but which prove impractical. The model is an over-simplification, of course – very few things in the chaotic life of schools and universities are so neatly or linearly arranged – but each gate is an opportunity for senior managers to liaise with each project's promoters alongside other stakeholders to add an iterative layer to each part of the 'line'.

The Change Quadrants communications model

Moving back from linear representations like the Phase-Gate model to the more usual two-by-two matrix format, the Change Quadrants (CQ) model tries to capture the tension between an organisation being 'hot' or 'cold', and whether the motivation for change is 'hot' or 'cold'.

*   A *cold organisation* is one where regulations, systems, line management structures and procedures drive the organization. This is common in the university sector.

- A *hot organisation* is one where shared norms, values and understandings drive the organisation (Van den Berg & Pietersma, 2016). This is more common in the school sector.

The CQ model tries to capture an organisation's motivation for change in a similar way:

- A *cold motivation* is an 'objective response to an emergency' (ibid) such as a drop in market share or fee revenue or reputation in the face of competition from other schools, colleges or universities.
- A *hot motivation* for change is driven by personal and professional ambition.

This leads to four quadrants and four possible change communication strategies (see Figure 10.5): cold–cold is the 'Intervention' communication strategy; hot–hot is the 'Innovation and Renewal' communication strategy; cold organisation–hot change is the 'Implementation' communication strategy; and hot organisation–cold change is the 'Transformation' communication strategy.

The grid is used to analyse both the type of organisation-motivation and the type of change-motivation, and then to choose an appropriate change strategy and a 'matching approach' for communicating its aims and objectives.

- The *Intervention* communication strategy comes from *cold* organisation-motivation and *cold* change-motivation; that is to say, the school or university is responding to an emergency of sorts, and the culture of the organisation is one where rules and structures are paramount. This communication strategy

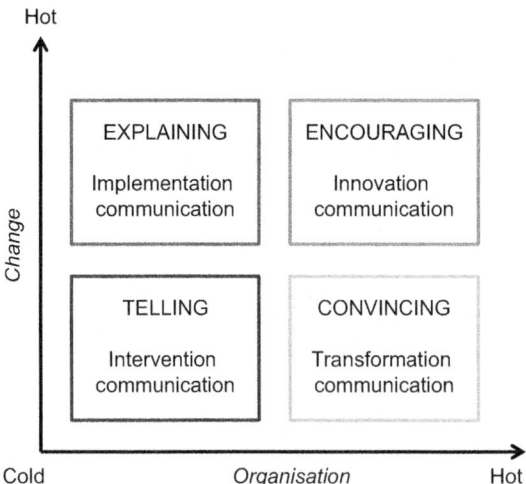

FIGURE 10.5 The Change Quadrants model.

is characterised by '*telling*', shown in the bottom-left quadrant of Figure 10.5. Van den Berg and Pietersma (2016: 240) suggest that this quadrant requires 'a balance between mass communication and personal attention, with clear and direct group-communication, and attentive and specific one-to-one communication'. Intervention is about change being urgent and top-down. Managers decide on the goals, and staff are consulted only insofar as the operational consequences of those goals are concerned.

- The *Implementation* communication strategy comes from *cold* organisation-motivation and *hot* change-motivation; that is to say, the school or university is responding to an emergency of sorts and the culture is one where motivation for change is driven more by personal/professional ambition than by the necessity of a crisis. The communication style is therefore about convincing staff of the benefits of the change and motivating them to help realise it. Information is shared openly, and everyone is kept motivated towards the same end result. Van den Berg and Pietersma (2016: 241) characterise this as 'a public relations style of communication' characterised by '*explaining*', shown in the top-left quadrant of Figure 10.5. Implementation is about change being urgent and top-down, driven by the ambition of managers to be successful.

- The *Transformation* communication strategy comes from *hot* organisation-motivation and *cold* change-motivation; that is, the school or university is driven by shared norms, values and understandings, and the culture of the organisation is one where rules and structures are paramount. The defining characteristic in this quadrant (on the bottom-right of Figure 10.5) is '*convincing*'. Management takes the initiative for change, and the appropriate staff are invited to contribute and say what can be best done within the organisation's rules and structures to actualise the desired change. Transformation is about efficiency of participation, based on established rules and structures, and clear aims.

- The *Innovation and Renewal* communication strategy comes from *hot* organisation-motivation and *hot* change-motivation; that is, the school, college or university is driven by shared norms, values and understandings, and the organisational culture is one where motivation for change is driven more by personal and professional ambition than by crises (see the top-right quadrant of Figure 10.5). Communication is bottom-up and the change is the result of ambition within the organisation. The focus of communications is the actualisation of the desired change, and the defining characteristic in this quadrant is '*encouraging*'. Innovation and renewal is about staff being motivated to create something together, and the school or university being open to creative suggestions from junior employees and utilising their ambition and creativity to build a long-term vision.

In summary, the four quadrants are used to decide qualitatively who the change agents should be, who the active stakeholders are and the scope and timing of the change process. All four quadrants want to maximise the chances of success by choosing the correct strategy, the most appropriate style of communication for the type of school or university in question; for example, it will be different for a research-intensive university than for a teaching-only university. A cold organisation (driven by regulations and management structures) and cold motivation (in response to an emergency) is easier to plan and communicate than a 'hot–hot' one, although typically many schools and universities consider themselves to be hotter and less managerialist than is actually the case. In any case, the model facilitates a matching communication strategy to support change. Most teachers and lecturers – perhaps less so with researchers – have a natural inclination towards social interaction, so communication strategy is usually more a case of facilitating a *natural* inclination than seeking an *unnatural* reversal.

On a practical level, there are many measures that can be taken to develop effective communication networks in schools and universities, though they are only cosmetic unless a culture of sharing is first developed:

- There should be formal structures for sharing knowledge. Staff meetings, in-service days and off-campus training are recommended at all levels.
- Agenda items should be categorised for staff meetings according to importance. Not everything warrants a full discussion; some items should be 'for information' only. Research (Angelides, 2003) has shown that generally, teachers and academics find staff meetings unhelpful and are frustrated by the amount of time spent needlessly discussing that which cannot be changed. The simplest method of categorisation is to asterisk some items 'for information' and others 'for discussion'.
- Staff should be afforded structured opportunities for *casual* communication. When the new mathematics faculty building at the University of Cambridge was built, for example, canteen tables were installed with writing surfaces.
- A well-designed and well-equipped common room is essential in schools, colleges and university departments.
- Junior staff should be encouraged to perform the difficult task of sharing opinions and engaging in critical discussion with senior colleagues. Experience suggests that this is easier, in the initial stages at least, in informal settings. Perhaps surprisingly, input from *newly appointed* staff is often more valuable in relation to *strategic* matters, where they have the least experience, because they bring less professional and political baggage to the discussion.

Education managers should avail of every opportunity to open communication networks within and without the school or university for the benefit of staff, no matter how counter-intuitive it might seem to encourage what appears at first sight to be frivolity. The meta-skill of learning how to learn, which transforms 'experience' into 'learning', is a skill that is very difficult to transfer among colleagues, so despite the fact that every instance of non-directive communication entails some loss of structure, principals and deans should strive not to curtail involvement, but to steer it. Otherwise, there can be no sharing of vision and therefore no leadership, only management.

Kotter's Change model

The Change Quadrants model is often used in combination with Kotter's Change model, which is based on eight identifiable phases of change (Kotter, 1990, 1996, 2002). Kotter distinguished between the leadership of change and the management of change. The latter is essentially a set of processes that keep a holistic system of people and processes running smoothly; the former creates a vision, aligns employees with that vision, defines the future for the organisation and inspires people to buy into it (Van den Berg & Pietersma, 2016). The Kotter Change model suggests that the most common pitfalls are being too complacent, failing to create a coalition in support of change, not having a clear enough vision and failing to communicate that vision, failing to create short-term wins and not embedding the change in the culture of the organisation. The model's eight phases are:

1. The first phase is aimed at creating a sense of urgency to eliminate complacency. Managers should eliminate any false sense of security.
2. The second phase is to create a coalition to support the desired change across the school or university. Members need to recognise the value of the proposed change, trust and commit to achieving it, and have the credibility, skill and formal authority to lead others in pursuit of it.
3. The third phase is to develop a clear vision, provide a sense of direction and align everyone's efforts.
4. The next phase is to share that vision, communicating it consistently to everyone.
5. The fifth phase is to empower tutors and researchers to overcome the inevitable obstacles. The idea is to get everyone to participate in the effort to implement change.
6. The next phase is to 'secure short-term wins' (Van den Berg & Pietersma, 2016) to encourage staff towards greater directed effort. Short-term wins should be visible, unambiguous and linked like stepping-stones to the desired change in the minds of those working in the organisation.
7. The seventh phase is to consolidate the gains and continue towards the vision. The idea is to build and maintain momentum.
8. The final phase is to embed new approaches into the culture of the school or university, to make the changes permanent and prevent recidivism. The key to lasting change is to change the culture itself.

In relation to Phase Eight, change will fail when there is no shared vision and it has not been embedded. Change must be planned well in advance; managers need to imagine and specify what success looks like. What will the school, college or university look like if and when the change is actualised successfully? This then needs to be translated into detailed processes and practical structures: to engineer and embed strategic change, but also to learn from and improve upon it when necessary.

The PDCA improvement cycle

The change cycle of strategic planning, actualisation, embedding and learning is reflected in the Walton and Deming (1986) 'Plan–Do–Check–Act' (PDCA) cycle for structuring improvement. *Planning* the improvement is followed by *doing* the improvement, which is followed by measuring and checking the results coming from the improvement, and finally learning from data so that 'action' can then be taken to adapt and re-engineer it.

- *Planning* for change involves analysing an existing situation and the potential effects of any proposed change on the school, college or university.
- *Doing* the change involves looking at modular bits of the actualisation and attributing the various effects of improvement to particular elements of the change process.
- *Measuring and checking* the change is about looking at the results of the change, like looking at the emerging results of a scientific experiment. The main question, of course, is whether or not the change has had the intended improvement effect. Dynamic leaders go further to analyse why success is realised – and if not, finding out why not.
- *Learning from and acting upon* the change is about re-engineering the change when results are not what was desired. The modular approach to the second ('doing') step above is a help in re-engineering.

Of course, one of the learning outcomes of the PDCA cycle is that it is *itself* a learning process and practice for future iterations. Learning how to be specific in planning and setting objectives and in modularising and monitoring the 'doing of change', as well as knowing how to re-engineer it systematically and consistently, is itself a discipline, helping to avoid the unhelpful habit of firefighting and crisis management.

The PDCA cycle is closely associated with the implementation of 'kaizen' in Japanese-style management. For his pioneering work on the introduction and implementation of kaizen in Japan, the Emperor of Japan awarded Deming, the primary designer of the PDCA cycle, the Order of the Sacred Treasure in 1960, and to this day the Union of Japanese Scientists and Engineers has annual 'Deming Prizes' for achievement in quality management.

Notes

1 Moore's Laws are often used in the IT manufacturing sector. His first 'law' is the observation that the number of transistors in an integrated circuit doubles (as an historical trend) every two years approximately. The observation is named after Gordon Moore, the co-founder of Intel, who suggested in 1965 a doubling every year in the number of components per integrated circuit. Ten years later he revised the forecast to doubling every *two* years. His predictions have been used in the semiconductor industry to guide long-term planning and research and development. Moore's second 'law' states that as the cost of computer power to the consumer falls over time, the cost to manufacturers (in research and development, marketing, etc.) increases exponentially.

2 'Hype' in the media sense of the term, meaning intensive or exaggerated publicity or promotion.

11

APPROACHES TO INTELLECTUAL CAPITAL

Capital, at its most basic, is the wealth that an organisation has at its disposal to carry out its functions.[1] Traditionally, it is the sum of an organisation's resources and is its primary source of influence and competitive advantage. It is the knowledge and utility that comes from the interactions that arise when people work and learn together. There are many definitions and many types of capital – intellectual, social, cultural, financial, structural and physical, to name but a few – and there have been attempts to link some of them together in terms that relate to educational outcomes (Hargreaves, 2001, 2003). Intellectual capital is at the core of what society deems to be the purpose and definition of successful education. It is the resource that comes from relationships between the school or university and its stakeholders, from its ability to innovate and manage change, from its infrastructure and from the knowledge, experience and transferable competencies of its staff. Being largely internal to the organisation, it promises maximum leverage in the search for educational improvement and effectiveness (Kelly, 2004). Intellectual capital is a language for thinking and doing something about an organisation's potential for adding value (Roos & Roos, 1997), and in recent years it has considerably increased its role in the value-creation process. In part at least, this is due to fundamental changes in society and the global economy, where services (of which education is said to be one) have replaced manufacturing as the primary source of wealth in the gig economy. Knowledge is now acknowledged as a very important resource, and what stakeholders think of it reflects their perception of how well knowledge management is integrated into the organisation proper.

The management of intellectual capital in schools and universities is an amalgam of two different theoretical perspectives: one that focuses on generating and exploiting knowledge and intangibles in the manner of *educational improvement*; and one that focuses on measuring output in terms of determinants in the manner of

DOI: 10.4324/9781003217220-11

educational effectiveness research. It should have its foundation in strategy since it is possible to measure effectiveness only against the strategic objectives of an organisation. They are the only sensible guide to the selection of appropriate indicators for measuring the forms and flows of intellectual capital that are deemed important. Since to capture progress, these indicators must eventually be coalesced into a single overall index, they should be coherent with the strategic aims. There is not likely to be a shortage of suitable intellectual capital indicators; the tricky thing for a senior management team is to be able to reduce them to a few important ones. In general, intellectual capital indices should be:

- Sensitive, but not overly so. They should be able to respond to changes fairly quickly, but not be so sensitive that they react unduly to the temporary fluctuations that are a natural part of life in schools and university.
- Accurate, insofar as they should be able to differentiate between levels of change and degrees of success.
- Reliable, in that they do actually measure what they purport to measure.

Intellectual capital represents the potential within an organisation for generating value as well as being an asset in the traditional sense. It is the imperative of dynamic leadership to manage invisible assets, so the concept of intellectual capital implies more than just knowledge about the competencies of employees. In the gig economy in which schools and particularly universities operate, the principal agent for change is the fact that information is no longer precious, the possession of the privileged professional few, but freely available to everyone and available in real time. And, of course, there is a much greater demand for information today due to increased parental sophistication and a better-educated and more consumerist student body. Within reason, geographical separation is today less of a barrier to choosing a preferred school, college or university, at least for those with the wherewithal to travel. In addition, parents and students now have free access to information that would previously have been confined to teachers, lecturers, principals, deans and senior university staff, or would have been expensive and troublesome to obtain (Kelly, 2004).

Intellectual capital and transformational change

The practicalities of managing intellectual capital are complicated by the fact that employees can be both a decreasing and an increasing return factor, depending on whether they are regarded as labour or as a source of knowledge respectively. But one essential skill of intellectual capital management is the ability to lead and respond quickly to change. This is obviously more easily achieved within a learning organisation, as we discussed in the previous chapter in relation to Kotter's work, and we will discuss this further in coming chapters: in relation to the Six Sigma approach (in Chapter 13); Covey's habits of effective managers (Chapter 15); the Core Competence model (Chapter 22); transformational theory and team advocacy (Chapter 23); the work of Bennis (Chapter 24); and, most pertinently, to Senge's work (Chapter 25). The link between transformational leadership theory and intellectual capital management is that in a traditional controlling organisation, people learn only what they know they need to learn; in a learning organisation, committed to the management of its intellectual capital, they learn how to learn, which is what transformational leadership is all about. In education especially, professionals need to attach personal meaning to experience, and initiatives need to be assimilated over time before meaning can be shared. The impetus for change in schools and universities might come from small groups, as we will see in Greiner's Organisational Growth model in Chapter 15; but the momentum to sustain it comes from a bias for action within the whole organisation. Change needs both pressure and support to sustain it. For teachers, lecturers and researchers, that means developing a collaborative culture that converts tacit knowledge to explicit knowledge. For dynamic managers, it means coping with the chaos and conflict that is inherent in education management, as we discussed in Chapter 8, pulled towards stability by collegiality and towards *in*stability by individualism. Success in managing intellectual capital in schools, colleges and universities lies in maintaining the organisation on the cusp of both (Kelly, 2004).

Competition and cooperation

In terms of competition, first-move and fast-response confer an advantage in the marketplace with innovations like MOOCs and MOODs, but layers of middle management are barriers to success in this respect. Whether or not such barriers exist in a school or university setting depends on organisational maturity, size and operational requirements. But it is certain that layers of middle management whose existence serves only to buffer leadership from the unpleasantness of decision-making, and to provide a comfort zone for those at both ends of the responsibility spectrum, can have no place in competitive learning organisations.

In terms of cooperation, success in the marketplace today can be achieved in partnership with other organisations more easily than in the past, because knowledge-based enterprises like schools and universities are more closely related to each other than organisations in (say) the manufacturing sector. However, cooperation is under-exploited in the education sector as a result of an externally imposed accountability structure that pits schools or universities against each other without conferring any real advantage on students, stakeholders or society in general. The league-table compliance mentality that currently prevails in education actually serves to *discourage* cooperation. A high-achieving organisation helping an under-performing one guarantees only to pull itself back towards the median. There is little incentive to cooperate. Notwithstanding, there are many possible areas for cooperation between educational institutions, and between educational institutions and commercial organisations, that can (and need to) be exploited in the future (Kelly, 2004). Schools and universities driven by an intellectual capital outlook and dynamic leadership will look for them.

Note

1 Some parts of this chapters on intellectual capital were previously discussed in Kelly (2004).

12

DYNAMIC LEADERSHIP AND INTELLECTUAL CAPITAL

The central concerns for those charged with measuring intellectual capital in schools and universities are how to account for collective and individual performance, how to track changes in intellectual capital and how to evaluate productivity. No metric will capture all three aspects perfectly of course, since correlations between activity and consequence in education are often hard to find and seldom causal. Productivity – defined simply as the ratio of output to input – is a long-standing concern. In the commercial sector, it is measured as output per unit of labour (perhaps including materials and equipment), but that does not have any direct analogy for teachers and researchers in schools and universities. Too much is unknown. However, if any indicator is to be chosen to measure the importance of knowledge to individual institutions, then the best approaches, which are described in this chapter, are undoubtedly those that link output to strategic priorities (Kelly, 2004).

The Value Added Intellectual Coefficient and value added measures

The Value Added Intellectual Coefficient is a measure of return on investment in thinking capital developed by Ante Pulic (1999) at the University of Graz, Austria, and the University of Zagreb, Croatia. It is based on the premise that the role of labour is different in post-Fordist organisations. Whereas in the past a given amount of work consistently produced a given quantity and value of product, today a given amount of work can result in various outputs. Labour used to be a commodity whose value depended simply on the number of hours an employee worked, which became a proxy measurement for output and was why workers were paid on the basis of time – usually an hourly rate or a salary based on an estimated hourly

DOI: 10.4324/9781003217220-12

rate – but in intellectual-capital-intensive organisations like schools, colleges and universities, output cannot be properly judged (either in terms of quality or value to the organisation) solely on time worked; it must be inferred from things like value added. This is one of the problems with workload models in university departments and with lecturing contracts that notionally divide 'research', 'teaching and 'administration' into percentages:[1] firstly, the total number of hours is not known (or knowable), so a percentage of it is a meaningless figure; secondly, the number of hours spent on any particular activity in a school or university is not linked in any meaningful way with either quality or value.

The Value Added Intellectual Coefficient is calculated by subtracting non-employee inputs (like expenses) from outputs (like revenue from fees, consultancy and research funding). This produces a measure of value added, which is then divided by total payroll costs to give a coefficient measure of how much value has been added per monetary unit of investment in staff. Although the coefficient is imperfect as a pure measure of investment in thinking capital, it is an acceptable way of gauging the importance of intellectual capital to an organisation like a school or a university: the higher the value added per unit of labour cost, the greater the importance of knowledge to the endeavour.

Over the past decade or so, the UK has devised analogous methods for measuring added value in its schools. They measure the progress pupils make between Key Stage 2 and Key Stage 3 (i.e. across the first three years of secondary school),[2] and between Key Stage 3 and the GCSE[3] examination (i.e. across the fourth and fifth years of secondary school). These value added measures allow comparisons to be made between schools with different pupil intakes. Value added scores then compare Key Stage 3 performance with the median performance for all pupils with similar results at Key Stage 2 (or compares their GCSE examination performance with the median performance for other pupils with similar results at Key Stage 3). Individual value added scores are then averaged to give a Value Added Measure for the whole school. Positive scores indicate schools where pupils on average make more progress than similar pupils nationally, while negative scores represent schools where pupils made less progress.[4] Extending such a scheme to colleges and universities would be problematic, not least because the educational outcomes in higher education, mainly degree classification or grade point average (GPA), are not fine-grained enough to differentiate students, and the correlation with prior attainment in secondary school is uncertain.

Expenditure on intellectual capital

Value Added Measures such as the UK model for public schools are complicated – some would say unnecessarily so – and are declining in popularity. Expenditure on intellectual capital is a simpler measure. Keeping track of spending on knowledge workers, on importing outside expertise and on know-how enhancement and training, can give a fairly accurate indication of the extent to which intellectual capital is core to the mission of the school or university. In his book *The Wealth of Knowledge*, Thomas Stewart (2002), one of the pioneers of intellectual capital, describes a diagram developed by British Nuclear Fuels for mapping expenditure as part of their quality management procedures. The horizontal axis has time and major expenditure decision points for the school or university. As costs are incurred, they are marked on the vertical axis in four categories, which together make up the total expenditure on intellectual capital. The hard asset elements first, in two parts:

- *Fixed* hard capital (estate, plant, 'ed tech' equipment, materials).
- *Liquid* hard capital (cash reserves, lines of credit).

And the intellectual capital elements, in two parts:

- *Thinking* capital (teaching and lecturing, research, analysis, planning, marketing).
- *Structural* non-thinking capital (library, support and IT expenditure, staff development and training, infrastructure).

Admittedly, it is difficult for schools and universities to disentangle and categorise expenditure in these four ways, but dynamic managers will find it a worthwhile exercise to see the relative size of spends, and it can facilitate a reduction or increase in expenditure if and when it is required. It is known from experience in the commercial sector that knowledge-intensive work incurs the highest up-front costs (Drucker, 1999; Stewart, 2002), so it is important for managers to check that they are falling over time, as they should.

Identifying and analysing intangible assets

One way of identifying and analysing intangible assets, and comparing them with those of other organisations, is the notion of 'Company IQ', developed by the Norwegian advertising agency Bates Gruppen. The first step in calculating Company IQ for schools and universities is to identify what they do that gives them an advantage over competitors; not core skills, but unique aspects to its services, like student-friendly design, assessment flexibility, reliability of course delivery and cutting-edge research expertise. Managers can draw up a list of attributes unique to the organisation, and this list then goes to staff, students and stakeholders as a questionnaire. Each attribute is rated on a Likert scale for *uniqueness* and *value to customers*, and the results are tabulated on a two-by-two matrix. The horizontal axis has 'value to students or funders', while the vertical axis has 'uniqueness'. The attributes in the High–High quadrant are what everyone perceives to be the most valuable manifestations of the organisation's intellectual capital, and the important thing for management is to discover the knowledge assets that produce them. Workshops can be convened to compile a set of knowledge asset measurements distributed among the various forms of intellectual capital. Typically, these will include training costs, the extent of dependence on a small number of employees, customer perceptions, innovativeness and the ability to change, administrative costs, investment in new educational technology, response to student issues, time to solve problems, measures of loyalty and so on. The measurements chosen should represent knowledge assets that relate strongly to what gives the school, college or university the edge over its competitors. They should be measurable on at least an ordinal scale, and preferably on an interval or ratio scale. In this way, comparisons can be made between departments within the institution or between institutions, with a view to boosting strengths and overcoming weaknesses (Kelly, 2004).

An alternative way to analyse and evaluate knowledge assets is the 'Intellectual Capital Rating', a concept developed by the Swedish company Intellectual Capital Sweden. Unlike Company IQ, the results from the Intellectual Capital Rating approach, though quantifiable, are purely subjective, and external comparisons are difficult. How an educational organisation differentiates itself is important to an Intellectual Capital Rating approach. A questionnaire, adapted for use in schools and universities, is given to managers, teachers, lecturers, researchers, administration and support staff, parents, alumni, students, strategic partners and suppliers. It measures each form of intellectual capital in terms of efficiency, renewal and risk (Stewart, 2002):

- *Efficiency* is scaled from 'extremely good' to 'limited', depending on whether or not the school or university has efficient processes and high-reputation tutors and researchers.
- *Renewal* measures on a Likert scale how strong are the school or university's efforts to rejuvenate and grow its assets, the number of new courses and services offered, the extent to which it hires good new teachers, lecturers and researchers, the extent to which it has a rolling staff development programme for existing staff and the number of curriculum initiatives pursued.
- *Risk* is the danger that the intellectual assets of the school or university will lose value as new technologies, adverse societal developments and yet more government regulation threaten its well-being. Risk is graded from 'negligible', through 'moderate', to 'high'.

In the commercial sector, a high correlation has been found between Intellectual Capital Rating and economic growth (Stewart, 2002), but the approach does not by itself force an organisation to connect output to specific knowledge. It lacks the facility to make comparisons with other organisations, and it is only as good as the questions asked and the honesty of the answers given, but at least it is easy to apply at the level of the individual school, college or university and can point a clear way forward in terms of remedial action (Kelly, 2004).

Exploiting intangible assets

Educational institutions must exploit their intellectual capital assets and invest in them to increase their potential for adding value to the educative experience of students, and the intellectual and professional experience of staff. Rather than look to develop new skills in existing staff or import expertise from outside, schools and universities should utilise their *existing* skills and experience to link their intangible assets to value creation (Clare & DeTore, 2000; Stewart, 2002). Knowledge creates value in schools and universities by adding intelligence to the service they provide, by sharing expertise through networks and by improving ways of working. In commercial companies, this can be measured in *options*, which confer the right to do something without imposing an obligation to do it, and this can be transferred to an education setting without much adjustment. The value of an 'option' to a school or university, greatest in times of uncertainty, is largely fixed by its time span; in other words, the time remaining until the option expires in usefulness, like a lease. Certain options, such as the freedom to participate in government education strategies and membership of research advisory committees, have specific expiry dates; others, like the fashion for certain curriculum initiatives, have less specific time limits but are limited nevertheless. Options can lose value as time passes. In schools, for example, a curriculum option might seem like an attractive proposition today, but actually exercising it in the future when resources are scarcer or more urgently needed elsewhere might not be such a good idea. Options can also lose prestige due to delays in exercising them, and hanging on to them can impede progress if competitor schools and universities develop more fashionable alternatives (Kelly, 2004).

Of course, individual knowledge investment in schools and universities can be analysed simply in a ledger-style manner, with costs on one side and benefits on the other. For example, an investment in staff training can increase student satisfaction and lower delivery costs, and targeted recruitment and higher entry pay for researchers in key projects can result in immediate improvement and make the learning curve less steep for other newcomers. However, it is very difficult to measure on the benefit side how well talent is being exploited at any given time in a school or university, or how satisfied tutors and researchers are in their jobs. One potential measurement approach from the commercial sector is the Watson-Wyatt Human Capital Index, which correlates organisational value with human relations practices (Stewart, 2002). School improvement research suggests that it could be adapted to an education setting since it is known that *improving* schools have different human relations practices to *failing* schools. The index is based on detailed feedback from more than 400 publicly quoted US companies. They ranked themselves according to some 30 weighted factors: the ability to recruit well; to offer performance-related rewards to employees; to be transparent with regard to promotions; to sustain integrity in communications; to use resources prudently; to offer job-sharing and flexible working; to encourage a shared sense of ownership among employees; and so on. In commercial companies, these factors have direct correlations with measures of financial well-being like market capitalisation and shareholder return; the higher the index, the better a company is performing. The index suggests that good recruitment is the most important determinant of success. In fact, it is claimed that each of the five points on its Likert scale equates to a 10% difference in company value; that is, after controlling for other factors, companies that score 'five' on recruiting have market values 10% higher than companies who score 'four', and so on.

This has some important implications for educational management and leadership, where anecdotal evidence suggests that recruitment of good staff to schools, colleges and universities is similarly critical. The same research has found that other factors have a big influence too: a transparent system of rewards has a 9% impact on perceived value; a collegial atmosphere and flexible work practices an 8% impact; and good communications a 4% impact. Somewhat curiously, managing resources prudently does not appear to have any positive impact on the value of an organisation (Stewart, 2002).

In terms of recruiting the best people and keeping them, other independent research (Bontis, 1998, 2001, 2002) has found that nearly 70% of the variation in an organisation's ability to recruit and retain good staff in key positions is exercised through two factors: leadership and employee commitment. Leadership is the more important of the two because it affects retention both directly and indirectly: people want to work for effective leaders, effective leaders get employees to share the mission, and people who share tend to stay together. Bontis further found that the two biggest contributors to thinking capital are employee education and employee satisfaction, but for these to make a difference to adding value, employees have to be engaged directly with customers; in other words, staff satisfaction in schools and universities is an important generator of thinking capital as long as the satisfied teachers and lecturers are engaged directly with students at the chalk-face. Employee satisfaction and employee commitment are directly related; together they increase the motivation necessary for successful knowledge sharing (Stewart, 2002).

Measuring the efficiency of knowledge work and knowledge workers

There are two principal ways of measuring the efficiency and productivity of knowledge in an organisation: one is to assess its infrastructure; the other is to assess its vitality. To have an effective *knowledge infrastructure*, the know-how required for each job must be codified somewhere within the school or university department. Research by Speel et al. (1999) suggests that factors critical to the success of knowledge management include having vision, connecting know-how to output, creating a 'sharing' team culture, having adequate resources and appropriate management tools, developing a shared vocabulary, motivating employees with clear objectives, having the support of a critical friend in the upper echelons of the organisation, and having the ability to break through organisational barriers when the need arises. Knowledge infrastructure is appraised by asking managers, students and academic staff to rate these critical factors on a Likert scale and plotting the results on a diagram like the one in Figure 12.1. The measure is subjective, of course, but it has the benefit of simplicity, and it is easy to spot trends (Stewart, 2002).

Assessing *organisational vitality* as a way of measuring the efficiency and productivity of knowledge was developed by the US company General Electric. It measures the talent of individuals in a workforce and differentiates between members of

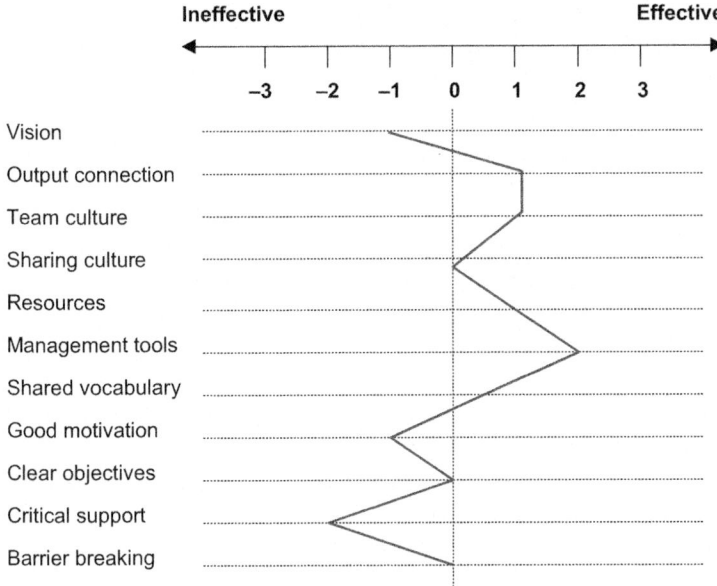

FIGURE 12.1 An example of a Knowledge Infrastructure against critical factors. *Source:* Kelly (2004).

staff on the basis of performance. Managers rank employees as being in one of three categories, which determine pay, promotion and benefits:

- The 'top' 20%
- The 'productive' 70%
- The 'bottom' 10%.

A tarnished version of something similar is quite common in universities, at least in the UK, where tenured professors are placed in one of several salary bands following *criterion-based* appraisal. This is unproblematic as far as it goes; but then, in order to save money, the appraisals are adjusted using *norm-based* criteria by senior managers, completely destroying the integrity of both the appraisal and the reward system. The *post facto* norm-referencing is almost totally subjective and tends to abject corruption when all the usual cultural biases are let loose: gender, sexual orientation, religious adherence and race. Professional bodies and trade unions are silent on the matter because it affects only a few senior (and aging) staff. It is a strictly internal measure, of course. There is no claim to comparison with other organisations (Kelly, 2004).

Putting a value on intellectual capital

Stewart's (1997) concept of Calculated Intangible Value is an attempt to put a monetary value on intellectual capital by means of a return-on-assets calculation; that is, calculating the portion of income (or income minus costs) an organisation earns over and above its generic activities. Unfortunately, this approach cannot usefully be transferred to not-for-profit organisations like schools and universities because in educational organisations, knowledge assets are typically developed by individuals outside the organisation, and no market transaction takes place. Baruch Lev (2001) of New York University adapted the approach to develop an alternative. He infers the value of intangible assets from the returns they produce so that an amount is arrived at that can be attributed to intellectual capital. The first step in Lev's approach is to estimate the organisation's normalised earnings by taking three years of past earnings and adding three years of forecasted earnings.[5] The next step is to see what assets produce these earnings. Financial capital earns a known rate of interest, as does hard, fixed, property capital, so it is relatively easy to subtract the earnings attributable to financial and hard assets from total earnings, and whatever remains must have come from intangibles. Finally, the amount of knowledge capital can be inferred from its earnings by dividing knowledge earnings by the discount rate.[6] The efficacy of Lev's approach is supported by stock market research in that there appears to be a strong correlation between knowledge earnings and performance, and we know anecdotally that this is also the case in universities.

Notes

1 For example, the common "balanced 40/40/20" contracts in UK universities.
2 Compulsory schooling in England is divided into Key Stages: KS1 (Years 1 and 2) for ages 5–7; KS2 (Years 3–6) for ages 7–11; KS3 (Years 7–9) for ages 11–14; KS4 (Years 10 and 11) for ages 14–16. Age 11 is the end of Key Stage 2 (KS2) and is the marker for secondary school attainment.
3 The General Certificate in Secondary Education is the examination taken by nearly all 16-year-old students in England and Wales after five years of secondary schooling. It is the most widely used student attainment measure in educational effectiveness research in the UK.
4 For the KS2 to KS3 Value Added Measures, a result of +1. say, means that on average each pupil at the school made one term's more progress between Key Stage 2 and Key Stage 3 than the median for pupils with similar Key Stage 2 attainment.
5 Lev gives extra weight to anticipated earnings because this is what the market does.
6 The discount rate is a proxy derived from the average after-tax profit of the sector in question, which depends on knowledge assets to the exclusion of all else. Lev acknowledges that returns on knowledge capital wane over time. After five years, it is assumed that the return declines until after ten years, it reaches the growth rate of the economy as a whole. The discount rate is therefore lower for *older* knowledge assets.

13

PROCESS IMPROVEMENT

The Five Why approach

The 'Five Why' approach is an iterative technique used to explore the cause-and-effect relationships behind a particular problem. The goal is to determine the root cause of a problem by repeatedly (five times) asking the 'why' question. Each answer informs the next question. If a problem does not have a single root cause, then the Five Why approach must be repeated asking a different set of questions for each cause. The success of the approach depends on the skill, perseverance and know-how of the team because there are no fixed why questions. The questioning takes place at five levels, progressing from the statement of the problem to the root cause. Five iterations are usually sufficient to get to a root cause; thus the "five whys" in the title. The key is to avoid preconceptions and inherited assumptions instead of following the chain of causality in increments through the levels.

Uncovering a causal behaviour that is alterable is usually indicative of having found the root-cause *level*. The real root cause should point to a process that is not working well, or a process that *should* exist but does not.

One of two primary techniques is used to perform a Five Why analysis: an Ishikawa fishbone diagram; or a tabular format. In order to carry out the analysis properly, it is necessary to:

- Engage management dynamically in the Five Why process and for the analysis itself, assemble the right working group, bringing in an external facilitator as necessary. Lack of support to help the team provide the right answers to 'why questions' is a common failing.
- Try to display all the ideas and diagrams simultaneously to aid discussion, so remote/online teamworking is not ideal.

DOI: 10.4324/9781003217220-13

- Write down the problem and make sure that everyone understands it.
- Differentiate between causes and symptoms. There is a tendency in schools and colleges to stop at symptoms – this is what's wrong – rather than going to the next level of root causes.
- Pay close attention to the logic of cause-and-effect relationships.
- Ensure that root causes definitely cause the problem by reversing the conclusion of the analysis to test it.
- Keep answers precise.
- Follow the logic and the facts step by step. Do not jump to conclusions.
- Assess processes, not the people who operate the processes. Assess the job, not the jobber.
- Never accept human error or employee inattention as root causes.
- Foster an atmosphere of openness, trust, willingness and polite truthfulness.
- Ask the question 'why' repeatedly until the root cause is found. Remember that the elimination of a root cause should *by definition* prevent the error from occurring again. Bear in mind that some questions can elicit several different root causes.
- Formulate the answers to the 'why' questions as if the answers were coming from students, research funders, stakeholders, parents or staff, as appropriate, depending on the issue.

The Five Why technique was developed by Toyota, and it remains a critical component of that company's problem-solving training. The architect, Taiichi Ohno, described the Five Whys approach 'as part of Toyota's scientific approach', 'repeating five times the nature of the problem' as well as its solution. The tool is now use widely outside Toyota, within kaizen, which we discussed in Chapter 9, and the Six Sigma approach, which we discuss next.

The Six Sigma approach

The Six Sigma (6σ) approach is a set of techniques for process improvement invented at (and registered as a trademark by) Motorola[1] in 1986 and later adopted by companies like General Electric. It was singled out for mention in the seminal High Reliability Schools longitudinal study[2] by Stringfield et al. (2008), discussed in Chapter 1. The process is one where 99.99966% of production – but it could also be applied to delivery of services – is expected to be free of defects. The term 'six sigma' comes from statistics and refers to an organisation's ability to produce a very high proportion of outputs within specification, with defect levels fewer than 3.4 per million; that is, within six standard deviations ($\pm 6\sigma$) of either side of the mean of a normal distribution.[3] The idea is that even if the average were to shift up or down by 1.5σ at some point, there would still be a good safety margin in terms of quality.

The application of the Six Sigma approach to education speaks to a broader issue in the leadership and management of schools and universities; namely, why an education system should tolerate poor-quality outcomes and unreliability in its processes, and the extent to which shortcomings should be accepted. Six Sigma is a set of strategies seeking to improve the quality of outputs by identifying and removing the causes of defects and minimising variability in an organisation's processes. It creates a special expert team within the organisation to oversee the modelling of its processes. Projects typically include reducing student-assessment cycle time, reducing energy overheads and carbon footprint across the school or university campus, reducing general costs, increasing staff and student satisfaction, and increasing fee income. In the commercial sector, processes are eventually branded with a 'Sigma Rating' to indicate their defect-free percentage; that is to say, to within how many standard deviations of a normal distribution the fraction of defect-free outcomes corresponds. The goal is not necessarily to improve all processes to the 3.4 (6σ) level; organisations must determine an appropriate sigma level for each of their significant processes and strive to achieve these levels, so it is a question of managers prioritising certain areas for improvement.

Dynamic leadership is about the introduction of Six Sigma – or a version of it – in schools and universities as part of a move to higher reliability. Applying Six Sigma in universities is relatively easy because universities are large multifaceted organisations with substantial estate, plant, engineering, scientific and technical facilities that need to be managed in the same way as large industrial and commercial outfits (Pyzdek & Keller, 2009): making admin and support cycles more efficient; reducing energy overheads and estate costs; increasing staff satisfaction rates and student evaluations; diversifying courses; increasing fee and research income streams; and so on. While the same focus of tolerance-management is not as easily applied in schools, it is still applicable in terms of setting tolerance levels for strategic objectives like pupil attainment figures, examination grades and progression rates to higher education.

As a quality-improvement drive, Six Sigma stresses the importance of:

- Continuous improvement to achieve stable and predictable processes, and reduce quality variation.
- Defining service delivery processes so that they can be measured, analysed, improved and managed.
- Achieving sustained quality improvement across the entire organisation, and from managers and staff.

There is a clear focus in Six Sigma on the measurable and the quantifiable, on strong management and leadership, on good support for colleagues and on making decisions on the basis of verifiable data (Tennant, 2001), very much in the fashion of educational effectiveness research methods.

By the late 1990s, about two-thirds of Fortune 500 organisations were using Six Sigma to reduce costs and improve quality (De Feo & Barnard, 2005) and it acquired an ISO number (International Organisation for Standardization, 2011). It has more recently been combined with lean production to create 'Lean Six Sigma', which looks at reducing wastage, although Lean Management (like Genba Kaizen) and Six Sigma are two different programmes: the former is focused on eliminating waste using proven standardised tools and performance improvement methodologies that target organisational efficiencies; the latter focuses on eliminating defects and reducing variation. Both systems have a Japanese provenance and both are driven by data, but Six Sigma more so.

Six Sigma follows one of two methodologies: DMAIC or DMADV. DMAIC is used for projects to *improve existing* processes. It has five steps:

1. *Define* the system, the voice of students and other stakeholders and their requirements, and the project's specific goals.
2. *Measure* key aspects of current processes and collect relevant data.
3. *Analyse* the data to investigate and verify cause-and-effect relationships, describe those relationships and seek out root causes of the defect under investigation.
4. *Improve* current processes based on the data analysis and set up pilots to improve processes and capability.
5. *Control* future processes to ensure that any deviations are corrected before they result in defects. Implement control systems and continuously monitor the educative and research processes. Repeat the procedure until the desired quality level is obtained.

DMADV is used for projects to *create new* process designs. It is sometimes called DFSS (**D**esign **F**or **S**ix **S**igma). This also has five steps:

1. *Define* design goals consistent with student and stakeholder demands.
2. *Measure* and identify characteristics that are critical to quality, taking risk into account.
3. *Analyse* to come up with possible alternatives.
4. *Design* an improved alternative.
5. *Verify* the design, set up pilots and implement the new processes.

Within the individual phases of both DMAIC and DMADV methodologies, Six Sigma uses established quality-management tools such as the Five Whys approach discussed earlier. Typical statistical tools include analysis of variance, regression and correlational analyses, and chi-square tests (Breyfogle, 1999).

Six Sigma uses an elite ranking nomenclature, familiar to those who enjoy Japanese martial arts. It defines a hierarchy and career pathways that include all management levels and functions. The key roles of Six Sigma (for which special training is required) include:

- *Executive Leadership.* They are responsible for the organisation's vision for the Six Sigma project and they give other role holders the freedom and resources to explore their ideas for improvement.
- *Champions* take responsibility for Six Sigma implementation and its integration across the school, college or university. The Executive Leadership draws

Champions from the ranks of senior management. Champions act as mentors to the next layer down, Master Black Belts.

- *Master Black Belts* are identified by Champions and act as coaches on the Six Sigma programme. They devote all of their time to Six Sigma projects, assisting the Champions and guiding the two lower ranks (Black Belts and Green Belts). They take on statistical tasks and ensure the consistent application of Six Sigma across the organisation.
- *Black Belts* operate under Master Black Belts to apply Six Sigma methodology to specific projects. They devote most or all of their time to Six Sigma, focusing on project execution and special tasks (whereas Champions and Master Black Belts focus on *identifying* projects for Six Sigma).
- *Green Belts* are the employees who take on Six Sigma implementation alongside their other responsibilities, operating under the guidance of Black Belts.

Some organisations use additional belt colours – yellow, white and orange – for lower functions and develop certification programmes for individuals at the relevant skill 'belt' level based on experience and participation in Six Sigma projects.

As explained earlier, the term 'Six Sigma' comes from the idea that if an organisation has six standard deviations (6σ) between the mean and the upper limit, and between the mean and the lower limit, as shown in Figure 13.1, very few items will fail to meet quality specifications. Capability studies measure the number of standard deviations between the mean and the nearest specification limit in multiples of sigma. As standard deviation goes up, or the mean moves away from the centre, fewer standard deviations will fit between the mean and the nearest limit, decreasing the sigma number and increasing the likelihood of items failing the quality specification.

In the centre at 0, the mean μ is zero, with the horizontal axis showing distance from the mean in standard deviations (σ). It goes from −6σ (the lower specification limit, LSL) to +6σ (the upper specification limit, USL). The greater the standard deviation, the greater the spread of values encountered. For the curve in the middle, μ = 0 and σ = 1. The upper and lower specification limits are at a distance of ±6σ

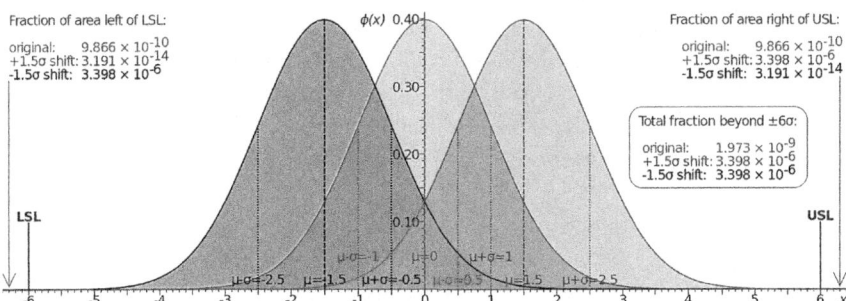

FIGURE 13.1 Graph showing six standard deviations between the mean and the upper and lower limits in a normal distribution. *Source*: Cmglee (n.d.), Wikipedia.

from the mean. Values lying that far away from the mean are extremely unlikely: approximately 1 in a billion (10^{10}) too low or too high. Even if the mean were (at some point in the future) to shift to the right by 1.5σ (the right-hand curve) or to the left by 1.5σ (the left-hand curve), there is still a good safety margin for quality. This is why the Six Sigma approach *aims* to have processes where the mean is at least 6σ away from the nearest (upper or lower) specification limit.

We know that processes usually do not perform as well in the long term as they do in the short term, so the number of σ that will fit between the mean and the nearest specification limit usually drops over time. To account for this real-life increase in quality variation over time, the 1.5 sigma shift referred to earlier is deliberately introduced into the calculation. According to the model, a process that fits 6σ between the process mean and the nearest specification limit in the short term will in the long term fit only 4.5σ on either side because the mean will shift over time or because the observed standard deviation in the long term will be greater than that observed in the short term.

The sigma shift is practical, but its role is mainly academic. The purpose of the Six Sigma approach is to generate organisational improvement, so it is up to the organisation to determine what the appropriate sigma level of their processes should be. The purpose of the sigma value is as a comparative figure to determine whether a process is improving or deteriorating. Having defects fewer than 3.4 per million (equivalent to 6σ) is not *per se* the goal of the approach, which is why it is worth applying to education settings like schools and universities. *Striving for* high reliability is the real aim.

After its first application at Motorola in the late 1980s, other famous companies – Johnson and Johnson, Texas Instruments, Sony and Boeing – have applied Six Sigma and have recorded significant savings (Kwak & Anbari, 2006). It has also been applied in financial service companies such as Bank of America, American Express, GE Capital and JP Morgan, improving the accuracy of cash allocation, reducing bank charges, improving reporting, reducing credit and collection defects, and increasing customer satisfaction. The healthcare sector is also well suited to Six Sigma because of its zero tolerance for mistakes and the overriding imperative to reduce errors and medical negligence claims, but the approach can also reduce time waiting for medical appointments while increasing the number of examinations. A similar approach in education with the high reliability schooling approach (McREL, n.d.; Reynolds et al., 2002; Stringfield et al., 2008) introduced in Chapter 1, would seem like an obvious extension. In applying High Reliability Organisation Theory to schools, Stringfield et al. (2008) agree with the general view that reliability is socially constructed, dynamic and evolving, and that many schools exhibit some high reliability characteristics[4] even though policy reform in education generally has not prioritised reliability of service (Reynolds et al., 2006). Where high reliability procedures do exist, these researchers found a very significant improvement[5] in pupil attainment and that such improvement was sustained over time.[6] It is one of the most significant findings in educational effectiveness research, which for some reason has stayed under the policy radar and has gone largely unreported outside academia.

Stringfield et al. (2008) identified several themes in the leadership and management of High Reliability Schools (HRS):

- The importance of a finite and modest number of goals that evolve and are shared school-wide.
- The centrality of data and data analysis.
- Standard operating procedures were found to benefit the organisation and staff in responding to recurring problems: student and teacher absences, behaviour management, data collection, and other daily or weekly activities.
- Seeking out best practice by observing other higher achieving departments in the same school or university, or in other organisations.
- Skilfully managed leadership succession, particularly with charismatic leaders leaving (see Chapter 3). A new leader must immediately recommit to HRS practices, especially when unfamiliar with the original effort.
- Rather than pushing relentlessly for 'fidelity' of implementation of the original set of ideas, staff pursuing HRS development co-construct their own locally developed reforms, following the doctrine of 'mission command' discussed in Chapter 5.
- HRS processes are cyclical in their effect. Initial gains must be built in layers. Teacher enthusiasm and leadership authority are also cyclical, as are staff expectations for achievement. They must all be monitored, while recognising that student attainment and examination results are only a surface reflections of deeper achievement. As Stringfield et al. (2008: 20) put it:

> The quantitative goals are nothing more than measurable artifacts of larger, less readily quantifiable but equally laudable goals. In each case, the achievement of a readily observable goal has allowed the upward re-benchmarking of a range of desirable outcomes. When asked in 2006 about their initial goals, the great majority of HRS-school personnel smiled and stated confidence in their ability to achieve new, much higher goals. These are, in themselves, laudable achievements.

It is a similar situation in universities – degree classification is only one student outcome from four years of attendance, and perhaps a minor one at that – but there are theoretical problems with Six Sigma. For one thing it is better suited to *existing* processes; and secondly, it does not help to develop new or so-called 'disruptive innovation' practices discussed in Chapter 10. Its reliance on statistical tools is not a problem in education since most of these techniques are already in use in school effectiveness research, but Six Sigma typically pays more attention to reducing variation than to the inherent benefits of a learning organisation: adaptability, creativity and continuing professional development. And of course, statistical approaches such as Six Sigma cannot predict rare events, which in education might be the gifted child or the exceptionally deprived catchment area of a school or Nobel Prize-winning breakthrough research in a university. Correspondingly in universities, in their search for 'less variability', Six Sigma as a top-down method can stifle creativity in research environments, resulting in more 'sameness', albeit at a higher level of quality. Six Sigma, like high reliability itself, results in less 'exceptionality' and fewer left-field innovations. Reducing variability waters down the discovery process, the 'free-wheeling nature of brainstorming' (Hindo, 2007) and the serendipitous nature of discovery. Inconveniently, research is not something that can be dulled and at the same time remain exceptional.

Notes

1 In 2005 Motorola attributed over $17 billion in savings to Six Sigma!
2 Conducted first (2006) in England and later (2008) transferred to Wales.
3 This figure was originally based on the tolerance in the height of a stack of discs.
4 These are listed in Chapter 1.
5 High Reliability Schools raised their average percentage of students obtaining top grades by 75% more than the national average, which itself had risen over the same period, and nearly half the schools involved in the project made gains more than double the national average.
6 Five full years after the initial high-reliability intervention.

14

SCORECARDS AND DASHBOARDS

The Balanced Scorecard system is a semi-structured performance dashboard for strategy and processes, tracking staff activities and their consequences (Epstein & Manzoni, 1997). A Balanced Scorecard focuses on the strategic agenda of a school or university, measures and monitors performance and looks at financial matters, student-related issues, internal processes and learning opportunities that impact on the achievement of objectives (Kaplan & Norton, 1992, 1993, 1996a). It is an example of a closed-loop control – a control where *actual* performance is measured and compared to a reference value – applied to the management of strategy implementation (Muralidharan, 2004) and is a mixture of financial and non-financial measures (Lawrie & Cobbold, 2004). The Balanced Scorecard was designed as an alternative to traditional performance measures that focus solely on fiscal indicators or are based on past performance, and as such, Balanced Scorecards are particularly suited to organisations like schools and universities where objectives are not primarily financial.

Balanced Scorecards and strategic maps

A Balanced Scorecard identifies a small number of measures – typically no more than 20 – and attaches targets to them, so that when they are reviewed, it is possible to determine whether performance has or has not met expectations. Depending on the role of the appraisee within the school or university, financial measures may be included; for example, one would expect budgetary control to be one element of a college principal's review, but not for a lecturer, say. By alerting managers to areas where performance does not meet expectations, the scorecard focuses attention on underperforming areas.

DOI: 10.4324/9781003217220-14

The characteristic feature of a Balanced Scorecard is the summative and concise presentation of a mix of measures, each one compared to a target reference value. It gives an insight into an organisation's strategy by requiring general strategic statements to be distilled into more tangible practical forms. The first version of the Balanced Scorecard by Kaplan and Norton (1992, 1993) suggested choosing targets for the main activities required to implement the organisation's strategy in four categories – financial, non-financial customer, non-financial internal processes, non-financial learning opportunities and people – but for an education setting like a university, an alternative four categories are shown in Figure 14.1:

- *Teaching*, which is student-stakeholder-focused and internal. It includes working with colleagues in the delivery of courses.
- *Research* is funder-focused and external. It includes measures of impact on society, on the academic discipline and on policy-makers.
- *Enterprise and citizenship* are both internally and externally focused. Entrepreneurship can mean gaining access to internal university funding or bringing in external funding to support new initiatives. 'Citizenship' refers to the contribution made by the appraisee to the management and administration of the department. It is also both internally and externally focused: being in charge of postgraduate courses, for example, is an internal function; liaising with local community schools is an external function.
- *Personal development* is about growth and learning for the individual: career ambitions, personal challenges, achievement and interests, and skills development. It should include salary, reward and recognition. The idea is to try to align personal targets with desirable organisational targets.

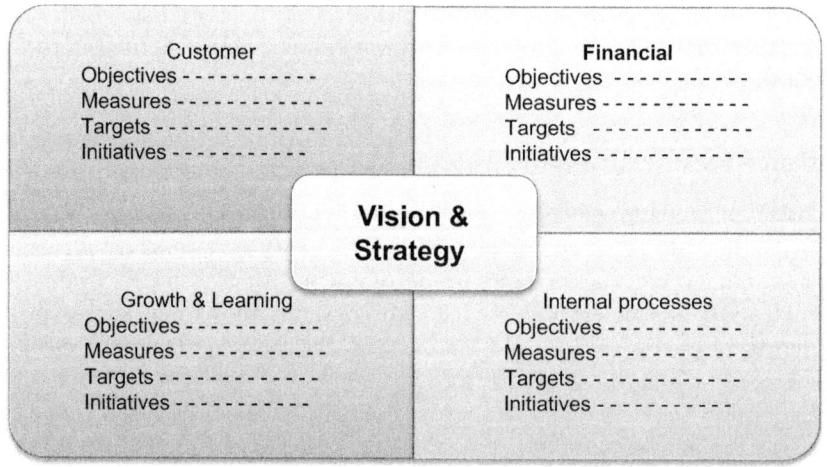

FIGURE 14.1 The Balanced Scorecard.

Construction of the scorecard usually starts with the last one, Personal Development, and builds towards the two external ones, Teaching and Research. Not surprisingly, with the first generation of Scorecards, the focus was on commercial companies and their finances (Butler et al., 1997; Irwin, 2002; Moulin, 2017), but modern Balanced Scorecards have made their way into public sector organisations (Northcott & Taulapapa, 2012) and health care management (Moullin et al., 2007). They are now flexible enough to fit a wide range of organisations, taking account of aspects of strategy that have social, human resource and political dimensions, and can be adapted to reflect the distinctive nature of competition and collaboration in not-for-profit settings. They now come in three types (Lawrie & Cobbold, 2004):

1. The original four-box type shown in Figure 14.1. The measures that track the implementation of strategy within each of the four boxes might include:
    ○   High-level and accurate income measures, including value added metrics. The aim is to choose measures that gauge how the organisation appears *from the perspective of external stakeholders* like prospective students, their parents, research funders and policy-makers.
    ○   Customer measures, like the take-up of new services, recruitment to new courses, student satisfaction ratings, the handling of staff and student complaints, market share, employability or progression to higher education, and on-time completion of courses. The aim is to choose measures that judge what is important to staff and to external stakeholders.
    ○   Internal processes like course cycle time, unit cost per student or per A-level grade or per degree, response time for complaints, cost and time for new course development, and the percentage of new students from certain demographics. The aim is to choose measures that identify what the organisation should excel at looking forward. These metrics essentially look at internal effectiveness.
    ○   Learning and growth measures like human resources, the management of new ideas, staff satisfaction, promotions and turnover. The aim is to choose measures that identify how the organisation can continue to improve, create value and innovate.
    Managers choose and use categories like these to select a small number of measurements that inform one aspect of the organisation's strategic performance. The choice of metric should be justified so that users have confidence in the scorecard. It was not common to do this in the early years of the Balanced Scorecard, which ultimately led to its redesign.
2. Types that include a 'strategic map' or 'strategic linkages' like the Performance Prism model (Neely et al., 2002). This is an improved version of the Balanced Scorecard that dates from the mid-1990s (Olve et al., 1999). In this version, metrics are selected based on a set of strategic objectives plotted on a strategy map. The objectives are distributed across the Kaplan and Norton (1996b) measurements listed in the previous point. Managers choose a few strategic objectives

within each area and then define the cause-effect chain between these objectives to create 'strategic linkages' (Lawrie & Cobbold, 2004). The approach provides greater justification for the metrics chosen, and users have more confidence in the process because they are more involved at an earlier stage.

3. Types that include a 'destination statement' to augment the strategic maps and linkages. These statements are separate documents describing the long-term outcomes sought from the strategy. This design emerged in the late 1990s to address an issue with the second-generation scorecard described earlier; namely, that plotting causal links between twenty or so strategic goals was difficult and somewhat abstract. The 'strategic map' type scorecard (point 2) also ignores the fact that opportunities intervene to influence strategic goals. This third-generation type tests the impact of objectives using a so-called 'destination statement', which is simply a statement of what strategic success looks like and if created at the beginning of the process, makes it easier to select strategic activities and objectives to correspond to the desired end-state. Metrics and performance targets can then be chosen and tracked. This scorecard design is significantly different from the earlier two designs (Lawrie & Cobbold, 2004) and is more suitable for third-sector and non-commercial organisations like schools and universities.

The Balanced Scorecard approach can be criticised as a list of metrics that fails to provide clear recommendations for improvement; also, that it does not address those aspects of strategy that have social, human resource and political dimensions, nor does it reflect the distinctive nature of competition and collaboration in the not-for-profit sector. However, when coupled with strategic maps, they are more than the simple 'stacking' of (financial and non-financial) metrics. Strategic maps have become integral to the more recent, improved versions of the Balanced Scorecard (Kaplan & Norton, 2004). These maps are patterns of effect from drivers that generate strategic outcomes and can describe the process of transforming intangible assets, discussed at length in the previous chapters, into tangible outcomes. Figure 14.2 is an example of a strategic map, showing two strategic 'themes': operational efficiency; and development of service leaders. (There are usually more than two themes, and they usually include things like growing market share in a particular sector or geographical area.) The themes reflect what needs to be done within an organisation. Starting at the bottom left, the school or university wishes to have less variability in teaching and more targeted delivery of its courses. This requires improved quality assurance and, from the student point of view, will provide better quality and lead to fee-income growth. Of course, having less variability also reduces duplication and remediation, which is a type of waste. This will require improved delivery processes so that fees are kept to a minimum and students think that they get good value. This will also lead to fee-income growth, and ultimately happy stakeholders (Van den Berg & Pietersma, 2016: 56).

Strategic maps show in a single, easily understood overview the value-adding elements and processes of a school, college or university, and the importance of

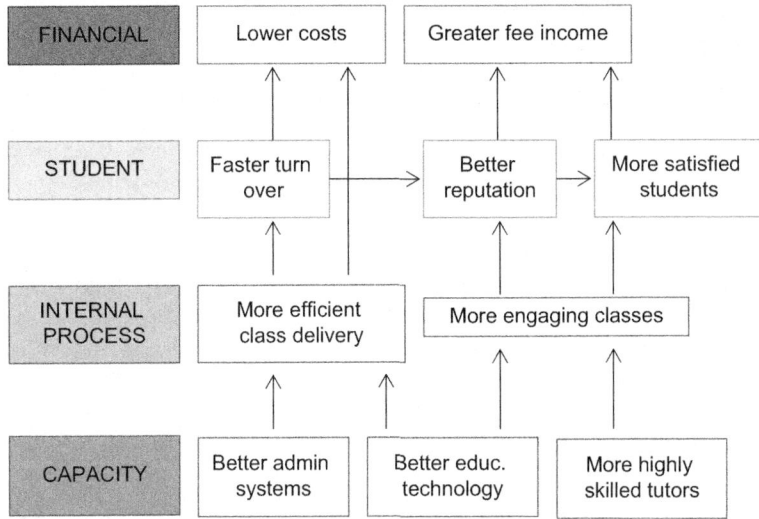

FIGURE 14.2 Example of a strategic map.

intangible assets in what is a knowledge-intensive world. The internal processes are driven by these intangible assets, which in turn determine how the organisation delivers on the student and stakeholder perspective (Van den Berg & Pietersma, 2016). This is ultimately what drives outcomes, but dynamic managers need to use these maps alongside their Balanced Scorecards to translate strategy into targets. Knowing how strategic objectives hang together holistically is not enough. Strategic objectives need performance targets that are challenging but attainable at the level of the individual academic in order to be realised. This need not result in a surveillance or performativity culture but, if coupled with the right support and training, can encourage a shared sense of ownership.

SWOT analysis

The four measures on the Balanced Scorecard are similar to the four facets of the popular SWOT analysis approach – Strengths, Weaknesses, Opportunities and Threats – which is used to create strategy and make decisions. The first two are *internal* to the organisation; the last two are *external*. Strengths and weaknesses refer to the skills and assets that the organisation possesses or does not possess that add to, or take away from, the value of the organisation. Mostly, these strengths and weaknesses are gauged relative to the competition rather than gauged in the abstract. Opportunities and threats emerge due to the activity of competitors and change constantly so that any particular SWOT analysis is fixed at a point in time. They occur because of external environmental forces or changes – demographic, economic, technological, political, legal, social and cultural – as well as external sector-specific environmental forces such as changing customer demands, bigger or different competitors, new grant providers, and changes in supply (Van den Berg & Pietersma, 2016).

- *Strengths.* What the school or university does well, what it has a *good* reputation for, and the research and teaching skills and experience of its staff.
- *Weaknesses.* What the organisation does badly, what it has a *bad* reputation for, relative to the competition, and the skills deficit of its staff.
- *Opportunities.* How the school or university can benefit from potential part-nerships, synergies, technological developments and demographic changes, and how its assets can be used differently and more effectively.
- *Threats.* Changes that the school or university faces in new market regulations, in society, in the introduction of new technologies, the cost base or from other competitive forces.

The second step in the SWOT analysis is to score each finding in each of the four categories according to importance, and then put them on a two-by-two matrix (see Figure 14.3). This identifies the organisation's most urgent and most important strategic issues by juxtaposing the internal (S&W) and the external (O&T). It is about finding a good strategic fit with existing capabilities, in the existing market context.

The aims here are fourfold: on the top row, (a) to use strengths to take advantage of opportunities, and (b) to overcome weaknesses to take advantage of opportunities; and on the bottom row, (c) to use strengths to overcome threats, and (d) to minimise weaknesses to overcome threats.

The third step is to decide what to do as a result of the SWOT analysis. Both (a) and (d) are straightforward. Although (a) is the ideal (internal strengths combined

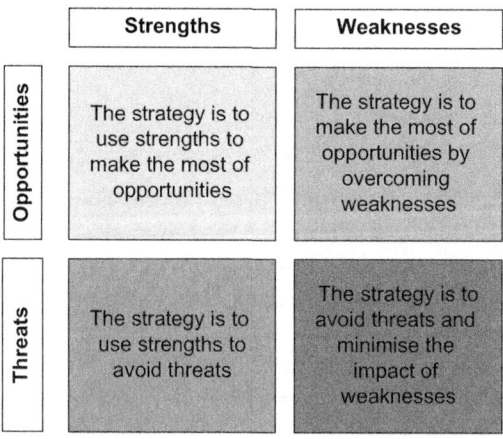

FIGURE 14.3 The SWOT two-by-two matrix.

with external opportunities), it still requires an understanding of how those strengths can support weaknesses in other areas so that the whole mission does not suffer or become unbalanced in its activities. A school or university should do what it is good at when the opportunity arises, and avoid activities for which it does not have the competencies. Conversely, (d) is the worst-case scenario – existing internal weaknesses combined with threats – and usually requires radical change such as divestment in certain courses, subject disciplines or activities.

Less obvious and much more risky are the strategies in (b); that is, when an organisation takes on an opportunity despite not having the required skills at the time but intending to develop them later. Existing weaknesses combined with opportunities must be judged on investment effectiveness to determine whether the gain is worth the effort of bringing in new people or the cost of developing the skills of existing tutors, researchers and support staff.

Schools and universities that use strengths to overcome threats (c) tend to 'bully' their way to prosperity by using their reputation, size or financial clout to fend off the competition (Van den Berg & Pietersma, 2016). Existing strengths combined with external threats essentially requires changing the threat into an opportunity.

The final step is to decide on a school-wide or university-wide action plan based on the SWOT analysis, assigning managers to their tasks, allocating resources and monitoring progress towards strategic objectives; while remembering that SWOT analysis is an iterative process and, because it captures existing strengths, weaknesses, opportunities and threats *at a particular point in time*, needs to be redone regularly.

The problem with the SWOT analysis model, apart from the fact that it does not generate strategic alternatives, is that it requires skills that may be absent from the school of university that is trying to use it to find what skills are missing! There is a risk of making wrong assumptions but not knowing that they are wrong.

15

STRUCTURES AND SYSTEMS

One of the most popular diagnostic models for structure and systems is the '7-S Framework'. This model, designed to structure effectively the systems of an organisation, views the organisation as a holistic entity with seven different interconnected strands that must be 'aligned' so that they can reinforce each other: strategy; structure; systems; skills; staff; style; and shared values. The last strand – shared values – is like Senge's 'Fifth Discipline' (see Chapter 25); it is the unifying element at the centre of the framework (see Figure 15.1).

The 7-S framework

The model defines and analyses the most important elements of an organisation. Like the Value Chain model (to be discussed in Chapter 17), it looks at the existing structure and at the desired future structure, and how to get to the latter from the former by identifying gaps and inconsistencies in the organisation's strategic plans.

- *Strategy* refers to the aims of the school or university (faculty or department, say) and the choices that must be done to achieve them; for example, by prioritising certain courses and target markets and deciding on the allocation of resources. Strategy can be planned or opportunistic.
- *Structure* refers to the hierarchy of the school or university and the integration of work and activities within it. Structure ranges from elitist to pluralist.
- *Systems* refer to the primary and secondary processes that the school or university uses to achieve its objectives; for example, its course delivery and student support systems. Systems range from directive to discretionary.
- *Style* refers to the culture of how management chooses priorities and what it will do (or *not* do) to achieve its objectives; for example, the behaviour of management towards research or specialist teaching.

DOI: 10.4324/9781003217220-15

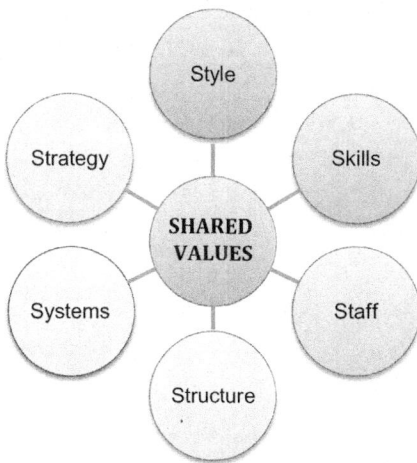

FIGURE 15.1 The 7-S framework.

- *Staff* refers to the people within the school or university, both as individuals and in the collective sense.
- *Skills* refer to the distinctive capabilities of staff, individually and collectively.
- *Shared values* refers to those values that underpin the organisation's behaviour, culture and modus operandi – its shared beliefs. Shared values are at the centre of the framework. They include core beliefs and the expectations that staff have of the organisation.

The first three of the seven elements – strategy, structure and systems – are scientific, tangible and task-centred ('hard'). The other four elements – style, staff, skills and shared values – are emotional, intangible and person-centred ('soft') and are harder to measure. The usual analytic approach involves looking for conflicts between the seven elements and their opposites, called 'vectors of contention' (Pascale, 1990). The idea is not to resolve those conflicts but to be aware of and understand them, and to use them to the organisation's advantage.

Greiner's Organisational Growth model

Solving problems is particularly important for organisations that are *growing*, and Greiner's (1998) Organisational Growth model is a suitable diagnostic in such circumstances. In an education setting, the model suggests that schools and universities go through six 'phases' of growth, with five 'crises' at the transition points between the phases (see Figure 15.2). Each phase of growth has a steady state at the start and an unstable change-intensive state at the end. The six phases of growth are:

1. Creativity
2. Direction

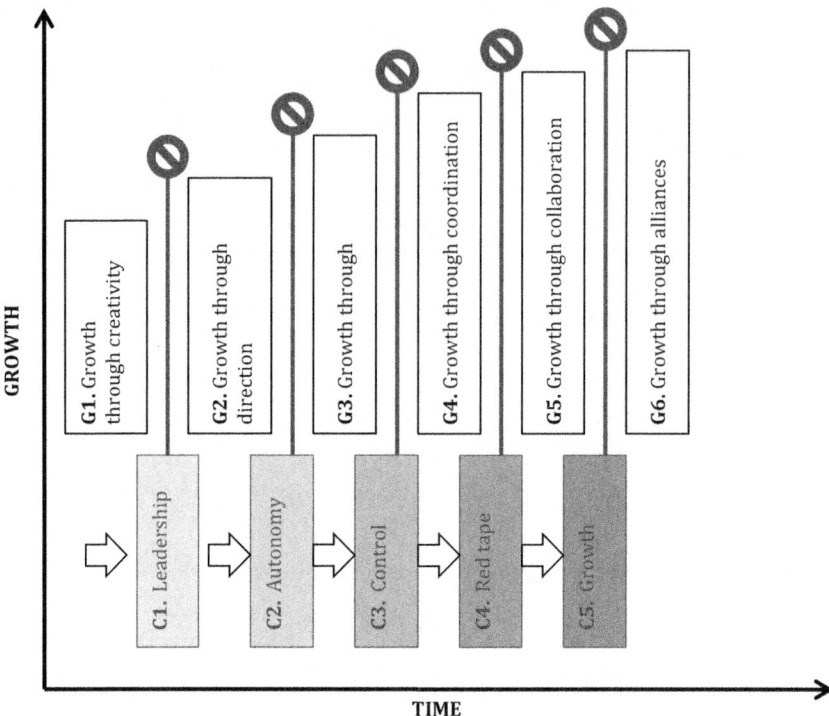

FIGURE 15.2 Greiner's six growth phases and five crises.

3. Delegation
4. Coordination
5. Collaboration
6. Alliances

The crisis that occurs at the transition point between two phases is what moves the school, college or university from one phase to the next:

From phase 1 to phase 2 is driven by a crisis of leadership. Initially, the emphasis is on creativity; specifically, creating a new course or service or research expertise, and generating a market for it. The person or group initiating the new offering is still solely in charge, and the school or university is behaving technically and entrepreneurially. Communication is informal, reward is modest and satisfaction is accrued by the sense of ownership of the innovation and its potential contribution to the mission of the school or university. However, as the innovation grows, it becomes more complex, and internal disputes arise about its direction of travel. The new activity gets too big to be sustained any longer by the creativity of the initial team who cannot keep their hands on all the rudders. The need to move to the next phase – the 'direction' phase – is pressing and the need for decisiveness is urgent. The formation of a management structure begins; typically, by bringing in experts not originally involved to pull the whole thing together. This second phase is character-ised by a more formal functional structure, reward incentives, quality assurance, for-mal communication, a more traditional hierarchy and more directive management.

From phase 2 to phase 3 is driven by a crisis of autonomy. The directive management style of the second phase focuses everyone on growth. As the new course or service becomes more complex, senior managers are no longer able to oversee all opera-tions, but they are not willing to let go. The experts brought in at the first crisis want autonomy and more control. They cannot do their jobs effectively and a crisis of autonomy is created, so the organisation is pushed towards greater delegation. Delegation is part of a decentralised structure. It trickles down decision-making subject to periodic reviews. Communication becomes less frequent and more for-mal, and the job of leadership becomes one of coordination as middle managers act more independently and with increasing autonomy.

From phase 3 to phase 4 is driven by a crisis of control. As the school or university adds more layers and starts to recruit middle managers to run the new offering with autonomy, the structure of the school or university gets taller, so senior managers are not as well informed. This leads to a crisis of control as they struggle to coordinate the activities of autonomous subordinates. There are reviews of activities and struc-tures, formal line management and accountability structures are introduced, support and admin functions are centralised, and the delivery of courses and services is ration-alised. Eventually, after endless tweaking of command-and-control management sys-tems, with an ever-increasing admin department that increases bureaucracy in order to perpetuate itself, the admin becomes a core activity *in itself* rather than an enabler of core activities like teaching and research. The organisation is moving towards its next crisis, with which everyone working in a university today is familiar: red tape!

From phase 4 to phase 5 is driven by a crisis of red tape. As the school or university adds more features, there is greater emphasis on communications and more and more meetings; again, something with which everyone working in a university is familiar. The added bureaucracy leads to a crisis of red tape, characterised by slow decision-making and management teams that become less aware of their external environment. This is not what the organisation needs. Costs increase; there are too many bureaucratic layers and too many managers. The school or university must be more agile in the market and more flexible in its working practices. Managers now start to take out the layers that had earlier been added, and the organisation moves into a fifth, collaborative phase characterised by team management, a focus on task-centred problem-solving, the decentralisation of admin staff to support those teams, simpler and lighter-touch management systems, and in-house staff development programmes. Incentives tend to be at the team level, rather than at the level of the individual.

From phase 5 to phase 6 is driven by a crisis of growth. This is where the school or uni-versity starts to run out of ideas and starts to look for alternative methods of growth through research alliances, acquisitions to enlarge the estate facilities, franchising courses and big developments like overseas 'campuses'. The de-layering continues and the red tape decreases. Costs eventually decline and growth is stimulated.

Greiner's growth model is simplistic: not every organisation goes through all six phases or all five crises, and the model does not take account of *pace* of growth. It is essentially a theory about the growth of an organisation and the problems that arise in each growth phase, showing that changes in management style and organisational structure are required for different stages and for different crises, and helping organisations understand transitioning from one phase of development to another (Van den Berg & Pietersma, 2016).

Mintzberg's Organisational Framework model

The way the Greiner model is structured is similar to the six configurations of an Organisational Framework model developed by Henry Mintzberg (1989, 1992), which helps managers understand an organisation's core problems, and coordinate its structures and processes. The model sees organisations as comprising six fundamental building blocks:

1. Operational core
2. Senior strategic management
3. Middle management
4. Technology infrastructure
5. Support staff
6. Ideology

The first three blocks form the core and are connected by a single chain of command. The technology infrastructure block (4) and the support staff block (5) act to influence the core indirectly. The organisation's ideology (6) represents the cultural values that permeate the school or university, in the manner of Hofstede's Cultural Dimensions model and the Competing Values model, which will both be discussed in Chapter 17. Together with external stakeholders and circumstances, these six configurations or blocks determine how a school or university evolves. Therefore, the job of management is to coordinate the blocks and distribute authority and delegation between them, which (according to the theory) is what gives each organisation its uniqueness.

Mintzberg's identifies seven different types of organisation – ignoring hybrid combinations of types – each with its own primary coordinating mechanism, its own primary block and its own type of distribution of power, the most important parameter in the model.

- An *entrepreneurial* configuration is characterised by direct supervision as its primary coordinating mechanism. The most important part of the school or university is the senior management team in charge of strategy, and there is both vertical and horizontal centralisation and little distribution of authority.
- A *machine* configuration is characterised by the standardisation of work as its primary coordinating mechanism. The most important part of the school or

university is its technological and support structure, and there is some horizontal centralisation of authority.

- A *professional* configuration is characterised by the standardisation of skills and competencies as its primary coordinating mechanism. The most important part of the school or university is the operational core, and there is horizontal *decentralisation*.
- A *diversified* configuration is characterised by the standardisation of outputs and outcomes as the primary coordinating mechanism. The most important part of the school or university is middle management, and there is some vertical centralisation of authority.
- An *innovative* configuration is characterised by mutual adjustment as its primary coordinating mechanism. Mutual adjustment is the way in which both managers and staff accommodate and adapt to each other's work practices and relationships. The most important part of the organisation is its support staff, and there is some select *decentralisation* of authority.
- A *missionary* configuration is very common in education. It is characterised by the standardisation of norms and values as the primary coordinating mechanism. The most important aspect of the school or university is its mission and ideology, and there is full *decentralisation* of authority.
- A *political* configuration is characterised by the absence of a primary coordinating mechanism and a random *decentralisation* of authority. The model holds that when organisations lack appropriate coordination, a power vacuum forms, and the organisation becomes politicised.

The EFQM model

The European Foundation for Quality Management (EFQM) developed a non-prescriptive model to translate strategy into five organisational categories called 'enablers' and four performance areas called 'results' (Hakes, 2007). The five organisational categories are:

- *Leadership and purposefulness.* This requires managers and leaders to have a vision, moral values and a sense of mission. Managers should lead the school, college or university by example, fostering a culture of excellence, being personally involved in developing and improving the organisation, and motivating and supporting staff.
- *Policy and strategy.* This requires current and future needs to be identified through research data, and measured and acted upon in terms of performance. Good communication is critical.
- *The involvement and professional development of staff within an environment of continuous organisational learning and innovation.* Staff should be encouraged and developed having identified their knowledge, interests and skill sets. They should be empowered to act appropriately at all levels of the organisation, and be rewarded for doing so.

- *Partnerships and resources, accepting the organisation's civic responsibility.* This is particularly appropriate for educational organisations like schools and universities. It is essentially the management of external relations, communications and IT, which needs to be strategically and functionally integrated into the structure of the organisation, and the intellectual, physical, financial and cultural capital of the school or university.
- *The design and management of processes in a systematic way to meet customer demands and increase value.* Managers should produce services that meet customer expectations and, while doing so, build a loyal base.

These five 'enablers' are key elements in effectively managing an organisation. The aim is to align them by having a good strategy effectively implemented so that the school or university has satisfied students, teachers, researchers, funders and external stakeholders, and an efficient organisation (EFQM, 1992).

The EFQM model is based on Total Quality Management (Oakland, 2000), aiming to re-design an organisation's systemic architecture and understand the interrelationships between its various parts. The model can explain underperformance and identify areas for improvement (Van den Berg & Pietersma, 2016), called 'results'. These go with the five 'enablers' just described. They look at outcomes from different perspectives. In an education setting, these are:

- The student or external stakeholder (parents, research funders, etc.) perspective
- The staff perspective, including that of alumni
- The social perspective, including that of policy-makers and the local community
- The perspective of performance results.

All five organisational enablers contribute to all four result areas. Actual results are measured using key performance indicators, including measures of perception. Any underperformance is identified and suggestions for improvement made in the appropriate organisational arena, to be actualised in the organisation's structure and through feedback learning loops between the result areas and the organisational enablers. All of these require effective managers – and managers with effective 'habits'.

Covey's Seven Habits of Effective Managers

Covey (1989) claimed that effective managers have seven habits – they are really 'steps' – that make them successful. The first three are about creating independence; the next three are about interdependence and increasing effectiveness with others; the final one is, like Senge's Fifth Discipline (see Chapter 25), overarching.

1. Effective managers are proactive, taking responsibility for their own behaviour and not blaming circumstances or others. They take charge of their own responses to situations, and they don't mind feeling uncomfortable.

2. Effective managers keep the objective in mind. They visualise the result and the success they want to achieve. They have a clear vision of where they want to go and know exactly what they want to achieve. In education, they are driven by a sense of moral leadership.
3. They prioritise. They focus on the important and not on the most urgent. They build relationships and plan in advance in a professional manner. They prepare, and they are independent and selective in what they choose to do and in what order. They tick off activities in order of importance, but do not grow their 'to do' lists by taking on relatively unimportant tasks even if they are urgent.
4. They know that effective management is not a zero-sum game: one colleague's success in, say, winning research funding does not create someone else's failure. It is a cooperative game. They seek solutions to problems that enable cooperation. They include others and create benefits for all involved.
5. Effective managers 'diagnose' by understanding, and they then 'prescribe' while making themselves understood. They make others feel good, and at the same time, they learn from others. They listen, not in the manner of the confessional, but in order to understand others on a human level.
6. They synergise. They are open to creative ideas and are agents for change and innovation within the school or university. They value differences between people and try to build upon those divergences in the belief that an effective organisation is one in which the whole is greater than the sum of the parts. They tend to resolve conflict in creative ways and have the 'street cred' as a good teacher or lecturer or as a successful researcher to carry it off.
7. Effective managers have reached 'interdependence' and are admired by colleagues for their effectiveness, but they never rest on their laurels. To them, improvement is not an end in itself, but a continuous process built on a belief in the intrinsic value of a learning organisation.

While Covey (1989) presents these as seven habits, they are more akin to steps in that they are sequenced as managers work from being 'dependent' to being 'independent' to being 'interdependent', and then securing that success in the final step by committing to continuous learning for improvement. The Seven Habits model seeks to enable dynamic managers to understand what makes staff do the things they do, and how they can be incentivised to do better. The model can be applied equally – perhaps even *more* usefully – to managers *themselves* in the spirit of *self-knowledge*. Know thyself, and know thy situation!

16

THREE LEVELS LEADERSHIP AND SELF-MASTERY

The Three Levels Leadership model was formulated by James Scouller (2011) as a management tool for developing leadership presence, know-how and skill. It summarises what leaders must do to lead their teams and organisations and to develop themselves technically and psychologically as leaders. It is also known as the '3P Model' of leadership (Public, Private and Personal leadership). The model attempts to combine the strengths of trait, behavioural and situational-contingency leadership theories, while at the same time offering a foundation for leaders wanting to employ authentic leadership (see Chapter 6) and servant leadership (discussed in the next chapter) approaches.

The limitations of the various leadership theories are well established in the literature. Trait theory (discussed in Chapter 2) fails to provide a universal list of desirable leadership characteristics (Buchanan & Huczynski, 1997; Stogdill, 1948), reflecting a 19th-century 'Great Man' view of events; and in that theoretical sense, it is particularly unsuited to educational organisations like schools. Even by its own claims and standards, trait theory only *finds* those born to lead; it does not claim to *develop* them. Behavioural theory (see Chapters 5 and 6) – for example, Blake and Mouton's managerial grid which tries to capture the tension between concern for task and concern for people – does not suit circumstances where a school, college or university is failing or facing a crisis. Situational-contingency theory (see Chapter 7) – for example, Hersey and Blanchard's model and Tannenbaum and Schmidt's leadership continuum – assume that leaders can change behaviour at will to meet changing circumstances, but in practice this is hard to do because of fixed beliefs or unconscious ingrained habits. Functional theory – for example, Adair's Action-Centred leadership theory – is a subset of situational-contingency theory, which assumes that once leaders understand and have been trained in the necessary leadership behaviours, they will be able to apply them as and when they are needed,

DOI: 10.4324/9781003217220-16

regardless of their personalities. Again, this is hard to do in practice because of unconscious bias and ingrained habits. The Three Levels model claims to overcome these theoretical limitations – the ways in which it does so are shown in Table 16.1 – but the model includes an additional consideration: leadership presence.

Leadership presence

Effective leadership is something more than behaviour or situation; there is something distinctive about certain leaders that wins trust and enables them to lead successfully. This is often called 'presence' (Scouller, 2011). It could be conceived as a 'trait' except that its nature varies from person to person, and research has shown that it is not defined in terms of personality characteristics. Other leadership theories – trait, behavioural, situational or, indeed, transformational (see Chapters 23–25) – do not consider 'presence' as part of their constructs.

The three levels

The three leadership levels in the model's name are 'public', 'private' and 'personal', usually presented diagrammatically as three concentric layers (see Figure 16.1).

The public and private leadership levels or layers are outer and behavioural. Scouller (2011) distinguished between public leadership, where the behaviours involve influencing two or more people simultaneously, and private leadership, where the behaviours involve influencing individuals one-to-one. (Scouller listed 34 distinct public leadership behaviours and a further 14 private leadership behaviours.) Personal leadership is the inner layer and concerns a person's leadership presence, know-how, skills, beliefs, emotions, unconscious habits, self-awareness, self-mastery, technical competence and a sense of connection with colleagues. The theory is that if leaders want to be effective, they must work on all three layers simultaneously, but this inner core is the source of the leader's outer effectiveness (Scouller, 2011).

The two outer layers of public and private leadership are what the leader must *do* – how she or he must *behave* – to address Scouller's four dimensions of leadership:

- A shared vision or purpose that motivates teachers, lecturers and researchers collectively – addressed by public leadership.
- Action and results – addressed by public leadership.
- Collective unity or team spirit – addressed by public leadership.
- Individual selection and motivation – addressed by private leadership.

The inner layer (personal leadership) refers to what leaders should do to grow their presence, know-how and skill. It has three aspects:

- Developing technical know-how and skill.
- Cultivating the right attitude toward others.
- Working on self-mastery.

TABLE 16.1 The Three Levels model and the theoretical limitations of other leadership theories

Theory	Limitations	How the Three Levels model addresses limitations
Trait	• Cannot provide a definitive list of personality characteristics. • Even if they could agree, trait theory does not develop leaders (even if traits *could* be found). • Ignores leadership presence.	The Three Levels model accepts that the best leaders have something about them – leadership presence – that inspires followers. Presence is unique to each person and cannot be pinned down to a shortlist of common personality traits. The model's solution to developing a leader's presence is the practice of 'personal leadership' and 'self-mastery'.
Behavioural	• Wrongly proposes one ideal style that may not be best in all circumstances. • Ignores leadership presence.	The Three Levels model agrees with Blake and Mouton's grid for balancing task-centredness with person-centredness, but it additionally allows for changing the emphasis if the situation requires it. Leadership presence is an integral part of the model.
Situational-contingency and Functional	• Wrongly assumes that everyone can change their behaviour at will to suit different situations. • Ignores a leader's controlling psychology. • Ignores leadership presence.	The Three Levels model supports the idea of behavioural flexibility as circumstances demand but believes that the key to achieving this is to work on one's own limiting beliefs and emotions, which control the tendency to cling to rigid, defensive behaviours. The Three Levels model is 'functional' in that it concentrates on what leaders must *do* in order to provide leadership, and what leaders can do to develop themselves technically and psychologically. The idea is to help leaders translate functional theory into practice by freeing themselves from rigid, fear-based mindsets, enabling them to flex and extend their behavioural range when they need to. Again, leadership presence is an integral part of the model.

Source: Scouller (2011).

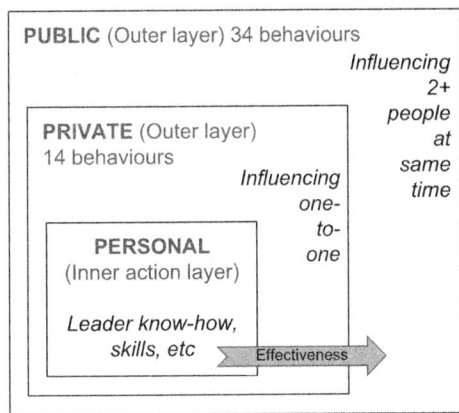

FIGURE 16.1 The three leadership levels.

The Three Levels model holds that personal leadership is the most powerful of the three levels. Scouller likened its effect to dropping a pebble in a pond and seeing the ripples spreading out from the centre. This is why Figure 16.1 has an arrow pointing outward in the diagram. The pebble represents inner, personal leadership, and the ripples represent the flow to the two outer levels. Inner change and personal leadership and growth affect positively the two outer levels of public and private leadership (Scouller, 2011).

Public leadership

Public leadership is what the leader must *do* or how the leader must *behave* in order to influence two or more people simultaneously; most commonly in meetings or by addressing a larger group. Public leadership in education is about setting a motivating vision and a desired future direction for the school, college or university. Its purpose is to ensure unity of direction and effort. It is also about creating positive peer pressure towards shared goals; sharing best practice, especially in teaching and course delivery; having high expectations of students; high standards and impactful outcomes in research; and building an atmosphere of trust and *esprit de corps*. Public leadership drives collective action and produces effectiveness and efficiency. Overall it addresses the first three dimensions of leadership mentioned earlier: building a shared vision or purpose that motivates employees collectively, focusing on action and results, and building a collective unifying team spirit.

The 34 distinct public leadership behaviours listed by Scouller (2011) can be grouped as follows:

- 4 behaviours in setting the *vision* and staying focused: briefing, challenging, navigating and prioritising.
- 2 behaviours in *organising*, planning and giving power to others: assigning and organising.

- 10 behaviours in *ideation*, problem-solving and decision-making. Ideation is the creative process of generating, developing and communicating new ideas. Ideation comprises all stages of a thought cycle, from innovation, through development, to actualisation.
- 6 behaviours in *executing*: educating, energising, doing, measuring, following up and tolerating.
- 12 behaviours in *group building and maintenance*.

Leaders need to balance their time between the 22 behaviours in the first four categories and the 12 behaviours in the final ('group building and maintenance') category. According to the Three Levels model, the key to leaders widening their repertoire of public leadership behaviours (and the skill with which they are performed) is attention to personal leadership, the third and final 'P'.

Private leadership

Private leadership is what the leader must *do* or how the leader must *behave* to handle individuals one-to-one. This addresses the fourth and last of Scouller's dimensions of leadership: individual selection and motivation. Although leadership involves creating group unity, groups are composed of individuals who vary in their ambitions, confidence, experience and personality; hence, the importance of private leadership. There are 14 private leadership behaviours (Scouller, 2011):

- 5 behaviours in *individual purpose and task*; for example, in appraising teaching quality and research productivity of colleagues.
- 9 behaviours in *individual building and maintenance*; for example, in recognising rising talent in early career researchers.

Some people find the powerful one-to-one conversations demanded by private leadership uncomfortable. In education, this commonly presents itself in annual appraisals, fallout from school inspection reports, student course evaluations and research output assessment in higher education. Consequently, leaders try to avoid some of the more difficult private leadership behaviours, which reduces their effectiveness. Scouller (2011) argues that the 'intimacy' of private leadership leads to 'avoidance behaviour' either because of a lack of skill or because of negative self-image beliefs that give rise to powerful fears about what might happen during (or as a result of) these encounters. This is why personal leadership is so important to improving a leader's one-to-one person skills and reducing their interpersonal fears.

Personal leadership

Personal leadership addresses the leader's technical, psychological and moral development and its impact on leadership presence, skill and behaviour. Personal leadership is how to turn the theoretical two outer behavioural levels into practice. Personal leadership is about inner development. It has three elements: technical know-how and skill, the right attitude towards others and psychological self-mastery.

- *Technical know-how and skill* is about leaders knowing their technical weaknesses and taking action to update their knowledge and skills. Scouller (2011) suggests that there are three areas of know-how that all leaders should learn: time management, individual psychology and group psychology. In the model, there are six skill sets that underlie both public leadership and private leadership behaviours:
  - Group problem-solving and planning
  - Group decision-making
  - Interpersonal ability and emotional intelligence
  - Managing group process
  - Assertiveness
  - Goal-setting
- *Attitude toward others* is about developing the right attitude toward colleagues in order to maintain the leader's relationships as the school, college or university moves towards its goals. Having the right attitude is the belief that other people are as important as the leader and that leadership is primarily an act of service (Scouller, 2011). This is servant leadership, formulated in 1970 by Greenleaf (2002, 2003), which we will discuss in the next chapter. In education, a servant leader shares power, puts the needs of staff first and helps teachers, lecturers and researchers develop. Servant leadership turns leadership upside-down: instead of staff working to serve the leader, the leader works to serve staff. Although there is a moral, altruistic aspect to this in the Three Levels model, there is also a practical side. A leader's attitude and behaviour toward others largely determine how much followers respect and trust the leader, and are happy to be directed. Scouller outlined the five parts of the right attitude:
  - Interdependence
  - Appreciation
  - Caring
  - Service
  - Balance
  The two keys to developing these five aspects are to ensure that (a) there is a demanding but achievable shared vision, and (b) that the leader works on self-mastery.
- *Self-mastery* is a psychological process that emphasises self-awareness. Through mindfulness and meditation, it allows the leader to let go of previously unconscious limiting beliefs and their associated defensive habits; for example, avoiding powerful conversations such as annual appraisal discussions. It enables leaders to connect more strongly with their values, to let their leadership presence flow and to act authentically. Self-mastery is the key to growing leadership

presence, building trust and enabling behavioural flexibility as circumstances change, while staying connected to one's core values and remaining authentic. It is essential in educational leadership.

Leadership presence

Leadership presence is a central feature of the Three Levels model. The key tenet is that it takes more than the right know-how, skills and behaviours to be an effective leader. It also takes leadership presence: the 'inner alignment' of self-identity and purpose that dissolves fear; a magnetic, radiating effect on others when being authentic; having teaching and research staff give their full respect and attention; speaking honestly; letting character traits flow. Leaders must of course be technically competent, but it is their unique presence and genuineness that inspires staff and prompts them to want the leader to lead (Scouller, 2011).

Presence is not the same as charisma. According to Scouller's model, leaders can be charismatic by relying on a job title, fame, prior achievement and skilfully acting out the halo effect of 'specialness'. Presence is deeper than this and is more authentic. It does not depend on social status and has a powerful mental and moral resilience. Charismatic leaders are apt to abandon moral and ethical leadership when their charisma is based on acting skills and their power is based on what their followers give them. This is not the case with leadership presence because it goes deeper than acting behaviour.

A leader's presence is developed by practising personal leadership. It is a unique and different combination for every leader, but it has seven qualities:

- Personal power and command over thoughts, feelings and actions
- High self-esteem
- A drive to *be* more, to *learn* more and to grow
- Energetic sense of purpose combined with concern for others
- Intuition
- The ability to live 'in the now'
- Inner peace of mind and a sense of fulfilment from the job of leadership

The link with authentic leadership discussed in Chapter 6 is clear. Leadership presence is synonymous with authenticity; that is, with being genuine and expressing one's highest values (Scouller, 2011). So in proposing self-mastery to develop the right attitude toward colleagues as a means of developing presence, the Three Levels model offers a more practical ('how to') extension to authentic leadership. The model shifts away from the view of leadership as 'Great Person' or 'Hero'. It does not deny the possibility of a hero leader, but it suggests that shared leadership is a more realistic model.

Scouller's view is that leadership is 'bigger than the leader' and is not the same as the *role* of leader. Situational and contingency theories were discussed in Chapter 7, and specifically the functional approach of John Adair's three-circle Action-centred model, which holds that leadership need not rely on one person because anyone in a group can exercise it. Scouller goes further by suggesting that not only *can* others exercise leadership, but *must* exercise it. Sharing leadership is not an option; it is a practical necessity, for three reasons:

- The number of different behaviours needed by leaders means that they are unlikely to be equally proficient at all of them, so it is sensible to let colleagues lead occasionally.
- It is foolish to make one person responsible for every leadership behaviour, as it would overburden them and frustrate those colleagues who are willing and better able to lead in a given situation.
- It is beneficial to have more people involved in the big decisions. It promotes joint accountability, which is a feature of high-performance teams.

Of course, sharing leadership duties potentially undermines the leader's position. The Three Levels model therefore suggests a new purpose for leaders: to make sure that there *is* leadership, and that the four dimensions of leadership discussed earlier are being addressed. The leader can act solely, can delegate or can share, and the responsibility for deciding whether it is delegating or sharing (and with whom) is the essence of leadership. So although leaders can share leadership, they cannot shirk what Weber would call their 'legal' responsibility.

Self-mastery

Leadership self-mastery is about the leader getting to know their own negative impulses and then overcoming them in order to steer the school or university towards its desired future. It requires leaders to have a vision for themselves and to actualise their potential; to be the best they can be. Self-mastery is both a path and an orientation, and a commitment to never-ending improvement. It is a 'process of becoming' (Jeffrey, n.d.). Leaders who have self-mastery are self-aware and can identify their own fears and resistances, and have the creativity to find ways to overcome them.

Jeffrey (ibid) claims that everyone can have an intrinsic motivational drive to grow, develop new skills and get to the top of Maslow's hierarchy, the 'self-actualising' level (see Chapter 6). Adapting Maslow's theory of motivation to dynamic leadership, we have two powerful forces shaping the practice of leadership and management: the drive for growth and, opposing it, the desire for safety. Growth moves the leader forward; the opposing desire motivates the leader to defend the current self, clinging to safety, avoiding the unknown and being averse to risk. This safety force is afraid of independence and freedom, which the growth impulse is demanding. According to Jeffrey, if the focus is on the dangers of growth, the need for safety will dominate. It is legitimate to fear growth because although it brings reward and gratification, it also brings pain and possible danger, and an expectation to give up the familiar. What we know seems simple to us, so with growth, there is an accompanying increase in complexity and responsibility.

According to Maslow, safety is a more basic human need than growth, but a leader who always chooses safety over growth, in the long run, will be disappointed, and disappointing, in the role because leadership is about risk and change (see Chapter 24). Leadership for growth is characterised by feelings of achievement, calmness and a zest for activity. Effective leaders have confidence in their ability to handle problems and anxieties. Leadership for safety, on the other hand, is characterised by feelings of anxiety, boredom, self-betrayal, disappointment, aimlessness and shame at not making the most of opportunity.

Leadership homeostasis

The fear of failure is a mindset that can evoke emotions of embarrassment, humiliation and frustration, and damage self-esteem, but some leaders fear success to the extent that they even sabotage their own development. The cause is homeostasis: the ability or tendency to maintain a steady internal state in the face of external change. Biologically, all living organisms have it. They must regulate their internal state to survive; for example, by maintaining a steady body temperature. For a leader, and for followers, movement out of the familiar and into the unknown is a disruption to the equilibrium. Our internal systems – psychological as well as physiological – are designed to maintain homeostasis in the face of that disruption. Workwise, we are all wired to stay in sync with what is known and familiar, and return to equilibrium when there is movement outside the narrow limits of professional comfort. Schools, colleges and universities are more or less self-regulating organisations, and they have ways of maintaining homeostasis and staying in familiar and safe territory. Unfortunately for leadership and management praxis, homeostasis does not distinguish between improvement-change and *dis*improvement-change. Homeostasis is allied to social inertia and the natural gravitational pull of staff, students and stakeholders such as research councils who are resistant to change and innovative practice. It has its own alarm signals, but leaders need to persist through the discomfort, slowly shifting their institution's equilibrium state to a new, improved normal. It was jokingly said by Chesterton that it was the function of Progressives to make mistakes and the function of Conservatives to prevent those mistakes from being rectified. In leadership, that function is performed by leadership homeostasis: the conservative force designed to maintain whatever is the current state.

Differential self-growth

The growth of leaders can cause discomfort for followers if they do not grow alongside each other. Opposing homeostasis and safety is the desire for growth and adventure; but growth means change, and change sometimes means growing apart. The working environment is disrupted by change, perhaps for the better in the long run, but disrupted nonetheless. Followers look at the leader differently, and followers look different to the leader. Followers may admire the leader's growth – the effort at change might even inspire them – but this can be accompanied by envy. Leaders seeking self-mastery learn to be aware of these tendencies, learn to be emotionally intelligent and feel these social homeostasis pressures without letting them determine their behaviour. Self-mastery is about the evolution of self, even though change can bring with it feelings of uncertainty, risk and fear. It can also be isolating for the leader, cultivating inner strength instead of seeking support from colleagues in the normal fashion. The unfamiliar is an uncomfortable burden, and the familiar is always attractive, so self-mastery is about setting new, higher homeostasis 'normals'. Leaders should aim to transform themselves slowly, recognising the natural need for safety, but consciously and courageously guiding themselves, in spite of homeostasis, into a better (but as yet unknown) place.

Self-mastery is linked to Maslow's notion of self-actualisation, the ultimate need that must be satisfied in his hierarchy, and the path to self-mastery is the path to self-actualisation. According to Maslow (1954), there are 13 interconnected qualities or markers on that path.

- *Superior perception of reality.* Self-actualising leaders have the ability to judge others accurately. They have superior perception and the capacity to make effective decisions on behalf of others.
- *Increased acceptance of self and of others.* Self-actualising leaders have less guilt and do not suffer severe anxiety. They accept their nature, including their shortcomings, without shame. Successful leaders operate within their own capabilities at any given moment with due regard for their shortcomings, but with the ambition to develop the former and overcome the latter.
- *Increased spontaneity.* Self-actualising leaders are more spontaneous in their behaviour, thoughts and impulses, but simplicity and being natural characterises their behaviour. 'Being natural' in education settings is important, especially when dealing with students and parents.
- *Increased problem-focus.* Self-actualising leaders are more focused on problems outside themselves as opposed to personal, ego-centred issues. They have a mission in life, and tasks that serve their mission use up most of their energies. They do not aim at too many targets or dissipate their purposes on too many ideas. They do not let those ideas wander too far into the future, but they keep their eyes and hands on the immediate task and discharge it with patience and tenacity.
- *Increased detachment.* Self-actualising leaders are comfortable being on their own. They accept solitude and privacy to a greater degree than other teachers, academics and researchers.
- *Increased autonomy and resistance to enculturation.* Self-actualising leaders are relatively independent of cultural forces and the social environment. They are motivated by the drive for personal mastery and growth, and are more focused on the development of their potential.

- *Greater appreciation.* Self-actualising leaders appreciate 'life's rich tapestry'. They are more interested in everything.
- *Intense experiences.* Self-actualising leaders have intense experiences more frequently than other colleagues.
- *Increased identification.* Self-actualising leaders go from identifying exclusively with themselves (egocentricity), to identification with a group (socio-centricity), to identification with everyone (world-centricity).
- *Improved interpersonal relations.* Self-actualising leaders have deeper relationships with a select few others, maintaining a small but close circle of friends.
- *More democratic character structure.* Self-actualising leaders make friends irrespective of social class, education, political belief, race or creed.
- *Increased creativeness.* Self-actualising leaders are more creative and are more spontaneous.
- *A firm value system.* Self-actualising leaders have a robust moral and values structure.

Mirroring these 13 markers on the path to Maslow's self-actualisation, Jeffrey (n.d.) listed some instructions – he called them 'secrets' – for overcoming resistance and building momentum on the path to self-mastery. Applied to an education setting, they include:

- *Accepting resistance.* Dynamic leaders accept the fact that resistance to change exists in schools and universities. Feelings of shame and guilt delay progress because they reinforce bad habits in teaching and scholarship. Self-acceptance and self-compassion are important when working to overcome the resistance of others.
- *Creating a compelling vision.* A clear vision and clear direction are always needed in education because, unlike the commercial sector, it is driven by a strong moral imperative. The vision must inspire both the leader and the teaching and research staff.
- *Committing to sustained improvement.* Dynamic leaders understand that lasting transformation does not just happen – certainly not immediately – and is difficult to sustain. Long-term improvement in schools and university departments requires good communication skills and vigilance. However, setting interim shorter-term goals can help leaders and staff to stay focused. Having short-term goals avoids practice for its own sake and makes practice fun.
- *Expecting backsliding.* Even when dynamic leaders understand and expect homeostasis, it is still an influence, and backsliding is inevitable on the path to self-mastery. Leaders should not be too discouraged when it happens.
- *Moderating their behaviour.* Homeostasis often happens when there is a surge of enthusiasm at the start of the improvement process; typically with a new headteacher, principal, dean or vice-chancellor. Typically, the leader is pushing ahead too quickly and selling the vision too enthusiastically. This creates commensurately greater resistance. As Jeffrey (n.d.) says, self-mastery is not a sprint;

it's a long-distance run. Dynamic leaders should moderate their behaviour and curb their enthusiasm a little. Those who seek personal mastery should avoid extremes.

- *Relaxing and practising.* Dynamic leaders should not take themselves too seriously. Proceed with humour and be willing to share a joke among colleagues. Effective leaders see the humorous side and are willing to laugh at themselves. They find ways to have fun practising their skills among colleagues who in schools and universities are equally qualified.
- *Learning to learn.* Aside from lists of things to do and things to avoid, the essence of self-mastery is learning to learn, learning to lead and setting up a learning organisation (MacBeath, 2011; MacBeath & Dempster, 2008). Leaders who stop learning lose their creativity and destroy it in others, and inhibit personal mastery.
- *Cultivating fitness and energy.* Leaders must be fit, mentally and physically, have the energy to manage stress (and help others manage stress), overcome resistance and keep everyone engaged.
- *Being honest.* Self-assessment is essential for leaders pursuing self-mastery, so honesty and self-awareness are essential. Dynamic leaders avoid self-inflation and self-deflation equally. Jeffrey (ibid) makes a great suggestion: leaders should keep a journal where they can express their aims and hopes, their failures and fears.
- *Establishing empowering rituals.* Like good athletes, dynamic leaders have rituals for getting ready to perform: they go through the agenda before meetings; they decide what needs to be said and what needs to go *un*said; they leave adequate time between meetings in order to meet and reassure colleagues in the aftermath of meetings and presentations, which is often the more formative part of the event; and they use similar approaches in similar situations. These rituals are perfected through practice. From my own research, I would go so far as to say that establishing and perfecting rituals is the *purpose* of practice, and *practice itself is the most important ritual.*

17

MORAL LEADERSHIP AND CULTURAL LEADERSHIP

Although Max Weber, the founder of bureaucratic management, was fascinated with heroic leadership at the level of the individual, his scorn was reserved for those who believed in nothing and regarded compromise as an end in itself.

> What is possible would never have been achieved if people had not repeatedly reached for the impossible.
>
> (Weber, cited in Whimster, 2004: 269)

Even for Weber, whose name is not generally associated with this theoretical approach, leadership is about striving for something in a moral sense. He did not distinguish between it and management in this sense, but perhaps we could say that management is about *value*, whereas leadership is about *values*. There can be a moral dimension to both, but the term 'value' is used in education in two different senses: in the ethical sense, when schools and universities consider the proper thing to do and how to conduct themselves culturally; and in the economic sense, when schools and universities consider how to maximise the value they add through their teaching and research. In education, effective managers do the right thing for the right reasons and in the right way, and it is in the search for what is 'right' that leadership acquires its morality. Moral leadership is about providing values and meaning for staff to live and work by, providing teaching and academic colleagues with the inspiration to act and the motivation to hold themselves accountable. Ultimately, it is about taking responsibility. It is a purpose-driven leadership that aligns decision-making with core principles and values. It prioritises purpose, character and integrity, with leaders believing deeply in causes, like improving the quality of education for all children or widening access to selective universities for disadvantaged students, not just because they are important to the school or the university, but because they

DOI: 10.4324/9781003217220-17

matter to society. Students and other stakeholders respond well to such an approach and generally give their support.

Moral leadership can be developed by leaders in five ways:

- *By identifying a set of values.* In education, moral leaders know (or should know) the principles by which they live and work. They guide themselves with values and professional ethics that they have developed over time: professional integrity; self-respect and respect for others; a belief in being accountable; an ethic of service to the academic community, the local community and society; a sense of fair play; a commitment to equity and dispassionate service. These are *not* innate characteristics in the 'trait theory' sense but instead are developed from experience.
- *By managing own ego.* Moral leaders have self-esteem and are not threatened by the esteem of others. They do not see themselves as the most important part of the equation. They believe that educational leadership is not about self or personal aggrandisement; it is about 'servant leadership' (see the next section) and serving others. Moral leaders in an education setting put the interest of others before themselves, which is an extension of what teachers do in the normal course of their professional lives so they are not strangers to the idea.
- *By including the views of diverse groups.* Moral leaders do not impose their values on others. They consider the views of others, interact and empathise with them, and understand their points of view. Their values and contributions inform the organisation's vision under the moral leader.
- *By embracing change.* Moral leaders do not fear change and organisations like schools and universities need (and seek out) moral leaders when they want change. Moral leaders have the courage and conviction to share their vision to generate improvement.
- *By building consensus and establishing unity.* Moral leaders know not to create divisions. They communicate a purpose that can inspire as many people as possible. A moral leader listens to people with different views, although it is usually impossible to win everyone over. The moral leader is aware of the 20/60/20 rule, which states that in any organisation, 20% of staff will be ready to embrace change, 60% will 'sit on the fence', and 20% will oppose change.
  - ○ The Positive 20% already has an understanding that is aligned with the leader's view. The leader does not need to sell the vision to them; they already get it. Dynamic leaders leave this group alone and do not over-lead them.
  - ○ The Negative 20% has already decided before the leader starts to sell the vision. A leader – even an effective one – will not be able to convince this negative group, so the tactic is the same as with the positive 20% group: leave them alone. All effort will be wasted and could be better spent on the most important middle group.
  - ○ The middle, workable 60% can be won over. This is where the leader should try to, and can, make a difference. It will depend on good

communications, a supportive environment and a bit of luck. This is where the leader should spend time, finding out why these colleagues are 'on the fence'. The leader should create a safe environment where staff can give honest answers without fear of retribution, and incorporate their input in order to get their buy-in. In most cases, followers just want to vent their concerns or reservations. They do not expect all their issues to be addressed or all their suggestions to be incorporated, but they do appreciate being listened to.

Applying the 20/60/20 rule is a great tool for dynamic leaders in schools and universities to determine where to spend the most time to greatest effect. Resistance is a natural component of change. Moral leaders expect it, but do not let it derail their efforts.

Servant leadership

Servant leadership is where the overriding practical objective of leadership is to serve colleagues, stakeholders and students, as opposed to traditional leadership where the main purpose is to benefit the organisation. In education, a servant leader shares power, puts the needs of staff first and helps teachers, lecturers and researchers to develop and perform as highly as possible. Servant leadership, formulated in 1970 by Robert Greenleaf (2002, 2003), turns traditional leadership upside-down: instead of followers working to serve the leader, the leader works to serve followers to help them grow as more autonomous people (Sendjaya & Sarros, 2002). This in turn helps the school or university grow because staff are better motivated, feel a shared ownership of the organisation, and are more effective at delivering education to students and research to the academic community.

Servant leadership is a form of moral or ethical leadership – in fact, Greenleaf's 'Center for Servant Leadership' was originally called the 'Center for Applied Ethics' – and is practised by some of the world's top commercial companies (Sendjaya & Sarros, 2002).[1] Unusually, it has a German rather than a North American provenance. In the mid-18th century, Frederick the Great famously declared himself as 'the first servant of the state', and Greenleaf himself credited Hermann Hesse, the German novelist and winner of the 1946 Nobel Prize in Literature, as his inspiration for his theory (Dittmar, 2006). Leo, the main character in Hesse's 1932 book *Journey to the East*, is a servant like all the other characters in the book. They all work well together until Leo disappears, when they realise that things are not the same without Leo and that he was more than just another colleague-servant; he was their leader. Greenleaf's inference was that a leader should be someone that colleagues and subordinates can relate to; a teacher who develops their followers.

Servant leaders find success and 'power' in the growth of others, guiding them toward self-improvement. Servant leaders care for the needs of others around them and ensure the growth of future leaders who in turn copy (and perpetuate) the servantship style for themselves. The betterment of others is 'the true intention' of servant leadership. Leaders serve because they are leaders, and they are leaders because they serve. The first premise – that servant leaders serve because they are leaders – is rooted in altruism: the disinterested and selfless concern for the well-being of others. Only through the act of serving does the leader lead other people to *be* what they *can be*. The second premise – that servant leaders are leaders because they serve – is rooted in the personal ambition to be leader.

Servant leadership is a more prevalent form of leadership in schools than in universities. It is a model that is inspirational, moral, altruistic and self-sacrificing, and it represents the link between moral leadership and the transformational leadership described later in Chapters 23, 24 and 25. Reflecting its origins in Hesse's work, servant leadership is also quasi-spiritual: a transformative change of heart or metanoia. Commentators have recognised this spiritual conceptualisation and have listed values such as love, humility, altruism and being visionary as core. Sen et al. (2019) even developed a six-item *Servant Leadership Behavior Scale* (SLBS-6), akin to Blanchard's *Leader Behaviour Analysis Questionnaire* described in Chapter 7, to measure it. It is also argued that servant leadership comes from and is inextricably linked to Christianity and that servant leaders have a particularly 'scriptural' view of themselves as 'stewards' entrusted to enable followers to reach their fullest potential, but overall the trend has been to list quantifiable – or at least *identifiable* – elements of servant leadership like trait theory. Spears (2010), for example, lists ten characteristics of servant leaders: listening, empathy, healing, awareness, persuasion, conceptualisation, foresight, stewardship, commitment to the growth of people, and building community.

- *Listening.* Leaders in schools, colleges and universities are traditionally valued for their communication skills. For the *servant* leader in education, this involves listening *intently* to others. The servant leader seeks to identify the will of the group and help to clarify it, listening receptively to what is being said and what is being left unsaid. Listening also involves listening to one's own inner voice. Listening, coupled with periods of reflection, is essential to the growth and well-being of the servant leader.
- *Empathy.* The servant leader empathises with teachers, researchers, stakeholders and students. Everyone is recognised for their special qualities, and their good intentions are assumed. The leader does not reject them as colleagues, even when rejecting certain of their behaviours or their underperformances. The servant leader hates the 'sin' but loves the 'sinner', in the Christian tradition of St. Augustine.[2]
- *Healing.* The healing of relationships is a powerful force for transformation and change in education. It is one of the strengths of servant leadership. It is about taking opportunities to 'heal' others; to make them happier and more content. Greenleaf held that there was 'something subtle' communicated between leader and follower: an understanding that participation in the mission of the school or university results in greater satisfaction for *everyone* and not just for the leader and the institution (Rodríguez-Carvajal et al., 2018).

- *Awareness.* Awareness and self-awareness strengthen the servant leader. Awareness helps servant leaders understand issues involving ethics and power. It enables them to view situations from an integrated holistic position. This can disturb – I would say *shake-up* – complacent academic staff and students, which is not always a bad thing.
- *Persuasion.* Another characteristic of servant leadership is the belief in, and reliance upon, persuasion rather than authority in forming strategy and making decisions. The servant leader seeks to convince rather than coerce. Servant leadership is not about compliance. It is about consensus.
- *Conceptualisation.* Servant leaders seek to nurture their own ability to look at issues and to look at the organisation, from a conceptual perspective, beyond mundane day-to-day problems. This requires discipline and practice. The traditional leader is consumed by the need to achieve short-term operational goals, whereas the servant leader must stretch to conceptual thinking. This in turn puts a headteacher or a college principal or a faculty dean in the position of a governor or trustee. Traditional leaders are mostly conceptual in their orientation; traditional subordinates are mostly operational in theirs. Servant leaders, being dynamic, need to develop both as 'managership': that delicate balance between conceptual leadership thinking and day-to-day operational management.
- *Foresight.* The ability to foresee the likely outcome of a proposed action is a trait of servant leadership. Foresight is an intuitive skill closely related to conceptualisation and is a characteristic that enables a leader to understand and interpret lessons from the past, the realities of the present and the likely consequences of decisions.
- *Stewardship.* Stewardship is holding something in trust for another generation or for the successor, or for the greater good of the community. Servant leadership, like stewardship, assumes a commitment to serving the needs of other generations (Eva et al., 2019) of students and staff, as well as current cohorts. In research terms, servant leadership is about stewarding the academy or the discipline for following generations of researchers.
- *Commitment to the growth of people.* Servant leaders believe that everyone has an intrinsic value beyond their utility value as workers and are therefore committed to the growth of each colleague within the school or university. This view carries with it a responsibility to do everything to nurture the personal and professional growth of colleagues and students. This involves taking a personal interest in ideas and suggestions from everyone and encouraging everyone's involvement in, and contribution to, decision-making (Yang et al., 2017).
- *Building community.* The servant leader is always looking out for the means to build community among those who work in the school, college or university. Servant leadership holds that a learning organisation – a community of practice – can be created among those who work there. This is particularly the case, and is relatively easy to do, in educational institutions.

Well-known educational leadership experts Michael Fullan (1991), author of *The New Meaning of Educational Change*, and Tom Sergiovanni (1992), author of *Moral Leadership*, cite some or all of these as characteristics of *effective* (rather than specifically *servant*) leadership. The ten characteristics just described are not exhaustive and are not all unique to servant leadership, but they do serve to communicate the promise that servant leadership offers to those who are open to it. Iarocci (2017) came up with something similar in identifying nine features that distinguish servant leadership:

- Three key priorities: developing people; building a trusting team; achieving results.
- Three key principles: serve first; persuasion; empowerment.
- Three key practices: listening; delegating; connecting followers to mission.

The literature and research on servant leadership suggests that a leader's core personal beliefs and values are its key antecedents, but there is a lack of empirical evidence to support the model more specifically. Servant leadership could be treated as a hierarchical cyclical process with behavioural (vision, service) and relational (influence, credibility, trust) components, very much in the style of transformational leadership but distinguishable from trait, behavioural and contingency approaches. Servant leadership has many positive effects, but it is possible for it to have a negative effect if the leader appears to be, or is, unethical. Despite assumptions to the contrary, it is not axiomatic that those who put service to others above service to the organisation are necessarily ethical or honest.

Values in the ethical sense: the Competing Values model

Every organisation is unique with its own culture, but University of Michigan academics Cameron and Quinn (1999) suggest that these seemingly unique cultures are actually different combinations of four basic types under one dominant style.

There are four basic competing values within every organisation: values of collaboration; values of creativity; values of competition; and values of control. This Competing Values model asks whether the organisation has an internal focus and integration, or an external focus and differentiation; and whether it strives for flexibility and individual discretion, or stability and control (see Figure 17.1). The model is predicated on several organisational culture dimensions, for which Cameron and Quinn (1999) developed their Organisational Culture Assessment Instrument (OCAI), and based on these parameters, a two-by-two matrix framework divides organisational cultures into four distinct types: a Clan culture; an Adhocracy culture; a Market culture; and a Hierarchy culture:

- A *Clan* culture (top-left quadrant) is one where the organisation concentrates on *internal* maintenance with *flexibility*, and on concern for staff and students. This culture is rooted in collaboration, where staff and students see themselves are part of 'one big family'. Everyone is actively involved. Leadership here is about

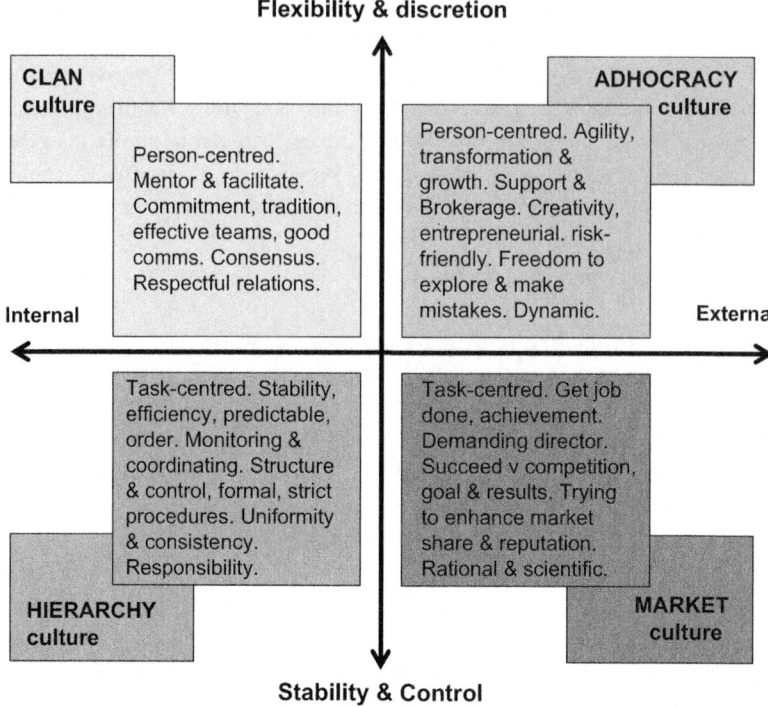

Flexibility & discretion

CLAN culture

Person-centred. Mentor & facilitate. Commitment, tradition, effective teams, good comms. Consensus. Respectful relations.

ADHOCRACY culture

Person-centred. Agility, transformation & growth. Support & Brokerage. Creativity, entrepreneurial. risk-friendly. Freedom to explore & make mistakes. Dynamic.

Internal

Task-centred. Stability, efficiency, predictable, order. Monitoring & coordinating. Structure & control, formal, strict procedures. Uniformity & consistency. Responsibility.

Task-centred. Get job done, achievement. Demanding director. Succeed v competition, goal & results. Trying to enhance market share & reputation. Rational & scientific.

External

HIERARCHY culture

MARKET culture

Stability & Control

FIGURE 17.1 Competing Values framework.

mentorship and facilitation, and the organisation is held together by widespread commitment, tradition, effective teamwork, good communication and a belief in consensus. Relationships with staff, students, external stakeholders and significant others are respectful. It is a person–centred, human relationship model.

- An *Adhocracy* culture (top-right quadrant) is one where the organisation concentrates on *external* positioning with a high degree of *flexibility* and individuality. This culture is based on energy and creativity. Employees are encouraged to take risks, be dynamic, be entrepreneurial and value innovation. Leadership is about brokerage and supporting entrepreneurship. The organisation is held together by experimentation, with an emphasis on individual freedom to explore. The core values are agility, change and transformation (to be discussed in Chapter 25), and growth. It is a person–centred, open–systems model with a monitoring culture that is not afraid to make mistakes as long as everyone learns from them.

- A *Market* culture (bottom-right quadrant) is one where the organisation concentrates on *external* maintenance with a need for *stability and control*. This culture is built on succeeding against competition, getting the job done and valuing achievement. It is goal- and results–oriented and focused on productivity. Leadership here is about being a director, and being tough and demanding.

The organisation is united by a common goal to succeed and beat the competition. The main value-driver is increasing market share, enhancing reputation and finishing at the top of teaching and research league tables such as the UK's National Student Survey (NSS) and Research Excellence Framework (REF). It is a task-centred, rational-goal model, objective and scientific after Max Weber (discussed in Chapter 3).

- A *Hierarchy* culture (bottom-left quadrant) is one where the organisation focuses on *internal* maintenance with a need for *stability and control*. This culture is founded on structure and control with a formal work environment and strict procedures. Leadership is about monitoring and coordinating. The emphasis is on efficiency, stability, order and predictability. The organisation values include consistency and uniformity. It is a task-centred, internal-process model, with a rule culture that documents responsibility and how jobs are measured (see Chapters 20 and 21). It is a stereotypical bureaucratic organisation.

The OCAI is a validated survey method for assessing both current and preferred organisational cultures, which can be mapped together for an organisation and has been used by more than 10,000 companies worldwide. It establishes an organisation's dominant culture type and constructs a cultural profile, which is known from research to be linked to performance (Kotter & Heskett, 1992; Wagner & Spencer, 1996). The Competing Values framework is not solely for commercial companies. It has also been used in the public sector too; for example, examining the culture at Ohio State University in the United States (Berrio & Henderson, 1998).

It is rare for organisations to have more than one dominant cultural type, but within any large departmental organisation like a university, it is likely that individual departments within the organisation will have their own different dominant cultural types. For example, the dominant culture in the Mathematics Department is not necessarily the same as the dominant culture in the Modern Languages Department within the same university, and the overall university dominant culture may be different again. The unit of analysis is obviously critical.

Values in the ethical sense: the Hofstede Cultural Dimensions model

Of course, there is a societal context to cultural values and values management in schools and universities. Hofstede's Cultural Dimensions model helps in this respect: to develop a strategy for employees from different cultures (Hofstede, 1991, 2001) who can (and do) perceive problems and interpret solutions in different ways. Hofstede's model identifies five cultural tensions: power distance; individualism versus collectivism; masculinity versus femininity; uncertainty avoidance; and long-term versus short-term orientation.

- *Power distance* is the extent to which the less powerful accept that power is distributed *unequally* among individuals. In some cultures, the expectation is that power is very centralised, and there is little or no expectation of sharing.

- The *individualism-collectivism* continuum describes the general relationship in a given culture between employees and society. Individualism is dominant in societies (like the United States, say) where the ties between individuals are loose and self-interest prevails. Collectivism is dominant in societies (like Japan, say) where people are integrated into strong cohesive groups that protect people in exchange for loyal membership.
- The *masculinity-femininity* continuum describes the differences between the binary sexes. In masculine cultures, assertiveness, ambition and competitiveness are (supposedly) dominant characteristics; feminine cultures are (supposedly) characterised by personal goals, nurturing relationships and concern for quality of life.
- *Uncertainty avoidance* refers to the extent that members of a culture feel threatened by ambiguity and uncertainty. Cultures that want to avoid uncertainty tend to minimise it by strict laws, rules and regulations. Cultures that are uncertainty-friendly are more willing to take risks.
- *Long-term versus short-term orientation.* Long-term orientation is characterised by thrift and perseverance. The values most associated with short-term orientation is respect for tradition and the pressure to fulfil social obligations.

The Hofstede Cultural Dimensions model is not a guideline for interaction between people, but is designed as an aide to understanding and managing culture-driven behaviour, and for avoiding cultural misunderstandings with international stakeholders.

Values in the ethical sense: the Trompenaars–Hampden-Turner model

Trompenaars and Hampden-Turner (1993) worked on understanding cultural diversity in a seven-dimension model. The premise is that employees from different cultures differ in specific predictable ways according to their own values and ways of thinking (see Figure 17.2). All cultural models underplay differences *within* (rather than *between*) cultures. Cultures are not homogenous entities and individuals do not always (or usually) conform to their stereotypes, but understanding the differences between cultures and how to overcome them is key; specifically, how to reconcile the dilemmas that result from one or more of the following seven 'tensions'.

- *Universalism v. particularism.* Universalist cultures regard general rules and obligations as their moral reference. They follow rules and not relationships and believe that their values are superior to others and therefore that others should adjust *their* beliefs. Particularist cultures put relationships, family and friends above rules and regulations, and tend to act in any given situation according to *who* is involved.
- *The community v. the individual.* An individualist culture tells people to take care of themselves and sees group-effort mostly as a means to achieve selfish

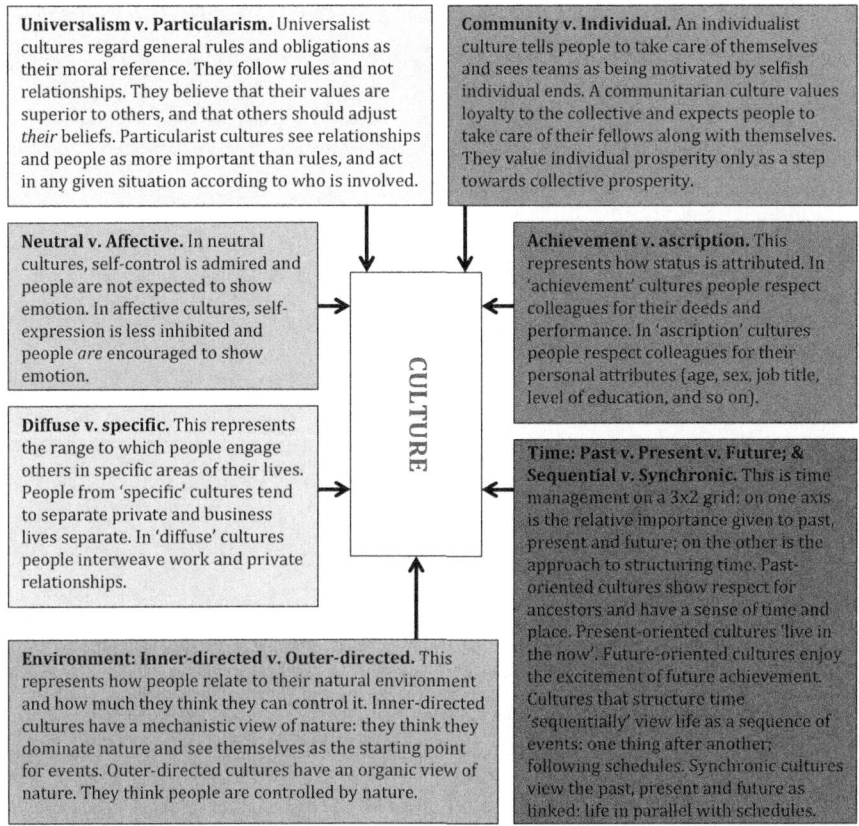

Universalism v. Particularism. Universalist cultures regard general rules and obligations as their moral reference. They follow rules and not relationships. They believe that their values are superior to others, and that others should adjust *their* beliefs. Particularist cultures see relationships and people as more important than rules, and act in any given situation according to who is involved.

Community v. Individual. An individualist culture tells people to take care of themselves and sees teams as being motivated by selfish individual ends. A communitarian culture values loyalty to the collective and expects people to take care of their fellows along with themselves. They value individual prosperity only as a step towards collective prosperity.

Neutral v. Affective. In neutral cultures, self-control is admired and people are not expected to show emotion. In affective cultures, self-expression is less inhibited and people *are* encouraged to show emotion.

Achievement v. ascription. This represents how status is attributed. In 'achievement' cultures people respect colleagues for their deeds and performance. In 'ascription' cultures people respect colleagues for their personal attributes (age, sex, job title, level of education, and so on).

Diffuse v. specific. This represents the range to which people engage others in specific areas of their lives. People from 'specific' cultures tend to separate private and business lives separate. In 'diffuse' cultures people interweave work and private relationships.

Time: Past v. Present v. Future; & Sequential v. Synchronic. This is time management on a 3x2 grid: on one axis is the relative importance given to past, present and future; on the other is the approach to structuring time. Past-oriented cultures show respect for ancestors and have a sense of time and place. Present-oriented cultures 'live in the now'. Future-oriented cultures enjoy the excitement of future achievement. Cultures that structure time 'sequentially' view life as a sequence of events: one thing after another; following schedules. Synchronic cultures view the past, present and future as linked: life in parallel with schedules.

Environment: Inner-directed v. Outer-directed. This represents how people relate to their natural environment and how much they think they can control it. Inner-directed cultures have a mechanistic view of nature: they think they dominate nature and see themselves as the starting point for events. Outer-directed cultures have an organic view of nature. They think people are controlled by nature.

CULTURE

FIGURE 17.2 The Trompenaars and Hampden–Turner model of culture differences.

(not in a pejorative sense) individual ends. A communitarian culture values a strong sense of loyalty within society and expects people to take care of their fellow human beings alongside themselves. They value individual progress and prosperity mostly as a step towards *group* progress and prosperity.

- *Neutral v. affective.* This represents the range of expressed feelings and emotions. In 'neutral' cultures, self-control is admired and people are not expected to show emotion. In 'affective' cultures, self-expression is less inhibited, and people are encouraged to show emotions.

- *Diffuse v. specific.* This represents the extent to which people engage others in specific areas of their lives. People from 'specific' cultures tend to keep private and professional lives separate. In 'diffuse' cultures, people interweave work and private relationships.

- *Achievement v. ascription.* This represents how status is attributed. In 'achievement' cultures, people respect colleagues for their deeds and performance. In 'ascription' cultures, people respect colleagues for their personal attributes (age, job title, level of education and so on).

- *Time: past v. present v. future; and sequential v. synchronic.* This represents how time is managed on a 3×2 grid: on one axis is the relative importance given to past, present and future, and on the other axis is the approach to structuring time. Past-oriented cultures show respect for ancestors and more senior colleagues, and have an acute sense of history. Present-oriented cultures enjoy the present moment and current relationships. Future-oriented cultures enjoy the potential and excitement of future achievement.

  Cultures that structure time 'sequentially' view life as a series of events: one thing at a time and one thing after another, following plans and schedules. Cultures that structure time 'synchronically' view things in parallel with schedules being desirable but not binding.

- *Environment: inner-directed v. outer-directed.* This represents how people relate to their natural environment and the extent to which they believe they can control it. 'Inner-directed' cultures have a mechanistic view of nature: they think they dominate nature and see themselves as the starting point for events. 'Outer-directed' cultures have an external organic view of nature. They think humans are controlled by nature and that external others are the starting point for events.

Van den Berg and Pietersma (2016: 297) explain how the model works:

- Each employee has a culture identified.
- Those cultures are assessed on each of the seven dimensions and then positioned on seven sliding scales.
- The cultures are then compared to the 'home' culture of the organisation and the dimensions on which the two differ are identified and a conversation started to see how differences can be overcome using appropriate strategies.

Cultural responsiveness

Culturally responsive models do not apply solely to staff; in education, they apply also, and perhaps more importantly, to students. Culturally responsive leadership in schools and universities applies cultural diversity to practices and policies and incorporates aspects of different cultures – specifically, the history, values and cultural capital *of students' own backgrounds* – into the formal curriculum. Culturally responsive leadership supports improved learning for students from culturally diverse racial, ethnic and linguistic communities while emphasising high expectations for achievement. It seeks to develop a critical consciousness among students and staff to challenge inequality in society by creating inclusive organisational structures in the school or university that empower students and stakeholders from diverse socio-economic, racial and ethnic communities.

Culturally responsive managers have an ethic to develop cultural awareness in the school or university and in the local community. They demonstrate and promote inclusive practice, and they challenge established principles and practices when those have not reduced things like attainment gaps. They actively respond to cultural and socio-economic diversity in their schools and universities, see different student backgrounds as positive and legitimate, and seek to personalise instruction in light of that diversity. Cultural responsiveness is often associated with social activism, but at a practical level it depends on having the right people on staff to innovate the curriculum and reflect the diversity of the community served by the organisation. It is sometimes spoken of as a form of leadership, but to reduce it to yet another inchoate adjective is to trivialise it. Doing things right, as Peter Drucker might say, is what *every* competent education leader does: encouraging staff to sign up to being culturally aware and responsive, focusing on making the curriculum 'relevant' and having high expectations for student achievement. This is not to diminish its importance – quite the opposite, in fact, because cultural awareness should be part of *every* leader's practice – but the practical problems of 'mainstreaming' cultural diversity into the *formal* curriculum have gone unchallenged and remain unresolved: whether cultures that are themselves intolerant of diversity should be included in what we teach students; whether it is desirable to teach demonstrably false 'flat-earth' beliefs as part of the curriculum; whether schools should treat abusive cultural practices as being on a par with the jurisprudence of democratic societies; and whether liberal democratic values and tolerance can ever be passed on to the next generation through formal schooling if schools treat diametrically opposed totalitarian values as being on an equal footing.

Values in the ethical sense: the Stakeholder Management model

All stakeholders and not just employees from different cultures need to be 'managed'. The Stakeholder Management model does this by assessing (a) the power of stakeholders, (b) the legitimacy of their demands and (c) the urgency of their demands (Freeman, 2010). The term 'stakeholder' describes those who have a direct stake in the welfare and performance of the school or university and whose judgements stem from self-interest. They are not objective, neutral, disinterested observers. The organisation assesses which stakeholders are most important, the power they exert on the school or university, how they interact with one other, what they contribute to the organisation, how the organisation should act in relation to their interests, and the desirability, appropriateness and urgency of their demands.

- The model categorises stakeholders that score highly on *only one* of the three characteristics as 'latent' (power only), 'demanding' (urgency only) or 'discrete' (discrete only).
- Stakeholders that score highly on *all three* are called 'crucial', and their needs and wants should always be prioritised.

- Stakeholders that score highly on both power and urgency but not legitimacy are termed 'dangerous'; those that score highly on both power and legitimacy but not urgency are termed 'dominant'; those that score highly on both urgency and legitimacy but not power are termed 'dependent'.

Following an assessment of power, each stakeholder is assessed for their relationship with the organisation, their potential coalitions with other stakeholders, their position in the market and their concerns and priorities. Based on these assessments, the school or university can gauge which stakeholders will:

- Support the organisation's objectives. These are called 'movers' who will contribute actively and will encourage others to do likewise.
- Not support the organisation's objectives. These are called 'blockers'.
- Neither oppose nor support the organisation's aims. These are the 'floaters', lying between the movers and the blockers.

Movers need to be informed about an organisation's objectives and strategies so that they can contribute and encourage others to contribute. Floaters need to be won over by explaining how their interests will be served by the organisation's plans. Blockers also need to be consulted, but not overly so if they are very resistant, to find out what they perceive to be threats and what the school or university can do to allay their fears. Typically, too much attention is given to blockers and too little to floaters (Van den Berg & Pietersma, 2016).

The purpose of all this communication with stakeholders is to create win–win scenarios for the school or university, and for students and external stakeholders. To help with this, key performance indicators are designed for each aspect of the strategy, and progress is tracked using 'stakeholder action cards', which give a good overview of the interests, needs and roles of stakeholders, and the organisation's progress and development.

Values in the economic sense: the Value Disciplines model

Various management techniques are associated with value in the economic sense, and the Value Disciplines model is one of them. It uses valuation techniques for performance and rewards, setting goals and aiding decision-making. It is used for financial reporting, and in that respect is beyond the scope of this book, but it has some relevance in relation to performance pay and reward, discussed in Chapter 19, and unlike other traditional accounting systems, it takes account of effectiveness. Value-based management links the right levers to effect improvement with management and measurement. Managers are motivated to think and act as if they were owners (Van den Berg & Pietersma, 2016), with penalties for underperformance and bonuses to reward achievement. The focus is on better operational decisions, *creating* value and not just *measuring* it, and avoiding unnecessary complexity.

In this context, there are three 'value-disciplines' that enable a school or university to deliver value to its students and external stakeholders:

- Excellence operationally by optimising the efficiency of delivery.
- Leadership in offering the best service and/or being the first in a particular market with an innovation like a MOOC.
- Customer-facing in offering the best educational service, and being the most dependable and responsive to student/stakeholder needs.

The model focuses on value for the student and research funder, and emphasises the natural tendency of schools, colleges and universities to change with changing needs, expectations and demographics. Market-leading schools and universities are successful because they do not pursue all three value-disciplines simultaneously. The model helps organisations review the needs of stakeholders and the value of what the organisation offers them by way of fulfilling those needs. There are typically three steps to the process:

- *Step 1*. The focus is explicitly on students and competitors in the sector. Management identifies which type of value means the most to current students and stakeholders, how many focus on each type of value, what the sector standard is, whether there are any competitors doing a better job, and why the home school or university is worse (or better) than competitors.
- *Step 2*. The focus is on the school or university itself. Middle management determines what the three value-disciplines mean for their own disciplines or departments, including any major changes that might be required. This results in several options for consideration:
  - Excellence in operations offers high-quality education at relatively low fees, but these organisations do not offer the *latest* mode of delivery or cutting-edge content. Instead, they observe the market's direction, and they focus on efficiency, streamlining and integration. Standardisation of delivery and processes is the key.
  - Leading schools and universities experiment with new modes of delivery. Their markets are either unknown or very dynamic. Risk is high, and as a result, so are the potential gains. The focus is on research and development, good design and jumping the market. Innovation and life-cycle management are the keys.
  - Student-facing schools and research-intensive universities satisfy their customers (students and funders, respectively) at all costs. They invest time and money in building long-term relationships with a few select others (feeder and partner schools, university networks and industrial partners) and work closely with them (Van den Berg & Pietersma, 2016). The focus is on retention and delivering satisfaction to the existing base.

∘   *Step 3*. The school or university chooses its main value-discipline involving the main internal stakeholders. The organisation's processes, structure, culture, management and information systems must be aligned with the chosen value-discipline, as well as the corresponding value-drivers, but should not ignore internal skills and competencies.

Values in the economic sense: the Value Chain model

It is sometimes best to look at an organisation holistically by considering the chain of activities that delivers value to students, research funders and other stakeholders. This Value Chain model divides value-adding activities into five primary and four secondary activities.

- Primary activities:
  1. Internal logistics about course delivery and things like student accommodation and catering.
  2. Operations including design, maintenance and operational management.
  3. External logistics like managing the delivery of research projects.
  4. Marketing and advertising.
  5. Service – alumni relations and ongoing careers support.
- Secondary activities:
  1. Organisational structure, including general management structure, planning procedures, finance, simulation exercises and quality assurance of courses and research.
  2. HR management, including recruitment and retention of staff, and training and professional development.
  3. Educational and research technology, including online assessment platforms, publications databases and library provision.
  4. Procurement, including hardware servicing, IT support for staff and students, general supplies, and negotiating contracts.

Together, these primary and secondary activities generate competitive advantage by maximising value creation and minimising costs. Overall, value chains separate an organisation's activities into discrete activities, each of which is analysed for its added value and cost. The issue of waste and avoiding non-value-adding activities is a related issue and needs to be addressed also as part of the Value Chain model. The idea is to map both the value-adding and the non-value-adding processes and create a lean organisation, as discussed in Chapter 9. Value Chains identify opportunities for improvement, as well as waste and inefficiencies – for example, ignoring synergies when tutors are travelling to deliver university courses off campus – by first mapping the *existing* situation and then mapping the *desired-future* situation. The critical stage is to change things so that the current map starts to look like the desired-future map. Usually this involves redesigning delivery systems to meet student demand and market expectation (and not for the convenience of staff), which will need to be mapped as well. The use of supporting data is key to success, as the organisation seeks to reduce variability and increase flexibility, which often demands strategic planning for introducing new ways of working, the subject of the next chapter.

Notes

1 Greenleaf first applied his theory of servant leadership while working as an executive at AT&T, the world's largest telecommunications company.
2 Greenleaf was a practising Quaker.

18

MATRICES AND GRIDS

The Ansoff Matrix

It should be apparent from previous chapters – in particular from seminal work by contingency theorists Tannenbaum and Schmidt, and Blake and Mouton, who developed the concept of leadership orientation and its measurement – that two-by-two matrices and grids are useful tools for presenting theoretical frameworks. Actually, the famous grid model developed by Blake and Mouton in 1964 was preceded seven years earlier by a similar model by US mathematician Igor Ansoff (1957). It plotted 'product' against 'market strategy' and has become famous as a strategic planning tool to help leaders and managers devise strategies for future growth (see Figure 18.1). It can help an organisation avoid overlooking available growth and diversification strategies or misunderstanding the implications of pursuing a particular course.

The Ansoff Matrix describes four alternatives for growing an organisation either in existing or in new markets, with either existing or new services, each alternative posing a differing level of risk for the organisation. Selecting a growth strategy is a three-step process. First, all available strategies are set out. Then qualitative criteria are used to shortlist the favoured alternatives. Finally, return on investment – in education, fee income or research funding in relation to staffing and set-up costs, for example – is examined in order to narrow the alternatives still further.

(1,1) Market Penetration

The Market Penetration strategy is the least risky strategy for growth. In it the organisation tries to grow using its existing services in existing markets; that is, it tries to increase its market share in the current marketplace without departing

DOI: 10.4324/9781003217220-18

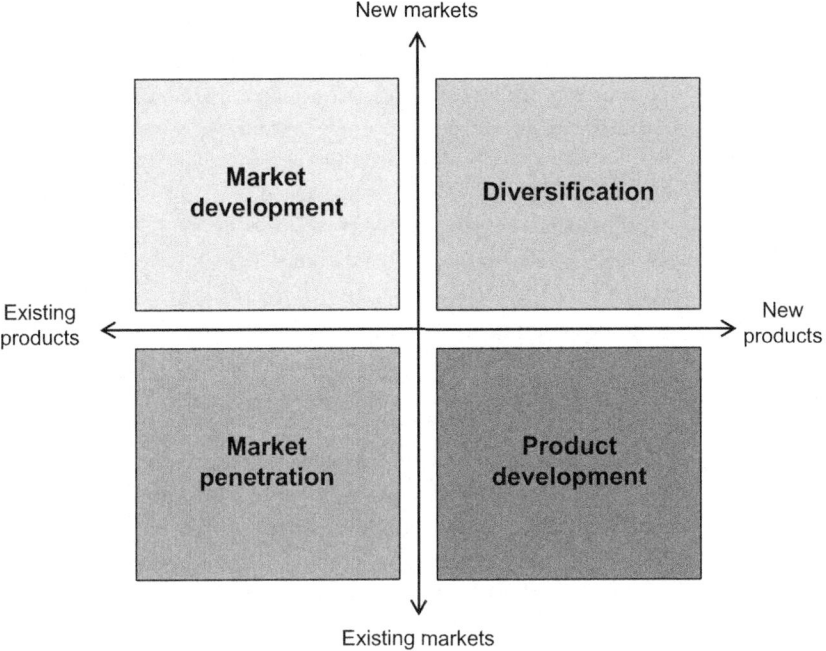

FIGURE 18.1 The Ansoff Matrix.

from the original service-market strategy. This can be achieved by selling more education and research services to an established student and stakeholder base or by finding new students within existing markets. The school or university looks to increase recruitment for its present offerings in its present markets through more aggressive promotion: by lowering fees, improving student support and research dissemination, merging with a rival or refining the education service in small ways. Common examples include refreshing a college's publicity material or more aggressively recruiting from traditional feeder schools.

Market Penetration is the strategy that can most easily leverage *existing* resources and capabilities. It makes greatest sense if the school or university already has a strong competitive advantage or if the overall size of a market (e.g. professional doctorates) is growing or can be made to grow. Market Penetration can be pursued by: increasing advertising to promote or to re-position courses; by offering special scholarships and bursaries; by introducing alumni schemes; by improving the quality of teaching; by changing how the courses are structured (e.g. by introducing exit diplomas into master's degree programmes); by improving online delivery to reach more customers within existing markets (e.g. MOOCs); by targeting a niche if the school or university is relatively small; by changing fee structure; by improving operational efficiency so that surplus can be increased through economies of scale and rationalisation.

(1,2) Market Development

In this strategy, the organisation expands into new markets, sectors and demographics using existing offerings (with some modifications). Examples in education might be a university recruiting students from emerging economies or a state school introducing a Sixth Form (senior) cycle. This strategy is more likely to be successful where the school or university has a unique service that it can leverage in new markets so that it can benefit from economies of scale if delivery increases. It is best if new markets are fairly similar to existing ones, but it is a slightly riskier strategy than the previous one (Market Penetration). Ansoff described this as a strategy 'to adapt current lines to new missions'. For example, aircraft manufacturer Boeing might adapt an existing model of passenger aircraft and sell it for cargo transportation (Spencer, 2013).

Market Development makes sense as a strategy where: the school or university's core competencies relate to existing courses and services, and it has a strong marketing team; where the school or university can identify opportunities for market development including chances to reposition the brand, exploit new uses for the service or expand into new areas. Market Development can be pursued by marketing services in new locations, by advertising through different media to reach new customers and by modifying fee policy to appeal to different student demographics.

(2,1) Product Development

In this growth strategy, an organisation tries to create new services with new (or altered) features targeted at existing markets. As such, it is a strategy of 'horizontal diversification', which can increase an organisation's dependence on certain markets. It is an equally risky strategy to the previous one (Market Development) and involves extending the service range in existing markets. Extending the range of services may be achieved by developing new services jointly with another school or university.

Product Development is a good strategy when: a school or college understands the needs of its students and research stakeholders and identifies an opportunity to offer new courses or services to satisfy changing needs; when the organisation operates in a competitive market where continuous innovation is necessary; when the school or university has a large market share and a strong brand; when the organisation's services benefit from network effects, and new offerings can gain a significant edge by being first to market; when the market has strong growth potential.

(2,2) Diversification

In Diversification, a school or university tries to grow its market share by introducing new services into new markets. It is the riskiest strategy because the organisation is simultaneously developing new courses *and* entering new markets, and may be operating outside its area of expertise. If the new courses are unrelated to existing courses, it is called 'lateral diversification'.

Diversification can enable an organisation to achieve growth, stability and flexibility. There are three kinds of diversification:

- *Vertical integration*, where an organisation expands its services to different points; for example, a university offering pre-university courses usually provided by schools or colleges.
- *Horizontal diversification*, where a school or university adds new courses that are unrelated to existing ones but are likely to appeal to existing students and using existing delivery structures.
- *Lateral diversification*, where a school or university adds new courses which are unrelated to existing courses and are likely to appeal to completely different students. While lateral diversification has little relationship to an organisation's current activities, the school or university might adopt this strategy in order to enter a more lucrative growth sector, to poach top academic talent, to expand fee income or a research-funding base or to reduce risk by spreading activities across multiple programmes and markets.

Each of these strategies represents a different path that a school or university can take to pursue growth, but in practice, an institution will often implement more than one strategy at any given time. Ansoff noted that a 'simultaneous pursuit of market penetration, market development and product development is usually a sign of a progressive, well-run' organisation and may be 'essential to survival in the face of competition' (Spencer, 2013). The Ansoff Matrix is useful for organisations wanting to identify and explore these growth options. Although the risk varies between quadrants, with Diversification (2,2) being the riskiest, it can be argued that if a school or university diversifies its offering successfully into multiple unrelated markets, then, in fact, its overall risk is *lowered*. However, the Ansoff Matrix can be misleading in this respect because it does not take into account the activities of competitors and *their* ability to counter-move. It also fails to consider the challenges and risks of changes to existing programmes while the new programme is being developed or the move into new markets is taking place. The leader of an organisation hoping to move into new markets or create new teaching or research offerings (or both) must consider whether staff have the necessary skills, structures and stakeholders to make the strategy a success. The way the matrix defines 'new', if indeed it does at all, has also been questioned. If a service really *is* new, then it should *ipso facto* take the school or university into new markets anyway. Is there any such quadrant as (2,1) – new services confined to an existing market – and indeed, is there any meaning to (2,2), the Diversification quadrant, since any new service will simultaneously take the organisation into an unfamiliar market (Dawes, 2018)?

The Growth–Share BCG matrix

The Growth–Share matrix, also known as the Boston Consulting Group (BCG) matrix, is a chart created by Bruce Henderson for the BCG in 1970 to help organisations analyse their activities and allocate resources (Henderson, 1968, 1970, 1973). Based on the assumption that economies of scale apply, the Growth–Share matrix is used as an analytical tool in brand marketing, strategic management and portfolio analysis (see Figure 18.2). It helps organisations decide which markets and activities to invest in on the basis of two factors, 'competitiveness' and 'market attractiveness', with the underlying drivers for these being relative market share and growth rate respectively. The logic is that market leadership, expressed through high relative market share, results in sustainable superior returns. In the long run, a market leader obtains a self-reinforcing cost-advantage through scale and experience, which competitors find difficult to replicate. High growth rates, on the other hand, signal the markets in which leadership can most easily be built. Putting these drivers in a matrix generates four quadrants, each with a specific strategic imperative.

To use the chart, analysts plot a scatter graph to rank the school or university's courses and research projects on the basis of their relative market share, which is on

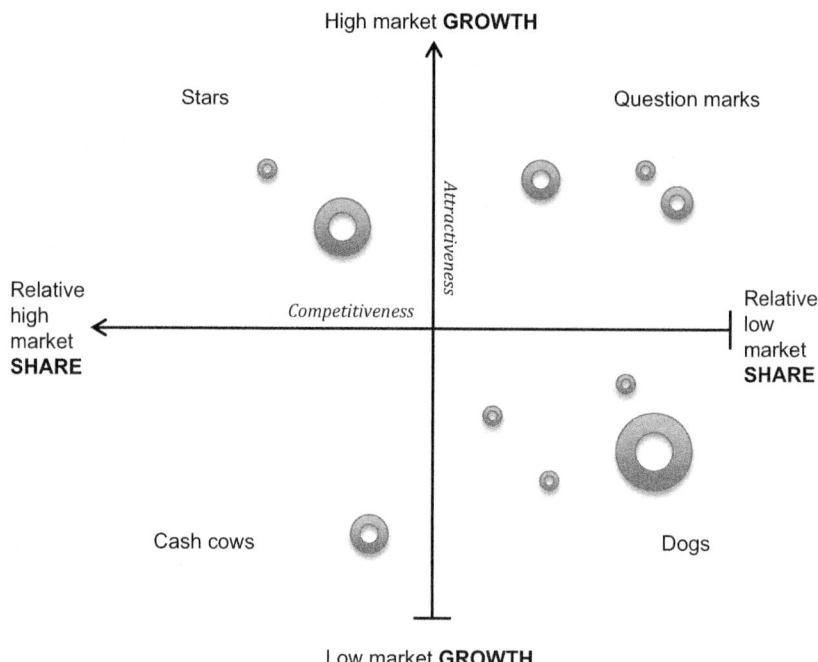

FIGURE 18.2 The Growth–Share matrix (circles show revenue).

the horizontal axis. Counter-intuitively, the left hand side is higher. Growth rate is on the vertical axis, with the top being faster growth.

- (High share, Slow growth – bottom-left quadrant): *Cash Cows* are where a school or university course or research project has high market share with slow growth. These activities typically generate profit; that is to say, fee income or research funding exceeds the amount needed to maintain delivery of the course or research output. Cash Cows are regarded as boring and the market is typically 'mature', but they are desirable activities because of their ability to generate income and be milked, requiring little additional inward investment. An example of a Cash Cow in the education sector (although, strictly speaking, it was not-for-profit) is the Centre for Evaluation and Monitoring (CEM), founded at Durham University but sold to Cambridge University Press in 2019 (Hazell, 2019).
- (Low, Slow – bottom-right quadrant): *Dogs*, also known as *Pets*, have low relative market share and are mature and slow-growing. They are courses or research activities that typically just break even, generating barely enough cash to maintain their market share. They might offer some synergies with other units in the school or university, but are otherwise pretty worthless. They depress the organisation's return on assets, although it should be remembered that Dogs can be 'loss-leaders'; that is to say, while not profitable themselves, they increase prestige – like having a medical research facility in the university – and boost recruitment in other more profitable disciplines or activities.
- (Low, Fast – top-right quadrant): *Question Marks* (also known as *Wild Dogs*) are school or university courses or research areas operating with a low relative market share in a high-growth market. They are the starting point for most activities. They have the potential to gain market share and become Stars, and eventually Cash Cows when growth slows. If Question Marks do not succeed in becoming market leaders after years of cash consumption, they degenerate into Dogs when growth declines.
- (High, Fast – top-left quadrant): *Stars* are courses or research activities with a big market share in a fast-growing area. They are graduated Question Marks with a market-leading trajectory or have a monopolistic or dominant unique selling proposition. They have novelty value, are topical or fashionable and have research-funder loyalty and student goodwill. The hope is that Stars become Cash Cows (when growth slows in that field and if they are still among the sector leaders), but they need high funding to fight off competitor schools and universities and maintain growth.

As a particular sector matures and growth slows, all courses and research activities become either Cash Cows or Dogs, the lower two quadrants on the matrix. The natural cycle for most is that they start as Question Marks, then turn anticlockwise into Stars. Eventually, the market stops growing, so the particular project or course becomes a Cash Cow; and at the end of the cycle, the Cash Cow turns into a Dog.

A diversified organisation will have a balanced portfolio of courses and research centres: with Stars whose high share and fast growth can assure the future, with Cash Cows that supply income for future growth, and with Question Marks to be converted into Stars.

On the Growth–Share matrix, for each course and research activity, the size of the circle represents its 'value' in some way: fee income or research funding or student recruitment, say. The matrix thus also offers a map of an organisation's strengths and weaknesses. One of the main indicators of fee-income and research-income generation is relative market share, and one of the main indicators of income usage is market growth rate (Spencer, 2015).

Relative market share

The higher the market share, the more fee income and research income is generated. As a result of economies of scale, income will grow faster the greater the market share. The critical measure is the school or university's share *relative to its largest competitor*. For example, if the 'home' brand has a 10% share of the market, but the main competitor has a 40% share, the ratio is 1:4, implying that the home brand is in a relatively weak position. On the other hand, if the largest competitor has only a 5% share, the ratio is 2:1, implying that the home brand owned is in a relatively strong position. What constitutes a 'high relative market share' is a matter of dispute. The most stable position is thought to be the 'Rule of 1–2–3'; namely, for the brand leader to have a share double that of the second brand, and triple that of the third. Brand leaders in this position tend to be very stable and profitable (Fripp, n.d.).

Choosing relative market share, rather than simply income, is that it carries more information. It shows where the brand is positioned against other competitor schools and universities, and indicates where it is likely to go in the future and what type of marketing activities might be effective (BCG, 1970).

Market growth rate

Organisations want to be fast-growing in fast-growing markets, but they need investment. Growth is essentially 'bought' by investment with the expectation that a higher market share will in future turn into higher income. The theory behind the matrix assumes, therefore, that a higher growth rate indicates demand for investment. Market growth rate is really about 'brand position'. It is a good indicator of the school or university's strength in the market, of future potential and of its attractiveness to potential partners.

Some research has called into question whether the Growth–Share matrix actually helps businesses succeed (Armstrong & Brodie, 1994). Slater and Zwirlein (1992) looked at more than 100 companies and found that those that used portfolio planning models like the Growth–Share matrix actually had *lower* shareholder returns. Another problem is that the matrix defines Dogs as having low market share and low growth, but several Dogs still alive in the market today are very profitable and retain their share of the market *without dominating it* (Duica et al., 2014). They can still produce substantial income.

The Growth–Share matrix as originally designed by BCG was for situations where it could graphically illustrate the composition of a portfolio as a function of the balance between different income streams (Spencer, 2015). If the matrix is used under its originally intended conditions, it is still valid. The problem is that over the years, it has become over-simplified and over-used, creating two major problems: the income-stream techniques are applicable only to a very limited number of sectors where growth is high, and a definite pattern of life cycles can be observed in courses and research trends; and the belief that the brand-leading Cash Cow courses and programmes should be milked to fund new courses and research activities despite the fact that a brand-leading programme is the one, above all others, that needs to be defended. The Growth–Share matrix intends that there should be a balance of activities across all four quadrants, so income should be diverted from Cash Cows to fund future Stars, since Cash Cows inevitably decline to become Dogs. Unfortunately, the matrix focuses attention and investment onto the Star programmes, ignoring the reality that Cash Cows are the most important element in the school or university and it would be foolish to divert support away from them when the school or university needs to extend them for reasons of prestige.

Updating the Growth–Share matrix

Recently, BCG has revisited its matrix to adapt it for today's environment (Reeves et al., 2014). BCG sees the concept as being 'very much alive' while acknowledging that the world has changed 'in ways that have had a fundamental impact on the original matrix: the pace of change has accelerated; and competitive advantage has become less durable'. The practical utility of the *original* matrix is twofold:

- It provides diversified organisations like universities with a rationale for redeploying support/resources from Cash Cows to other taught and research programmes with higher growth potential. This idea came at a time when organisations hoarded and then reinvested their income. Organisations that allocated their income smartly gained an advantage.
- The original matrix also provides organisations with a simple but powerful tool for maximising competitiveness and sustainability by striking the right balance between the exploitation of mature programmes and the exploration of new ones to secure future growth.

However, the environment has since changed for both commercial and public sector enterprises. Organisations today face circumstances that change more rapidly and unpredictably than before because of educational technology advances and globalisation, as a result of which organisations need constantly to renew their advantage and increase the speed at which they shift resources between different courses and research activities. In addition, market share is no longer a direct predictor of sustained performance. Today, we see new drivers of competitive advantage, such as the ability to adapt to changing circumstances or indeed to shape them.

BCG looked at what these two shifts mean for the original concept (Reeves et al., 2014). As change accelerates, BCG found in their research[1] that businesses move around the matrix quadrants more quickly, and as the disruption of mature businesses increases with change and unpredictability, they found that there were proportionately fewer Cash Cows today[2] because their longevity was curtailed. Income generation today is less tied to mature activities with high market share, so BCG suggest that an updated version of the matrix should have a new measure of '*Competitiveness*' to replace its original horizontal axis.

Successful organisations today need to explore new services, new markets and different service models more frequently to renew their advantage 'through disciplined experimentation' (Reeves et al., 2014). This new experimental approach requires organisations like universities to invest in more Question Marks, experiment with them in a quicker and more economical way than competitors and systematically select promising ones to grow into Stars. At the same time, they need to be prepared to respond to changes in the marketplace; for example, by retiring Cash Cows more quickly.

To get the most out of the new 'experimentation' version of the BCG matrix, organisations need to focus on four practical imperatives according to BCG:

1. *Accelerate.* It is critical to evaluate the portfolio of activities and services frequently. Organisations should increase their 'strategic clock-speed' to match that of the environment, with shorter planning cycles and feedback loops from students and research funders requiring simplified approval processes for investment and divestment decisions.
2. *Balance exploration and exploitation.* This requires having an adequate number of Question Marks while simultaneously maximising the benefits of both Cows and Dogs. This requires: a culture within the college or university that encourages risk-taking, tolerates unsuccessful innovations (e.g. courses that did not prove popular) and allows challenges to the status quo; by using rapid (and if possible, virtual) tests that limit the cost of failure; by not neglecting the need to exploit *existing* sources of advantage and prestige; and capturing 'failure signals' from Dogs to inform future decisions on where and how to experiment, lower exit barriers and move quickly to squeeze out remaining value before divestment.
3. *Select rigorously.* Organisations must carefully select investments as well as divestments by leveraging a wide range of data sources and predictive analytics to determine which Question Marks should be scaled up and which Dogs and Cash Cows should be culled.
4. *Measure and manage the experimentation portfolio.* Understanding the experimentation level required to maintain growth is important for long-term sustainability. Organisations like colleges and universities need to: continually measure and manage the number and costs of their Question Marks to ensure the pipeline

stays filled; ensure that the probability that Question Marks become Stars is high enough and that the cost of failure for these Question Marks is acceptable; look for today's Stars (and Question Marks) to generate at least enough fee income to replace Cash Cows (and Dogs) that are late in their life cycle so that the portfolio of activities and programmes generates sufficient income in the long run.

The GE–McKinsey matrix

In the 1970s, General Electric (GE) asked its consultants, McKinsey, to develop a portfolio management model to guide a systematic approach to prioritise its multi-activity operations. The GE–McKinsey three-by-three matrix was the result. GE was at that time an umbrella corporation with about 150 business units and had been using the BCG Matrix, but it felt the need for a more sophisticated model to help it decide which of its units deserved development funding and which did not. As resources become scarcer in organisations, decisions are needed to make the best use of income. For enterprises like universities, diversified by subject-area rather than by service – all the constituent parts teach and do research, just in different fields – the fight for resources is complex because multiple reputations (the educational equivalent of brands) and multiple activity portfolios need to be managed. The GE–McKinsey matrix can help educational organisations make these decisions in a systematic and informed manner (Luenendonk, 2015).

Like the BCG matrix, the GE–McKinsey matrix helps organisations make investment and disinvestment decisions related to their activities or business units, but whereas the BCG matrix uses 'growth' and 'market share' on its two axes, the GE–McKinsey matrix uses Sector Attractiveness and Competitive Strength (see Figure 18.3).

The GE–McKinsey matrix is slightly more difficult than the BCG matrix to put into practice because of the larger number of cells. The analysis looks like a two-dimensional matrix, but the dimensions are multifactor with 9 Attractiveness measures and 12 Competitive Strength measures (Luenendonk, 2015). It typically involves five steps.

1. *Identify the Attractiveness of each activity*. This dimension helps determine the attractiveness of the market by analysing the benefits a college or university is likely to get by entering and competing within the market (Luenendonk, 2015).
    - First, list the factors. To determine Attractiveness, there are nine measures to be taken into account: long-term sector growth rate; size of the market and strength of competition within it; entry and exit barriers; the threat from less prestigious competitors; fee and income structure of the sector; programme life cycle; course demand; fee and research income trends; labour and market segmentation.

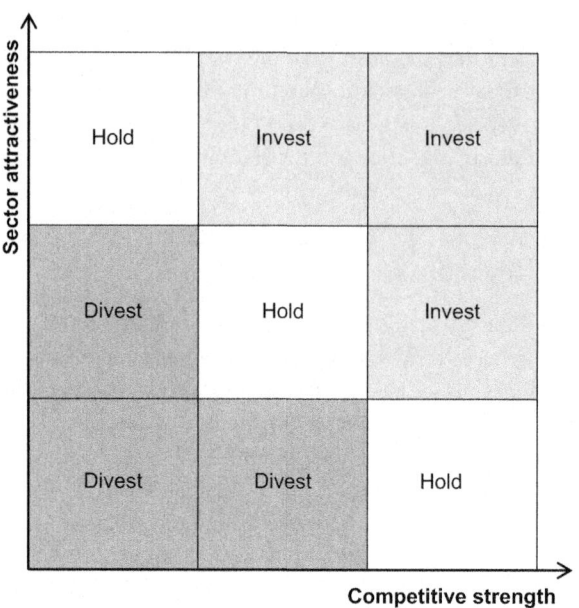

FIGURE 18.3 The GE–McKinsey matrix.

-   Secondly, decide on the relative *weights* of these factors on a scale of one to ten, say. These weights determine the importance of the factor to Attractiveness and whatever factors *are chosen* should be assigned a weight. The total of these weights should be ten. For example, 'Activity X' might have Profitability weighted as 5, Industry Growth weighted as 3 and low Competition weighted as 2. In contrast, 'Activity Y' might have Profitability = 7, Industry Growth = 2 and low Competition = 1.

-   Thirdly, rate each factor for each activity on a scale of one to ten (10 = very attractive) but this time (unlike the sum of the weights) the *ratings* need *not* add up to ten. For example, for 'Activity X', low competition might be the most attractive factor at 6, profitability less so at 5 and sector growth at 3. For 'Activity Y', profitability might be the most attractive factor at 8, low competition less so at 3 and sector growth at 2.

-   Finally, to get the *weighted scores* for Sector Attractiveness for each activity in the organisation, multiply the *weight* by *rating* for the activity. These are added up to achieve one figure for each organisational activity or unit. In the above examples, 'Activity X' has a weighted score of 5 × 5 + 3 × 3 + 2 × 6 = 46 and 'Activity Y' has a weighted score of 7 × 8 + 2 × 2 + 1 × 3 = 63.

2. *Determine the Competitive Strength of each activity.* This dimension helps understand the extent to which a college or university has the required competence to compete in a particular market. This can be determined by internal factors such as assets and resources, market share, reputation and creative strengths,

and by external factors such as government regulations and some estate taxes (Luenendonk, 2015). The second step is similar to the first step.

   ° *List the factors.* To determine the Competitive Strengths of the different activities, there are 12 measures to be taken into account, including total market share, market share growth compared to competitor colleges and universities, profitability, reputation, staff, student and alumni loyalty and service differentiation.

   ° *Decide on the weights.* As in the first step, the *chosen* factors are assigned weights according to their importance in helping the organisation achieve sustainable competitive advantage. As before, the weights can be between 1 and 10, with the total summing to 10.

   ° *Decide on the ratings.* As in the first step, once the weights have been assigned, the rating for each factor needs to be determined for each service or activity.

   ° *Weighted score.* As in the first step, to get the weighted score for each factor of Competitive Strength for each activity, multiply the *weight* by *rating* for each of the activities and add up to achieve a total score.

3. *Determine the position of the activities on the matrix.* Once the weighted scores for the activities or units within the organization have been determined, these are plotted on the matrix. Each activity can be represented by a box or disc whose size represents (say) the proportion as the organisation's overall revenue that the activity brings in or (say) its share of the market. The future outlook for each activity is also included – this is explained in Step 5.

4. *Determine the strategy option for the units or activities.* Depending on the position of the teaching activity or research unit (say) on the matrix, three categories of decision can be made: invest/grow; hold; harvest/divest. Organisations should make resources available to activities in the Invest/Grow category, as they promise high fee generation in the future. These units or activities also require investment to allow them to maintain their share if the sector if growing (Luenendonk, 2015). Investments include expansion in service delivery/capacity.

   In the Hold category, organisations should invest in them only if they appear to have a future and if resources are available, which is not often the situation in education. These activities are in an ambiguous position because it is unclear whether they will grow in the future or stagnate. Investments in this category can happen only after resources have already been put into the Invest/Grow category units or if there is a strategic purpose (like prestige) in maintaining the Hold activities.

   In the Harvest/Divest category, colleges and universities should axe activities or units if they are not showing any promise or not generating income. Services in this category may be poor performers or operate in less attractive fields and markets, with little or no sustainable competitive advantage. Investment should be put into them only if they generate revenue to equal the investment. If this does not happen, then these activities or units need to be 'liquidated' (Luenendonk, 2015).

5.   *Forecast the future of the activities.* Notwithstanding the location of the 'weight-by-rating scores' for different activities, some further analysis is required going forward. For an activity in the Invest category (top-right of the matrix) where the outlook is that the market is likely to shrink and that the activity will lose Competitive Strength (i.e. move 'down' to the left), then that activity might become much less attractive for investment in the medium term. Managers will need to keep a watching brief on it. On the other hand, if an activity were in a sector that was poised for growth, that activity, although perhaps currently in the 'hold' category on the matrix, might become attractive for investment in the medium term.

The matrix itself only helps an organisation determine the current state of the sector and Competitive Strength, with no indication of future positioning, so within the matrix, an arrow is usually added to each box/disc showing its likely future direction (Luenendonk, 2015).

The main advantage of the GE–McKinsey matrix as a strategy tool is that it tries to answer the question of where resources should be invested. In Chapter 22 we will see how it can be used in parallel with an analysis of competition in the university sector, so it is a powerful adaptable tool even in education. The GE–McKinsey matrix is more refined than the BCG matrix as it replaces a single factor, Market Growth, with many factors under Market Attractiveness. Similarly, Competitive Strength in the GE–McKinsey matrix includes many more factors than just Market Share. However, like the BCG matrix, it fails to consider the intersectionality between activities and their core competencies. Potential synergies and (sometimes unusual) dynamics between two or more activities or units in a university – for example, between Demography and Medicine – are not taken into account (Luenendonk, 2015), and for complex organisations the two axes factors and their weights (at best, a very subjective exercise) can be accurately determined only by an external consultant, which is usually costly.

Notes

1   BCG found that companies in 75% of industries circulated through the matrix quadrants faster in the five-year period 2008–2012 than in the five-year period 1988–1992; and in those industries, the average time spent in a quadrant halved, from four years in 1992 to less than two years in 2012. Only a few stable industries, such as food retail and health-care equipment, saw fewer disruptions and did *not* show faster circulation.
2   The share of total profits captured by Cash Cows in 2012 was 25% lower than it was in 1982.

19

PAY AND REWARD

Pay and reward is a fraught area in education – especially in Further Education colleges in the UK where union power was broken in the 1980s and 1990s – and is a common problem area for managers. It goes to the heart of motivation, discussed in previous chapters, and how the leadership of an organisation views work and workers. It is not just a question of salary, which across the education sector and the public sector generally is usually set by national agreements and therefore beyond the remit of an organisation's senior management team, but it also involves discretionary annual increments or (for managers) performance bonuses, which are usually internal matters, and personal esteem. Teachers, lecturers and researchers who are supportive of, and contributors to, improvement initiatives are already likely to be hard-working and conscientious, so they are probably working to capacity anyway. They do not need *more* work, just *different* work. For these and other staff, where salary increases are impossible, there should be linkage between desired organisational outcomes and personal esteem. If outcomes shift in terms of importance, management must be prepared to refocus incentives and promotion criteria in such a way as to drive the school or college in the desired direction in an efficient manner. It is nonsensical to reward performance *in an incidental area*. Schools, colleges and universities must be focused going forward, and management must engage with the process knowing that difficult decisions lie ahead.

The Compensation Model

Before looking at the theory and practice of performance-related pay and reward, which can be quite complex, and the Human Relations departments that oversee it, we will look at a relatively simple model for the design, operation and assessment

DOI: 10.4324/9781003217220-19

of pay and reward strategies; namely, the Compensation Model (Milkovich & Newman, 2013). It has three dimensions:

- *Policies to outline the basis for the pay and reward system and guidelines for managing compensation in ways that accomplish the organisation's goals.* Internal alignment compares relative pay for different employees within the school or university, based on output, skill and experience (or seniority), but the organisation also needs to be externally competitive and pay an attractive rate in the market. And the entire pay and reward system must be managed and maintained.
- *Techniques to link policies and objectives in a reward system.* These techniques include job analyses, promotion criteria and monitoring for bias. External comparisons can easily be done using benchmarking techniques (Kelly, 2001), and this can be used to gauge the school or university's competitiveness in the recruitment market, but the most important function is to have proper internal alignment for the various jobs and positions, and to have techniques for installing and maintaining a *fair* remuneration-reward scheme.
- *Goals for a reward system are efficiency, effectiveness and equity (in both ethical and legal senses).* Efficiency is the ratio of output to input, and as far as pay and reward is concerned, it is about controlling staff costs. Effectiveness is the extent to which the school or university is achieving its desired outcomes, and as far as pay and reward is concerned, it is about maintaining quality and improving performance to the satisfaction of students and stakeholders, while still being efficient. Equity refers to treating employees fairly in terms of their pay and reward, irrespective of religion, race, gender or sexual orientation, because that is the moral thing to do *and* because it is a legal requirement in most jurisdictions.

In many ways, pay and reward both *reflects* and *creates* the culture of a school or university. The problem is usually in the area of promotion. Most public sector organisations like universities have criteria for promotion that are so generic that they could enable anyone both to gain promotion and to have their promotion declined, depending on the interpretation. Of course, overly generic and vague criteria are to blame and not the aspiration to have transparent guidelines. The vagueness comes from a desire not to exclude anyone for any reason, forgetting that promotion, like appointment, is by definition *about* excluding people! The result is that promotion in these organisations is often not a matter of fact, but of narrative. The system suits employees who know how to write up their career stories to best effect and who know the right people who will smile favourably on their narratives as referees. It is an irony that the very criteria designed to help disadvantaged sections of the workforce have the opposite effect, while of course keeping human resources departments gainfully employed and growing in size.

The Ulrich Business Partner model for HR departments

In general, HR departments give support and advice to the organisation as their 'administrative experts'. They also act as strategic partners to senior managers, as champions for employees and as agents for change (the subject of Chapter 24). Ulrich (1996) laid out these four roles on a grid (see Figure 19.1) to capture the balance between supporting the organisation as a whole and specifically supporting senior managers.

HR as administrative experts. The role of HR staff as administrative experts is immediate and aimed at helping the school or university with its pay and reward services to both managers and employees. Administration within the HR department must be organised efficiently and up-to-date on the law and best practice in terms of equity. A shoddy HR department means a shoddy organisation. It is a process-oriented role, as show on the vertical axis of Figure 19.1, and operationally focused, as shown on the horizontal axis.

HR as 'strategic partner' within an organisation. The role of the HR department as a strategic 'business partner' within the school or university is long-term, operationally focused (like the 'administrative expert' role), but (unlike that role) focused on *people* rather than on *processes* (see the axes on Figure 19.1). The simple aim is to enable the organisation to achieve its strategic goals (Van den Berg & Pietersma, 2016) using performance indicators at a level below the strategic – at the level of the employee – and using scorecard models (see Chapter 14) for departments within the organisation.

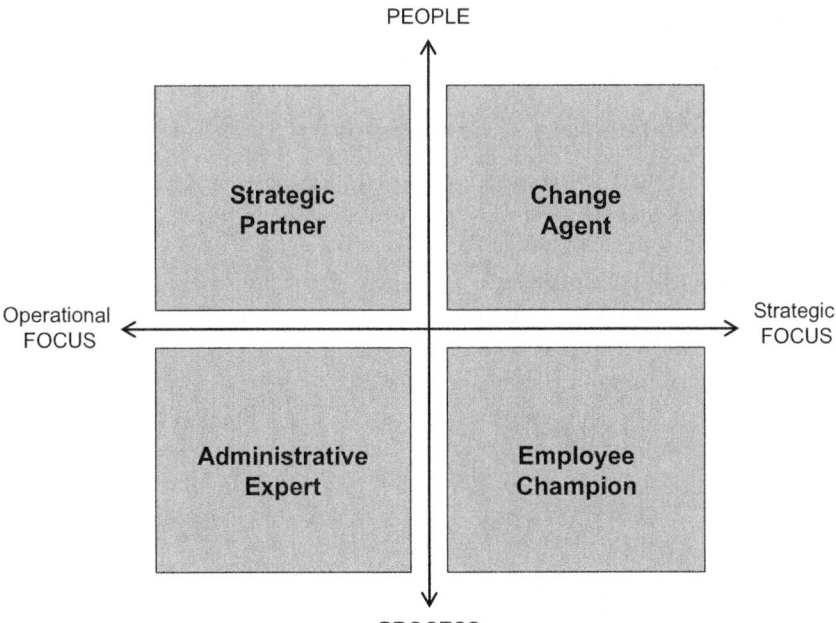

FIGURE 19.1 The Ulrich HR business partner model.

HR as champion for employees. The role of HR as a champion *for employees* is short-term, process-focused (on the vertical axis) and strategic (on the horizontal axis). The main aim is to provide an effective employee–organisation relationship, to recruit and retain the best employees for the school or university, and to up-skill and develop teachers, lecturers and researchers when they are recruited. In many ways, the HR department is an advisory counsel to both employees and management.

HR as agent for change. The role of a HR department as an agent for change is long-term, strategic and focused on people. The key aim is to provide the organisational capability to manage and facilitate change. The HR department as a change-agent positions it as a facilitator to senior managers to actualise strategic changes across the school or university (Van den Berg & Pietersma, 2016).

The Ulrich HR model is designed to plug HR departments into organisations and embed HR in the organisation's processes from top to bottom. The model offers a typology of roles for the HR department against two tensions – the 'operational' versus the 'strategic', and the 'people-focused' versus the 'process-focused' – but ultimately a HR department is only as good as its staff and the willingness of senior managers to trust their judgements. It can be a fine balancing act to support and advise employees and management simultaneously while retaining the trust of both parties. A *bad* HR department will almost certainly wreck an organisation or, at a minimum, reduce confidence in its systems among employees, but the extent to which a *good* HR department will make an organisation successful is debatable. The model does not address this question or the question of resolving ethical conflicts between advising employees and guiding managers *when the two parties are at odds*, but it is likely that success is contingent on circumstance and on the maturity of the school or university, as we saw with the situational leadership model in Chapter 7.

Performance-related pay and incentives in education

Over the past two decades, universities (and, to a lesser extent, schools) have come under attack in the media for offering very large compensation packages to their top executives; both the fixed salary part and the ancillary components. Like most things, it began in the commercial sector. In May 2003, for example, telecommunications provider Cable & Wireless announced plans to shed more than a quarter of its UK workforce, halt all dividend payments to shareholders and pull out of the US market as the full extent of the failure of the outgoing chief executive's period in office became known. The company made a record £6.5 billion annual loss, spent £9 billion over three years building a failed internet business (C&W Global) and in the year to the end of March 2003, made an operating loss of £303 million on revenues of £1.7 million (Wray, 2003). The outgoing chief executive received a performance bonus of £1.5 million under his contract! That same month, the shareholders of pharmaceutical giant GlaxoSmithKline rebelled over its CEO's remuneration package: a regular salary of £2.4 million and a 'golden parachute' of £22 million. More recently, in the public sector, after months of controversy and protest, the University of Bath replaced its vice-chancellor, Dame Glynis Breakwell, who was the highest-paid vice-chancellor in the UK. She was replaced by Professor Ian White, then deputy vice-chancellor at the University of Cambridge and Master of Jesus College. In response to the public outrage at Dame Breakwell's salary, Professor White's salary was set at £266,000 compared to his predecessor's £468,000 (BBC, 2008). Today, the fixed component of salary for top managers can be less than the incentive component, and although commentators and analysts are concerned at the extent to which the use of incentives actually results in better management, manager pay below that of vice-chancellor has followed the same pattern, though naturally at a lower level of remuneration. Pay and bonuses for managers like deans and heads of university departments are now increasingly tied to targets and to increased student recruitment and decreased absenteeism (McKenzie & Lee, 1998).

Whatever its efficacy, the use of incentives as components of pay continues to grow in importance because of the increased complexity of organisations. In schools and universities, as in other service sector organisations, employees on the frontline have know-how and expertise that managers do not – information about students, curriculum delivery and pedagogy, marking examination papers, educational technology, research methods and so on – and managers now rely more on this intellectual capital to maintain effective and efficient output. At the same time, increasingly, managers must be sure that employees are developing their intellectual capital *with the interests of the organisation in mind*, so there is an increasing tendency to use incentives as part of remuneration.

In both commercial and public sectors, the perceived need for performance-related pay is caused at least in part by the fact that services have become globalised and more complex, and students and staff more mobile and more international. Workforces can now be physically remote from management, just as students can be from lecturers, in a way that makes direct supervision inessential and sometimes impossible on a daily basis, and as a consequence, some organisations have had to become less hierarchical. Employees have had to be trusted to act in the interests of the organisation and the pace of that change has meant that decision-making has had to be devolved to lower levels. There simply isn't the time to pass everything up the chain of command for decision. Old style 'command-and-control' approaches are no longer an option for dynamic managers. The new style is one of enticement. Furthermore, for reasons of economy, organisations like universities have had to outsource many of their services – for example, IT support and occupational health services – so there is sometimes an asymmetry between the business goals of service *providers* and those of service *consumers*, which can be rectified only by incentivising the workforce at the service level.

It is claimed that tying remuneration to objective measures of performance can cause productivity to rise and can increase an organisation's ability to add value (Aboud, 1990). In the commercial sector, even the *announcement* that executive compensation is to be tied to performance can cause share value, which is a measure of stakeholder confidence, to rise. Performance-related pay encourages risk-taking, whereas fixed salaries encourage risk-aversion; but as McKenzie and Lee (1998) and others have pointed out, the danger with incentive pay is that it can encourage short-term gain at the expense of long-term well-being. Managers can feel induced by performance pay to sacrifice higher long-term pay-offs in favour of smaller immediate pay-offs that ripen within the performance assessment period. Nowhere is this more evident than in the application of performance-related pay to schools and universities, where academics, parents and teacher unions have documented a shift away from the traditional values of long-term learning towards short-term assessment success. Despite government rhetoric, lifelong *learning* has been usurped by lifelong *assessment* where fixed dispassionate salary has been supplanted by short-term inducements (Kelly, 2004).

In the commercial sector, short-termism is overcome by obliging managers to retain financial benefits like share options until a date well into the future, thus lengthening their time horizons. Something similar is needed in not-for-profit organisations like schools and universities. Headteachers, principals and senior managers in universities should, initially at least, be fixed into a medium-length contract – with safeguards, of course – when being tied to performance. Performance-related incentive structures should be used with a certain amount of circumspection to avoid inadvertently generating perverse incentives, like short-termism and situations where employees are incentivised to hide faults. Incentives can have a negative effect if used in the wrong way or if incorrectly structured.

The best approach to incentivisation in the education sector is to involve as many stakeholders as possible: national and local trustees; employees and governors; parents and students. It is not a zero-sum game, as is generally thought, where one stakeholder's loss is another's gain. It is in part a cooperative, mixed-motive game in which collegiality and individualism can both be nurtured to everyone's benefit. Inducement pay does not necessarily work in opposition to teamwork. Whereas commercial organisations compete with each other by producing similar services at lower prices or services supplied with greater convenience to the consumer, schools and universities compete on the basis of matching service to expectation and reputation. Within reason, cost has nothing to do with it, and although schools, colleges and universities can make themselves friendlier, they cannot make themselves more convenient.

Not all schools operate in the same market, of course. Different schools cater for different expectations. Many of England's leading *private* schools are comprehensive in terms of academic ability, but selective in terms of wealth and social class; and many of England's leading *state* schools are selective in terms of academic ability, but socially comprehensive. Leading private schools sell a product that prepares students to be confident 'public people' in a patristic sense. Typically, their students look forward to inherited wealth, so escaping penury is not a measure of success for them. Leading state schools, on the other hand, provide a product that, for many students, is the silver bullet that can slay the evils of poverty and ignorance. Different services for different markets; different incentives for different measures of success. It is crucial for managers to employ smart incentives and to understand them. For educational institutions planning to introduce an element of performance-related pay, this means employing different inducements in different sectors.

In theory, incentive schemes are necessary because the interests of employees do not always coincide with the interests of employers or managers. Good incentives encourage reluctant staff to act not in their own selfish interests, but in the interests of the school or university. Management by diktat cannot carry the day in education, even if staff feel a sense of obligation to do what they are paid to do to the best of their abilities. Incentives are simply a cheaper substitute for giving orders that would otherwise go unheeded (McKenzie & Lee, 1998). Incentive schemes can also be used to reinforce objectives and strengthen an organisation's collective effort towards achieving them. They can be an aid to good communication. This author's experience suggests that the dissemination of critical information by internal memoranda is not successful: importance and urgency are seldom communicated effectively, and there is a certain perverse credibility to be gained among staff by ignoring them (Kelly, 2004).

In communities of (more-or-less) equally qualified professionals, like schools and universities, the motivation generated by incentive schemes frees staff to use their specialist/localised knowledge to overcome resistance to organisational aims; in other words, to reconcile the conflict between individual and collective interest. Without incentives, and in the absence of command-and-control management, individual know-how cannot be properly coordinated to the benefit of both the organisation and the individual. The ideal is to operate a system of incentives that encourages employees to pursue their own selfish interests, but at the same time benefit the organisation and colleagues. The greater the perception of compatibility between individual and collective interest, the more desirable it is to have greater freedom for individuals. In a perfect world, staff would be given complete freedom to act in their own interest, and this would coincide fully with the collective organisational interest. In the real world, however, motivating teachers, lecturers and researchers is a mixture of market incentivisation and government control, so full coincidence of motivation is impossible.

The benefits accruing from incentives accumulate over time as incremental differentials are compounded. Incentive schemes can be the difference between success and failure, and although they are difficult to get right in schools and universities, and no one size fits all, there are some underlying principles that should be adhered to. One of the most important is the desirability and importance of creating *residual claimants* out of staff in receipt of performance-related pay; in other words, it is desirable that staff are given ownership rights to their own benefits. They should receive benefit in a form that allows them ownership of it; otherwise, there is no incentive to use resources sparingly, to reduce waste or to help maintain a lean organisation as described in Chapter 9. It is one of the difficulties with incentivisation in education. In universities, for example, it is common practice to allow researchers who win external research funding to retain a small percentage of project income, but typically this can be kept only in a 'retained contribution' or 'services rendered' account owned by the university and can be used only for work-related things like conference travel. Such funds are gradually forfeited to the university on a sliding scale as the years go by, and in the hurly-burly of academic life, as good researchers act opportunistically in pursuit of research funding, this can be a source of grievance as the 'incentive pot' drains away through no fault of the beneficiary. In such a system, there is no residual claim and no ownership of the performance reward.[1] It is a similar situation in schools, where senior managers cannot be made the beneficiaries of their own good decisions and cannot act as residual claimants. Admittedly, there are good reasons for this, as financial scandals like that in the Roslyn School District in New York, demonstrate. Frank Tassone, the district's charismatic superintendent, stole (with an associate) more than $11 million from the school budget in the largest public school embezzlement in US history. Dr Tassone was a very effective leader. During his 12 years in charge, Roslyn High School entered the top ten in national rankings of the best public schools! A month before the embezzlement was exposed (in May 2004), the *Wall Street Journal* ranked Roslyn the sixth-best public high school in America (Kim, 2020).

Incentives of course, need not be financial. They can be benefits in kind, such as more convenient annual leave or relief from some unpalatable admin work; and simple politeness can also go a long way towards encouraging more and better work from employees. No set of incentives, financial or other, is ever perfect, and this gives rise in the education sector to the question of meta-incentives; the incentive to find the right incentives for others. Typically, systems do not currently incentivise local authority education managers and university vice-chancellors to find the best set of incentives for teachers, lecturers and researchers.

Moral hazard, adverse selection and principal-agent resistance

In the UK, when the introduction of performance-related pay for staff in schools was proposed, it was claimed that it would 'modernise the teaching profession' by recruiting, retaining and promoting effective practitioners, and would 'raise the status of teachers' in their own eyes and in the eyes of the public (Barber, 2001). It was intended to create a culture in which teachers would take prime responsibility for pupil performance and be rewarded accordingly. The obvious difficulty is one of measurement; specifically, how to reward teachers in schools serving challenging communities where 'obvious' metrics like examination results cannot fairly be applied. One suggested answer was a 'contextualised value added' (CVA) metric that would measure the value added by a school in the social context of its community during the course of the year and reward teachers accordingly. The problem with this was finding a reliable measure of CVA that would command the confidence of teachers – necessary to prevent them from deserting poorly performing schools – that would not itself become a driver of (low) pupil attainment. For example, if teachers were rewarded for achieving relatively poor *raw* exam results, which were then deemed to be good when context was taken into account because the school had a high percentage of (say) Bangladeshi boys, this would lower the expectation that society had of that section of the population and the expectation that Bangladeshi boys had of themselves. Another solution might have been simply to add a salary weighting to teacher salaries for working in poorly performing schools, but the concern here was that it might create a perverse incentive – especially at the boundary of 'poor' and 'good' performance – to keep a school 'poor-performing' in order to retain the additional salary. The whole idea was fraught with difficulties and unsurprisingly, in the UK school sector at least, it withered on the vine.

Traditionally, for cultural reasons and as a result of the instincts aroused by the issues described earlier, time-based seniority systems have predominated in schools and colleges, although West (2001) has argued that it was the failure of managers properly *to use existing* mechanisms to reward performance, rather than any inherent flaws in the system, that was largely to blame for its ineffectiveness. The old monolithic incremental pay scales, which afforded so few opportunities for advancement outside the mere fact of getting older, were never intended to provide automatic progression to the top of some notional ladder (Marsden et al., 2000). It was simply that checks and sanctions, which existed, were rarely invoked (Megaw Inquiry, 1982). It was not that the old seniority-based system was inherently flawed; it is rather that it was badly managed and compounded by a promotion structure that rewarded good teachers by taking them out of the classroom.

Whatever the relative importance of the various cultural and practical influences on the old, traditional, time-based promotion system, the introduction of performance-related pay for teachers likely would require, and be facilitated by, the break-up of large education bureaucracies like local education authorities and school districts. *School-level* performance targets are more easily set and appraised than *nationwide* or *city-wide* or *regional* ones, though this in itself is not sufficient to overcome opposition to the ethos of individual self-interest that underpins performance-related pay. Schools are subject to a tension in this respect: on the one hand, the need for team-based approaches to improvement because research (Teddlie & Reynolds, 2000) and instinct suggest that it makes for better schools; and on the other hand, a performance-related pay disposition towards individualism as a means of raising classroom performance (Kelly, 2004).

The link between incentives and performance

When staff have significant discretion in the performance of their duties, the two main links between incentives and performance are the ability to recruit and retain effective workers, and motivation (see Figure 19.2). These two parallel claims need to be examined in some detail in connection with performance pay and reward. Firstly, while in theory at least, performance-related pay offers schools and universities a greater opportunity to retain effective staff, its success depends on the extent to which experienced teachers, lecturers and researchers are motivated by money (and to a lesser extent, the esteem and recognition of others) to stay when they would otherwise leave. Secondly, performance-related pay purports to increase motivation, although even in the commercial sector, where performance bonuses have supplanted security and loyalty as the main motivation for recruitment, the veracity of that assertion has been questioned (Marsden et al., 2000). Whether justified or not, the supposed link between performance-related pay and motivation for teachers and academics depends largely on the transferability (to the not-for-profit sector) of performance-related pay's two supporting tenets: moral hazard and adverse selection; and principal-agent resistance.

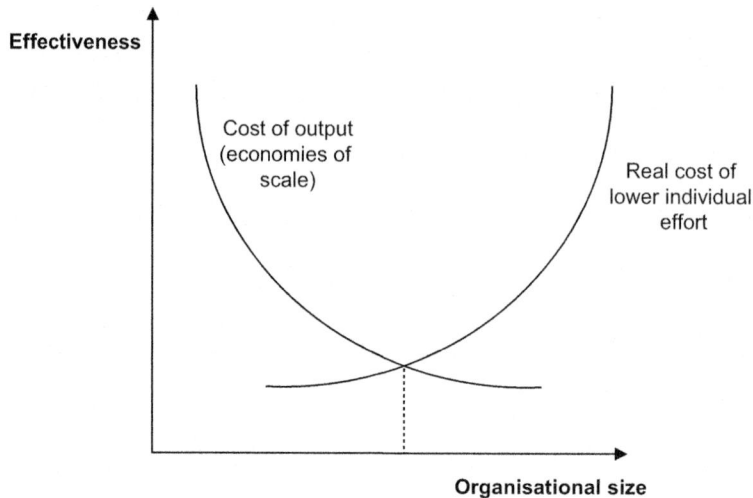

FIGURE 19.2 The optimal size of an educational organisation.

Moral hazard and adverse selection

In any situation where payment is made by an organisation to an employee, labour and expertise are sold by the employee at a notional market value. Teaching and academic employment is no exception. Properly qualified teachers and researchers sell their labour and expertise under a warranty-type arrangement whereby their postgraduate status and pedagogic qualifications underwrite, initially at least, a certain minimum standard of performance.[2] While this reduces the incentive for academic staff (the sellers of their labour and expertise) to act dishonestly, since they can be held accountable professionally, an environment in which performance bonuses constitute a significant element of pay simultaneously offers two distinct opportunities for schools and universities (the buyers of the same labour and expertise) to act dishonestly:

- School or university authorities can unfairly withhold performance bonuses from teachers or lecturers safe in the excuse that, since their labour is under 'warranty', they can be blamed for not coming up to some arbitrary level of performance. Shifting criteria thus creates a *moral hazard* for the unfortunate teachers or academics who, as with every warranty, must rely on systemic restrictions to avoid spurious claims of failure made against them. For an incentive system to function properly under such conditions of moral hazard, teachers, lecturers and researchers need to be confident that they can rely on regulation for protection. The same restrictions on individual schools and universities that are needed for the protection of staff against the moral hazard have an additional beneficial effect: they serve to encourage honesty among institutions *collectively*, for they know that if they act dishonestly towards staff now, all schools and universities in the future will have to pay higher salaries with more easily attainable assessment criteria. Collectively, therefore, schools and universities have a rational incentive to act socially rather than selfishly; a situation analogous to the

Prisoner's Dilemma in game theory (Kelly, 2003), and one that is considerably in teachers' favour.

- The second opportunity for schools and universities to act dishonestly through an incentive pay and reward scheme arises from an 'information imbalance'. Managers have more useful information at their disposal about the pay-off structure than do staff, especially if central or local government intervenes, as it must, to complicate the system with limits and guidelines. Some schools and universities use obfuscation to set more difficult criteria or demand more work for a given bonus. If a local authority offers performance bonuses just equal to the pay for the average amount of extra work required to earn the bonuses, then only those schools and universities who know that they will get more than the average amount of extra work from staff will offer performance-related pay at all. This amounts to a problem of *adverse selection*; only those teachers and researchers who estimate that they can earn their bonuses for an amount of work *less than they would do anyway* benefit from it. An analogous situation exists in the commercial sector with warranties. Some users are naturally harder on a product than others, without being downright abusive. If a manufacturer offers a warranty equal to the cost of the average repair bill, only those buyers who think they will be harder than average will purchase the warranty. Therefore, by definition, warranties will always be sold at a loss, and if any attempt is made to increase the price, ever more reasonable users will drop out of the market. Only the worst users will find value in them. Inducement pay may therefore have the opposite effect to that which is intended. It may merely create a following of teachers and academics who can achieve their targets and bonuses without doing what they perceive as additional work.

Principal–agent resistance and organisational size

Incentive schemes exist in all sectors of the economy, though sometimes in latent forms. They are not confined to commercial companies. In schools, for example, inducements are generated by the prospect and process of advancement to deputy headship and headship, despite the impression being created that teachers and lecturers just get on with the business of being efficient and effective without the need for 'vulgar' inducement. This is a convenient simplification. On the one hand, it ignores human psychology; on the other, it contradicts the rationale for organisations existing at all. Large organisations like local education authorities and school districts exist because the cost of replacing their internally organised activities – cleaning, administration, finance and accounting, catering and so on – with market-driven ones is higher or the delivery is less secure or more unstable. Large organisations benefit from economies of scale. In schools and universities, when tasks are divided among a larger number of staff along the lines of specialism, they become more efficient at what they do and can service more students in any given period of time. Effectively, large organisations swap control for a type of free market exchange that would exist if everyone were driven solely by individual need.

However, large organisations cannot grow ever larger and expect economy-of-scale benefits to increase in line with that expansion (Kelly, 2004). Firstly, larger organisations have more communication problems: the bureaucratic pyramid becomes depersonalised, and individuals within it start to resent being directed only as part of a huge monolith. Entropy increases, and consequently, employees must be offered bigger and better inducements to stay effective within the expanding structure.

Secondly, within larger organisations, conflicts of interest arise between certain identifiable groups. The goals of *principals*, who organise staff to pursue the interests of the organisation, and those of *agents*, who deliver the outcomes on the front line, can sometimes be in direct conflict. Principals must get agents to work with the best interests of the organisation in mind, and more frequently in large organisations, agents resist this and create a consequent 'resistance cost'.

Thirdly, employees have more opportunity to shirk responsibility in larger organisations because their lack of contribution is less noticeable (Coase, 1988). It is not that workers become more dishonest; it is rather that their incentive deteriorates as the group expands (Isaac & Walker, 1988; McKenzie & Lee, 1998; Olson, 1965). Group size and individual effort are inversely related (Furnham, 1993), so to get the same amount of work from each agent, it becomes necessary for large organisations to offer ever-larger incentives like performance-related pay.

Economy-of-scale functions, which for schools and universities depend on the nature and extent of their taught courses and research activities, the built environment and the support services offered, are decreasing ones (see Figure 19.2). In contrast, the extent to which size lowers individual teacher and researcher effort and increases communication and coordination costs is an *increasing* function, influenced by the quality of dynamic leadership in the institution and the extent to which staff feel ownership of the changes that have resulted from the expansion (Fullan, 1991). These two complimentary functions intersect at a point that indicates the optimal size of the institution, and indeed the perceived need for performance-related reward, and the practice of paying it in the education sector suggests that schools and universities may have exceeded their optimal size, although that varies with context and situation.

Transplanting incentive systems into the education sector

A good appraisal system should have clear objectives, be capable of accurate measurement of outcomes and have transparent assessment criteria supported by a culture of responsibility. The search for such a system for schools and universities is made all the more important by the fact that schools and universities simply do not have the resources or the freedom to gear the performance element of staff pay highly enough. Research in the commercial sector has shown that performance-related pay is sometimes regarded by employees as a device for cutting expenditure, that it is used to reward favoured employees, that management have quotas for recipients, and that good work is not always rewarded (Marsden et al., 2000; Milkovitch & Wigdor, 1991). Sadly, this is very commonly the case in universities, where annual appraisal is criterion-referenced at departmental level but then adjusted normatively afterwards at faculty level to reduce the number of staff who get rewarded for exceeding agreed performance targets. Exceptions are made for a coterie of favoured halo-effected staff so that the overall effect is to make incentive systems in universities ridiculous and amateurish. And, of course, not all of the assumptions that underpin incentive systems in the commercial sector translate well to an education. Firstly, many graduates go into teaching for altruistic reasons and are driven by a strong desire for independence. To that extent, they may resent the assumption that relatively small performance-related increments in pay would motivate them to greater effort. In addition, the principal–agent/moral hazard model of performance-related pay assumes a Theory X view of staff and their work (see Chapter 6), but there is no evidence to suggest that this simplistic and somewhat outmoded view represents reality in schools and universities any better than other models. The Theory X assumption that teachers and academics are lazy and do the least amount of work they can get away with is not borne out by research, which suggests that a mixture of commitment to individual institutions and to individual students is enough to overcome any supposed tendency towards sloth (Scott et al., 2000).

Finally, it is difficult to measure output in the education sector, especially in the university sector where degree classifications are crude and not fine-grained like examination grades in schools, and employment prospects are not easily attributable in any causal way to input variables. What distinguishes schools and universities from manufacturing and commercial service activities is the profusion and confusion of influences. In education, it is not axiomatic that low effort results in low output. There is, almost by the very nature of the endeavour, a large overlap between high and low performances, representing an area where, for a wide variety of reasons, high tutor effort results in low student achievement (and more rarely, the converse). In education, the variables are simply not controllable.

Conflict between the individual and the collective

It could be said that moves towards greater accountability in schools, colleges and universities is a manifestation of the fact that teachers and academics are not trusted by policy-makers with conducting the business of education. It has resulted in a culture of compliance across the sector and an expectation of surveillance through appraisal by managers fixated with workload models, but it would be a mistake to think that these phenomena are unique to education. In the commercial sector, there has similarly been a fear that principals and agents could collude to exploit their position at the expense of stakeholders. To reassure themselves, principals bond themselves voluntarily to stakeholders' interests. They throw in their lot with them and, in this way, stakeholders are reassured to know that managers will suffer almost as much as they will if things go wrong. A potentially *competitive* situation is transformed into a *cooperative* one 'by declaration'. Regular accountability, inspection and assessment reporting are as much a benefit to managers in this respect as they are to stakeholders; they reduce the opportunity for corruption, but more importantly, they reduce the *suspicion* of corruption. That is why in the commercial sector, the market looks unfavourably on directors selling their holdings in listed companies: it lessens the prospect that managers will suffer alongside shareholders if things should go wrong.

Ultimately, success is a question of cooperation, but it doesn't just happen, despite the moral obligation some staff feel to do their best for the collegiate. Cooperation comes about largely as a result of inducements. Good incentives motivate individuals to act in the interest of the collective while at the same time being selfish, but sometimes the situation is complicated by conflict between individual teachers and researchers, and between organisations. Game theory suggests that incentivising cooperation is something that comes about of itself in situations where colleagues agree in advance to arrangements that punish those who choose non-cooperation. It is important that headteachers, principals, deans and vice-chancellors are able to identify dilemmas as they arise within and between institutions, and with external agencies. Schools and universities that have evolved through cooperation are generally stronger because staff have developed an innate sense of belonging to something bigger than themselves, though they might still wish to work independently. This offers education managers the potential to develop synergies, but they must be harnessed carefully because ultimately, staff cooperate effectively only when their own interests are *also* served. The trick for managers, therefore, is to arrange incentives so that this happy coincidence of interests comes about. The natural instinct is for personal survival, and good incentives are those that cater to that instinct through cooperation with like-minded people.

Paying employees on the basis of output

Incentives do not affect *all* forms of behaviour, but as a general principle, if employees are rewarded for doing something, they will do more of it, even if it is unsociable. There is a rate of pay at which most people would work any time of the day or night, and within reason, managers have to find that level of remuneration and ensure that it is tied in some way to performance.

In theory, those who are self-employed have the perfect incentive scheme. They bear all the risk and reap all the benefits in line with the performance of the business, but this is a rare congruence (McKenzie & Lee, 1998) and is not the situation in education. Usually, there is a difference between what managers want and what staff want, and the bigger the workforce, the greater the divergence. In large organisations especially, staff are separated from senior managers by layers of bureaucracy, good communications are more difficult and the time between discovering faults and correcting them is longer. In addition, employees perceive (correctly) that as a proportion of overall output, their contribution is relatively small, and opportunities for shirking are many. Supervision is also more difficult, and staff can exploit that, so managers must design and maintain appropriate incentive schemes to maintain productivity.

Some ways of incentivising employees involve money; others do not. Loyalty, trust and honour all have important roles to play in management, especially in schools and universities, but they are sometimes insufficient in themselves to maintain staff commitment to the aims of the organisation. The simplest way of complementing these virtues is to make employees stakeholders in the organisation. As such, their reputational reward is conditional on the success of the enterprise and therefore on their own output. The greater the output from employees collectively, the greater is each individual's reward.

Ideally then, in theory, it might appear that organisations should dispense with salaries altogether and just pay piece-rate; that is to say, pay staff *solely* on the basis of output. In the case of teachers, lecturers and researchers, this would mean payment by examination results or similar. Such piece-rate remuneration is rare, even in sectors like sales and marketing where it is most easily applied. Most pay is tied simply to time, though of course *all* employment is contingent in some way on the economic success of the enterprise. If employees do not add to an organisation's output, everyone will eventually be made redundant, and that goes for academics in a university department as easily as staff in a high street department store.

There are many explanations why piece-rate pay is not more widely used. Firstly, the output of employees cannot always be reduced to 'pieces'. In particular, it is difficult to measure objectively the output of workers like teachers, academics, researchers and educational support administrators. Some would say it is difficult even to *define* their work. Secondly, while employees might be fully motivated towards organisational goals by piece-rate pay, the complexity of service processes today, even in education, is such that there is no guarantee that proper motivation brings about an increase in actual output. In addition, it is likely that the complexity of these internal processes results in less than adequate job appraisal because so few managers can understand every aspect of every job, so there is uncertainty as to who exactly is to be held responsible for each outcome, good or bad. In university faculties, for example, does any single line manager understand the intricacies of every field within every discipline within the faculty? At the end of the day, what gets assessed is what can be measured; everything else is ignored. And in jobs like teaching, lecturing and researching, that is pretty much everything!

Thirdly, if employees were paid solely on the basis of quantity – for example, the throughput of master's students or the generation of fee income – there would be an incentive to sacrifice quality in order to increase output 'count'. In schools, if teachers were paid on the number of top grades in state examinations, there would be little incentive to teach weak students or to teach anyone anything that is not examinable. It would be the same for university lecturers who would quickly abandon any extra encouragement for their brightest students, concentrating instead solely on the number and classification of degree results. This situation is further compounded by the fact that teachers and lecturers are not always in control of the factors that affect their own success in terms of output. It is not reasonable to pay (or refuse to pay) people for something that is outside their spheres of influence. Being sensible about this can in itself result in increased productivity as a result of increased goodwill between management and workforce.

In education, piece-rate systems can have the opposite effect from that intended: they can reduce output as employees are induced to lower productivity for the same rate of pay, rather than raise productivity for greater pay. It is important for managers to get incentives right and to be perceived as dependable in terms of sticking to agreements. Changing the terms and conditions of productivity agreements should be attempted only when the way of doing a particular job has fundamentally changed since the agreement was drawn up. Delivering university degree courses and online teaching by schools during the Covid epidemic is a case in point. The unpopularity of the performance-related element of teacher pay in the UK proposed in 2000 can be traced to something similar. The job had not changed significantly since previous pay and conditions agreements were made, yet at a stroke, the system of reward was altered. In fact, so blatant was this breach of procedure that the new pay system, which was intended to be introduced in September 2000, had to be delayed initially for two years because it failed to meet the *legal* obligation to engage in prior consultation (West, 2001). Thus it was that the paymaster – in this case the government – came to be perceived by teacher unions as undependable, with the result that some teachers and heads lowered their levels of performance so that they just met the targets set for them and thereby preserved the option of achieving the following year's targets more easily. Clearly, these employees felt that any increased 'productivity' would be used against them in the future and that their employers would take advantage of them. Effectively, teachers were perversely induced to lower productivity.

In jurisdictions where it does exist, incentive pay for education workers has both a fixed salary component and a performance element. It is a compromise between fixed time-based salary and performance-based pay. Generally, such compromises are beneficial to both employers and staff because they reflect the fact that output depends not just on the behaviour of teachers, lecturers and researchers, but on external factors as well. In education, for example, examination results depend not just on an individual teacher's classroom performance or on the quality of the formal lectures given in a university, but on the whole-school, whole-faculty or whole-university performance of senior managers, the performance of academic colleagues, peer-support, the general work ethos and support systems that pervade the school or university, and so on.

The overall problem for managers in schools and universities that have an element of performance-related pay – for example, the award of salary increments – is how to set challenging but appropriate targets by getting staff to reveal the full potential of their students when they know that that information can adversely affect performance criteria and reward. Common sense suggests that if there is a 'game to play', staff will underestimate the innate potential of their students or overestimate the difficulties of winning research funding so as to preserve the greatest potential for 'exceeding targets', with the minimum of effort, when it comes to their annual appraisal.

Notes

1 It should be said that there are tax incentives for operating a 'services rendered' account as (at the time of writing) it is not taxable as a benefit-in-kind.

2 This warranty arrangement works both ways, of course – the reputation of teachers and researchers affects the reputation of the school or university – but it is usually the school/ university that warrants the teacher/researcher, and not the other way round.

20

MEASURING RESPONSIBILITY

A 'job' is defined as a set of recognisable, recurring duties and responsibilities assigned to an 'incumbent'. These duties and responsibilities, discharged through 'work', are collectively the 'functions' of a job, and a 'job description' is a public narrative statement of these functions. The term 'job' is not commonly used for salaried professions who prefer euphemistic terms like 'position' or 'role' to imply something over and above what waged non-professionals do, but except for these subtle social distinctions, they have the same meaning. A 'job profile' is an extended, contextualised description. It should include general information about the working environment and the management structure, and it should describe the skills and 'know-how' required to do the job successfully (Kelly, 2004).[1]

Know-how is a form of competence capital. It is the sum of technical or scientific knowledge, managerial and human relations skill, and problem-solving ability.

- For schools, colleges and universities, *technical knowledge* ranges from simple familiarity with routines to externally recognised expertise and professional eminence in pedagogy or an academic discipline.
- *Managerial skill* ranges from doing or directing activities similar to each other to managing disparate groups of jobs with different and varied functions.
- *Human relations skill* ranges from normal courtesy in dealing with colleagues to motivating, understanding and influencing reluctant stakeholders to act not in their own interest, but in the interest of the institution.
- *Problem-solving* is the extent to which know-how is required by the incumbent to overcome the difficulties thrown up by the job. People think with what they know, so problem-solving can be thought of simply as a percentage of know-how.

DOI: 10.4324/9781003217220-20

There is a distinction to be made between 'duties' and 'responsibilities'. Responsibilities are the activities that define a job; duties are activities done in pursuit of the responsibility.

A 'manager' is an employee who acts legally on behalf of an employer, and in the sense that managers have authority over 'subordinates', are of a higher rank within the organisation. So job descriptions for managers should concentrate on responsibilities, not duties.

Job descriptions for salaried jobs

The first step in measuring responsibility is to describe it (Kelly, 2004). Job descriptions for salaried jobs in schools and universities should recognise the fact that management jobs exist not only to perform prescribed tasks, but also to play a part in leading development across the whole institution. In that sense, dynamic leadership and management are two facets of the same activity, as argued in Chapter 1. Environment, situation and circumstance change from institution to institution and from manager to manager, but the basic *raisons d'être* remain the same. A job description should clarify that which an incumbent is paid to accomplish. It is the legal basis for agreement between the staff member and the school or university, so it should be a statement about goals and objectives, and it should give stakeholders like students, trustees, governors and the public a clear and understandable picture of the nature and scope of the job. Apart from their obvious legal significance, job descriptions are part of the process of record keeping. In general, they should:

- Specify why a job exists and its primary objectives.
- List accountabilities and the impact of the job on the mission of the school or university; in other words, the effect that the job has on outcomes.
- Specify the extent of the job's freedom to act, and the nature and sources of control limiting the incumbent's ability to take decisions.
- Specify the role of the job in the overall scheme of things and the context in which the incumbent is expected to operate.
- Bring out the technical, managerial, problem-solving and human relations skills required. (These terms and their measurement are discussed in the next section).
- Give a general idea of the magnitude of the job and its 'prescribed' and 'discretionary' elements. The discretionary content of a job consists of those elements where choice is left to an incumbent and where the best course of action must be chosen by the incumbent. It is the part that is perceived by staff to be their *level* of work. The prescribed content, on the other hand, consists of those elements about which an incumbent has no choice.
- Specify the size, scope and nature of each subordinate position reporting to the job.
- Define the job in its own terms and not solely in terms of how it assists or relates to a more senior position.

- Make it known what is needed by way of education, experience, know-how and human relations skills to do the job to an acceptable standard.
- Describe the types of policy and procedure that the incumbent is expected to initiate, interpret or work within.
- State the type of guidance, supervision and direction that will be given to the incumbent by the school or university.

Most educational institutions rely on government circulars and sector-wide agreements regarding conditions of employment for their generic job descriptions. If there are specific personal characteristics associated with the probability of success in doing a job, these should be included in the job description and defined relative to some standard of success; for example, the completion of a professional teaching qualification or a research training programme. In schools and universities, job descriptions give colleagues and outsiders a clear understanding of each role within the institution and clarify accountability for outcomes. While the changing needs of schools, colleges and universities mean that some adjustments usually have to be made to job descriptions over time, at any given instance they should give accurate snapshots of jobs as they are currently constituted. They should state the effect of the job on the quality and quantity of the educational provision to students or to the research community and how the job's primary objectives affect the institutional mission.

The discretionary element of a job is difficult to describe fully in a job description, because the relationship between the member of staff and the job cannot be fully established in advance. However, an initial job description should give some indication as to the areas in which an incumbent can expect to exercise discretion; if not immediately, then at some future stage. The description of the discretionary element is more than just an addendum to the job description. The discretionary element is the part of the job that gives the greatest satisfaction to employees and most enhances the quality of the work done, irrespective of quantity (Kelly, 2004).

The measurement of responsibility

Central to the idea of job evaluation and responsibility analysis is the question of determining appropriate reward and status for staff in their jobs, the subject of the previous chapter. This is an emotive issue, questioning as it does an employee's security, value and usefulness, but before it can even be attempted, it is necessary to distinguish between 'level' and 'quantity' of work. *Level* of work is a measure of the intensity of responsibility in a job. *Quantity* of work is the amount of work done irrespective of the level of responsibility. Research shows that level of work rather than quantity is the aspect of a job that staff think merits differentiation in status and pay (Jaques, 1956). Most people have an intuitive idea about the relative importance of jobs, and critics of job evaluation and responsibility analysis say that to try to quantify it further is virtually impossible and in any case undesirable, but some degree of differentiation must be achieved. Typically, job evaluation ranks jobs by seniority for the purposes of establishing a hierarchy, whereas job *analysis* additionally quantifies the differential between them; in other words, it places a numerical value on each job in an organisation. The complexity of the job and the organisation will determine which is the more appropriate tool in each case.

Job content changes over time, as do job titles, so it is important to have yardsticks that measure level of work that are flexible enough to adapt to changing circumstances. The most accurate and equitable approach to gauging level of work is to use the concepts of 'maximum time span of discretion' and 'range of level of work' (Kelly, 2004).

- *The maximum time span of discretion*
  The level of work in a job can be assessed by teasing out the discretionary content of the job, evaluating how staff review their use of discretion, and then discovering the maximum time that elapses during which the incumbent is authorised or expected to use discretion in relation to the job. The 'prescribed' content of a job in a school, college or university consists of those elements about which the teacher, lecturer, researcher or manager has no choice. There are normally two factors which remove the element of discretion: the fact that targets are set by the headteacher, principal, dean or vice-chancellor and not by the incumbent; and the fact that the methods by which the desired outcomes are to be achieved are themselves more or less predetermined. The 'discretionary' content of a job, on the other hand, consists of those elements about which the teacher, lecturer, researcher or manager *has* freedom; in other words, those elements for which the work itself does not automatically determine the best method. Whatever the relative sizes of the discretionary and prescribed elements of a job, a period of time elapses before the effects of discretion become apparent to a line manager. This is what is meant by 'time-span of discretion', and its maximum for any given job is a measure of the value of that job to the organisation. For example, in business, it may take several weeks before the return of unsatisfactory goods alerts a sales manager to a production problem; or in a school setting, it may take a certain period of time for the inappropriate behaviour of a teacher to come to the attention of the principal. Serious errors of judgement result in quicker reviews of discretion because consequences come to light sooner. Marginal errors do not attract the same attention unless consciously sought out, but cumulatively, they do have a significant impact – a festering incompetence – if a long period of time elapses between error and effect. A dean, headteacher, principal or vice-chancellor can keep time span of discretion to a minimum by reviewing reports as soon as they arrive or can lengthen it by postponing reviews, tending towards the latter as confidence in the work of the subordinate increases. Traditionally, a job with a maximum time span of discretion of less than one month does not carry any managerial responsibility (Kelly, 2004), and research has shown that time span of discretion is not applicable to jobs where the maximum is shorter than a couple of days.

○ *Review of work by a manager.* The mechanisms by which a manager reviews an incumbent's use of discretion can be divided into two categories: a *direct* review of work by a manager and an *indirect* review. A direct review of work occurs when all discretionary elements are examined by the relevant line manager. Merely countersigning something does not constitute a review. An *indirect* review of work occurs when the outcome of work done by an incumbent moves unreviewed to a manager outside the direct line of 'command'. For example, a faculty dean might review the work of a lecturer after dealing with a complaint from students, leapfrogging the Head of Department's role as the lecturer's immediate line manager.

○ *Measuring the relative status of jobs.* The prescribed element of a job should not be used as a determinant of status or remuneration. The relative importance of jobs should only be judged by the amount of discretion exercised. This in turn requires accurate job descriptions so that discretionary components can be singled out for comparison. Every education job has a discretionary component. If a job becomes so automatic that it no longer has any discretionary element, then it should no longer exist as a job for a teacher, lecturer or academic. Generally, the higher the rank of a job, the greater the maximum time span of discretion, and time spans of discretion decrease as one goes 'down the ranks'. This is inevitable, as a line manager could not reasonably work at a shorter time span of discretion than a line managee, since the former must oversee the latter. In education, employees with similar time spans of discretion, irrespective of rank, typically claim parity of status and remuneration. Conversely, incumbents whose remuneration is perceived as being below that commensurate with their time spans of discretion think themselves unfairly treated, and research shows they are the major instigators of grievance procedures (Jaques, 1956). Workers and jobs can be grouped by like time spans of discretion, and an increase in an employee's time span of discretion within the group should be what defines an increase in workload rather than the current fashion for facile 'workload models' that count hours of student contact and other assorted 'beans'. And if such an increase in workload brings the teacher, lecturer or researcher to the next higher-ranking group, then there should be formal promotion. In fact, promotion should be *defined* as the movement from one group to another group with a longer time span of discretion (Kelly, 2004).

○ *The elements of a job that confer status and cause difficulties.* Schools and universities face difficulties as a result of changes in policy, political climate, marketisation, the need for continuous professional development and the expansion and contraction of the education system. Changes nationally in the status and remuneration of teachers and academics, and changes locally in personnel, are fluctuations that can subject a school or university to pressures that disturb its equilibrium. Occasionally, *amount* and *level* of work increase simultaneously without incumbents becoming aware of it (or compensated for it) until subordinates end up doing similar work to managers but without the status or pay. In such a scenario, found predominantly in schools, colleges and university departments that have expanded rapidly over a short period of time, the situation is embarrassing for line managers and line managees alike. From the senior leader's point of view, grievances tend to become very disruptive; from the subordinate's point of view, fair performance appraisal becomes impossible. Teachers, lecturers and researchers usually have an intuitive grasp of the value of their own work in a school or university department, which is kept current by the influx of new staff and the exodus of old colleagues. Furthermore, incumbents test their current status and pay relative to similar positions in other institutions through social contact at conferences or by applying for external jobs as they occur. It is a natural moderation process and the direct result of mobility of labour. So when an academic advances in a personal capacity, but the level of work available within the institution remains the same or decreases, that incumbent either leaves for another job or accepts work at a level below his or her full capacity, which leads to frustration. Equally serious is the phenomenon of losing staff to another school or university who are working at a higher level than their status/rank warrants. These are the people who keep operational standards high. The rump of what remains after these good people leave usually sees a dramatic fall in performance unless top-quality replacements are bought in. Most universities have acute experience of this phenomenon, as the poaching of research-active staff becomes ever more acceptable in a competitive marketised higher education environment (see Chapter 22). And difficulties arise when such vacancies are filled from outside, especially when they command a higher remuneration than was the case previously. It is not that the new higher salary and status is unjustified – the job may have developed a scarcity value – but there can be an awareness among staff that the higher salary is no more than what should have been paid to the previous incumbent anyway if level of work had been properly assessed!

- *Range of level of work*

Increased sensitivity to the concept of maximum time span of discretion brings another evaluative concept into focus: 'range of level of work'. Range of level of work is the widest range within which work can be allocated to a staff member, from the lowest level compatible with the work merely being done to the highest level available to be assigned. Range of level of work cannot be expanded or contracted at will. The upper level is set by the availability of work, and the lower level by the fact that when an incumbent's line manager is doing more than a certain amount of reviewing, there is no time left for the line manager to do his or her own job. At this lower point, it is just as easy for a line manager to do the subordinate's job as to supervise it. The measurement of range of level of work requires leaders and managers to specify the upper and lower limits for all the jobs they supervise and thus lay the foundation for an open and transparent system of appraisal (Kelly, 2004).

The totality of work

Work is the sum of the prescribed and discretionary activities that employees do in discharging their responsibilities. What employees experience as their own level of work is only the discretionary part, but both prescribed and discretionary components interact as part of the totality of work in educational organisations. The prescribed component can be thought of as a boundary around the discretionary component, setting limits for it and stipulating what teachers, lecturers, researchers and academic managers must (or must not) do and the regulations to which they must conform. Within these prescribed limits, incumbents can use their discretion in selecting the best course of action from alternatives. Setting limits for a job is not necessarily a bad thing. It allows staff to concentrate their judgement on their own fields of operation and expertise (Kelly, 2004).

- *Decision-making and choice*
  Dynamic management in schools and universities involves selecting the best course of action from those available and rejecting the alternatives, and only when a task has been completed is it possible to put everything into perspective and discover which action would have been optimal. In jobs with long time spans of discretion, there is always more than one task to be done at any given time, and decisions with respect to entirely different topics must be made in quick succession. In such circumstances, more optimal choices can remain unrecognised for a long period of time. There is a fine balance to be struck between, on the one hand, selecting a course of action immediately in order to get a job done and, on the other, experimenting with novel approaches in the hope that one of them will do the same job more effectively or more efficiently. This is something that in truth has gone unrecognised among the change advocates within the transformational leadership camp (to be discussed in Chapters 23–25).
- Time-span capacity and job size
  The capacity to tolerate uncertainty plays an important part for those who work in schools and universities (Chapters 10 and 24). As tolerance of uncertainty grows, a greater capacity develops to put off decisions in the hope of something better. 'Time-span capacity' is the length of time an incumbent is able to tolerate the delaying effects of exercising discretion; in other words, the length of time that an incumbent can postpone a decision. The capacity to exercise discretion for longer or shorter periods of time is a function of the ability to anticipate consequences. The greater the time-span capacity of a teacher or researcher, the greater is their ability to use past experience as a bridge over uncertainty. Maximum time-span capacity is a measure of the *size* of a job. The greater the tolerance for making decisions in the face of continuing uncertainty, the more senior the position. When principals, deans, headteachers and heads of department talk of being 'weighed down with responsibility', they reflect the fact that they are experiencing too much uncertainty for too long and they feel insecure

as a result. Work is a kind of investment behaviour for schools and universities, investing in the foresight of staff and the ability of tutors and researchers to lengthen their time-span capacities. As such, it is a form of intellectual capital. The bigger the job, the more complex the decision tree, the longer the required period of foresight and the greater the uncertainty. A characteristic feature of management and leadership in schools and universities is the proliferation of alternatives in the decision-making process and the complexity of selecting one course of action from many without the benefit of any quantitative calculation. Good educational decisions, whether in a school, a college, a faculty or across a university, require a considerable amount of foresight.

- *Current and potential time-span capacity*

Research suggests that time-span capacity – the toleration of uncertainty – increases with an incumbent's age until middle age when it slows down, though it depends on the level at which an incumbent is operating. For staff in schools and universities, the growth in time-span capacity tails off sooner, which suggests a need for two differentiating concepts: '*current* time-span capacity' and '*potential* time-span capacity'. The difference between them is in a way a measure of the intellectual capital of a school or university, and the job of education managers is to devise interventions so that potential is both developed and realised. Time-span capacity exerts a strong influence on the level of work an employee seeks out. Ambitious teachers, lecturers and researchers will naturally (but perhaps subconsciously) come to jobs that satisfy their current time-span capacity until a level of work is reached that corresponds to it. Current time-span capacity increases with learning and will eventually outgrow a role so that an employee will look to move on and up. Time-span capacity is the engine of ambition, and managers should have a promotion system in place that recognises the benefits to the institution of restless dynamic learning (Kelly, 2004).

- *The pressure to work at the correct time-span level*

Teachers, lecturers and researchers exert pressure on management to work at their correct time-span capacities by seeking job change within (and sometimes outside) the organisation, by attending training courses and by obtaining additional qualifications. Unfortunately, it is common for many education staff to then change *careers*, despite an initial drop in status and remuneration. The desire to have freedom to act independently is a powerful driving force behind ambition; but too much responsibility leads to anxiety, and this creates a tension for employees between the uncertainty that breeds a desire for supervision and the ambition that encourages independence. It is unlikely that any organisation where there is an absence of ambition and low morale will survive; so it is for managers to see to it that fear and anxiety do not blight the ambition of junior staff. In schools, colleges and universities, there is peer pressure to accept additional responsibility in a way that does not occur in the commercial sector. Teachers want to see school-wide difficulties overcome as effectively as possible, researchers in one discipline want to see all their university departments do well so that the reputation of the *whole* institution is enhanced, and there is a general expectation in staff common rooms that those with the ability to solve problems should use their abilities *pro bono*. Frustration is most common in schools and universities where teachers and relatively junior lecturers foresee difficulties that senior managers do not.

- *Time-span capacity and growth*
  Whether or not a school or university grows depends, among other things, on the collective time-span capacity of its senior management team. If management's time-span capacity is growing beyond the level of work available, management will grow the organisation. If management's time-span capacity is stable, the organisation will be stable in growth terms. And if management's time-span capacity is growing too slowly for the available level of work, the organisation will contract.

Note

1 The technical aspects of this chapter have been described previously in Kelly (2004).

21

A PROFILE GUIDE CHART METHOD FOR JOB EVALUATION

There are three general approaches to job analysis.[1] The first, 'task-centred job analysis', describes work in terms of the outcomes to be achieved, which are themselves enumerated by carrying out a functional analysis of the job or by compiling a task checklist. Task-centred job analysis is limited in its ability to identify similarities across sectors or between job types. The second, 'behaviour-centred job analysis', describes work in terms of processes and behaviours. It is based on the behavioural theories of leadership discussed in Chapters 5 and 6 and focuses on the job holder rather than on job outcomes. It is less specific than the task–centred approach but more transferable, enabling comparisons to be made. The third, *'trait-centred job analysis'*, describes work in terms of the personality traits required to perform the job's functions successfully. This approach, based on the trait theories of leadership discussed in Chapter 2, suffers from the disadvantage of having to find a direct correspondence between job content and human attributes.

Job evaluation falls into the first category; that is to say, it is a form of task-centred analysis. It is basically a systematic way of determining the relative importance of jobs by describing each one piecemeal in terms of its component parts. It is a derivative of classical management and is rooted in the logic of bureaucracy. As a result, its shortcoming is that it sees itself as being entirely scientific, but it is nevertheless a useful tool. Job evaluation starts with the preparation of the job description. Each job is formally described according to its duties, requirements, responsibilities and measurement. Techniques then calculate the value of each to the organisation. The

DOI: 10.4324/9781003217220-21

manner of carrying out this measurement is what distinguishes one type of job evaluation from another (Kelly, 2004). There are three main types:

- *Analytical methods* break down jobs into component factors. The most popular analytical approach is to use a *'points rating'* scheme, which involves choosing compensable factors such as skill, effort and responsibility, and attaching weights to them according to their perceived importance.
- *Non-analytical methods* compare jobs holistically. The most popular non-analytical approaches are 'ranking schemes' and 'classification schemes'. In ranking schemes, jobs are ranked from the highest to the lowest, based on an assessment of each job as a whole and not as an amalgam of component factors. In classification schemes, jobs are divided into classes or families, each of which has a generic classification. Each job is then matched to the nearest class according to its duties.
- *Hybrid methods* are combinations of analytical and non-analytical approaches. They include the time span of discretion approach described in the previous chapter and Profile Guide Chart schemes, which is the subject of this chapter. A new hybrid scheme for evaluating jobs in schools, colleges and universities, which takes account of both time span of discretion and profile guide charts, is developed in this chapter.

A Profile Guide Chart method for education management

The original Profile Guide Chart method of job evaluation had its roots in earlier factor comparison methods. It is widely regarded as the industry standard. The fundamental ways in which jobs can equate with (or differ from) one another are arranged on scales and a 'guide chart' is put together consisting of two or more of these scales brought together in a grid. While each scale is defined only in general terms, each step on it is a progressive refinement in detail (Kelly, 2004).

An evaluation system based on guide charts has a number of underpinning features, some of which require an understanding of scaling techniques as well as an understanding of organisations.

- There are many factors to be considered in the evaluation of a job, but the most important three are:
  - The knowledge required to do the job.
  - The kind of thinking required to solve the challenges commonly faced in the job.
  - The responsibilities assigned to the job.
- A good evaluation system should be able not only to rank jobs in order of importance, but also to measure their relative size; in other words, a good evaluation system should be able to measure the significant *difference* between jobs.
- The focus of job evaluation as a process is on the nature and requirement of a job, not on the skills and characteristics of the member of staff doing it.

These underpinning features suggest a three-factor codification of jobs,[2] each of which has a corresponding guide chart to measure it: know-how, problem-solving and accountability.

Know-how

'Know-how' is the sum of every kind of knowledge and skill required for the acceptable performance of the job (see Table 21.1). Its three dimensions are 'practical scientific know-how', 'managerial know-how' and 'human relations skills':

- *Practical scientific know-how* is the sum of scientific knowledge and teaching and research experience in the field of education. It consists largely of specialised techniques and procedures, and is categorised according to its variety (width) and complexity (depth). Exemplars are given in Table 21.2. Some jobs require a little knowledge of many things; others require a deep knowledge about only a few things. To reflect this fact, practical scientific know-how, on the vertical axis of Table 21.1, ranges from 'Basic Understanding' (A) to 'Professional Eminence' (H).
- *Managerial know-how* is the ability to integrate and harmonise the diverse functions of a job in order to produce desired outcomes for the school or university. It involves, in some combination, skills in planning, organising, co-ordinating, executing, evaluating, directing and controlling resources. Managerial know-how is on the *upper* horizontal axis of Table 21.1 and ranges from 'Non-supervisory' (N) to 'Total' (V).
- *Human Relations skills* comprise the person-to-person and social skills essential to jobs that involve working with people. It is on the *lower* horizontal axis of Table 21.1 and ranges from 'Basic' (1) to 'Critical' (3).

Problem-solving

Problem-solving is the use of know-how to identify, define and resolve problems (see Table 21.3). Teachers, lecturers and researchers think with what they know, even in the most creative aspects of what they do, so problem-solving can be thought of as a simple percentage of know-how. Problem-solving is less important when results can be obtained by the automatic application of skill, rather than by the application of a thinking process to knowledge, so this guide chart measures the extent to which thinking processes must be applied to a job's required knowledge in order to get the desired results (Kelly, 2004). It has two dimensions: 'Thinking Environment' and 'Thinking Challenge':

- *Thinking environment* represents the extent to which assistance is available from colleagues or from precedent. This dimension is on the vertical axis of Table 21.3 and ranges from 'Highly Structured' (A) to 'Abstract' (H).
- *Thinking Challenge* represents the complexity and novelty of the thinking that is required for a job. It is represented on the horizontal axis of Table 21.3 and ranges from 'Repetitive' (1) to 'Uncharted' (5).

TABLE 21.1 Evaluating know-how in schools, colleges and universities

Managerial Know-how

Guide Chart for Evaluating Know-how	N. Non-supervisory: Performance of activities as an individual, not as a professional manager.			I. Minimal: Performance or direction of a group of duties similar in content and aims, being aware of other school or university activities.			II. Related: Incumbent directs a team with variety of duties and aims, or guides group of like sub-duties across several teams.			III. Diverse: Incumbent directs a large team with various duties. Or guides some duties that affect all or most of the school or university.			IV. Broad: Incumbent directs a management team with large functional diversity. Or guides policy that affect all or most of the school or university.			V. Total: Leadership of all management teams, functions, policies and decisions i.e. incumbent is acting as 'head' or chief executive.		
	1	2	3	1	2	3	1	2	3	1	2	3	1	2	3	1	2	3
A. Basic understanding: Incumbent has a basic familiarity with simple school/university routines.	38	43	50	50	57	66	66	76	87	87	100	115	115	132	152	152	175	200
	43	50	57	57	66	76	76	87	100	100	115	132	132	152	175	175	200	230
	50	57	66	66	76	87	87	100	115	115	132	152	152	175	200	200	230	264
B. Elementary skill/ knowledge: Capable of carrying out standard school/university procedures. Use of simple programmes.	50	57	66	66	76	87	87	100	115	115	132	152	152	175	200	200	230	264
	57	66	76	76	87	100	100	115	132	132	152	175	175	200	230	230	264	304
	66	76	87	87	100	115	115	132	152	152	175	200	200	230	264	264	304	350
C. Intermediate skill/ knowledge: Experienced in applying procedures with some deviation. Use of specialist programmes.	66	76	87	87	100	115	115	132	152	152	175	200	200	230	264	264	304	350
	76	87	100	100	115	132	132	152	175	175	200	230	230	264	304	304	350	400
	87	100	115	115	132	152	152	175	200	200	230	264	264	304	350	350	400	460
D. Extended skill/knowledge: Good at implementing school/university systems, with skills requiring technical knowledge.	87	100	115	115	132	152	152	175	200	200	230	264	264	304	350	350	400	460
	100	115	132	132	152	175	175	200	230	230	264	304	304	350	400	400	460	528
	115	132	152	152	175	200	200	230	264	264	304	350	350	400	460	460	528	608

PRACTICAL SCIENTIFIC KNOW–HOW

(Continued)

TABLE 21.1 Continued

PRACTICAL SCIENTIFIC KNOW-HOW

E. Diverse/specialised: Understanding and skill in a variety of activities. Needs command of basic management theory.	115	132	152	152	175	200	200	230	264	264	304	350	350	400	460	460	528	608
	132	152	175	175	200	230	230	264	304	304	350	400	400	460	528	528	608	700
	152	175	200	200	230	264	264	304	350	350	400	460	460	528	608	608	700	800
F. Seasoned diverse/ specialised: Needs command of management theory, a very experienced manager or both.	152	175	200	200	230	264	264	304	350	350	400	460	460	528	608	608	700	800
	175	200	230	230	264	304	304	350	400	400	460	528	528	608	700	700	800	920
	200	230	264	264	304	350	350	400	460	460	528	608	608	700	800	800	920	1056
G. Broad or specialised mastery: Command of educational or management theory through professional development.	200	230	264	264	304	350	350	400	460	460	528	608	608	700	800	800	920	1056
	230	264	304	304	350	400	400	460	528	528	608	700	700	800	920	920	1056	1216
	264	304	350	350	400	460	460	528	608	608	700	800	800	920	1056	1056	1216	1400
H. Professional eminence: Externally recognised expertise in some aspect of management or educational leadership.	264	304	350	350	400	460	460	528	608	608	700	800	800	920	1056	1056	1216	1400
	304	350	400	400	460	528	528	608	700	700	800	920	920	1056	1216	1216	1400	1610
	350	400	460	460	528	608	608	700	800	800	920	1056	1056	1216	1400	1400	1610	1852

1. **Basic:** Ordinary courtesy and effectiveness in dealing with colleagues.	2. **Important:** Influence over and understanding of tutors or researchers and managing subordinates peers are important aspects of the job.	3. **Critical:** Advanced skills have been developed by incumbent in understanding and motivating people, and this is extremely important for the job.

Human Relations Skills

TABLE 21.2 Evaluating know-how in schools, colleges and universities

	Evaluating Know-How	*Exemplars*
P R A C T I C A L **S C I E N T I F I C** **K N O W - H O W**	**A. Basic understanding**: Incumbent has a basic familiarity with simple school or university routines.	**A. Basic**: Attendance records
	B. Elementary skill/knowledge: Capable of carrying out standard school/university procedures. Use of simple programmes.	**B. Elementary**: Administrative returns; preparing basic documentation for school inspection or university REF return.
	C. Intermediate skill/knowledge: Experienced in applying procedures with some deviation. Use of specialist programmes.	**C. Intermediate**: Timetable construction; organising open days, but typically not designing them.
	D. Extended skill/knowledge: Good at implementing school/university systems, with skills requiring technical knowledge.	**D. Extended**: Introducing established systems of pastoral care and student support in schools or universities.
	E. Diverse/specialised: Understanding and skill in a variety of activities. Needs command of basic management theory.	**E. Diverse**: Managing groups or fairly wide-ranging management activities.
	F. Seasoned diverse/specialised: Needs command of management theory or a very experienced manager, or both.	**F. Seasoned**: Managing small changes and problems that are not everyday or predictable; e.g. staff absence and disruption due to strikes.
	G. Broad or specialised mastery: Command of educational or management theory through professional development.	**G. Mastery**: Managing significant changes and problems arising from unusual circumstances such as the Covid-19 lockdown of 2020.
	H. Professional eminence: Externally recognised expertise in some aspect of management or educational leadership.	**H. Eminence**: Leading change in a school/university involved in some innovation or pilot; leading other institutions in the area or nationally.

TABLE 21.3 Evaluating problem-solving in schools, colleges and universities

Thinking challenge

Guide Chart for Evaluating Problem-solving	1. Repetitive Identical situations requiring the incumbent to make simple choices between known things.	2. Patterned Similar situations requiring the incumbent to make discriminating choices between known things.	3. Varied Differing situations requiring the incumbent to search for solutions within an area of known things.	4. Adaptive Variable situations requiring analytical, interpretive, evaluative and/or constructive thinking.	5. Uncharted New or non-recurring path-finding situations requiring development of new concepts and imaginative approaches.
A. Highly structured: Thinking within detailed school/university rules or instructions. Or constant supervision/help.	10% 12%	14% 16%	19% 22%	25% 29%	33% 38%
B. Routine: Thinking within detailed school/university practice. Or immediate help or examples available.	12% 14%	16% 19%	22% 25%	29% 33%	38% 43%
C. Semi-routine: Thinking within well-defined school/university procedures. Precedence helps or ready assistance.	14% 16%	19% 22%	25% 29%	33% 38%	43% 50%

THINKING ENVIRONMENT

Thinking challenge

THINKING ENVIRONMENT					
D. Standardised: Thinking within substantially diverse procedures. Precedence helps or access to assistance.	16% / 19%	22% / 25%	29% / 33%	38% / 43%	50% / 57%
E. Clearly defined: Thinking within a remit of the head/CEO towards specific goals. Guided a lot by practice and precedent.	19% / 22%	25% / 29%	33% / 38%	43% / 50%	57% / 66%
F. Generally defined: Thinking within remit of leader towards specific goals. Some intangible unstructured aspects.	22% / 25%	29% / 33%	38% / 43%	50% / 57%	66% / 76%
G. Broadly defined: Thinking in education management concepts. Broadly towards institutional goals. Much intangible.	25% / 29%	33% / 38%	43% / 50%	57% / 66%	76% / 87%
H. Abstract: Thinking within education or management philosophy or human relations theory.	29% / 33%	38% / 43%	50% / 57%	66% / 76%	87%

Accountability

Accountability is the extent to which incumbent tutors and researchers are answerable for their actions. For university researchers, this echoes the definition of 'independent researcher' used by the UK Research Councils in its REF assessment of university research productivity.[3] It is the measured effect of a job on the output of an institution (see Table 21.4) and is related to the opportunity the job provides for bringing about results that are important to the school or university. There are three components to accountability, in the following decreasing order of importance: 'Freedom to Act'; 'Job Impact'; and 'Magnitude'.

- *Freedom to Act* is the degree to which personal or procedural control exists (or does not exist) in a job. It is represented on the vertical axis of Table 21.4 and ranges from 'Restricted' (R) to 'General Guidance' (H). (Exemplars are given in Table 21.5.)
- *Job Impact* is the degree to which a job affects organisational outcomes, in one of four categories:
   - *Primary impact* (P) occurs when a job exercises control over the resources and activities that produce the end results.
   - *Shared impact* (S) occurs when a job that controls the resources that produce the end results is shared equally with one other person, or where there is control of most, but not all, of the significant variables that bring about the end results.
   - *Contributory impact* (C) occurs when a job provides advice, interpretation or support to others so that the desired results can be achieved.
   - *Ancillary impact* (A) occurs when supplementary assistance, information or an auxiliary service is given in support of others.
   Job impact is represented on the *lower* horizontal axis of Table 21.4. There are A, C, S and P categories in each of the six Magnitude categories.
- *Magnitude* (or *Size*) represents the extent to which the school, college or university is encompassed by a job. For example, deputy headship usually encompasses whole-school duties, but it can in other cases be confined to the Sixth Form or to the Junior School. This dimension is represented on the *upper* horizontal axis of Table 21.4, parallel to the Impact dimension. It ranges in six steps from 'Very Small' (1) to 'Very Large' (6). I have designed it to correspond to the UK government's categorisation of schools by size, but it can be adjusted for any jurisdiction.

The scales on the guide charts

The scales on the know-how and accountability charts (Tables 21.1 and 21.4) – but not on the problem-solving chart (Table 21.3) – are expandable to reflect the size and complexity of the school, college or university; and the nomenclature can be adjusted to suit individual circumstance. This is called 'sizing' the guide charts (Kelly, 2004).

TABLE 21.4 Evaluating accountability in schools, colleges and universities

Institution size

Guide Chart for Evaluating Accountability	1. Very small Group 1				2. Small Group 1				3. Medium small Group 3				4. Medium large Group 4				5. Large Group 5				6. Very large Group 6			
Impact =	A	C	S	P	A	C	S	P	A	C	S	P	A	C	S	P	A	C	S	P	A	C	S	P
R. Restricted: Duties subject to explicit instructions or constant personal or procedural supervision.	5	7	9	12	7	9	12	16	9	12	16	22	12	16	22	29	16	22	29	38	22	29	38	50
	6	8	10	14	8	10	14	19	10	14	19	25	14	19	25	33	19	25	33	43	25	33	43	57
	7	9	12	16	9	12	16	22	12	16	22	29	16	22	29	38	22	29	38	50	29	38	50	66
A. Prescribed: Duties subject to direct detailed instructions or very close supervision.	8	10	14	19	10	14	19	25	14	19	25	33	19	25	33	43	25	33	43	57	33	43	57	76
	9	12	16	22	12	16	22	29	16	22	29	38	22	29	38	50	29	38	50	66	38	50	66	87
	10	14	19	25	14	19	25	33	19	25	33	43	25	33	43	57	33	43	57	76	43	57	76	100
B. Controlled: Duties subject to instructions, established routines or close supervision.	12	16	22	29	16	22	29	38	22	29	38	50	29	38	50	66	38	50	66	87	50	66	87	115
	14	19	25	33	19	25	33	43	25	33	43	57	33	43	57	76	43	57	76	100	57	76	100	132
	16	22	29	38	22	29	38	50	29	38	50	66	38	50	66	87	50	66	87	115	66	87	115	152
C. Standardised: Duties subject to standard practices and procedures, and supervision of progress and results.	19	25	33	43	25	33	43	57	33	43	57	76	43	57	76	100	57	76	100	132	76	100	132	175
	22	29	38	50	29	38	50	66	38	50	66	87	50	66	87	115	66	87	115	152	87	115	152	200
	25	33	43	57	33	43	57	76	43	57	76	100	57	76	100	132	76	100	132	175	100	132	175	230
D. Generally regulated: Duties subject to definite procedures. Supervision of short-term results.	29	38	50	66	38	50	66	87	50	66	87	115	66	87	115	152	87	115	152	200	115	152	200	264
	33	43	57	76	43	57	76	100	57	76	100	132	76	100	132	175	100	132	175	230	132	175	230	304
	38	50	66	87	50	66	87	115	66	87	115	152	87	115	152	200	115	132	200	264	152	200	264	350

F R E E D O M   T O   A C T

(*Continued*)

TABLE 21.4 Continued

FREEDOM TO ACT

Freedom to Act	A	C	S	P	A	C	S	P	A	C	S	P	A	C	S	P	A	C	S	P	A	C	S	P
E. Directed: Duties subject to broad policy. Leader directs the incumbent's medium-term results.	43	57	76	100	57	76	100	132	76	100	132	175	100	132	175	230	132	175	230	304	175	230	304	400
	50	66	87	115	66	87	115	152	87	115	152	200	115	152	200	264	152	200	264	350	200	264	350	460
	57	76	100	132	76	100	132	175	100	132	175	230	132	175	230	304	175	230	304	400	230	304	400	528
F. General direction: Duties subject to functional policies. Head, dean/VC directs long-term results.	66	87	115	152	87	115	152	200	115	152	200	264	152	200	264	350	200	264	350	460	264	350	460	608
	76	100	132	175	100	132	175	230	132	175	230	304	175	230	304	400	230	304	400	528	304	400	528	700
	87	115	152	200	115	152	200	264	152	200	264	350	200	264	350	460	264	350	460	608	350	460	608	800
G. Guidance: Duties subject to the guidance of school policy and direction from head, dean or VC.	100	132	175	230	132	175	230	304	175	230	304	400	230	304	400	528	304	400	528	700	400	528	700	920
	115	152	200	264	152	200	264	350	200	264	350	460	264	350	460	608	350	460	608	800	460	608	800	1056
	132	175	230	304	175	230	304	400	230	304	400	528	304	400	528	700	400	528	700	920	528	700	920	1216
H. General guidance: Duties subject to guidance of educational policy and legal limits.	152	200	264	350	200	264	350	460	264	350	460	608	350	460	608	800	460	608	800	1056	608	800	1056	1400
	175	230	304	400	230	304	400	528	304	400	528	700	400	528	700	920	528	700	920	1216	700	920	1216	1610
	200	264	350	460	264	350	460	608	350	460	608	800	460	608	800	1056	608	800	1056	1400	800	1056	1400	1852
Impact =	A	C	S	P	A	C	S	P	A	C	S	P	A	C	S	P	A	C	S	P	A	C	S	P

A = ancillary
C = contributory
S = shared
P = primary

TABLE 21.5 Evaluating accountability in schools, colleges and universities

	Evaluating Accountability	Exemplars
F	**R. Restricted**: Duties subject to explicit instructions or constant personal or procedural supervision.	Admin tasks done immediately upon request from the leader or by events. There is explicit instruction as to method and outcome, both of which are checked constantly. E.g. organising cover for a student group unexpectedly left without a teacher or lecturer.
R	**A. Prescribed**: Duties subject to direct detailed instructions or very close supervision.	Admin tasks that come with detailed instructions, but no explanation or relevancy explained. Tasks are purely bureaucratic. Head, principal, dean of VC checks during the task or at certain stages. E.g. the preparation of a parents' evening.
E	**B. Elementary skill/knowledge**: Duties subject to instructions and established routines or close supervision.	Admin tasks are checked before implementation. Head, principal, dean of VC makes the internal checks in a summative way and gives general instruction as to the best method – the established way of performing the tasks. E.g. checking department budgets for overspend.
E	**C. Standardised**: Duties subject to standard practices and procedures and supervision of progress and results.	The admin tasks typically reveal errors within the current year, next term/semester, say, typically when a complaint is made. There is a standard practice that is normally followed. E.g. a problem in the previous term's teaching rota was not corrected in the next version.
D	**D. Generally regulated**: Duties subject to definite procedures and past precedent. Short-term supervision of results.	E.g. Weekly or termly rosters. Some staff politics is involved and/or the admin tasks reveal errors before next year's equivalent is done. Has a discretionary time span of less than one academic year.
O	**E. Directed**: Duties subject to broad practices and defined policy. Medium-term supervision of results by head, principal, dean of vice-chancellor.	E.g. Main timetable for the year. Head, principal, dean of vice-chancellor works out staffing and curricular implications while the jobber does the rooms, tutors, etc. There is no policy review at year-end, but there may be early warnings. Has a discretionary time span of approximately one academic year.
M	**F. General directed**: Duties subject to definite functional policies. Long-term supervision of results by head, principal, dean of vice-chancellor.	Not a decision-making job, but a functionary one. E.g. does the timetable, but does not make the curriculum decisions. Makes recommendations to the head, principal, dean of vice-chancellor on staffing and other implications so there are long-term goals involved. Or admin tasks where errors go unnoticed for a year or longer, so there is a discretionary time span of more than one year.
T **O**	**G. Guidance**: Duties subject to guidance of the school's policy and direction from the head, principal, dean of vice-chancellor.	E.g. makes the curriculum decisions in addition to doing the timetable, say, but within existing institutional policy. Arranges subject/course options but from an existing list, say. Or constructs a student support programme, but within stated parameters that limit freedom to act.
A **C** **T**	**H. General guidance**: Duties subject to guidance of education policy, legal limits and the institution's official mandate.	E.g. makes and implements policy decisions in curriculum, pastoral and/or other areas. E.g. does the timetable and also decides on the course curriculum offered to various student groups.

For each factor, the reading is a single number. The numbers on the charts increase at the rate of 15% (except for the very small numbers) in order to conform to two general principles of psychometric scaling:

- *Weber's Law*, which states that when comparing objects, one perceives not *actual* difference but the *ratio* of difference to magnitude. So the relationship between numbers in more important than the numbers themselves.
- The concept of *Just Noticeable Difference*, which states that characteristic differences that are noticeable tend to be specific constant percentages. So an evaluator must have, say, a 15% difference between job characteristics in order to notice that one job is bigger than another.

Instinctively, managers also know the '*shape*' of jobs: uphill, flat or downhill. Using guide charts, jobs can be scientifically described on the basis of the relationship between know-how, problem-solving and accountability. An 'uphill' job is one for which the accountability score is greater than the problem-solving score. A 'downhill' job is one in which the accountability score is lower than the problem-solving score. And a 'flat' job is one where the two are equal in size. So an uphill job is one where results are more important than thinking – a *do* job – and a downhill job is one where the use of knowledge through thinking is more important that answerability for results – a *think* job.

Job evaluation using guide charts is a measuring *process*, not a measuring *instrument*, which is why it is possible to modify the scales on the charts to reflect the character and structure of particular schools and universities – for example, whether or not they are comprehensive in their intake of students – and why the charts have the ability to absorb new information on job content over time. It is a relative, not an absolute, measuring process based on four beliefs:

- Every job requires some know-how, some problem-solving and some accountability.
- Guide chart scales reflect degrees to which these three factors are developed and used in a job.
- A relative rank order can be produced for jobs, and differences that reflect their relative importance can be measured.
- Guide charts are driven by principles, rather than by immutable scales or rules, so the process of measurement can be adapted for use in different organisations.

Post-evaluation checks and correlation

The idea of *shape* is what gives the word 'profile' to the title of the guide chart method, and it is shape that controls their relative calibration; in other words, the numbering patterns on the guide charts are set such that proper use produces scores for the factors which, when arrayed for a given job, produce a shape or profile that is recognisable to the incumbent and has face validity. This provides important *post facto* checks on evaluations: the profile or shape of a job should make sense, and the guide chart scores should be compared to scores for bigger, smaller and similar jobs as part of a moderation process. After a job has been evaluated, if the relationship between problem-solving and accountability does not fit the incumbent's perception, there is a strong possibility that an error has occurred. For example, school or university administration jobs should be 'do' jobs; curriculum and course innovation jobs should be 'think' jobs; and personnel and accounting jobs should be 'flat'. And each job should then be compared to others above and below it to see if the scores in any of the three dimensions are too high or too low in comparison. These are what might be called 'sore-thumb checks' (Kelly, 2004).

Guide chart job evaluation has a second check – that of 'correlation' – which involves taking a sample of evaluations and comparing them with known jobs in *other* organisations. A correlation factor can then be worked out that allows a correspondence to be made between the two sets of jobs. Correlation is mostly used for the purpose of remuneration, comparing salaries in one organisation with those in another, but it is important that two spurious effects are first eliminated from the comparison: the *halo effect*, where an incumbent's above-average performance in a job increases the score allocated to a job; and the *horns effect*, where an incumbent's below-average performance decreases a score. Comparison should be between jobs, not between job-holders (Kelly, 2004).

Example of evaluation using guide charts

Highfield School is a large (Group 6) comprehensive school in England with a Senior/Sixth Form of approximately 150 pupils. According to its most recent inspection report, it has a well-established senior management team with two deputy heads. The position of Pastoral Deputy, the more junior of the two, is being evaluated using the guide charts (Kelly, 2004).

The job description is specific as to the deputy's sole and jointly held responsibilities. The incumbent is expected to undertake a significant amount of teaching. This varies from year to year, so the exact time commitment is not made explicit in the job specification. The most important managerial functions of the job include the design, development and implementation of a new whole-school system to monitor pupil progress, and promoting that system among staff, students and parents (see Table 21.6, Panel 2).

Responsibility analysis. The job description is thorough and the responsibilities described in it are onerous and of fundamental importance to the mission of the school. The discretionary element of the job is 'Large' and the maximum time span of discretion for substantive tasks such as the design and implementation of a whole-school system is relatively long – *in excess of one year* – so a large guide chart score can be anticipated. The range of level of work is 'Wide', from assisting the head in the preparation of reports to the design of the whole-school system for monitoring pupil progress (see Table 21.6, Panel 5).

Know-how. Since the job involves managing medium-size change with unpredictable problems and demands *at least* a good command of educational theory

TABLE 21.6 Example of a guide chart evaluation

PANEL 1		
School:	Highfield School	**Ofsted:** <date>
Type:	Comprehensive	
Size:	1300	**Group:** 6
Salary for job:	------	
Equivalent positions:	2 deputy heads	
Membership of SMT:	7: H + 2DH + 3 Senior Teachers + operations manager	

PANEL 2

Position: Deputy Head (Pastoral)
Duties mentioned in job description:
To raise achievement with regard to monitoring pupil progress.
To design & implement a new whole school system for monitoring pupil progress.
To develop base-line testing in Year 7.
To raise teacher awareness of the monitoring system and to gauge its effectiveness
To support teachers in their target setting.
To liaise with the curriculum deputy head.
To organise and chair meetings to discuss and disseminate policy.
To develop study programmes to encourage pupils.
To develop links with outside agencies.
To develop a range of celebratory events for achievement.
To work with department heads to ensure consistency.
To carry out administration for the post.
To assist the head in preparing reports.
To reinforce rules and ethos and to deal with discipline in Year 10.

PANEL 3

Personal qualities required: None specified in job description

PANEL 4

Guide Chart Analysis

Summary: To design, explore, develop, implement, monitor & support a whole-school system for monitoring pupil progress.

Know-how:	F+; III; 3	608		
Problem-solving:	F+; 4 (57%)	347		
Accountability:	F; 6; C+	460	**Total:**	1415

PANEL 5

Responsibility Analysis

Discretionary element:	Large
Max time-span of discretion:	Greater than 1 year
Range of level of work:	Wide

(see Tables 21.1 and 21.2), the assessment of the scientific know-how required for the job is on the boundary of 'Seasoned Diverse/Specialised' (F) and 'Broad or Specialised Mastery' (G). The F+ and G− scores are the same (see Table 21.1), so it can be scored as F+.

The job involves the direction of a large diverse school-wide team and affects the entire school, so managerial know-how is assessed as 'Diverse' (III) (see Table 21.1, upper horizontal axis).

Skills in motivating staff are 'Critical' to the success of the introduction of the system, so this is assessed as 3 (see Table 21.6, lower horizontal axis).

Know-how is scored as 608 (see Table 21.6, Panel 4).

Problem-solving. The job is under the headteacher's direction towards the goal of developing a whole-school system and there are many intangible aspects to the undertaking, so the thinking environment is assessed as being in the upper reaches of 'Generally Defined' (F) (see Table 21.3). As the job demands interpretative and constructive thinking by the incumbent, the Thinking Challenge is assessed as 'Adaptive' (4). It is not quite 'Uncharted' (5) since whole-school systems can be imported from other schools. The thinking required is not path-finding, however imaginative it may turn out to be. Problem-solving is scored as 57%. It is a percentage of know-how. and 57% of 608 is 347 (Table 21.6, Panel 4).

Accountability. The job is subject to functional policy as the head directs the incumbent towards the job's long-term goal. As the deputy is directed by the head rather than by general school policy, the Freedom to Act is classed as 'General Direction' (F) rather than as 'Guidance' (G) (see Tables 21.4 and 21.5).

The Impact of the job is essentially advisory and supportive, particularly in the context of the management structure of the school, and it is not a position shared equally with another. So it is assessed as 'Contributory' (C), but at the upper end (see Table 21.4).

The size of the school places it in the 'Very Large' (6) category (see Table 21.4), so the accountability score is 460 (see Table 21.6, Panel 4).

Notes

1 The technical aspects of this chapter have been described previously in Kelly (2004).

2 A fourth factor, 'working conditions', can be introduced if required to comply with employment legislation for jobs that are hazardous, unpleasant, unsociable or physically demanding.

3 Only staff with 'significant responsibility for research' are eligible to be returned for the REF. The REF definition of 'significant responsibility' is that they must be 'independent researchers'. This is defined as someone who 'undertakes self-directed research, rather than carrying out another individual's research programme'. The REF guidelines include the following indicators of 'independence' (although they vary *slightly* between academic disciplines): leading an externally funding research project as the principal investigator, leading a research group or having won a prestigious research fellowship.

22

MEASURING COMPETITION AND COMPETITIVENESS

The three most common issues for management teams are creating lean efficient organisations, rewarding staff and competing. The first two are internal issues (see Chapters 9 and 19), whereas competition is externally facing, and although much of the literature refers to competition between commercial organisations, schools and universities are no strangers to it.

Porter's Five Forces model

Competition is related to the relative attractiveness of a given market. Generally speaking, the more attractive a sector, the greater the competition. Porter (1980) developed a model to analyse competition based on five forces that determine the relative attractiveness of a market. It can be applied in an education setting; for example, attracting students onto new courses or competing for research funding.

1. Specific barriers for new market entrants.
   - The greater the importance of economies of scale, the higher the entry barrier will be.
   - It is harder to compete against established courses and reputations, and against existing customer loyalty.
   - High up-front funding makes entry into a new market or research area more difficult.
   - It is important for new entrants not to face legal restrictions like research data protection or government regulations like caps on student recruitment.
   - It is important for new entrants to know if existing players have cost advantages that are independent of economy of scale; for example, unique access to specialist facilities in training hospitals or to government subsidies.

DOI: 10.4324/9781003217220-22

- Obviously, it is better for new entrants if there is a low level of retaliation by existing players.

2. The bargaining power of buyers (students or research funders)
   - The easier a service like a taught course or a research facility can be set up, the more students or research funders have bargaining power.

3. The bargaining power of suppliers (schools, colleges and universities).
   - The more suppliers can bargain, the more power they have. On the other hand, when *buyers* like research councils fund in large volumes and are considered prestigious and career-enhancing, the more they can bargain with schools and universities for better prices (like lower research overheads, say).
   - Undifferentiated services make it easier for buyers to play schools or universities off against each other.
   - Higher switching costs increase supplier power.
   - The potential for 'backward integration' is a strong bargaining lever. Backward integration is the process by which an organisation acquires subsidiaries (e.g. student counselling and IT support) which provide certain inputs needed in its supply chain. 'Tapered integration' (partial in-house production) is also a strong bargaining tool.
   - The more a buyer's overall performance is affected by the service, the less price-sensitive the buyer will be.
   - The more information research funders and students have, the better is their bargaining position.

4. Substitute services.
   - A few schools or universities selling to relatively many buyers have more bargaining power.
   - The absence of substitutes increases supplier power because research funders and students have little choice.
   - Schools and universities with a wide customer base have more power.
   - Suppliers have more power when the service is indispensable or when switching is very expensive.

5. Rivalry between existing competitors.
   - It is important to know what advantages competitors have.
   - Rivalry between competitors can lead to aggressive pricing and competition for customers and profits.
   - High fixed costs encourage rivals to fill capacity.
   - When services like research and teaching are sold at low cost, buyers are encouraged to switch at no risk and buy on the basis of price.
   - Diversity of competition makes it difficult to anticipate what the competition will do next.
   - It is important to know if there are high *exit* barriers for strategic, financial or socio-legal reasons (Van den Berg & Pietersma, 2016). For example, having a medical school at a university is rarely profitable in itself; but the prestige of having it adds to other university departments, and *this* has a

financial value. It is similar for private schools offering classical languages like Latin. At other times it can be expensive to 'get out' of a particular market because specialised assets are difficult to sell or re-purpose, or there are binding trade union agreements in place that make it expensive to compensate staff.

Porter's Competitive Analysis model provides an insight into the dynamics of a sector or a market and allows an organisation to make strategic decisions regarding the most attractive position economically and in terms of being able to defend its position. The weaker the five forces, the more attractive the market. An organisation like a school or university can use Porter's model to identify whether new services are potentially profitable, and to evaluate their strategic position. By identifying the strength and direction of each of the five forces, it is easy to assess the strength of the organisation's position, and its ability to generate income profit (or maintain profitability) in a specific market or sector. Van den Berg and Pietersma (2016: 34–35) point out that although Porter's model is popular and powerful, it suffers from the disadvantage that it underplays an organisation's 'intrinsic strengths and ability to develop its core competencies independently of external forces' so that the model is 'reactive rather than proactive and is best used in combination' with other approaches.

The Core Competence model

This issue of core competences is also addressed by Prahalad and Hamel (1990) and Hamel and Prahalad (1994). These are skills and abilities unique to an organisation, and assessing them is an essential component of building strategy. Van den Berg and Pietersma (2016: 36) trace the concept to work by Barney (1991), who suggested that an organisation's tangible and intangible assets are key aspects of its competitive advantage. The core competence model is a strategic tool in determining the assets unique to an organisation; the strengths and capabilities that set it apart from competitors and create value for customers. Whereas Porter's Five Forces model uses the *external* environment as the starting point, the Core Competence model starts with the *internal* environment on the assumption that competitiveness derives ultimately from an organisation's own ability to build core competences from within. Every school, college and university should have something that it can do well, that provides benefits to its students and 'consumers of research', that cannot easily be imitated and that can be leveraged widely to many services. An organisation that 'identifies, develops or acquires unique assets with which to build valuable services can create a long-lasting competitive advantage' (Van den Berg & Pietersma, 2016: 37). The organisation should understand where this 'uniqueness' comes from and how it can be supported, the new skills and technologies that will be needed in the future and the implications for how it interacts with its stakeholders. The future will inevitably involve change and uncertainty management (to be discussed more fully in Chapter 24) to oversee the introduction of services that do not yet exist.

For research-intensive universities in particular, it is about futures thinking; namely, looking at the organisation not in terms of its constituent units, but as a collection of core competences, and looking at how it functions overall. It is about building and rebuilding the strategic architecture of the organisation, and to do this it is useful for managers to put themselves in the role of the customer to see how their needs are likely to unfold in the short-to-medium term.

The strategic architecture of an organisation is allied to Senge's 'systems thinking'. It is a framework that sets up a school or university to make the most of emerging opportunities. It addresses issues such as: the future skills and competences that need to be developed; how new stakeholder groups will (probably) behave in, and engage with, new markets; and which development opportunities should be prioritised. The process of looking at strategic architecture through the lens of core competences stimulates management to think about staff capabilities that give the organisation an edge over competitors. The core competences of a learning organisation range from the intellectual capital of employees (see Chapter 11) to synergising technologies. They include the ability to integrate multiple skills, to look at services from the student and research-funder perspective, and to learn from failures. The core competences themselves are difficult to define individually, but collectively, they offer competitive advantage and are unique to each school and university in the way they come together.

Regarding futures-thinking, organisations sometimes use road-mapping to create a common vision, to forecast future developments in technology and in the market, and to identify the consequences of those developments. Road-mapping clarifies future objectives based on a view of how technology and markets will develop, and how to achieve those objectives. Van den Berg and Pietersma (2016) identify four different types of road map: whole-sector road maps; service–market road maps; service–technology road maps; competence–research road maps.

- *Whole-sector road maps* are those in which the expected development of an entire sector is mapped out. The process minimises the risk to individual schools and universities.
- *Service–market road maps* combine the expected development of *services* with the expected development of *markets*.
- *Service–technology road maps* combine the expected development of *services* with the expected development of *technology*. They are combinations of market analyses, product assessments and technology scans and are used to set up an organisation's research and development plan.
- *Competence–research road maps* analyse and describe the core competences and research needed to create particular new technologies.

In schools and universities, road maps are planned visualisations of the future. They all start with brainstorming new ideas for services, courses and research; then doing an analysis of the rewards, unique selling points, risks, resources, and return-on-investment for each suggestion; rank-ordering those scores, choosing the ones with the highest rewards and the lowest risk and investment; and finally drawing up a plan, a timeline and a list of resources needed to bring one or more of those ideas to market. Market analysis looks from the *outside in* and is carried out to identify new and long-term trends and needs, but assessments and technology scans look from the *inside out* and identify possible new technologies (Van den Berg & Pietersma, 2016). A good road map will be based on accurate, well-structured information, both internal and external data, will include stakeholder viewpoints, a good alignment between research and development funding and service development, a focus on potential synergies between suppliers and buyers and the potential to adapt existing technology to deliver new courses and research.

Measuring competitiveness: the Herfindahl Index

The Herfindahl Index (HI) is a measure of the extent of competition between organisations in a sector.[1] It is widely applied in mergers, competition and antitrust law in the US (Lovett, 1988) and is used to measure economic concentration and diversity in investment portfolios. HI is defined as the sum of the squares of the market shares of the 'N' largest, most significant firms within an industry, where the market shares are expressed as fractions.

$$HI = \sum_{i=1}^{N} s_i^2$$

where s_i is the market share of firm i in the market.

HI can range from $1/N$ to 1, where N is the number of firms in the market, representing anything from a huge number of small firms to a single monopoly producer. If N is very large, the lower limit tends to zero. A high HI indicates a lack of competition, and an increasing HI over time suggests that some organisation is increasing its market power. The Herfindahl Index is superior to other competition metrics because it gives more weight to larger firms since market shares are squared prior to being summed.

When all firms have *equal* shares in the market, the *reciprocal* of the HI is simply the number of companies in a sector. For example, in a market with five competing organisations each with a 20% market share,

$$HI = 5\left(0.20^2\right) = 0.2$$

the reciprocal of the index is,

$$HI^{-1} = 5$$

When firms have *unequal* shares, the reciprocal of the index indicates the 'equivalent' number of firms in the sector, and the HI can distinguish between situations that otherwise might be regarded as similar. A simple example can illustrate this. Suppose that in one situation six large firms produce between them 90% of the goods in a market, 15% each, and the remaining 10% of the output is divided equally among 10 small producers (1% each). And suppose that in a second situation, one firm produces 80% of the goods in a market while five others produce 2% each and the remaining 10% of the output is divided among ten equally sized small producers (1% each). In both cases, there are 16 firms competing. If a simple descriptor were used instead of the HI, like the commonly used approach of measuring the market share of the 'biggest *six* companies', the 'Concentration Ratio' would be 90% in both situations. Yet the first scenario has significant competition, whereas the second scenario is close to a monopoly. Concentration Ratios, like the 'Six-Firm' measure, have very serious drawbacks according to the US Justice Department's Antitrust Division because they assume that size distribution *among* the top six organisations is irrelevant, 'which is obviously silly' (Calkins, 1983). The Herfindahl Index solves this shortcoming, as the following calculations show:

$$\text{Scenario 1:}$$
$$\text{HI} = 6\left(0.15^2\right) + 10\left(0.01^2\right)$$
$$= 0.136$$

$$\text{Scenario 2:}$$
$$\text{HI} = 0.80^2 + 5\left(0.02^2\right) + 10\left(0.01^2\right)$$
$$= 0.643$$

As we noted already, when firms have *unequal* shares as here, the reciprocal of the index indicates the 'equivalent' number of firms in the sector. In Scenario 2, the market structure (of having one firm produce 80% of the goods while five others produce 2% each, and the remaining 10% of output is divided among 10 equally sized small producers) is equivalent to having 1.56 organisations of equal size. In Scenario 1, the market structure is equivalent to having 7.35 organisations of equal size (Kelly, 2016).

The Herfindahl Index is correlated with the number of firms (N) in a sector because its lower limit (when all the organisations have equal market shares) is $1/N$. A sector with three competing organisations (say) must have a higher HI than a sector with 20 organisations (say) when organisations have equal market share, but as market shares within a sector diverge from equality, the HI can be bigger with a larger number of organisations.

In the world of antitrust regulation, if the Herfindahl Index is above a certain threshold regulators consider the market to be too concentrated with a correspondingly higher likelihood of collusion and monopoly. In the US, the *actual threshold* is considered critical, while in the EU regulators prefer to focus on *changes* to the HI. According to the Antitrust Division of the US Department of Justice guidelines on mergers: a HI below 0.01 indicates a 'highly competitive' market; between 0.01 and

0.15 indicates an 'unconcentrated' market; between 0.15 and 0.25 indicates a market of 'moderate concentration'; and a HI above 0.25 indicates 'high concentration'. Both the US Department of Justice and the US Federal Trade Commission use the Herfindahl Index as a screening tool to determine whether proposed mergers are likely to raise antitrust concerns, and HI increases greater than 0.01 generally trigger an investigation (Kelly, 2016).

It is possible, if required, to normalize the Herfindahl Index (assuming $N > 1$) using the formula

$$H_{\text{norm}} = \left(\text{HI} - \frac{1}{N} \right) \bigg/ \left(1 - \frac{1}{N} \right)$$

Unlike the HI (which ranges from $1/N$ to 1), the *normalised* HI ranges from 0 to 1. The disadvantage of normalising the Herfindahl Index is that information about the total number of competitors (N) is lost. For example, in a market with two players each with a 50% share, HI = 0.5 and the normalised HI is 0. Compare this to a situation with there are three firms with equal shares. The HI has changed to 0.333, but the normalised HI remains zero, the same as the two-firm case.

Of course, the usefulness of the HI in any market is dependent on *how a market is defined*, and in the commercial sector this hinges primarily on the notion of 'substitutability'. For example, if one were to look at the UK retail banking sector and find that it contained five firms each with a 20% market share, the sector would look fairly competitive, but one of these banks might handle 80% of all UK mortgages while another bank might handle 90% of all savings. Each of these banks, within a seemingly competitive market, can behave as a near monopoly, and in fact the entire market might as well be a monopoly as far as the unfortunate mortgage holder or saver is concerned. The problem is that the 'UK retail banking sector' needs to be more carefully defined as a 'sector'; perhaps in the example given, it should be defined as two *separate* sectors: mortgage and savings. Markets also need to be properly defined *geographically*. A particular 'high street bank' might have a 20% market share overall in the UK, but have a 95% market share in a particular region, like the North of England, say. To reiterate: the problem is to define the market carefully enough so that the HI can do its job (Kelly, 2016).

The Herfindahl Index has successfully been applied to university research assessments (Kelly, 2016) to measure the relative competitiveness of the different subject disciplines (or 'Units of Assessment') in the UK's research assessment exercises.

Note

1 A full worked example using the Herfindahl Index in the university sector was published as a peer-reviewed research paper (Kelly, 2016).

23

TRANSFORMATIONAL THEORY

Team and network leadership

In a sense, situational leadership guru John Hunt (see Chapter 7) is the link between situational/contingency theory and our final category, transformational theory. In pointing out the shortcomings of his own field, he both contributed to it and demonstrated the need to move away from it. It is not just a question of philosophy – the role of societal culture in organisational culture, the individualism of Western societies, and so on – but the practical requirement that situational theories must take account of the most important 'situation' of all: the working economy. It is ironic, to say the least, that while situational theorists were promoting the importance of 'situation', they were ignoring the fact that the nature of society and work was changing to a gig economy. In the first decade of the 21st century, the digitalisation of the economy was rapid due to the development of the Internet and the popularisation of smart technology. As a result, on-demand platform-based technology created jobs and modes of employment in a gig economy that were (and remain) markedly different from traditional, off-line hard transactions based on accessibility, convenience and price competitiveness. In old-fashioned Fordist economies, work was circumscribed by set working hours and a set rate of pay and reward. In the post-Fordist (Block, 1990; Piore & Sabel, 1984; Reich, 1991) gig economy, work is characterised by independent outsourced contract-based labour without a conventional working day and with variable rates of pay. In such an environment, from a leadership point of view, there is much more to a job than rates of pay, and in this new 'situation', the best managers focus on those aspects of work that are most attractive when hiring from an increasingly fluid labour force. Whereas traditional workers built long-term relationships with employers, gig-economy workers accept and welcome the fact that they are temporary and project-based, hired to complete a particular 'gig' in a fixed period of time. Work is more transitory today, and there is greater flexibility, autonomy, task variety and complexity. Freelancers sell their skills to maximise their

DOI: 10.4324/9781003217220-23

freedom and up-skilling, sometimes sacrificing a degree of income for a more interesting project that better leverages their skills.

It is not all positive, of course. There are fewer workplace benefits and weaker legal protections, and the terms 'employee' and 'employer' have been weakened in worker protection legislation in ways that could not have been foreseen when it was put in place in the latter part of the 20th century. The 2018 court case in the UK over whether Uber drivers are employed or self-employed is a case in point.[1] These changes have resulted in the casualisation of low-paid, menial work, with a commensurate lowering of pay and conditions, greater social isolation and longer and more unsociable working hours.

Against that background, we come to transformational leadership theory, which is characterised by the phrase: 'The only way to predict the future is to create it!' At its heart is the importance of imagination to leadership, and in that sense it follows from Hunt's work. It is a very gig economy attitude and reflects the criticism, mainly levelled at Adair and his followers, that previous theory was too Fordist in its world view: fine in a formal and old-fashioned manufacturing environment, but irrelevant in the modern context where leadership is about managing change and knowledge in learning organisations, and enabling and fostering innovation. Transformational theory holds that the demands on a leader centre on uncertainty and managing change. It reflects the changing nature of networks and communications, and the possible upturning of the law of diminishing returns. Demands made on leaders today include the need to:

- Transform organisations and change systems.
- Empower others and create empowering cultures.
- Work through teams in de-layered and high-tech environments.
- Change mindsets – what we can call 'metanoia'.[2]
- Understand and manage the meaning of situations.
- Drive the chosen vision forward.

Transformational theorists can be divided into three interrelated categories: team advocates, discussed in this chapter; change advocates, to be discussed in the next chapter; and vision advocates, to be discussed in Chapter 25.

Team advocacy

Outstanding researchers in this set include Meredith Belbin who wrote *Management Teams: Why They Succeed or Fail* (1981) with the help of Bill Hartston, a mathematician and international chess master, Jeanne Fisher, an anthropologist, and Roger Mottram, an occupational psychologist. Together, they conducted a seven-year study of teams, concluding that an effective team has members that cover eight (later nine) key management roles, which may be separate from the roles that they have in carrying out the work of the team. In summary, Belbin discovered that (what he called) 'Apollo teams' (i.e. teams with very intelligent members) often failed because they lacked the right spread of role types. He looked at individual personality types within teams, using personality tests, questionnaires and so on, and came up with his famous eight team roles.

1. *The coordinator.* The role of the coordinator (originally called 'the chairman') is to pull together and focus the team's efforts. People with high coordinator scores tend to be stable, extroverted, good judges of people and good at organising the efforts of others. They are adept at getting work done through the efforts of others. They like harmony and order, dislike confrontation and are better at bringing out the creativity in others than being original themselves. The coordinator is a leadership role and is essential when there is a need to focus on task, objectives and processes. In schools and universities, it is typically filled by the headteacher, head of department or dean.

2. *The shaper.* The shaper shapes a team's efforts. People with a high shaper score will be the drivers within any team. Typically, they lack patience, are anxious and very task-focused and tend to be domineering. They put the achievement of purpose above the maintenance of happy relationships or the feelings of teammates. They make life uncomfortable but ensure action and the achievement of goals. A typical example in a university might be a REF champion taking responsibility for a Unit of Assessment submission.

3. *The plant.* The plant is more introverted than other team members but contributes more in ideas, 'planting' creative seeds across the team. These team members score highly in intelligence tests, but they are typically ignored or put down by more extroverted colleagues, at which time they tend to withdraw from contributing.

4. *The monitor-evaluator.* These team members, typically lawyers and accountants, form the critical intelligence element in teams, but they can appear aloof and slightly removed. Monitor-evaluators do not engage as much in team discussions, but they typically come in on a point of order, sometimes in quite a curt fashion. They are a vital element for quality control, but are not popular.

5. *The company worker or implementer.* This is usually an underappreciated role, but it is vital in turning ideas and plans into reality. It is an actualising role. Implementers are good at timetables and schedules and budgets, but they are typically unimaginative. They are only interested in actualising what the team decides.

6. *The team worker.* These members are not dominant players in the team, but they enjoy being part of it. They foster harmony and good relations but, unlike shapers, have no interest in the top jobs. Team workers enjoy supporting other members' ideas, but do not themselves contribute to the direction of the team. They provide a groundswell of support for whatever is decided, enthusiastically getting behind the decisions that are made.

7. *The resource investigator.* These people are extroverts. They socialise outside the team and enjoy influencing outsiders and bringing back information or 'intel'. Belbin's view is that resource investigators are useful for making contacts. They are diplomatic but bad when it comes to the minutiae.

8. *The completer-finisher.* These people ensure that deadlines are met and project objectives are achieved. Essentially, the completer-finisher protects the team from its own shortcomings. They instil a sense of urgency in the team but are unpopular because they tend to nag!

Belbin went on to research *successful* teams, finding that they are characterised by having a good person in the chair, having one strong plant in the team, a fair spread of intellectual abilities, a spread of personal attributes offering wide role coverage, a good match between the skills of members and their responsibilities, and an ability to recognise when there is a shortcoming or imbalance in the team. Some roles are easily filled by more than one person; other roles are less compatible and are likely to be done well only by certain personality types. This means that a team need not have eight people, but is very likely to have at least three or four. While the eight team roles can be matched to certain personality types – for example, resource investigators are usually extroverts – it should be remembered that these eight roles represent *functions* in the management of a team's activities, and while questionnaires exist to identify ideal team roles and the personalities that best fill those roles, it is not predetermined. An extrovert can be a completer-finisher, and an introvert can be a resource investigator.

The Belbin model is useful in setting up teams to undertake specific assignments. Prospective members of the team should decide which roles they are best suited to and wish to fill, and apply to join. They are then assessed (by senior managers) as to suitability, which in itself is a useful exercise in terms of self-awareness for both organisation and individual. Assessment is usually done by a mixture of role play, team building and problem-solving exercises, assisted self-assessment and assessment by a neutral or external third party. The purpose of the assessment and the subsequent selection of team members is to avoid duplication and oversupply of one 'type'. The natural tendency for 'like' to select 'like' must be avoided, but at a minimum, it is useful for management to know in advance of any shortfall in, or deficit of, one type so that the team can play particular attention to certain roles during the process, remembering that the different roles are mutually complementary, not competing.

The strength of Belbin's team model is that people recognise themselves and others in the role descriptors – it has good face validity – and they understand team dynamics all the better for it. The model cannot resolve personality clashes or create good interpersonal relations where there is antipathy or acrimony – it is not a counselling service – but being aware, and more particularly being *self*-aware, makes it easier to create functioning, effective and efficient teams.

Networked leadership

It is assumed that the term 'teams' refers to groups of *individuals*, but logically it could refer to groups *of groups* or networks. Effective management necessarily involves bringing together groups of individuals *within* a school or university, or *between* schools or universities, and the manner in which they form a network is of obvious importance. Obvious examples in education include: the network of departments or colleges that make up a single university; a grouping of universities such the Russell Group in the UK; and Multi-Academy Trusts (MATs).

MATs are regulated charities that operate two or more 'academy' schools. These are state schools directly funded by the Department for Education and independent of local authority control. The schools in an MAT work together under a collective funding agreement with the government and are regulated by both company and charity law. The individual schools run by an MAT have no separate legal identity. Each one is in law simply a local 'site' through which the MAT delivers its government contract. Local staff, headteachers and governing bodies have only the roles assigned to them by the central MAT board; they are not appointed directly by government. The MATs are private, but they are not permitted to run schools for profit; and if they do a bad job, they lose their contracts and must return their buildings and assets to the central government. There are approximately 1,200 MATs in England: 29 are very large networks and have more than 25 schools; 85 have between 12 and 25 schools; 259 have between 6 and 11 schools; approximately 600 are small and have fewer than 6 schools (BESA, 2021).

A network such as an MAT or a university is an intermeshed system of information conduits involving individuals or groups of individuals working together towards a common goal. The network links together people or groups or departments or sites that have common interests, enabling them to share resources, ideas and experiences in an efficient manner. The complexity of networks varies, of course, but they all aspire to add value. They have two features that differentiate them from non-networked groupings that have a bearing on management: where the intelligence, experience and memory of the whole network organisation reside; and how the fluidity of its constituents' efforts affects its effectiveness.

- *The partition of intelligence, experience and memory in networks*
  Network intelligence is the ability of a network to accumulate, share, adapt and distribute data and information. It imparts value to the remedial actions that a school, college or university might decide to take. The conduits that distribute this data can be *passive*, where they simply transport the data, or *active*, where the conduits additionally interpret and add value to the data, turning it into information. Active networks enhance passing data and retain a memory of it.

  We can differentiate between *back-end* and *front-end* organisational intelligence in networks. The former is intelligence that becomes embedded in the shared infrastructure of the network core: in the case of an MAT or a university, by 'the centre' and its admin. Front-end intelligence, on the other hand, fragments into different forms at the periphery of a network: in the case of an MAT, at the individual school sites; in the case of a university, at individual departments or research groups. Front-end intelligence is decentralised, flexible and contextualised. The type of intelligence needed by an MAT or a university is back-end intelligence – the need and ability to store and process institutional memory – particularly in universities where senior management roles like Head of Department rotate on a voluntary basis. This is very different from the front-end intelligence an educational institution needs to handle its dealings with students and others at the customer interface (Kelly, 2004). If more than one kind of intelligence is required at any given place at any given time, then they may need to be coupled together; but with that exception, an education network needs to partition its two intelligences so that the core can efficiently store and process data/information and the periphery can be customised to meet the requirements of individual teachers, lecturers and researchers.

The *partition of intelligence* is one determinant of a network's efficiency. In an efficient network, back-end intelligence is pushed back to the core (where it belongs) while front-end intelligence is deliberately fragmented at the periphery of the network (where it belongs), and the conduits between the periphery and the core are hollowed out to become passive (see Figure 23.1).

- *The fluidity of effort in networks*
The 'fluidity' of a network – how easily it can respond to new demands – is another determinant of its effectiveness. It reflects the way an MAT or university organises its staff and its stakeholders, and the way it serves the local or wider community. In traditional school organisations and universities, individual

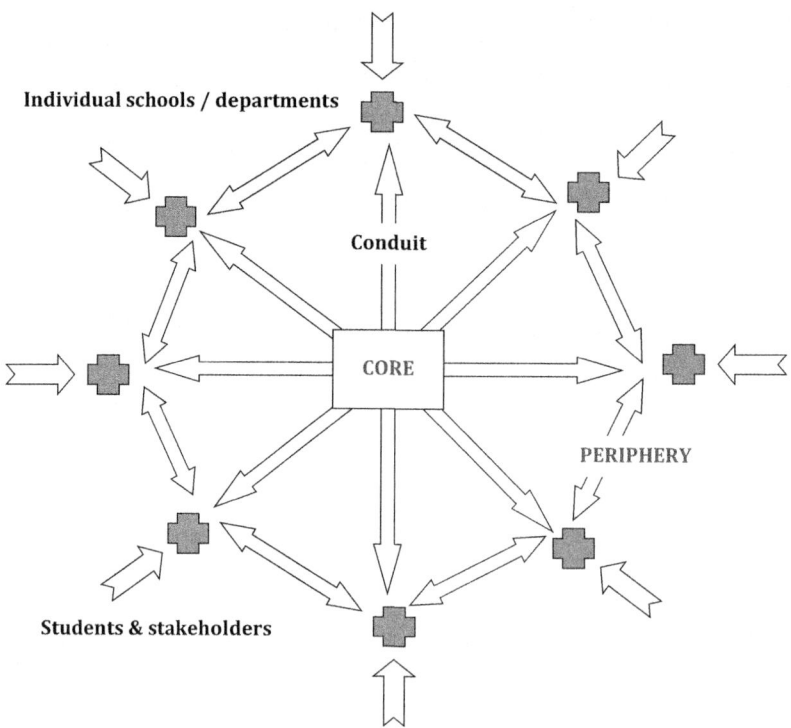

FIGURE 23.1 A networked organisation such as an MAT or a university.

teachers, lecturers and researchers are tightly grouped in large units of effort, iso-lated from each other in departments or faculties, in a crystalline-like structure. In contrast, a modern networked organisation has small free-floating units of effort that coalesce into temporary coalitions *around issues or priorities* whenever and wherever the need arises. Management then becomes primarily concerned with orchestrating and coordinating effort and the flow of intelligence, rather than with instructional leadership, and with ensuring that individual coalitions can communicate and collaborate through common protocols.

The changing location of value

Modern educational organisations need to be highly connected (to anyone and everyone who shares their mission) in order to be able to respond to change. For schools, colleges and universities, the ability to respond to student and external demands is now more important than the ability simply to teach or do research. The notion of adding and retaining value has altered too. In a network, everyone and everything is connected, and value behaves differently than in a traditional hierarchy:

- *Value is added at the ends and retained in the core.* Most added value is created at the periphery, facing the student or where research is having an impact, but it is important that the value generated by interactions at the periphery is retained at the core, where generic data-gathering functions consolidate know-how and competences.
- *Value in a common infrastructure.* Schools, colleges and universities as networked organisations have elements of their infrastructure brought together instead of being replicated among different sites or departmental units. This shared infra-structure typically takes the form of basic experiential storage-type functions as well as common business-type functions like administration, timetabling, marketing, student support, careers advisory services and alumni liaison.
- *Value in modularity.* In a network, organisational capabilities and processes are restructured as self-contained modules that can quickly and seamlessly con-nect together. If a value-adding process is conceptualised as a series of mod-ules operating sequentially, then success lies in creating modules that can be 'plugged into' as many different processes as possible.
- *Value in orchestration.* As modularisation within organisations becomes more prevalent, the ability to coordinate independent modules becomes a valuable new leadership skill.

Reshaping an organisation as a network of teams

Middle management in schools and universities will shrink as a consequence of what can be termed the 'pacification of network conduits', as intelligence gets pushed back to the core (senior admin managers) and out to the periphery (teachers and researchers). Networked organisations have less need for middle managers because communication is faster and easier, and collaboration almost unwitting (Kelly, 2004). In traditional organisations, middle managers are needed to package and distribute information on its way up and down the organisational structure between the core and the periphery. This 'information-sorting' function of middle management is redundant in schools and universities with networked pipework. Leadership and strategic functions are concentrated in a core of senior management, and day-to-day decision-making functions are pushed to the student-facing and stakeholder periphery. Fluidity of effort has an effect too. Leadership automatically becomes more 'distributed'. Passive conduits allow dispersed individuals to connect together dynamically to solve problems and respond to opportunities. Cooperation between previously unconnected departments or schools is no longer problematic or unusual; in fact, it becomes an expectation. Students, for example, are no longer shunted from one bureaucratic department to another, each claiming lack of jurisdiction! Networks allow remote and free access to information, and while such fundamental restructuring of an educational institution and the professions within it is threatening, it does offer certain opportunities:

- Stakeholders, staff and students become better informed and therefore more supportive.
- Previously competing institutions can come together in alliances around certain issues – for example, Russell Group universities coming together over the issue of rising student fees – to provide a better public service, safe in the knowledge that engagement and disengagement are easy.
- Since communication is more efficient and more immediate, the deposit of know-how and experience can be located anywhere within the institution's network and moved to a new 'site' as required.

Senior managers should dedicate resources both to the value-*retaining* core and the teaching and research, value-*adding* periphery, and they must support the processes that take place in both areas. Middle managers must change their role from filtration (sorting information as it passes up and down the organisation) to facilitation (orchestrating the interaction between the players at the periphery and the managers at the core). At the periphery, where the school or university interfaces with students, wider stakeholders and research-users, staff must accept more responsibility and self-direction. Action must be predicated on the doctrine of mission-command independent judgement (see Chapter 5) and informed by institutional strategy, which must include the institution's mission statement, what it aspires to and believes in, policy statements and aims, and how the school or university hopes to fulfil its mission. Failure to do this will manifest itself in an inability to adapt, an unwillingness to learn and inconsistent communications. In schools, colleges and universities, this will usually show as an increased number of complaints from staff, students and other stakeholders, a growing disinterest on the part of alumni, decision-making that is perceived as slow and unresponsive, growing organisational inflexibility and a failure to meet reasonable public expectations as evidenced by league tables of teaching and research. In addition, the cyclical flow of information and feedback will be seen to suffer thrombosis as boundaries grow between hierarchical levels and between departments and schools on the same hierarchical level (see Figure 23.2).

Networked organisations like MATs, single universities and university groupings typically adopt a multi-disciplinary approach to problem-solving, achieving outcomes by assembling, disassembling and reassembling coalitions and issue teams. Internal relationships make and break around issues and opportunities, rather than around competences and status. Ideally, they are characterised by interdependence and reciprocity, with responsibility devolved to autonomous modular groups and

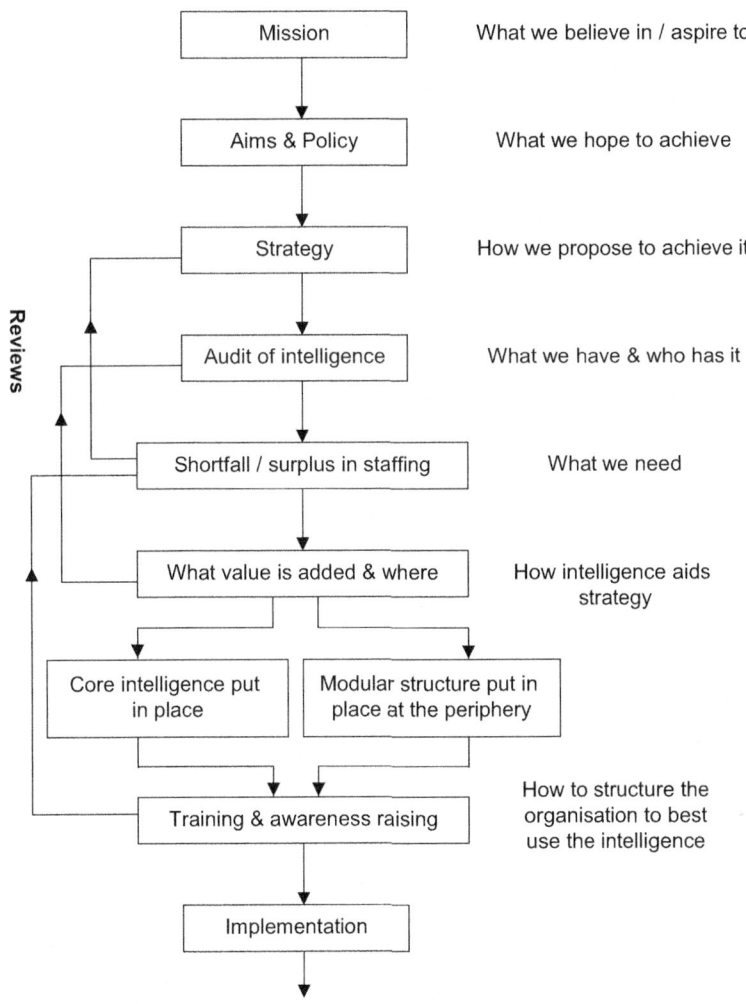

FIGURE 23.2 Preparing an organisation for change to a networked organisation.

individuals who are expected to exercise what can be called 'informed discretion'. These networked schools and universities have a greater shared sense of ownership. Performance appraisal is done in a transparent manner, and teams appraise their own performance relative to other teams in the network; for example, pastoral teams compare against each other in different schools in an MAT.

Supporting education networks with information technology

Although investment in it is usually expensive, information technology can be hugely supportive of networks in many different ways:

- Online databases allow stakeholders to identify key people and critical information with a minimum of fuss and run-around.
- E-mail allows contact with the core and with other schools, departments and universities along the periphery to be immediate and in real time.
- Students can use the intranet to track their own progress.
- Core administration and financial management can be made more efficient using dedicated software.
- Project and teaching teams can work together remotely, in planning and delivery, through electronic conferencing. This was particularly evident during the Covid pandemic of 2020–2021.
- Core data storage can be shared within and across institutions and accessed after office hours, subject to appropriate security restrictions, allowing staff to accommodate better the many different demands made on their time.
- An electronic bulletin board for staff can encourage shared ownership of information and maintain a sense of institutional identity.

Continuing professional development

Traditionally, the professional development of teachers and lecturers is aimed primarily at enhancing individual expertise and reinforcing specialism. This emphasis needs to shift if a school or university aspires to be an organisation intent on managing the retention of its know-how through networks. Professional development programmes in networks like MATs and universities focus instead on developing and distributing leadership, problem-solving, and communication and participation skills. As Hastings (1993) points out, the nature of an organisation can sometimes run ahead of the ability of individuals to operate within it. People must be given the skills to survive and prosper, and this includes the political skill to acquire critical friends to support individual projects. Individuals and task-centred teams need to be trained in network maintenance; oiling the wheels of information sharing. As a result, individual teachers, lecturers and researchers benefit from a more satisfying job despite the increased workload, they advance faster personally and professionally, they work flexibly with a wider range of projects and with a greater number of specialisms, they are challenged more, their knowledge and emotional intelligence are treated as organisational assets, and the process of peer appraisal and improvement creates the culture wherein performance measurement is supportive rather than adversarial. As an added benefit, these things also reduce staff turnover.

Barriers to networking

Staff in networked schools and universities need autonomy more than staff in traditional institutions. They need, and are usually given, that freedom. These institutions also need staff to share good practice and be able to work constructively together, and this creates a tension that is not always easy to resolve. The confidence necessary for autonomous endeavour to flourish is sometimes undermined by the need to work in teams.

Knowledge workers such as staff in schools, colleges and universities are usually driven by the need for recognition. In the past, this has come from the status conferred on incumbents by virtue of their specialism and hierarchical level: professor, senior tutor, headteacher, deputy principal, head of department. So when internal status barriers are removed or reduced, as they must be in a networked institution, part of the traditional reward system for education workers disappears with them, and a sense of insecurity replaces it. 'Network status' becomes the new motivation; a new cross-weave in the fabric of the school or university as a network-organisation. This can be seen in pan-organisational issue-related structures like steering committees for equality impact assessment in UK universities preparing for the REF; informal committees looking at mergers in the community college sector in the United States; expert staff preparing colleagues for inspection routines in schools. This new network status derives from an individual's ability to open doors for others and to collaborate over a wide spectrum of activities. In a networked organisation, individuals and modular teams are rewarded by being asked to undertake important projects, by being asked for advice and assistance, by having their contributions celebrated in public, by having good work publicised, by being asked to represent the organisation overseas, and by gaining access to more resources and greater remuneration. In traditional organisations, by contrast, experts identify only with their own areas of expertise, gaining recognition by visibly demonstrating that expertise to others. They either hide their professional know-how from outsiders to create a myth of private knowledge, or they frame the world in terms of what they want to tell rather than what others need to know: the senior professor, the deputy head in charge of the school timetable, the director of studies. Traditional organisations support an ethos of arrogance, removing from experts the obligation to *explain* to others what is afoot and why. Such an attitude is a barrier to networking and sharing intelligence. It provides a cultural veto on change, which many organisations find impossible to overcome and which explains why culture is such an important lever in educational improvement.

Another barrier lies in the cult of the maverick outsider; the teacher, lecturer or researcher as 'hero', achieving the seemingly impossible as a lone agent battling impossible odds. Seeking assistance is seen as an admission of failure – of disempowerment, even – despite the fact that the myth of the hero-innovator is just that – a myth! In fact, most successful innovators in science and industry relied on their ability to mobilise *other* people in pursuit of their objectives, rather than rely solely on their own efforts (Kanter, 1983); that, and not solitude, was their defining attribute! The media is also fond of portraying heroic hard-working individuals who have beaten the odds to succeed, overlooking the many people that may be similarly heroic and hard-working, but fail to find greatness or public acclaim simply because of random extraneous events. This is a type of 'survivor bias': most failures are not known to the public; only those who survive the competition for greatness are visible.

Finally, 'old school tie' networks are also barriers to effective networking. They occur when informal soft networks degenerate into personal advancement 'societies'. This, rather than *organisational* advancement, becomes their purpose: self-aggrandisement masquerading as altruism. They are typically closed and opaque to outsiders, and this is what marks them out as barriers. Ironically, we see this most frequently in universities practised by academics who themselves have benefited most by the dismantling of traditional prejudices! They form exclusive cabals themselves, entry to which can be gained only by demonstrating a shared woke-intolerance of dissent. By contrast, effective networks – from necessity and inclination – are open and actively seek out outsiders. They do not pathologise particular ways of thinking.

Team networking in schools and universities

Teams built around tasks necessarily evolve and dissolve as problems are solved and new ones present themselves. Although multi-functional and multi-disciplinary approaches are the result of a networking culture, a network is in many ways the product of a belief that improvement itself is an infinite series of incremental steps (to be discussed in the following chapter). These steps will sometimes be visible and formally instituted; at other times they will be *in*visible and have a very short shelf life. This will depend largely on the nature of the issue around which the team has been gathered, and the extent of its success will depend on how much its members share an understanding of the fundamental nature of the problem under consideration. A team's mix of expertise and experience, rather than the status of its members, is also critical to success, as we discussed earlier in this chapter in relation to Belbin's notion of Apollo teams. Individuals should belong to the team because they can contribute to its success, not because they enhance the team's status or are part of a personal advancement clique. Quality moderation within the team is not a hierarchical function, but a peer-imposed one. Members have the privilege of autonomy, but they also carry the burden of accountability and the pressure to perform for the common good. They are driven by the status of success and the need for achievement. Their reward is the status they get *out of it*, not the status they bring *to it*.

Of course, not every task in an MAT school, university or university grouping needs to be tackled by modular teams. There is still room for traditional hierarchical line management, and it would be as silly to complicate matters unnecessarily as it would be to oversimplify them. Teams work better in some areas than others. Anything that requires cross-functional thinking or is concerned with inter-departmental/inter-school issues is more suited to teamwork than individual endeavour. Strategic processes that re-shape the future of the school or university and issues relating to staff development are also typical team pursuits. Experience from school improvement research suggests that modular teams are most successful when they have more than a certain minimum threshold of experience and expertise, when they are steered by someone with an ability to achieve consensus and when they adopt a 'learning-to-learn' ethos for the institution (Kelly, 2004).

Notes

1 Uber is a US multinational ride-hailing company offering taxi-type peer-to-peer ride-sharing. Uber drivers are designated by the company as independent contractors and not employees, which affects taxation, working hours and overtime benefits, but several lawsuits in different jurisdictions have been filed by drivers alleging that they are entitled to the rights and remedies of employees under employment law. In *O'Connor v. Uber*, a lawsuit filed in the US District Court for the Northern District of California in 2013, Uber drivers pleaded that according to the California Labor Code, they should be classified as employees and receive reimbursement of business expenses such as gas and vehicle maintenance costs. In March 2019, Uber agreed to pay $20 million to settle the case. In October 2016, in the case of *Aslam v. Uber*, the Central London Employment tribunal ruled that Uber drivers are 'workers', rather than self-employed individuals, and are entitled to the minimum wage under the National Minimum Wage Act 1998, paid holiday and other normal worker entitlements. Two Uber drivers, James Farrar (chairman of the United Private Hire Drivers union) and Yaseen Aslam, had brought the test case to the employment tribunal on behalf of a group of drivers in London. Uber appealed the decision but, in December 2018, lost its appeal at the Court of Appeal and, in February 2021, lost the case again in the UK Supreme Court (Russon, 2021). In March 2018, the Swiss Department of Economic Affairs, Education and Research gave the legal opinion that under the conditions that bind drivers to Uber, they should be classified as employees.
2 Metanoia (from the Greek μετάνοια) means a transformative change of heart or mind. It can indicate not only a change of the heart, but also the manner of changing it.

24

TRANSFORMATIONAL THEORY AND CHANGE

The dynamic leadership of risk and choice

The outstanding writer in the area of transformational leadership is Warren Bennis, a well-respected academic and advisor to four US presidents. His work in the 1960s on group behaviour helped bring about the move to less hierarchical, more democratic and adaptive institutions, in both private and public sectors, and his article 'Revisionist Theory of Leadership' in the *Harvard Business Review* in 1961 challenged the prevailing wisdom by showing that humanistic, democratic-style leaders are better suited to dealing with complexity and change in modern organisations. Douglas McGregor, the founder of modern democratic management and a leading theorist in behavioural leadership (see Chapter 6), considered Bennis his protégé; in fact, they both later served as professors at the MIT Sloan School of Management. *The Wall Street Journal* (1993) named Bennis as one of the top-ten most-sought-after speakers on management, *Forbes* (1996) magazine referred to him as the 'dean of leadership gurus', *The Financial Times* (2000) referred to him as 'the professor who established leadership as a respectable academic field', and *Business Week* (August 2007) ranked him as one of the top thought leaders in business (International Leadership Association, 2008). Bennis wrote dozens of books, including: *The Leaning Ivory Tower* (1973); *The Unconscious Conspiracy: Why Leaders Can't Lead* (1976); *An Invented Life* (1993) which was nominated for a Pulitzer Prize; *Leaders: The Strategies for Taking Charge* (1985, with Burt Nanus); *Organizing Genius: The Secrets of Creative Collaboration* (1997, with Patricia Biederman); and *Geeks and Geezers* (2002, with Robert Thomas). *On Becoming a Leader* (1989) set out his theory that a leader must be 'authentic'; that is, the leader must be his or her own creation and have a combination of experience, self-knowledge and personal ethics. (This need for effective leaders to remain true to themselves was expanded later by others into what became known as 'authentic leadership'.) Bennis thought that experiencing struggle and hardship moulds leaders and that the journey to becoming one

DOI: 10.4324/9781003217220-24

comes as a result of going through a process of self-discovery. For Bennis, leadership is like beauty: hard to define, but you know it when you see it! He maintained that leadership was open to all. For Bennis, leadership was the mastery of confusion, embodying the management of meaning, trust, attention and self; and a willingness to learn from everything.

Bennis's purple patch was at the end of the 1980s. He himself places his work in both transformational and contingency camps, so he was really the one to open up this transformational category. For Bennis, leaders must master the context in which they operate. Pressure of work forces them to become bosses when they take high office, but leaders must recognise this trap! To master context, leaders must become self-expressive, listen to their inner voice, learn from the right mentors and give themselves over to a vision.

In other words, leaders must have a sense of purpose, and challenge and change their context. They should deploy themselves and not be deployed by others. Bennis says the basic ingredients of leadership are:

- *A guiding vision.* Leaders have a clear idea of what they want to achieve and the strength to persist on their course of action or change it in order to achieve their goals.
- *Passion.* Leaders need to have passion and communicate it. They need to inspire others.
- *Integrity.* Self-knowledge is the key to 'knowing oneself', and integrity is the basis of the trust that staff must have in their leader, a trust that must be earned. Knowing oneself is the first step towards *inventing* oneself.
- *Curiosity and risk-friendliness.* Leaders should be curious about everything and embrace mistakes as learning opportunities. They should be risk-friendly but not reckless, knowing the time and place to be conservative.

Bennis also outlined the differences for him between management and leadership in terms of these basic ingredients:

- A manager administers; a leader innovates.
- A manager is a copy; a leader is an original.
- A manager maintains; a leader develops.
- A manager focuses on structure and systems; a leader focuses on people.
- A manager focuses on control; a leader inspires trust.
- A manager has a short-term view; a leader has a long-term view.
- A manager asks 'how' and 'when'; a leader asks 'what' and 'why'.
- A manager has an eye on the bottom line; a leader has an eye on the horizon.
- A manager initiates; a leader originates.
- A manager accepts the status quo; a leader challenges it.
- A manager is a 'good soldier'; a leader is their own person.
- A manager does things right; a leader does the right thing.

Unfortunately, these distinctions are semantic and offer only false dichotomies in their appeal. There is no universal truth as to what leadership and management are *in themselves*; only various definitions of what they may or may not *include*. A manager may or may not have a short-term view, and a leader may or may not have a long-term view. This is not what distinguishes their roles or necessarily their incumbents. And the dichotomies are nonsensical in any case: the opposite of a 'good soldier' is a bad soldier, not someone 'who is their own person'; the opposite of 'control' is not 'trust'; and so on. These are essentially meaningless sound bites: catchy gibberish, but gibberish nonetheless. One would hope that *both* manager and leader would 'do things right', whatever the blandishments of high office. However, Bennis does occasionally deviate into sense in that in his bifurcation of (what he sees as) the two great contraries of leadership and management, he defines *what he means* by each. We are free to share his meanings, or not. He has not uncovered Great Secrets of what leadership and management are *per se*, but only what he *wants* them to mean for his own purposes, such as:

- Leaders formulate a clear vision; managers pursue goals shaped by others.
- Leaders keep daily sight of their vision; managers are concerned with daily administration.
- Leaders communicate their vision to others; managers monitor others carrying out their tasks.
- Leaders help subordinates to lead, and these subordinates have confidence in the leadership; managers do not inspire others necessarily.
- Leaders get others to work towards a common purpose; managers keep people working on task.
- Leaders are creative and take risks; managers work to guidelines.
- Leaders are prepared to question and be questioned; managers accept plans at face value and put them into action.
- Leaders initiate change; managers maintain the status quo.
- Leaders see failure as a learning opportunity; managers see failure as a problem to be overcome.
- Leaders are resolute in the face of setbacks; managers feel undermined by setbacks.
- Leaders have a realistic knowledge of self and surround themselves with colleagues with complementary skills; managers are just concerned with getting the job done.
- Leaders are interested in the development of their staff; managers share out tasks.
- Leaders give out responsibility; managers suppress responsibility in subordinates.
- Leaders are not afraid of new talent joining and plan for leadership succession; managers seek to control and tend to stifle talent in the search for efficiency.

In shifting from leader to manager, false dichotomies still permeate the contrast, but Bennis highlights an important feature of running an organisation; namely, the need to know oneself and the importance of self-knowledge. He lists four lessons:

- *Leaders are their own best teachers in the search for personal transformation.* It is about knowing the gap between what they are now and what they want to be, and accepting responsibility for their own re-education and up-skilling.
- *Accept responsibility.* Leaders don't pass the blame onto someone else, which impedes personal transformation.
- *Leaders can learn anything they want to learn.* This involves seeing the world both as it is and as it can be; understanding things and acting on that understanding; not being afraid of failure and learning from it; embracing the new.
- *Understanding comes from reflecting on experience.* This involves being a reflective practitioner in the art of leadership and management; of being self-critical in a constructive way and at the appropriate time.

Of course, leaders also need knowledge of the world and the ability to fill in the gaps in their education and experience. Leaders should seek broadening experiences so that they can trust to instinct *because their instinct is informed.* According to Bennis, the seven ingredients that constitute the process of leadership are therefore:

- *Resolution and reflection.* Reflecting on self and reflecting on task, and then set-tling on a course of action.
- *Perspective.* Taking the facts and looking at them from different perspectives.
- *Testing and measuring.* First asking the question, 'What do you want?'
- *Desire.* Desire is about self-expression. It needs to be coupled with drive, which is 'proofing oneself'.
- *Mastery.* Mastering the task and then articulating it.
- *Strategic thinking.* Getting a good overview, planning diligently and being prag-matic about the risks, then accepting and learning from failures along the way.
- *Synthesis.* This seventh ingredient is about bringing all the other six together, just as Senge would suggest years later with his Fifth Discipline (discussed in the following chapter).

Clearly, Bennis has a tendency to make lists! His final two are his ten organisa-tional and personal factors for creating a learning organisation, and his ten tips for avoiding disaster in a period of change. The ten organisational and personal factors for creating a learning organisation are:

- Leaders manage the dream. They have a compelling vision and know-how to make it a reality. They recruit to that vision.
- Leaders embrace error, and risk-taking is encouraged.
- Leaders encourage reflective feedback. They listen.

- Leaders encourage dissent and have people around them that will 'speak truth to power'.
- Leaders have faith, hope and optimism. People have no hope when they have no choices.
- Leaders expect the best from those around them; they stretch others without *over*stretching them.
- Leaders have a good instinctive touch with people; they are quite 'political'.
- Leaders see the longer view. They have vision and patience.
- Leaders balance the competing claims of various stakeholders.
- Leaders create strategic alliances and partnerships.

The ten tips for avoiding disaster in a period of change are:

- Recruit well and recruit with honesty.
- Avoid people who will distort the mission or ruin the prevailing positive atmosphere.
- Build support with like-minded people, new and old.
- Plan change from a solid conceptual base. Change should be planned and gradual.
- Don't settle for rhetorical (in-name-only) change.
- Don't allow those opposed to change or to the mission to appropriate the agenda, and make sure than nobody is frightened by what is proposed.
- Know your organisation inside out.
- Appreciate the context and the cultural environment.
- Avoid shock and remember the past. Proceed carefully, respectful of past success.
- Involve those most affected by change in the decision-making process. People resent change being imposed.

The management of risk and choice

Looking beyond the nonsense dichotomies and the hyperbole, leadership for Bennis is about embracing error and encouraging risk-taking. In education, there are risks associated with any action or effort at improvement. This is not the same as 'unintended consequences'. In schools and colleges, risk is a sign of action, whereas unintended consequences are the result of incomplete or inadequate analysis, or bad planning. There are many different types of risk. Some relate to the external context of the school or university – economic, socio-legal and the market itself; others are internal to the organisation – the management of change, technical and operational, recruitment and retention of staff, and project management. In all cases, a structured approach to the management of risk can help minimise its adverse effects.

First, risk must be identified and analysed, and then prioritised according to the size of the negative impact. Best practice is to use an approach that considers all stakeholder perspectives – students, staff, research users and the community – and all types of risks. The risks should be prioritised according to their potential negative impact; in particular, in schools and universities, the extent to which *reputation* – a critical aspect in both teaching and research – is put at risk by any particular change.

The prioritised risks are then analysed, the probability of occurrence and recurrence calculated and the triggers identified.

Next, appropriate responses to those risks are drawn up and analysed before deciding on responsive action. Only when risks are known and understood can an assessment be made of what the most appropriate responses are to them. Obviously, the most urgent and impactful threats require the most immediate and radical reaction. Some responsive actions will be aimed at prevention or elimination; other actions will aim to mitigate or reduce. Clearly, prevention is better than cure, subject of course to staffing limitations and cost curtailment, which are usual in schools and universities. Finally, following those actions, management should measure and closely monitor developments in case new risks emerge from the corrective action, or the initial actions prove to be ineffective, or unintended consequences emerge. It is often the low-probability risks and those with long-term impact that can 'sneak up' on an organisation, so managers need to be aware of them.

Many schools and universities operate in markets that are inherently risky or are becoming riskier as they morph into marketised economies and more competitive environments. To compete is to risk, but sometimes the negative impact is so severe that the organisation needs a designated risk management team from among academic staff. Ultimately in education, risk is regulated at societal level through legislation: the risks associated with the health and safety of staff and students, and proper data protection for research subjects are two recent examples. However, that's risk *regulation*, not risk *management*. The latter is a systematic set of methods and techniques that help an organisation to analyse, prevent, eliminate, mitigate or reduce the effect of risks. It provides a framework in which risks are deliberately sought out, identified and analysed, and appropriate actions taken pre-emptively. Taking risk is a consequence of being active in any marketplace, and its management should be a core function of any school (particularly in the fee-paying sector) or university, but over-the-top risk management, including obsessive health and safety training, can be counterproductive. There is no point to it if it reduces action to an insignificant level or inhibits innovation (Hopkin, 2012).

Of course, there is a link between, on the one hand, *risk and the activities* that cause it and, on the other, the *decisions* that precede and follow those activities. risk–reward analysis is one model for calculating the relative reward of assorted options assessed against risk. It can be very detailed or just a simple sketch. It is usually represented on a two-by-two grid formed by two perpendicular axes: one for risk, one for reward (see Figure 24.1). A list of feasible options (such as developing new degree courses or outsourcing a university's IT support) and their respective rewards (including savings) is compiled and quantified insofar as that is possible. Qualitative judgements are fine, if they are well-informed. Secondly, the associated risks are calculated for each option; in education, this is easier done if the risks are calculated *relative to each other* and not in absolute terms. These might include the level of investment required for a new degree, the opportunity costs of abandoning traditional courses and modes of delivery, the cost of exiting a course in terms of extra tuition and support for a diminishing student cohort as the course is 'taught-out', and the time

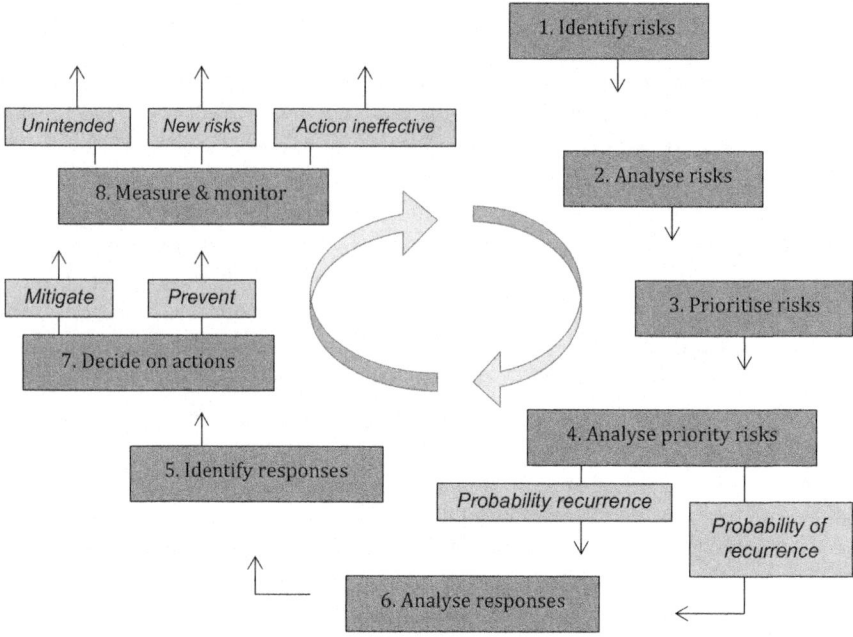

FIGURE 24.1 A risk management framework.

cost of keeping an eye on the competition. The options are then plotted on a risk–reward grid. The bottom-right corner is where the best options are located – low risk and high reward – and eventually some strategic options are selected.

The risk–reward grid can be given a third axis to represent the amount of resources required for each option. An alternative to a third axis is to give each option on the two-dimensional risk–reward chart a 'bubble' whose size represents the amount of resources required, as with the Growth–Share matrix (see Figure 18.2) and the GE–McKinsey matrix (see Figure 18.3). If larger bubbles represent options that need more resources, then ideally managers are looking for small bubbles in the bottom-right corner. Having said that, schools and universities should not be too risk-averse in looking only at options on the bottom of the chart, nor should they look only at high-reward strategies on the right-hand side. Sometimes the long-term health of an organisation like a university or a school is better served by a slow-burning, mid-reward option that has *longevity* in the market. It is all about finding a good balance between risk and reward, and between fee income/research income and resource expenditure. The typical danger is being unrealistic in overestimating the reward and being overly optimistic in underestimating the risk. There is also an unacknowledged (or ignored) interconnectedness between options as well as an emotional, sometimes defensive, element to the quantification of benefit by academics defending their particular 'patch'. As with all decision-making, the quality of the decision depends on the impartiality of the analysis (and the analyst), avoiding overcomplicating and oversimplifying things.

25

TRANSFORMATIONAL THEORY AND VISION LEADERSHIP

The third and final category within transformational theory – vision advocacy - is led by Peter Senge and those who followed him. Senge was Professor at the Sloan Business School at MIT and is famous for writing *The Fifth Discipline* (1990) and *The Dance of Change* (1999), which discuss the reasons why change often fails. He is co-founder of the Academy for Systems Change, a non-profit organisation that works with leaders to grow their ability to lead in complex social systems. The focus is on awareness-based, systems-thinking approaches.

Senge emerged in the 1990s as a major figure in organisational development with the publication of *The Fifth Discipline,* in which he developed the notion of a learning organisation. This conceptualised organisations as dynamic systems in various states of continuous adaptation and improvement. In 1997, the *Harvard Business Review* identified *The Fifth Discipline* as one of the seminal management books of the previous 75 years and Senge was named 'Strategist of the Century' by the *Journal of Business Strategy,* which described him as the person who 'had the greatest impact on the way we conduct business today' (Smith, 2001). It is certainly true that *The Fifth Discipline* changed the way we think about management and leadership, and that it gave birth to the movement to develop learning organisations and the management of change across many sectors, including education. The book's premise is that too many organisations are engaged in the search for heroic leaders who can inspire people to change, without realising that change creates resistance, born of cultural habits, which can overpower that effort. Organisations have opportunities, but they also have natural limits to their development, so it is essential to develop reflection and inquiry skills to discuss real problems. According to Senge, there are four challenges in initiating change:

- There must be a compelling *case* for change.
- There must be *time* to change.

DOI: 10.4324/9781003217220-25

- There must be *help* during the change process.
- As the perceived barriers to change are removed, it is important that some new problem, perhaps previously unrecognised, does not become the new critical barrier.

It should be said at this point that *learning* organisations are not *per se educational* organisations; in fact, schools and universities have been left behind somewhat in this respect compared to new-economy and repurposed commercial organisations. In Senge's view, learning organisations are those where staff continually expand their capacity to create the results they desire: where new patterns of thinking are nurtured; where collective aspiration is allowed full reign; where staff are continually learning to see the big picture together – a common challenge in universities where teaching and research staff tend to have their own distinct views. Only those schools and universities that can adapt quickly and effectively will be able to excel in their chosen fields.

In order to be a learning organisation, two conditions must be present at all times.

- The ability to design the organisation to match the desired goals and outcomes.
- The ability to recognise when the direction of the organisation is not aligned with its desired goals, and the ability to take the necessary steps to correct this misalignment.

According to Senge's gospel, what distinguishes a learning organisation from one run on a traditional authority basis is the mastery of five basic 'disciplines'. The fifth one, systems thinking, is the most important one because it underpins the other four, and because consequently they all must develop as an ensemble. The fifth discipline is really what could be called the 'discipline of integration'. The five disciplines are:

1. *Personal mastery.* This is the discipline of continually clarifying and deepening a leader's personal vision, of focusing one's energies, of developing patience and of seeing things objectively. Leaders with a high personal mastery are better able to realise the goals that matter most to them, so this discipline starts with them simply identifying what matters most.
2. *Working with mental models.* These are deeply ingrained assumptions and generalisations that influence how leaders understand the world and how they take action. Working with mental models begins with leaders finding out what those ingrained assumptions are, and opening themselves to the influence of others.
3. *Building a shared vision.* For Senge, building a shared vision is a common theme in all leadership models, even trait theory. Many leaders have *personal* visions that do not become *shared* visions, just as some other leaders have wrongly *imposed* their personal visions on their organisations. Building a shared vision is the practice of unearthing shared pictures of the future that foster genuine

commitment and enrolment rather than compliance. It is not about *imposing* a leader's vision, but of *agreeing and building* one.

4. *Team learning.* This discipline starts with dialogue, which is the capacity of staff in a team to suspend their ingrained assumptions and enter into genuine thinking together. An organisation cannot learn unless its teams can learn together. Team learning develops the ability to look at the big picture beyond individual perspectives.

5. *Systems thinking.* This is the discipline that integrates the other four. Similar summative, integrating approaches were used in Covey's Seven Habits of Effective Managers (discussed in Chapter 15), in the Core Competence model (discussed in Chapter 22) and in Warren Bennis's so-called 'synthesis', his seventh ingredient in his transformational change theory (discussed in the previous chapter). Implicit in them all is the view that it is only possible to understand a system by looking at it holistically rather than looking at its constituent parts. Systems thinking allows patterns to become clear and ways to improve to become better defined.

Senge lists the skills for a new form of leadership needed to manage a learning organisation. Traditional leadership assumes that there is a lack of subordinate vision and that there is an innate inability among staff to cope with change along the lines of the pathogenesis described in Chapter 8. Leadership of learning organisations, on the other hand, is based on three activities: designing, stewarding and teaching.

• *Designing.* The leader must design the organisational shape and methods of working. A good organisation should be felt everywhere. Design should not be the traditional command-and-control model, but an empowerment model. The leader should design the organisation's policies, strategies and systems by understanding how they all fit together as a coherent whole, and, in schools and universities, how the system is connected to external stakeholders. Education leaders must ensure and manage the interaction between the five disciplines. The first step, according to Senge, is to develop vision, values and purpose. Leaders must live the vision through what they say and do. They must remember that staff learn what they know they need to learn, not what someone else thinks they need to learn. So a leader should design in such a way that the learning processes develop the ability of teaching and research staff to cope with real-life critical issues and with their own ability to learn.

• *Stewarding.* According to Senge, good leaders 'develop a larger story' to give a sense of purpose to their vision. Visionary leaders regard their organisation as a vehicle for their story, and therefore a vehicle to deliver their vision. Education leaders feel a sense of destiny that they are stewards of that vision. In a learning organisation, the leader sees vision as part of something larger, while listening to others and adapting constantly. The leader must ensure that the vision is shared and must avoid being possessive about it in ownership terms.

- *Teaching*. Senge means this to help people achieve a certain view of reality by focusing on purpose and systemic structure. The leader must help staff to see the big picture and understand the interconnections within the organisation. For example, in schools, do teachers know *why* the timetable cannot give them Wednesday morning with a certain class? Do lecturers in a university know *why* their subject department never gets first call on a certain lecture theatre? Leaders must foster a systemic understanding of the forces that shape change in the school or university; otherwise, the system will be dominated by events and firefighting. The strategic insights of effective leaders should become 'public' knowledge, although that also means being open to challenge. Leadership-teaching is not about teaching people to achieve the vision, but about fostering learning so that the vision is achieved through understanding.

In addition to these three leadership activities, other issues emerge, like managing creative tension. The school or university leader must highlight for others the performance gap between vision and reality, which can be a source either of inspiration or of defeatism. It pulls staff between the reality (the status quo) and the vision (the preferred future). Managing this tension is the central tenet of personal mastery, the first principle in Senge's list of five disciplines. The skills required of leaders are:

- To see interrelationships and interconnectedness, not snapshots of things and processes. The latter leads to seeing events and things in isolation, not as systemic.
- To avoid the tendency to blame staff. Most organisational problems are caused by poorly designed systems.
- To distinguish between detail complexity and dynamic complexity. The former arises when there are many variables in a situation; the latter arises when cause and effect are separated in time or space so that consequences are unclear. Educational leadership involves understanding dynamic complexity first and foremost.
- To focus on areas of high leverage where small but effective actions have a disproportionately large impact on performance. Finding these 'long' levers is often the key to solving a problem effectively and efficiently with minimum effort.
- To avoid symptomatic solutions. When something goes wrong, the natural tendency is to fix the symptom and not, as Senge put it, the 'underlying illness'. This again echoes the critique, offered in Chapter 8, on adopting a salutogenic approach to educational leadership. Fixing the symptom only postpones resolution because the problem almost inevitably re-emerges. The correct course of action is to delay imposing a temporary solution, but to continue to work on finding an *enduring* solution.

Visible leadership

Although transformational leadership is quite a noticeable or visible activity, it is not the same as 'visible leadership'. Visible leadership is about ego: leading and managing *because* it elevates status and gives credit to the leader. *In*visible leadership, by contrast, is recognising that one will *not* get the credit for much of the work done – that much of it will go to subordinates – which is more closely aligned to the transformational approach. Visible leaders use command-and-control approaches. They play politics. Invisible leaders try to create an environment where subordinates can take decisions. It is about understanding problems, not finding solutions *per se*. Invisible leaders empower and create opportunity for others; for those who 'follow'. They have the ability to transform the lives of colleagues without being noticed and without wanting to be applauded.

- The invisible leader encourages autonomous critical thinking instead of prescribing solutions, thus creating an environment of trust where staff feel empowered to solve their own problems.
- The invisible leader provides a system where individuals are prepared, trained and supported in their role, and regularly exposed to opportunities to develop their skills.
- The invisible leader provides a non-judgemental space, encourages collaboration and teamworking, and breaks down silo environments. In schools and universities, they make themselves aware of how their actions influence teachers, lecturers and researchers, and adapt their behaviour accordingly.

Clearly, there are echoes of Warren Bennis's work in Senge's Five Disciplines, although it would be unfair to call it a *folie à deux*. Bennis said that 'synthesis', his seventh ingredient, was about bringing all his other six together (see the previous chapter) – resolution and reflection, perspective, testing and measuring, desire, mastery, and strategic thinking – so in a sense, what Bennis called 'synthesis' is what Senge called 'systems thinking'. In some ways, Senge invented a new leadership theory only to discover that it was an old one! His important contribution is in linking leadership as a transformative endeavour to the organisation as a learning entity. His theory holds that systems thinking is the cornerstone of a learning organisation because it focuses on how the individual *interacts* with the other constituents of the system. Rather than focusing on individuals within an organisation, it looks at the *interactions* within the organisation and between organisations. This idea is becoming more important and more relevant in an increasingly connected education sector where services are outsourced by schools, colleges and universities, which are themselves networked together in 'chains' like Multi-Academy Trusts and university groupings. Senge's work is also tied to Meredith Belbin's work in the importance it places on teams, so in many ways, Senge's work is the accumulation of several previous theories; the natural conclusion to the progression that was started after trait theories were abandoned (see Chapter 2). That progression was not linear but circular, and Senge's transformational theory is not as far removed from trait theory as the historical timeline might suggest. Actually, Senge comes close to closing a circle with trait theory by developing his own post-modern take on it. For Senge, leaders have traits like passion, an inner voice, a sense of destiny, the innate ability to instil faith and offer hope, and when an organisation becomes a learning organisation, it is an almost spiritual experience for those involved. It's almost as if the Great Man theory of leadership has been reinvented as the Great Revivalist theory of leadership. Senge even uses a theological term, 'metanoia', meaning a change of mind on the way to repentance, to describe his preferred type of leadership through which individuals are regenerated or born again. True, it is not exactly the Fuhrer Principal or the Divine Right of Kings, where all power was thought to radiate from a leader who could do no wrong and who embodied in their persona the organisation itself, but Senge's theory *is* describing a sort of missionary-trait leadership that has somehow sidestepped the usual criticism and attained an appeal that defies analysis: part quasi-religious; part New Age collective; part political and manipulative.

This is not to diminish Senge's contribution. All of leadership theory is a continuum of sorts. Just as Douglas McGregor, the philosopher of democratic management, considered Bennis his protégé, so too did Senge borrow from Bennis.[1] And before that, within the behaviourist camp, how Kurt Lewin influenced Tannenbaum and Schmidt, who gave birth to contingency theory, who in turn influenced Blake and Mouton, who developed the concept of leadership orientation. Senge's great contribution was to incorporate all this into a sense of moral purpose, which is an approach to leadership that is particularly appropriate in education and which we will discuss in the next chapter.

Note

1 Coincidentally, all three were professors at the MIT Sloan School of Management!

26

DISTRIBUTED, INSTRUCTIONAL AND VIRTUAL LEADERSHIP

Distributed leadership

Distributed leadership is a conceptual and analytical approach to understanding how the praxis of leadership takes place in complex organisations like schools and universities. Uniquely, the theory was developed *in the field of education* at the turn of the century (Gronn, 2000; Spillane, 2006; Spillane et al., 2001), but its three underpinning concepts – 'activity theory', 'distributed cognition' and Wenger's (1998) 'communities of practice', discussed in this section – go back much further. Instead of focusing on traits or behaviour or situation, it sees leadership as a social process that occurs at the intersection of leaders, followers and situation. It looks at how leaders and followers engage in tasks that are 'distributed' across the organisation. It is not a behaviour as such, it is a process, and what we call 'practice' is the product of these interactions.

Distributed leadership was conceived as a framework for studying educational leadership that focused explicitly on how leadership was enacted as an activity distributed across social and situational contexts. Most leadership research in education until that point concentrated primarily on the characteristics, behaviours and effects of individual headteachers and principals, with an unhealthy focus on the headteacher-as-hero, although there were many exceptional researchers (e.g. MacBeath, 2011) who imported novel alternative approaches from disciplines outside education, and heroic trait theory was by then a discredited theory just begging to be usurped. Until the development of distributed leadership, most research in the field was anecdotal, descriptive, atheoretical and lack structure.

Instructional leadership (discussed later in this chapter) and transformational leadership (discussed in the previous three chapters) are in many ways competing

DOI: 10.4324/9781003217220-26

theories to distributed leadership, but distributed leadership, although unique in that it understands leadership as the shared effort by many people, is substantively in the tradition of Belbin and the transformational team advocates discussed in Chapter 23. It looks at leadership *throughout* the school or university (Harris & Jones, 2007) and is allied to the shared and collaborative approach of Douglas McGregor, the founder of modern democratic management. Distributed leadership draws on a multi-agent perspective to describe how the various internal stakeholders work to improve teaching, learning and research in schools and universities. Important to this approach is the belief that the role of leader and follower is dynamic: a person might be a follower in one situation but a leader in another; and followers are not passive recipients of leadership, but they also influence and exercise it. This is the concept of 'Leader Plus'; the view that leadership activity is something that is stretched (i.e. distributed) across many people in a school or university and (unlike instructional leadership) is often enacted by those *not* in official leadership positions.

When distributed leadership looks at the enactments of leadership *activity* rather than leadership *roles*, the 'configurations' (which do *not* correspond to particular activities) include collaborated, collective or coordinated distribution.

- *Collaborated* distribution is where two or more leaders co-perform the leadership activity in the same place and time.
- *Collective* distribution is where the performance of leadership actions is separate but the actions are interdependent.
- *Coordinated* distribution is where the leadership activities are performed in a particular sequence.

Distributed leadership is partly a task-oriented approach. It breaks down practice into manageable units of analysis, and it is this link to practice that connects the model to Wenger's 'communities of practice' and to 'distributed cognition', where thinking and learning is a process composed of interactions with other people, rather than constructed independently. Distributed leadership is also situational – although 'situate*d*' is the preferred term – in that the model sees situation as the third intersected element, alongside leadership and followership. In distributed leadership, situation is seen as a mesh of material and socio-environmental elements that include organisational culture, the estate and physical environmental, policy, staff maturity, financial security, market position, demand for change, and organisational structure. In distributed leadership, situation shapes, enables and constrains the practice of leadership practice, but whereas situational/contingency theory (described in Chapter 7) sees situation just as the context in which leaders act, the distributed model sees it as a *constituent part* of leadership, in that situation both influences and is influenced by the actions of people within it. In this respect, distributed leadership sits between those who see leadership as almost wholly the outcome of the agency of the individual leader, and those who see leadership as almost wholly the outcome of situation. Its underpinning concepts are communities of practice (Wenger, 1998), distributed cognition and activity theory.

Communities of practice

A full explication of Wenger's 'communities of practice' is beyond the scope of this book, but put simply, it is a theory of learning which assumes that social participation is the basic process by which we all 'get to know what we know' and by which 'we become who we are'. It views learning as social participation, and the primary unit of analysis is neither the individual nor the social institution, but the informal (so-called) 'communities of practice' that people form as they pursue shared interests. The theory is a social account of learning, exploring the intersection of community, social practice, meaning and identity.

Distributed cognition

Distributed cognition was developed in anthropology by Ed Hutchins (1994) whose work on naturally situated cognition – knowing what to do – led to the conclusion that cognition is socially distributed. Rather than looking for knowledge structures within an individual, Hutchins showed that cognitive activity was a situated process, influenced by other people, by tools and by the situation.

'Tools' and 'routines' are two important aspects of situation in distributed leadership. Tools are objects (like a hammer in another context) designed with the purpose of enabling some action. In organisations, tools include the assorted management techniques described in this book, such as matrices and grids (see Chapter 18), scorecards and dashboards (Chapter 14), ways of measuring responsibility (Chapter 20) and metrics for evaluating jobs (Chapter 21). These are not just accessories: they shape, enable and constrain the practice of leadership. Tools can help focus attention on particular management tasks, but they can sometimes obscure other things. A tool is a constituent of the task, not just an accessory. On the other hand, routines are regular patterns in the use of tools; repetitions of action that may or may not align with the tools used in the action. Both tools and routines can be designed institutionally or locally, or they can be received or inherited from previous regimes. Tools and routines take a portion of the cognitive load required to complete a task. For example, in assessing the quality of teaching in a university, the colleague doing a peer observation may be prompted to pay attention to particular shortcomings mentioned by students in previous evaluations, the Head of Department will review the peer review, and the routine of peer observation will improve the practice of observation. Thus, the enactment of leadership is distributed across the task of being observed, the task of doing the observation, the task of reviewing by the Head of Department, and the routine itself. This is the link with Distributed Cognition: that knowledge and thinking are 'distributed' across tools, routines, people, situation and context.

Activity theory

Activity theory is an approach in the social sciences to understanding human actions and the relationship between them, contextualised according to situation. It is an approach that seeks to understand the individual by analysing the collective rather than the individual. There are three generations of activity theory: the first generation was Vygotsky's (1962, 1978) model, which focused on the *individual*; the second generation was developed by Leontiev (1979) and expanded Vygotsky's model to include *collective* action; the third generation was developed by Engestrom (1987) and proposed a *networked* understanding of interactive activity systems (Wertsch, 1985). Rogoff (1995, 2003) expands this tripartite structure by emphasising the individual *and* the interdependence of the system, and by using three different levels of resolution – the interpersonal, the community and the institutional – to understand the different activities. Distributed leadership theory adopts Rogoff's networked and multi-level approach to give context to action and understand the link between agency and distribution. The theory also draws on Henry Mintzberg's (1989, 1992) organisational framework model, described in Chapter 15, although the Mintzberg model does not differentiate between managerial and non-managerial work, nor does it explain leadership *effectiveness* (Gronn, 2000; Spillane, 2006; Spillane et al., 2001).

Distributed leadership is most commonly used to cover or include the subsets of shared, democratic and collaborative leadership, and the distribution of leadership roles among staff. Its popularity in education reflects the demands on schools, colleges and universities to reflect better the fact that they are complex organisations with (more or less) equally qualified communities of practitioners. In that sense, distributed leadership has morphed from a conceptual framework into a normative framework – a practical dynamic leadership framework in the spirit of this book – which focuses on optimising the distribution of leadership to improve educational outcomes.

Instructional leadership

Like distributed leadership, instructional leadership is an education-specific model. It is essentially the management of curriculum and instruction by a school headteacher, college principal or dean. The term first appeared in school effectiveness research in the 1980s, which suggested that one key element in an effective school lies in its formal leadership, especially in low socio-economic status contexts. The research found that the ideal principal was determined, directive and charismatic (Edmonds, 1979), and subsequent reviews of empirical research by two of the theory's great exponents, Philip Hallinger and Ronald Heck, found that the effect of instructional leadership in school effectiveness was a positive one (Hallinger & Heck, 1996a, 1998).

Instructional leadership replaced the 'principal-as-hero' view of educational leadership when the accountability movement of recent times, with its emphasis on learning outcomes, encouraged the targeted management of teaching and the curriculum. Since then, instructional leadership has extended itself to 'leadership that is distributed among staff' – we can see immediately the misinterpretation of the term 'distributed' as something shared democratically *among people* rather than stretched *among tasks* – and to transformational leadership (Hallinger, 2003, 2009).

Instructional leadership today has both 'exclusive' and 'inclusive' approaches. The former regards the principal as the sole, *exclusive* holder of responsibility when it comes to setting goals for the organisation and developing instruction that enhances student attainment. This perspective focuses only on the role of principals as instructional leaders, but Hallinger (2003) has suggested conjoining it with team-focused transformational leadership (see Chapter 23) for reasons of complementarity. The latter (inclusive instructional leadership) sees leadership as *including* other school staff, reflecting the importance of collaboration between leader and teachers to develop curriculum and teaching that enhances student attainment. This inclusive approach is a type of distributed instructional leadership where the job of leader is to instruct the instructors, so to speak.

Another way of slicing instructional leadership is according to its 'narrow' (direct) and 'broad' ('indirect) activities (Southworth, 2002). A narrow perspective focuses only on immediate actions related to instruction, such as classroom observation and curriculum development. A broad perspective focuses on indirect activities such as creating an appropriate organisational culture in addition to the direct activities.

The essential components of instructional leadership

Whatever the preferred method for differentiating its sub-types, instructional leadership has some recognised and accepted characteristics. The model developed by Hallinger and Murphy (1985) has proved the most popular in empirical studies. In this model, instructional leaders have three key roles and, within each, have different functions:

- *To define the school mission.* The functional focus here is twofold: framing clear goals, and communicating them.
- *To manage the instructional program.* The functional focus here is threefold: supervising and evaluating teaching, coordinating the curriculum and monitoring student progress.
- *To promote a positive learning climate in the school.* The functional focus here is fivefold: protecting teaching time, promoting professional development, being visible, providing incentives for teachers and providing incentives for learning.

Murphy (1988) later added a fourth one: developing a supportive work environment.

Andrews et al. (1991) defined four strategies that instructional leaders typically use to enhance student achievement:

- Providing resources to attain learning goals, including materials, time, support, and pay and reward (see Chapter 19), and distributing them.
- Providing strategies and skills to get better teaching, more opportunities for continuing professional development, supporting teacher growth, monitoring teaching and whole-school performance.

- Promoting discussion about the school's vision, goals and culture. This involves constructing (with others) and selling the vision, and developing and managing an organisational culture that is conducive to building and maintaining quality instruction.
- Having a visible presence through face-to-face interaction with colleagues.

Review of empirical research on instructional leadership

The reviews of empirical research by Hallinger and Heck (1996a, 1996b, 1998), mentioned earlier, about the effects of principalship on student attainment identified three models of instructional leadership from the research literature:

- A 'direct effects model', where heads, principals and deans directly affect student outcomes without mediating variables. Regarding the direct effect of principalship on student outcomes, the Hallinger and Heck (1996a: 37) review showed that the effect is 'non-existent or weak or conflicting or suspect in terms of validity'. Leaders generally do not *directly* affect student achievement, or if they do, the effects are small.
- A 'mediated effects model', where heads, principals and deans affect student outcomes *indirectly* through mediating variables such as the school, college or university organisation. The mediated effects model was found to be more sophisticated theoretically, with stronger research designs and more powerful statistical methods. Hallinger and Heck (ibid) found that leaders significantly impact student performance *through mediating variables*, such as teaching and teachers, and other assorted organisational factors.
- A 'reciprocal effects model', where leaders and their organisations have an interactive relationship. Hallinger and Heck (ibid) pointed out that as yet there is no research to demonstrate this effect, but they thought it important to include because heads, principals and deans not only carry out their functions in ways that influence student attainment, but student attainment affects leaders as well. The two have a reciprocal relationship.

Other studies have shown that instructional leadership has a positive effect on teacher and student outcomes, and on teacher commitment and innovation in schools (Sheppard, 1996), although it is controlled by the context of the school, its size, community and the socio-economic status of its catchment area (Heck, 1992).

Virtual team leadership

Virtual team leadership came into its own in schools and universities during the Covid pandemic lockdowns of 2020 and 2021. The style might be opportunistic and the application one of necessity rather than choice, but virtual leadership was well established long before Covid-19 and, like all leadership models, has defining characteristics. The leader of a virtual team must be able to inspire and lead individuals and teams without meeting them, without seeing them every day and without being able to model appropriate and desirable behaviour in a visible way. It is appropriate to mention 'visibility' here in contrast to the instructional leadership described in the previous section, which had it as one of its three essential roles. Virtual leaders must show their teams and followers that they can be trusted to get the job of management done without the usual visible demonstration. The most important task is to agree, set and track short-term and medium-term goals. This might seem like a throwback to earlier accountability-inspired leadership models, but when followers are not physically in the same location, the only way that employee performance can be judged is by outcome.

Miller (2018) and Grzeskowiak (2020) list some essential skills that define virtual or long-distance leadership:

- *Be able to use technology.* Teachers, lecturers and researchers, and their managers, need to use various forms of video telephony and online chat services through cloud-based peer-to-peer software platforms to communicate and collaborate remotely, usually in combination with e-mail and text messages. Having many ways to stay in contact and many ways to use technology enables effective remote working. A virtual leader must embrace the technology.
- *Recognise achievements and encourage collaboration.* Virtual workers often feel like their contributions are overlooked because they are not 'there' physically to get (and enjoy) recognition in front of co-workers. Virtual leaders need to be able to find ways to recognise the efforts of teachers, lecturers and researchers who are working from home. It can be easy for remote individuals to become withdrawn and work only on solitary tasks. Leaders need to promote teamwork by collaborating themselves.
- *Be proactive about staying in contact.* This could take any number of forms, such as setting up weekly catch-up calls or having frequent short meetings. The virtual leader needs to be proactive about staying in contact with the entire team and staying abreast of what everyone is working on, how projects are progressing for researchers, what difficulties colleagues are facing in teaching, and what they need to do to overcome the obstacles.
- *Have great communication skills.* There is a lot more room for misunderstandings when working from home. Colleagues don't have the benefit of nuanced vocal tones, facial expressions and body language to help decipher what someone means (or how strongly they feel) when there is disagreement or ambiguity. The likelihood of miscommunications is high. Headteachers, principals, heads of department and deans leading virtual teams need to sharpen their communication skills and online interpersonal relationships. They must ensure that the tone of communications is appropriate and supportive, that instructions are clear and, most importantly, that they are concise. Leaders should give feedback and provide enough detail and direction to avoid being ambiguous and eliminate confusion. Too much communication is overbearing and decreases productivity and employee satisfaction.

- *Show trust and motivate colleagues.* Virtual leaders in education must show their followers that they (the followers) are trusted to get the job done. The leader must be able to motivate staff to perform at their best. The difficulty will be getting more out of employees than just 'getting the job done'; in education, getting the job done is never enough. It must be the best job *possible* that gets done!

- *Set and track goals.* Setting and tracking goals is the most important task. When followers are not physically in the same location, the only way that performance can be judged is by outcome. Specific, measurable goals are crucial, and monitoring progress frequently can help ensure that everyone stays on track and that problems are flagged and sorted before they become roadblocks to progress.

- *Have realistic expectations.* This refers to being realistic as to what colleagues can do during working hours, assuming reasonable availability. Working from home does not imply an unlimited amount of time working, nor should that be assumed by managers. One of the few benefits of lockdown-enforced working is greater flexibility. If that flexibility is reduced to zero because every hour is filled with 60 minutes of work, the quality of that work will plummet. Virtual leaders should be aware of this and not set unrealistic expectations. The quality of teaching and research does not correlate to the number of hours spent answering e-mails. The virtual leader should lead with empathy, build and maintain good interpersonal connections, and take the time to listen to colleagues and understand how they can be set up for success by providing adequate resources and IT support.

- *Be self-motivated.* If team leaders and middle managers themselves need a lot of direction, it is much more difficult to motivate dispersed individuals. The leader needs to be proactive in managing the managers, and plan and act in deliberate ways. It may be necessary to make fresh appointments to put the right people in charge of the right teams, creating schedules to track progress and ensuring that everyone understands the plans and the schedules, and where to find them. This will provide a sense of transparency.

- *Develop emotional intelligence.* A leader with high emotional intelligence develops stronger relationships with employees and empowers their teams to the maximum extent possible. Building strong relationships is one of the most important things the virtual leader can do. Stronger connections improve culture, collaboration and engagement levels in an organisation. Leaders who continually develop their emotional intelligence are better equipped to overcome challenging situations and inspire those around them to become the best versions of themselves. Emotional intelligence is comprised of four major components: self-awareness, social awareness, self-management and relationship management. All components are equally important and can benefit both leaders and staff.

The experience in schools and universities of the Covid lockdowns of 2020 et seq. illuminated the shortcomings of virtual leadership, especially when *ad hoc*. The first and most obvious is the danger of communication overload and a widening communication disjoint. When the volume of e-mails exceeds the ability of staff to read and make sense of them, a perverse effect is created in that staff have not *absorbed* the communication, but management have assumed that they have. The solution is threefold: manage the volume and avoid long chatty e-mails; use personal one-to-one e-mails where possible; and check informally but regularly that the communications sent out are being read and acted upon, developing a routine that does not come across as surveillance. It is preposterous to assume that staff deluged by e-mails while maintaining a research agenda and delivering taught programmes during a pandemic have the time or incentive to read three-page missives, however encouraging and upbeat. Remember: *ignored* communication is *no* communication.

The second shortcoming of *ad hoc* virtual leadership is failing to ensure that the diary leaves enough time for meeting overruns, which are inevitable when online contributions from attendees are almost always sequential.

Finally, staff in schools and universities should be assured of their leaders' availability so that they feel that the leader values their relationship. Staff should discuss with managers when it is appropriate to use text messages, e-mails and webcam meetings, and understand when these are necessary and when they are not. Enforced remote working can increase what may already be a downward pressure on quality. It is the leader's job to make sure that hindrances are removed at source.

REFERENCES

Aboud, J.M. (February 1990) Does performance based managerial compensation affect corporate performance? *Industrial and Labor Relations Review.* 43, 52–73.

Adair, J. (1973) *Action-centre leadership.* London, McGraw-Hill.

Adair, J. (1983) *Effective leadership: A self-development manual.* London, Pan Books.

Adair, J. (1987a) *Effective motivation.* Guildford, Talbot Adair Press.

Adair, J. (1987b) *Effective teambuilding.* London, Pan Books.

Adair, J. (1988a) *The action-centred leader.* London, Industrial Society.

Adair, J. (1988b) *Developing leaders: The ten key principles.* Guildford, Talbot Press.

Adair, J. (1989) *Great leaders.* Guildford, Talbot Press.

Adair, J. (1990) *How to manage your times.* Guildford, Talbot Press.

Addi-Raccah, A. (2006) Accessing internal leadership positions at school: Testing the similarity-attraction approach regarding gender in three educational systems in Israel. *Educational Administration Quarterly.* 42(3), 291–323.

Alvesson, M. & Einola, K. (2019) Warning for excessive positivity: Authentic leadership and other traps in leadership studies. *The Leadership Quarterly.* 30(4), 383–95.

Andrews, R., Basom, M. & Basom, M. (1991) Instructional leadership: Supervision that makes a difference. *Theory into Practice.* 30(2), 97–101.

Angelides, P. (2003) *Changing the structure of staff meetings: An efficient approach to staff development.* [Presentation] International Congress of School Effectiveness and Improvement (ICSEI), Sydney. January.

Ansoff, I. (1957) Strategies for diversification. *Harvard Business Review.* 35(5), 113–24.

Antonovsky, A. (1979) *Health, stress and coping.* San Francisco, CA, Jossey-Bass.

Armstrong, J.S. & Brodie, R. (1994) Effects of portfolio planning methods on decision making: Experimental results. *International Journal of Research in Marketing.* 11(1), 73–84. Available at: https://repository.upenn.edu/cgi/viewcontent.cgi?referer=https://www.google.com/&httpsredir=1&article=1022&context=marketing_papers Accessed 10 April 2020.

Baker, S. (2007) Followership: The theoretical foundation of a contemporary construct. *Journal of Leadership and Organizational Studies.* 14(1), 50–60.

Barber, M. (2001) High expectations and standards for all, no matter what: Creating a world-class education service in England. In: M. Fielding (ed.) *Taking education really seriously: Four years' hard labour.* London, Routledge. pp. 17–43.

Barney, J. (1991) Firm resources and sustainable competitive advantage. *Journal of Management*. 17, 99–120.

Barty, K., Thomson, P., Blackmore, J. & Sachs, J. (2005) Unpacking the issues: Researching the shortage of school principals in two states in Australia. *The Australian Educational Researcher*. 32(3), 1–18.

Bass, F. (1969) A new product growth model for consumer durables. *Management Science*. 15(5), 215–27.

Bass, B.M. (1990) *Bass & Stogdill's handbook of leadership: Theory, research, and managerial applications* (3rd ed.). New York, NY, Free Press.

Bass, B.M. & Bass, R. (2008) *The Bass handbook of leadership: Theory, research, and managerial applications* (4th ed.). New York, NY, Free Press.

Bass, F., Trichy, V. & Dipak, C. (1994) Why the bass model fits without decision variables. *Marketing Science*. 13(2), 203–23.

Bassett-Jones, N. & Lloyd, G. (2005) Does Herzberg's motivation theory have staying power? *Journal of Management Development*. 24(10), 929–43.

BBC (2008) *University of Bath replaces 'highest paid' vice-chancellor*. September 4, 2008. Available at: https://www.bbc.co.uk/news/uk-england-somerset-45406697 Accessed August 25 2020.

BCG (Boston Consulting Group) (1970) *Product portfolio matrix*. Boston, MA, BCG.

Beck, D. & Cowan, C. (1996) *Spiral dynamics: Mastering values, leadership, and change*. Cambridge, MA, Blackwell.

Becker, C., Glascoff, M. & Felts, W. (2010) Salutogenesis 30 years later: Where do we go from here? *International Electronic Journal of Health Education*. 13, 25–32.

Bedeian, A. & Wren, D. (2001) Most influential management books of the 20th century. *Organisational Dynamics*. 29(3), 221–5.

Belbin, M. (1981) *Management teams: Why they succeed or fail*. London, Heinemann.

Bennis, W. (January–February 1961) Revisionist theory of leadership. *Harvard Business Review*. 39(1), 26–32.

Bennis, W. (1973) *The leaning ivory tower*. San Francisco, CA, Jossey-Bass.

Bennis, W. (1976) *The unconscious conspiracy: Why leaders can't lead*. New York, NY, Amacom.

Bennis, W. (1989) *On becoming a leader*. New York, NY, Basic Books.

Bennis, W. (1993) *An invented life: Reflections on leadership and change*. Reading, MA, Addison-Wesley.

Bennis, W. & Biederman, P. (1997) *Organizing genius: The secrets of creative collaboration*. Reading, MA, Addison-Wesley.

Bennis, W. & Nanus, B. (1985) *Leaders: the strategies for taking charge*. New York, NY, Harper Row.

Bennis, W. & Thomas, R. (2002) *Geeks & geezers*. Cambridge, MA, Harvard Business School Press.

Berrio, A. & Henderson, J. (1998) Assessing customer orientation in public, non-profit organisations: A profile of Ohio State University Extension. *Journal of Agricultural Education*. 39(4), 11–17.

BESA (2021) *Key UK education statistics*. Available at: https://www.besa.org.uk/key-uk-education-statistics/ Accessed March 31 2021.

Blake, R. & Mouton, J. (1964) *The managerial grid: The key to leadership excellence*. Houston, TX, Gulf Publishing Co.

Blake, R. & Mouton, J. (1985) *The managerial grid III: The key to leadership excellence*. Houston, TX, Gulf Publishing Co.

Blanchard, K. & Johnson, S. (1983) *The one-minute manager*. London, Fontana.

Blanchard, K. & Shula, D. (1995) *Everyone's a coach: Five business secrets for high-performance coaching*. New York, NY, Harper Business.

Blanchard, K., Zigarmi, P. & Zigarmi, D. (1985) *Leadership and the one minute manager: Increasing effectiveness through situational leadership*. New York, NY, Morrow.

Block, F. (1990) *Post-industrial possibilities: A critique of economic discourse*. Berkeley, CA, University of California Press.

Bontis, N. (1998) Intellectual capital: An exploratory study that develops measures and models. *Management Decision*. 36(2), 63–76.

Bontis, N. (2001) Assessing knowledge assets: A review of the models used to measure intellectual capital. *International Journal of Management Reviews*. 3(1), 41–60.

Bontis, N. (2002) *Human capital study*. Santa Clara, CA, Saratoga Institute and Accenture.

Bowyer, J. & Christensen, C. (1995) Disruptive technologies: Catching the wave. *Harvard Business Review*. 73(1), 43–53.

Breyfogle, F. (1999) *Implementing Six Sigma: Smarter solutions using statistical methods*. New York, NY, John Wiley.

Bruch, H. & Goshal, S. (February 2002) Beware the busy manager. *Harvard Business Review*. 80(2), 63–9.

Bruch, H. & Goshal, S. (2004) *A bias for action: How effective managers harness their willpower, achieve results, and stop wasting time*. Cambridge, MA, Harvard Business School Press.

Buchanan, D. & Huczynski, A. (1997) *Organizational behaviour*. London, Prentice Hall.

Butler, A., Letza, S. & Neale, B. (1997) Linking the Balanced Scorecard to strategy. *Long Range Planning*. 30(2), 241–53.

Cain, S. (2013) *Quiet: The power of introverts in a world that can't stop talking*. New York, NY, Broadway Books.

Calkins, S. (1983) The new merger guidelines and the Herfindahl-Hirschman index. *California Law Review*. 71(2), 402–29.

Cameron, K. & Quinn, R. (1999) *Diagnosing and changing organisational culture*. Reading, MA, Addison-Wesley.

Carlyle, T. (1841) *On heroes, hero-worship, and the heroic in history*. London, James Fraser.

Catano, N. & Stronge, J.H. (2007) What do we expect of school principals? Congruence between principal evaluation and performance standards. *International Journal of Leadership in Education*. 10(4), 379–99.

Chaleff, I. (2009) *The courageous follower*. San Francisco, CA, Barrett–Koehler.

Clare, M. & DeTore, A. (2000) *Knowledge assets professional's guide to valuation and financial management*. San Diego, CA, Harcourt.

Cleverley, G. (1971) *Managers and magic*. London, Longman.

Cmglee (n.d.) Wikipedia. Available at https://en.wikipedia.org/wiki/Six_Sigma#/media/File:6_Sigma_Normal_distribution.svg Accessed September 3 2021

Coase, R.H. (1988) *The firm, the market and the law*. Chicago, IL, Chicago University Press.

Cooper, R., Edgett, S. & Kleinschmidt, E. (2002) *Portfolio management for new products*. Reading, MA, Perseus.

Conger, J.A. & Kanungo, R.N. (1998) *Charismatic leadership in organizations*. Thousand Oaks, CA, Sage Publications.

Cotton, J., Vollrath, D., Froggatt, K., Lengnick-Hall, M. & Jennings, K. (1988) Employee participation: Diverse forms and different outcomes. *The Academy of Management Review*. 13(1), 8–22.

Covey, S. (1989) *The seven habits of highly effective people*. New York, NY, Simon & Schuster.

Dawes, J. (2018) *The Ansoff Matrix: A legendary tool, but with two logical problems* (February 27). Available at SSRN: https://ssrn.com/abstract=3130530 or http://dx.doi.org/10.2139/ssrn.3130530 Accessed September 4 2021

De Bono, E. (1971) *Lateral thinking for management: A handbook of creativity*. New York, NY, American Management Association.

De Bono, E. (1985) *Six thinking hats: An essential approach to business management*. London, Little Brown.

De Feo, J. & Barnard, W. (2005) *JURAN Institute's Six Sigma breakthrough and beyond: Quality performance breakthrough methods*. Delhi, Tata McGraw-Hill.

Derue, D.S., Nahrgang, J.D., Wellman, N. & Humphrey, S.E. (2011) Trait and behavioral theories of leadership: An integration and meta-analytic test of their relative validity. *Personnel Psychology*. 4(1), 7–52.

de Vries, R. (2012) Personality predictors of leadership styles and the self–other agreement problem. *The Leadership Quarterly*. 23(5), 809–21.

Drucker, P. (1999) *Management challenges for the 21st century*. Oxford, Butterworth-Heinemann.

Dittmar, J. (2006) An Interview with Larry Spears. *Journal of Leadership & Organizational Studies*. 13(1), 108–18.

Duica, A., Croitoru, G., Duica, M. & Robescu, O. (2014) *The rise and fall of the BCG model. Proceedings of the 8th International Management Conference: Management Challenges for Sustainable Development, November 6th & 7th*. Bucharest, Romania.

Edmonds, R. (1979) Effective schools for the urban poor. *Educational Leadership*. 37, 15–24.

EFQM (1992) *Total quality management: The European model for self-appraisal*. Brussels, European Foundation for Quality Management.

Engestrom, Y. (1987) *Learning by expanding: An activity-theoretical approach to developmental research*. Helsinki, Orienta-Konsultit.

Epstein, M. & Manzoni, J. (1997) The Balanced Scorecard and tableau de bord: Translating strategy into action. *Management Accounting*. 79(2), 28–36.

Eriksson, M. (2007) *Unravelling the mystery of salutogenesis*. Helsinki, Folkhalsan Research Centre.

Eva, N., Robin, M., Sen, S., Van Dierendonck, D. & Liden, R. (2019) Servant leadership: A systematic review and call for future research. *The Leadership Quarterly*. 30, 111–32.

Fenn, J. & Raskino, M. (2008) *Mastering the hype cycle: How to choose the right innovation at the right time*. Cambridge, MA, Harvard Business School Press.

Fernandez, C. & Vecchio, R. (1997) Situational leadership theory revisited: A test of an across-jobs perspective. *The Leadership Quarterly*. 8(1), 67–84.

Fiedler, F. (1958) *Leader attitudes and group effectiveness*. New York, NY, McGraw-Hill.

Fiedler, F. (1964) A contingency model of leadership effectiveness. *Advanced Experimental Social Psychology*. 1, 149–90.

Fiedler, F. (1966) The effect of leadership and cultural heterogeneity on group performance: A test of the contingency model. *Journal of Experimental and Social Psychology*. 2, 237–64.

Fiedler, F. (1967) *A theory of leadership effectiveness*. New York, NY, McGraw-Hill.

Frankl, V. (2006) *Man's search for meaning*. Boston, MA, Beacon Press. [First published in German in 1946.]

Freeman, R. (2010) *Strategic management: A stakeholder approach*. Cambridge, Cambridge University Press.

Fripp, G. (n.d.) *BCG Matrix and the experience curve guide to the BCG matrix*. Available at: https://www.marketingstudyguide.com/the-bcg-matrix-and-the-experience-curve/ Accessed April 9 2020.

Furnham, A. (Wednesday 10 March 1993) Wasting time in the board room. *Financial Times*. p. 10.

Fullan, M. (1991) *The new meaning of educational change*. New York, NY, Teachers' College Press.

Galton, F. (1869) *Hereditary genius*. New York, NY, Appleton.

Garbutt, G. & Davies, P. (2011) Should the practice of medicine be a deontological or utilitarian enterprise? *Journal of Medical Ethics*. 37(5), 267–70.

Gardner, W.L., Cogliser, C.C., Davis, K.M. & Dickens, M.P. (2011) Authentic leadership: A review of the literature and research agenda. *Leadership Quarterly.* 22, 1120–45.

Garner, R. (Friday 7 February 2014) *What is 'the Blob' and why is Michael Gove comparing his enemies to an unbeatable sci-fi mound of goo which once battled Steve McQueen? The Independent.* Available at: https://www.independent.co.uk/news/education/education-news/what-is-the-blob-and-why-is-michael-gove-comparing-his-enemies-to-an-unbeatable-sci-fi-mound-of-goo-9115600.html Accessed March 20 2020.

Gove, M. (2013) *New randomised controlled trials will drive forward evidence-based research.* London, DFE. Available at: https://www.gov.uk/government/news/new-randomised-controlled-trials-will-drive-forward-evidence-based-research Accessed May 21 2013.

Graves, C.W. (1970) Levels of existence: An open system theory of values. *Journal of Humanistic Psychology.* 10(2), 131–54.

Greenleaf, R.K. (2002) *Servant leadership: A journey into the nature of legitimate power and greatness.* New York, NY, Paulist Press.

Greenleaf, R.K. (2003) *The servant-leader within: A transformative path.* New York, NY, Paulist Press.

Greenwood, R., Bolton, A. & Greenwood, R. (1983) Hawthorne a half century later: Relay assembly participants remember. *Journal of Management.* 9(2), 217–31.

Greiner, L. (1998) Evolution and revolution as organizations grow. *Harvard Business Review.* 76(3), 55–68.

Gronn, P. (2000) Distributed properties: A new architecture for leadership. *Educational Management & Administration.* 28(3), 317–38.

Grzeskowiak, R. (2020) *4 essential skills for virtual leadership.* Available at: https://www.bizlibrary.com/blog/leadership/virtual-leadership-skills/ Accessed May 21 2020.

Gu, Q., Sammons, P. & Mehta, P. (2008) Leadership characteristics and practices in schools with different effectiveness and improvement profiles. *School Leadership and Management.* 28(1), 43–63.

Hackman, J. & Walton, R. (1986) Leading groups in organisations. In: P.S. Goodman & Associates (eds) *Designing effective work groups.* San Francisco, CA, Jossey-Bass. Chapter 3.

Hagerty, M. (1999) Testing Maslow's hierarchy of needs: National quality-of-life across time. *Social Indicators Research.* 46(3), 259–71.

Haggbloom, S., Warnick, R., Warnick, J., Jones, V., Yarbrough, G., Russell, T., Borecky, C., McGahey, R., Powell, J., Beavers, J. & Monte, E. (2002) The 100 most eminent psychologists of the 20th century. *Review of General Psychology.* 6(2), 139–52.

Hakes, C. (2007) *The EFQM excellence model: For assessing organisational performance: A management guide.* Hertogenbosch, NL, Van Haren Publishing.

Hall, J. (1972) A comparison of Halpin and Croft's organizational climates and Likert and Likert's organizational systems. *Administrative Science Quarterly.* 17(4), 586–90.

Hallinger, P. (2003) Leading educational change: Reflections on the practice of instructional and transformational leadership. *Cambridge Journal of Education.* 33(3), 329–52.

Hallinger, P. (2009) *Leadership for 21st century schools: From instructional leadership to leadership for learning.* Hong Kong, Hong Kong Institute of Education.

Hallinger, P. & Heck, R. (1996a) The principal's role in school effectiveness: An assessment of methodological progress, 1980–1995. In: K. Leithwood, J. Chapman, D. Corson, P. Hallinger, & A. Weaver-Hart (eds) *International handbook of educational leadership and administration.* Dordrecht, Kluwer. pp. 723–83.

Hallinger, P. & Heck, R. (1996b) Reassessing the principal's role in school effectiveness: A review of empirical research 1980–1995. *Educational Administration Quarterly.* 32(1), 5–44.

Hallinger, P. & Heck, R. (1998) Exploring the principal's contribution to school effectiveness: 1980–1995. *School Effectiveness and School Improvement.* 9(2), 157–91.

Hallinger, P. & Murphy, J. (1985) Assessing the instructional leadership behavior of principals. *Elementary School Journal*. 86(2), 217–48.

Hamel, G. & Prahalad, C. (1994) *Competing for the future: Breakthrough strategies for seizing control of your industry and creating the markets of tomorrow*. Cambridge, MA, Harvard Business School Press.

Hargreaves, D.H. (2001) A capital theory of school effectiveness & improvement. *British Educational Research Journal*. 27(4), 487–503.

Hargreaves, D.H. (2003) *From improvement to transformation*. [Keynote address] International Congress of School Effectiveness and Improvement (ICSEI), Sydney. January.

Harris, A. & Jones, M. (2007) Middle leaders matter: Reflections, recognition, and renaissance. *School Leadership and Management*. 37(3), 213–16.

Hastings, C. (1993) *The new organisation*. London, McGraw-Hill.

Hazell, W. (Tuesday 11 June 2019) *Cambridge buys Durham Uni 11-plus test provider: Cambridge Assessment acquires Durham University's not-for-profit Centre for Evaluation and Monitoring*. *Times Education Supplement*. Available at: https://www.tes.com/news/cambridge-buys-durham-uni-11-plus-test-provider Accessed May 27 2020.

Heck, R. (1992) Principals' instructional leadership and school performance: Implications for policy development. *Educational Evaluation and Policy Analysis*. 14(1), 21–34.

Henderson, B. (1968) The Product Portfolio. *BCG Perspectives*, 66.

Henderson, B. (1970) *The product portfolio*. Boston, MA, The Boston Consulting Group.

Henderson, B. (1973) The experience curve reviewed: The growth share matrix or product portfolio, *BCG Perspectives*, 135.

Henderson, J. & Hoy, W. (1983) Leader authenticity: The development and test of an operational measure. *Educational and Psychological Research*. 3(2), 63–75.

Henton, D. & Held, K. (2013) The dynamics of Silicon Valley: Creative destruction and the evolution of the innovation habitat. *Social Science Information*. 52(4), 539–57.

Hersey, P. (1985) *The situational leader*. New York, NY, Warner Books.

Hersey, P. & Blanchard, K. (1969a) *Management of organizational behaviour*. Upper Saddle River, NJ, Prentice Hall.

Hersey, P. & Blanchard, K. (1969b) Life cycle theory of leadership. *Training and Development Journal*. 23(5), 26–34.

Hersey, P. & Blanchard, K. (1977) *Management of organisational behaviour: utilizing human resources* (3rd ed.). Englewood Cliffs, NJ, Prentice Hall.

Herzberg, F. (1968) One more time, how do you motivate employees? *Harvard Business Review*. 46(1), 53–62.

Hindo, B. (Wednesday 6 June 2007) *At 3M, a struggle between efficiency and creativity*. *Business Week*. Available at: https://www.effectuation.org/wp-content/uploads/2016/06/3m-struggle-between-efficiency-and-creativity.pdf Accessed April 7 2021.

Hoffman, E. (1999) *The right to be human*. London, McGraw-Hill.

Hoffman, B.J., Woehr, D.J., Maldagen-Youngjohn, R. & Lyons, B.D. (2011) Great man or great myth? A quantitative review of the relationship between individual differences and leader effectiveness. *Journal of Occupational and Organizational Psychology*. 84(2), 347–81.

Hofstede, G. (1991) *Cultures and organisations: Software of the mind*. London, McGraw-Hill.

Hofstede, G. (2001) *Culture's consequences: Comparing values, behaviours, institutions, and organisations across nations*. Thousand Oaks, CA, Sage Publications.

Hopkin, P. (2012) *Fundamentals of risk management: Understanding, evaluating and implementing effective risk management*. London, Kogan Page.

House, R.J. & Aditya, R.N. (1997) The social scientific study of leadership: Quo-vadis? *Journal of Management*. 23(3), 409–73.

House, R. & Mitchell. T. (1974) Path-goal theory of leadership. *Journal of Contemporary Behavior.* 3, 81–97.

Hughes, R.L., Ginnett, R.C. & Curphy, G.J. (1996) *Leadership.* Boston, MA, Irwin McGraw-Hill.

Hunt, J. (1992) *Managing people at work* (3rd ed.). London, McGraw-Hill Education.

Hunt, J. & Larson, L. (1974) *Contingency approaches to leadership.* Carbondale, IL, Southern Illinois University Press.

Hurwitz, M. & Hurwitz, S. (2015) *Leadership is half the story: A fresh look at followership, leadership, and collaboration.* Toronto, University of Toronto Press.

Hutchins, E. (1994) *Cognition in the wild.* Cambridge, MA, MIT Press.

Hutchison, D. & Styles, B. (2010) *A guide to running randomised controlled trials for educational researchers.* Slough, NFER.

Iarocci, J. (2017) *Servant leadership in the workplace: A brief introduction.* Atlanta, GA, Cairnway.

Imai, M. (1986) *Kaizen: The key to Japan's competitive success.* New York, NY, Random House.

Imai, M. (1997) *Gemba Kaizen: A commonsense, low-cost approach to management.* New York, NY, McGraw-Hill.

Imai, M. (2012) *Gemba Kaizen: A commonsense approach to a continuous improvement strategy* (2nd ed.). New York, NY, McGraw-Hill.

Ingham, B. (2019) *The slow downfall of Margaret Thatcher: The diaries of Bernard Ingham.* London, Biteback.

International Leadership Association (2008) *Leadership legacy programme, lifetime achievement award winner Warren Bennis.* Los Angeles, CA. Available at http://www.ila-net.org/LeadershipLegacy/Warren_Bennis.html Accessed March 31 2020.

International Organisation for Standardization (2011) *ISO 13053-1:2011 Quantitative methods in process improvement – Six Sigma – Part 1: DMAIC methodology.* Available at https://www.iso.org/standard/52901.html Accessed September 3 2021.

Irwin, D. (2002) Strategy mapping in the public sector. *International Journal of Strategic Management.* 35(6), 563–72.

Isaac, R.M. & Walker, J.M. (February 1988) Group size effects in public goods provision: The voluntary contributions mechanism. *Quarterly Journal of Economics.* 103(1), 179–99.

Itami, H. & Roehl, T. (1987) *Mobilizing invisible assets.* Cambridge, MA, Harvard University Press.

Jaques, E. (1956) *Measurement of responsibility: A study of work, payment and individual capacity.* London, Tavistock.

Jeffrey, S. (n.d.) *A complete self-mastery guide to breaking through resistance so you can actualize your potential (CEOsage).* Available at: https://scottjeffrey.com/self-mastery/ Accessed September 17 2020.

Jensen, S. & Luthans, F. (2006) Relationship between entrepreneurs' psychological capital and their authentic leadership. *Journal of Managerial Issues.* 18, 254–73.

Jones, S. (1992) Was there a Hawthorne effect? *American Journal of Sociology.* 98(3), 451–68.

Judge, T.A., Bono, J.E., Ilies, R. & Gerhardt, M.W. (2002) Personality and leadership: A qualitative and quantitative review. *Journal of Applied Psychology.* 87(4), 765–80.

Judge, T.A., Colbert, A.E. & Ilies, R. (2004) Intelligence and leadership: A quantitative review and test of theoretical propositions. *Journal of Applied Psychology.* 89(3), 542–52.

Judge, T.A., Piccolo, R.F. & Kosalka, T. (2009) The bright and dark sides of leader traits, A review and theoretical extension of the leader trait paradigm. *The Leadership Quarterly.* 20(6), 855–75.

Kanter, R.M. (1983) *The change masters: Innovation for productivity in the american corporation.* New York, NY, Simon & Schuster.

Kaplan, R. & Norton, D. (January–February 1992) The Balanced Scorecard – Measures that drive performance. *Harvard Business Review.* 70(1), 71–9.

Kaplan, R. & Norton, D. (September–October 1993) Putting the Balanced Scorecard to work. *Harvard Business Review.* 71(5), 134–47.

Kaplan, R. & Norton, D. (1996a) *The Balanced Scorecard: Translating strategy into action.* Boston, MA, Harvard Business School Press.

Kaplan, R. & Norton, D. (1996b) Linking the Balanced Scorecard to strategy. *California Management Review.* 39(1), 53–79.

Kaplan, R. & Norton, D. (1997) *The Balanced Scorecard.* Boston, MA, Harvard Business School Press.

Kaplan, R. & Norton, D. (2004) *Strategy maps: Converting intangible assets into tangible outcomes.* Boston, MA, Harvard Business School Press.

Kelley, R. (November–December 1988) In praise of followers. *Harvard Business Review.* 66(6), 142–8. Available at: https://hbr.org/1988/11/in-praise-of-followers Accessed September 23 2020.

Kelley, R. (1992) *The power of followership: How to create leaders people want to follow and followers who lead themselves.* New York, NY, Doubleday.

Kelly, A. (2001) *Benchmarking for school improvement: A practical guide for comparing and improving effectiveness.* London, Routledge.

Kelly, A. (2003) *Decision-making using game theory: An introduction for managers.* Cambridge, Cambridge University Press.

Kelly, A. (2004) *The intellectual capital of schools: Measuring and managing knowledge, responsibility and reward.* Dordrecht, Kluwer Academic Press.

Kelly, A. (2015) Introducing the concept of Salutogenesis to school leadership research: Problematizing empirical methodologies and findings. *International Journal of Leadership in Education.* 18(2), 167–77.

Kelly, A. (2016) Measuring research competitiveness in UK universities: Introducing the Herfindahl Index to the 2008 and 2014 research assessment exercises. *Assessment & Evaluation in Higher Education.* 41(8), 1206–22.

Kelly, A. (2020) The fifth phase of educational effectiveness research: The philosophy and measurement of equity. In: J. Hall, A. Lindorff, & P. Sammons (eds) *International perspectives in educational effectiveness research.* Cham, Springer. pp. 71–99.

Kenny, D.A. & Zaccaro, S.J. (1983) An estimate of variance due to traits in leadership. *Journal of Applied Psychology.* 68(4), 678–85.

Kerr, S. & Jermier, J. (1978) Substitutes for leadership: Their meaning and measurement. *Organizational Behavior and Human Performance.* 12, 62–82.

Kim, L. (Wednesday 29 April 2020) The real Frank Tassone and the true story behind HBO's bad education, *Town and Country.* Available at: https://www.townandcountrymag.com/leisure/arts-and-culture/a32291684/bad-education-hbo-true-story-frank-tassone-pamela-gluckin/ Accessed August 30 2020.

Kleiner, K. (2008) Rethinking leadership and followership: A student's perspective. In: R. Riggio, I. Chaleff, & J. Lipman-Blumen (eds) *The art of followership: How great followers create great leaders and organizations.* San Francisco, CA, Jossey-Bass. pp. 89–94.

Kopelman, R., Prottas, D. & Davis, A. (2008) Douglas McGregor's Theory X and Y: Toward a construct-valid measure. *Journal of Managerial Issues.* 20(2), 255–71.

Kotter, J. (1990) *A force for change: How leadership differs from management.* New York, NY, Free Press.

Kotter, J. (1996) *Leading change.* Cambridge, MA, Harvard Business School Press.

Kotter, J. (2002) *The heart of change: Real-life stories of how people change their organisations.* Cambridge, MA, Harvard Business School Press.

Kouzes, J. & Posner, B. (2012) *The leadership challenge.* San Francisco, CA, Jossey-Bass.

Kotter, J. & Heskett, J. (1992) *Corporate culture and performance.* New York, NY, The Free Press.

Kwak, Y. & Anbari, F. (2006) Benefits, obstacles and future of Six Sigma approach. *Technovation*. 26(5–6), 708–15.

Kwan, P. (2011) Assessing school principal candidates: Perspectives of the hiring superintendents. *International Journal of Leadership in Education*. 15(3), 331–49.

Landsberger, H. (1958) *Hawthorne revisited*. Ithaca, NY, Cornell University Press.

Lawrie, G. & Cobbold, I. (2004) Third generation Balanced Scorecard: Evolution of an effective strategic control tool. *International Journal of Productivity and Performance Management*. 53(7), 611–23.

Leithwood, K. (2001) School leadership in the context of accountability policies. *International Journal of Leadership in Education*. 4(3), 217–35.

Leontiev [Leontyev], A.N. (1979) The problem of activity in psychology. In: J.V. Wertsch (ed.) *The concept of activity in Soviet psychology*. Armonk, NY, Sharpe. pp. 37–71. Available at: https://people.ucsc.edu/~gwells/Files/Courses_Folder/documents/LeontievProblemofactivity.pdf Accessed September 13 2020.

Lester, S., Meglino, B. & Korsgaard, M. (2002) The antecedents and consequences of group potency: A longitudinal investigation of newly formed work groups. *The Academy of Management Journal*. 45(2), 352–68.

Lev, B. (2001) *Intangibles: Management, measurement and reporting*. Washington, DC, Brookings Institution Press.

Levačić, R. (2005) Educational leadership as a causal factor. *Educational Management Administration & Leadership*. 33(2), 197–210.

Lewin, K. (1936) *Principles of topological psychology*. New York, NY, McGraw-Hill.

Lewin, K. (1948) *Resolving social conflicts: Selected papers on group dynamics*. New York, NY, Harper & Row.

Likert, R. (1967) *Human organization: Its management and value*. New York, NY, McGraw-Hill.

Locke, E.A. (1991) *The essence of leadership: The four keys to leading successfully*. New York, NY, Lexington Books.

Lord, R.G., De Vader, C.L. & Alliger, G.M. (1986) A meta-analysis of the relation between personality traits and leadership perceptions: An application of validity generalization procedures. *Journal of Applied Psychology*. 71, 402–10.

Lovett, W.A. (1988) *Banking and financial institutions law in a nutshell*. Eagan, MN, West Publishing.

Luenendonk, M. (2015) *GE McKinsey matrix: How to apply it to your business*. Available at: https://www.cleverism.com/ge-mckinsey-matrix-how-to-apply-it-to-your-business/ Accessed April 15 2020.

MacBeath, J. (2011) *Learning in and out of school: The selected works of John MacBeath*. London, Routledge.

MacBeath, J. & Dempster, N. (eds) (2008) *Connecting leadership and learning: Principles for practice*. London, Routledge.

Mann, R. (1959) A review of the relationship between personality and performance in small groups. *Psychological Bulletin*. 56, 241–70.

Marsden, D., French, S. & Kubo, K. (2000) *Why does performance pay de-motivate? LSE discussion paper*. London, London School of Economics.

Mascall, B. & Leithwood, K. (2010) Investing in leadership: The district's role in managing principal turnover. *Leadership and Policy in Schools*. 9(4), 367–83.

Maslow, A. (1954) *Motivation and personality*. New York, NY, Harper & Row.

Mayo, E. (1949) *Hawthorne and the Western electric company, the social problems of an industrial civilisation*. New York, NY, Routledge.

McClelland, D.C. & Boyatzis, R.E. (1982) Leadership motive pattern and long-term success in management. *Journal of Applied Psychology*. 67(6), 737–43.

McGrath, J. (1962) *Leadership behavior: Requirements for leadership training.* Washington, DC, U.S. Civil Service Commission Office of Career Development.

McGregor, D. (1960) *The human side of enterprise.* New York, NY, McGraw-Hill.

McGregor, D. (1967) *The professional manager.* New York, NY, McGraw-Hill.

McGregor, D. Bennis, W. & McGregor, C. (1970) *The professional manager.* New York, NY, McGraw-Hill.

McKenzie, R.B. & Lee, D.R. (1998) *Managing through incentives: How to develop a more collaborative, productive, and profitable organisation.* Oxford, Oxford University Press.

McLellan, D. (1970) *The Young Hegelians and Karl Marx.* London, Macmillan.

McREL (n.d.) *Noteworthy perspectives: high reliability organisations in education.* Denver, CO, McREL. Available at: https://files.eric.ed.gov/fulltext/ED544261.pdf Accessed March 6 2020.

Megaw Inquiry (1982) *Inquiry into civil service pay: Command 8590.* London, Stationery Office.

Milkovich, G. & Newman, J. (2013) *Compensation.* New York, NY, McGraw-Hill.

Milkovitch, G.T. & Wigdor, A.K. (1991) *Pay for performance: Evaluating performance appraisal and merit pay.* Washington, DC, National Academy Press.

Miller, B. (Friday 5 January 2018) *What are virtual leadership skills? Talent.* Available at: https://hrdailyadvisor.blr.com/2018/01/05/virtual-leadership-skills/ Accessed September 19 2020.

Misumi, J. (1985) *The behavioral science of leadership: An interdisciplinary Japanese research program.* Ann Arbor, MI, University of Michigan Press.

Mintzberg, H. (1989) *Mintzberg on management.* New York, NY, Free Press.

Mintzberg, H. (1992) *Structure in fives.* New York, NY, Prentice Hall.

Mitchell, T., Biglan, A., Oncken, G. & Fiedler, F. (1970) The contingency model: Criticism and suggestions. *Academy of Management Journal.* 13(September), 253–67.

Mittelman, W. (1991) Maslow's study of self-actualization: A reinterpretation. *Journal of Humanistic Psychology.* 31(1), 114–35.

Morgeson, F.P. & Ilies, R. (2007) *Correlations between leadership traits and leadership styles* [Unpublished raw data]. East Lansing, MI, Michigan State University.

Moulin, M. (2017) Improving and evaluating performance with the Public Sector Scorecard. *International Journal of Productivity and Performance Management.* 66(4), 442–58.

Moullin, M., Soady, J., Skinner, J., Price, C., Cullen, J. & Gilligan, C. (2007) Using the Public Sector Scorecard in public health. *Journal of Health Care Quality Assurance.* 20(4), 281–9.

Muralidharan, R. (2004) A framework for designing strategy content controls. *International Journal of Productivity and Performance Management.* 53(7), 590–601.

Murphy, J. (1988) Methodological, measurement, and conceptual problems in the study of instructional leadership. *Educational Evaluation and Policy Analysis.* 10(2), 117–39.

Mulder, P. (2012) *Core quadrant by Daniel Ofman* (Toolshero.com). Available at: https://www.toolshero.com/communication-skills/core-quadrant-ofman/ Accessed September 19 2020.

Neely, A., Adams, C. & Kennerley, M. (2002) *The performance prism: The scorecard for measuring and managing business success: The scorecard for measuring and managing stakeholder relationships.* London, Prentice Hall.

Ng, K.-Y., Ang, S. & Chan, K.-Y. (2008) Personality and leader effectiveness: A moderated mediation model of leadership self-efficacy, job demands, and job autonomy. *Journal of Applied Psychology.* 93(4), 733–43.

Northcott, D. & Taulapapa, T. (2012) Using the Balanced Scorecard to manage performance in public sector organisations. *The International Journal of Public Sector Management.* 25(3), 166–91.

Oakland, J. (2000) *Total quality management: Text with cases* (2nd ed.). Oxford, Butterworth Heinemann.

Ofman, D. (2001a) *Inspiration and quality in organisations* (12th ed.). Antwerp, Kosmos-Z&K.

Ofman, D. (2001b) *Core qualities – A gateway to human resources*. Bleiswijk, NL, Scriptum Publishers.

Ofman, D. (2004) *Core qualities: A gateway to human resources*. London, Cyan Communications.

Ohno, T. & Bodek, N. (1988) *The Toyota production system*. Boca Raton, FL, Productivity Press.

Olson, M. (1965) *The logic of collective action: Public goods and the theory of groups*. Cambridge, MA, Harvard University Press.

Olve, N., Roy, J. & Wetter, M. (1999) *Performance drivers: A practical guide to using the Balanced Scorecard*. New York, NY, John Wiley and Sons.

Pan, H-L.W. & Chen, P. (2011) Challenges and research agenda of school leadership in Taiwan. *School Leadership & Management*. 31(4), 339–53.

Parsons, H. (1974) What happened at Hawthorne? *Science*. 183(4128), 922–32.

Pascale, R. (1990) *Managing on the edge: How successful companies use conflict to stay ahead*. New York, NY, Simon & Schuster.

Pauchant, T. & Dumas, C. (1991) Abraham Maslow and Heinz Kohut: A comparison. *Journal of Humanistic Psychology*. 31(2), 58.

Petrovic, G. (1991) Praxis. In: T. Bottomore, L. Harris, V. Kiernan, & R. Miliband (eds) *The dictionary of Marxist thought* (2nd ed.). London, Blackwell. pp. 435–40.

Piore, M.J. & Sabel, C.F. (1984) *The second industrial divide: Possibilities for prosperity*. New York, NY, Basic Books.

Polanyi, M. (1956) *Personal knowledge*. London, Routledge.

Porter, M. (1980) *Competitive strategy: Techniques for analysing industries and competitors*. New York, NY, Free Press.

Prahalad, C. & Hamel, G. (1990) The core competence of corporation. *Harvard Business Review*. 68, 79–91.

Prittie, T. (1972) *Konrad Adenauer 1876–1967*. London, Tom Stacey.

Pulic, A. (1999) *An accounting tool for IC management*. Available at: http://www.measuring-ip.at/Papers/ham99txt.htm Accessed March 30 2021.

Pyzdek, T. & Keller, P. (2009) *The Six Sigma handbook* (3rd ed.). New York, NY, McGraw-Hill.

Reddin, W.J. (1983) *Managerial effectiveness and style: Individual or situation*. Cambridge, MA, MIT Press.

Reddin, W.J. (1989) *The output-oriented manager*. Aldershot, Gower.

Reeves, M., Moose, S. & Venema, T. (2014) *BCG classics revisited: The growth share matrix*. Boston, MA, Boston Consulting Group. Available at: https://www.bcg.com/en-gb/publications/2014/growth-share-matrix-bcg-classics-revisited.aspx Accessed April 13 2020.

Rego, A., Vitoria, A., Magalhaes, A., Ribeiro, N. & Cunha, M. (2013) Are authentic leaders associated with more virtuous, committed and potent teams? *Leadership Quarterly*. 24(1), 61–79.

Reich, R. (1991) *The work of nations*. New York, NY, Vintage.

Retraction Watch (2014a) *Leadership journal to retract five papers from FIU scholar*. Available at: http://retractionwatch.com/2014/02/07/leadership-journal-to-retract-five-papers-from-fiu-scholar/ Accessed September 23 2020.

Retraction Watch (2014b) *Florida leadership researcher Walumbwa notches sixth retraction*. Available at: http://retractionwatch.com/2014/04/30/florida-leadership-researcher-walumbwa-notches-sixth-retraction/ Accessed September 23 2020.

Retraction Watch (2014c) *Univ: No misconduct, but 'poor research practice' in mgt prof's work now subject to 7 retractions*. Available at: http://retractionwatch.com/2014/11/14/univ-no-mis-conduct-but-poor-research-practice-in-mgt-profs-work-now-subject-to-7-retractions/ Accessed September 23 2020.

Reynolds, D., Creemers, B., Stringfield, S., Teddlie, C. & Schaffer, E. (2002) *World class schools: International perspectives on school effectiveness*. New York, NY, Routledge Falmer.

Reynolds, D., Stringfield, S. & Schaffer, E. (2006) The high reliability schools project: Some preliminary results and analyses. In: J. Chrispeels & A. Harris (eds) *School improvement: International perspectives*. London, Routledge. pp. 56–76.

Riggio, R. (2014) Followership research: Looking back and looking forward. *Journal of Leadership Education*. 13(4), 15–20. [Special edition]

Roberts, K. (1989) New challenges in organizational research: High reliability organizations. *Organization & Environment*. 3(2), 111–25.

Roberts, K. & Rousseau, D. (1989) Research in nearly failure-free, high-reliability organizations: Having the bubble. *IEEE Transactions on Engineering Management*. 36(2), 132–9.

Rochlin, G. (1993) Defining high reliability organizations in practice: A taxonomic prologue. In: K. Roberts (ed.) *New challenges to understanding organizations*. New York, NY, Macmillan. pp. 11–32.

Rochlin, G. (1996) Reliable organizations: Present research and future directions. *Journal of Contingencies and Crisis Management*. 4(2), 55–9.

Rodríguez-Carvajal, R., Herrero, M., Van Dierendonck, D., de Rivas, S. & Moreno-Jiménez, B. (2018) Servant leadership and goal attainment through meaningful life and vitality: A diary study. *Journal of Happiness Studies*. 20(2), 499–521.

Rogoff, B. (1995) Observing sociocultural activity on three planes: participatory appropriation, guided participation, and apprenticeship. In: J. Wertsch & A. Alvarez (eds) *Sociocultural studies of mind*. Cambridge, Cambridge University Press. pp. 139–64.

Rogoff, B. (2003) *The cultural nature of human development*. New York, NY, Oxford University Press.

Roos, J. & Roos, G. (1997) Valuing intellectual capital: The next generation, *Financial Times Mastering Management Journal*. May.

Russon, M.-A. (2021) *Uber drivers are workers not self-employed, Supreme Court rules*. BBC News. Available at: https://www.bbc.co.uk/news/business-56123668 Accessed February 22 2021.

Schaubroeck, J., Lam, S.S.K. & Cha, S.E. (2007) Embracing transformational leadership: Team values and the impact of leader behavior on team performance. *Journal of Applied Psychology*. 92(4), 1020–30.

Schön, D. (1983) *The reflective practitioner: How professionals think in action*. London, Temple Smith.

Scott, C., Stone, B. & Dinham, S. (2000) *International patterns of teacher discontent*. [Presentation] American Educational Research Association. New Orleans, LA. 24–28 April.

Scouller, J. (2011) *The three levels of leadership: How to develop your leadership presence, know-how and skill*. Cirencester, Management Books.

Sen, S., Eva, N., Butar Butar, I., Robin, M. & Castles, S. (2019) SLBS-6: Validation of a short form of the servant leadership behavior scale. *Journal of Business Ethics*. 156(4), 941–56.

Sendjaya, S. & Sarros, J. (2002) Servant leadership: Its origin, development, and application in organizations. *Journal of Leadership & Organizational Studies*. 9(2), 57–64.

Senge, P. (1990) *The fifth discipline: The art and practice of the learning organisation*. London, Century Business.

Senge, P. (1999) *The dance of change: The challenges of sustaining momentum in learning organisations*. London, Nicholas Brealey.

Sergiovanni, T.J. (1992) *Moral leadership: Getting to the heart of school improvement*. San Francisco, CA, Jossey-Bass.

Shamir, B. & Eilam, G. (2005) What's your story? A life-stories approach to authentic leadership development. *Leadership Quarterly*. 16, 395–417.

Sheppard, B. (1996) Exploring the transformational nature of instructional leadership. *Alberta Journal of Educational Research.* 42(4), 325–44.

Sidani, Y. & Rowe, W. (2018) A reconceptualization of authentic leadership: Leader legitimation via follower-centred assessment of the moral dimension. *The Leadership Quarterly.* 29(6), 623–36.

Slater, S. & Zwirlein, T. (1992) Shareholder value and investment strategy using the general portfolio model. *Journal of Management.* 18(4), 717–32.

Smith, M.K. (2001) *Peter Senge and the learning organisation (Infed).* Available at: https://infed.org/mobi/peter-senge-and-the-learning-organisation/ Accessed April 4 2020.

Southworth, G. (2002) Instructional leadership in schools: Reflections and empirical evidence. *School Leadership & Management.* 22(1), 73–91.

Spears, L.C. (2010) Character and servant leadership: Ten characteristics of effective, caring leaders. *The Journal of Virtues & Leadership.* 1(1), 25–30. Available at: https://www.regent.edu/acad/global/publications/jvl/vol1_iss1/Spears_Final.pdf Accessed September 14 2020.

Speel, P.H., Shadbolt, N., de Vries, W., van Dam, P.H. & O'Hara, K. (1999) *Knowledge mapping for industrial purposes.* Available at: http://sern.ucalgary.ca/KSI/KAW/KAW99/papers/Speel1/ Accessed October 21 2020.

Spencer, H. (1873) *The study of sociology.* Ann Arbor, University of Michigan Press. Reprint, 1969.

Spencer, T. (2013) *Product / Market expansion matrix.* Available at: https://www.spencertom.com/2013/10/09/ansoff-matrix/#.U60YwZSSz3Q Accessed April 7 2020.

Spencer, T. (2015) *BCG growth/share matrix.* Available at: https://www.spencertom.com/?s=bcg+matrix Accessed April 9 2020.

Spillane, J. (2006) *Distributed leadership.* San Francisco, CA, Jossey-Bass.

Spillane, J., Halverson, R. & Diamond, J. (2001) Investigating school leadership practice: A distributed perspective. *Educational Researcher.* 30, 23–8.

Stewart, T.A. (1997) *Intellectual capital: The new wealth of organizations.* London, Nicholas Brealey.

Stewart, T.A. (2002) *The wealth of knowledge.* London, Nicholas Brealey.

Stogdill, R.M. (1948) Personal factors associated with leadership: A survey of the literature. *Journal of Psychology.* 25, 35–71.

Stringfield, S., Reynolds, D. & Schaffer, E. (2008) *Improving secondary students' academic achievement through a focus on reform reliability: Four- and nine-year findings from the High Reliability Schools project.* Reading, CfBT Education Trust.

Tannenbaum, R. & Schmidt, W. (March–April 1958) How to choose a leadership pattern. *Harvard Business Review.* 36, 95–101.

Taylor, F.W. (1911) *The principles of scientific management.* New York, NY, Harper & Bros.

Teddlie, C. & Reynolds, D. 2000 *The international handbook of school effectiveness research.* London, Falmer.

Tennant, G. (2001) *Six Sigma: SPC and TQM in manufacturing and services.* Aldershot, Gower Publishing.

Thompson, G. & Vecchio, R. (2009) Situational leadership theory: A test of three versions. *The Leadership Quarterly.* 20(5), 837–48.

Thomas, A. (2007) Self-report data in cross-cultural research: Issues of construct validity in questionnaires for quantitative research in educational leadership. *International Journal of Leadership in Education.* 10(2), 211–26.

Torres, M., Zellner, L. & Erlandson, D. (2008) Administrator perceptions of school Improvement policies in a high-impact policy setting. *International Journal of Education Policy and Leadership.* 3(7), 1–15.

Trompenaars, A. & Hampden-Turner, C. (1993) *Riding the waves of culture: understanding diversity in global business.* New York, NY, Random House.

Tuytens, M. & Devos, G. (2010) The influence of school leadership on teachers' perception of teacher evaluation policy. *Educational Studies.* 36(5), 521–36.

Uhl-Bien, M., Graen, G. & Scandura, T. (2000) Implications of Leader-Member Exchange (LMX) for strategic human resource management systems: Relationships as social capital for competitive advantage. *Research in Personnel and Human Resources Management.* 18, 137–85.

Ulrich, D. (1996) *Human resource champions.* Cambridge, MA, Harvard Business School Press.

Van den Berg, G. & Pietersma, P. (2016) *Key management models* (3rd ed.). Harlow, Pearson/FT Publishing.

Varela, F., Thompson, E. & Rosch, E. (1992) *The embodied mind.* Cambridge, MA, MIT Press.

Vecchio, R. (1987) Situational leadership theory: An examination of a prescriptive theory. *Journal of Applied Psychology.* 72(3), 444–51.

Vygotsky, L.S. (1962) *Thought and language.* Cambridge, MA, MIT Press.

Vygotsky, L.S. (1978) *Mind in society.* Cambridge, MA, Harvard University Press.

Walton, M. & Deming, W. (1986) *The Deming management method.* New York, NY, Dodd.

Waters, T. & Waters, D. (eds) (2015) *Weber's rationalism and modern society: New translations on politics, bureaucracy, and social stratification.* New York, NY, Palgrave MacMillan.

Weick, K. & Sutcliffe, K. (2001) *Managing the unexpected: Assuring high performance in an age of complexity.* San Francisco, CA, Jossey-Bass.

Weick, K., Sutcliffe, K. & Obstfeld, D. (1999) Organizing for high reliability: Processes of collective mindfulness. *Research in Organizational Behavior.* 21, 81–123.

Wenger, E. (1998) *Communities of practice: Learning, meaning, and identity.* Cambridge, Cambridge University Press.

Wagner, D. & Spencer, J. (1996) The role of surveys in transforming culture: Data, knowledge, and action. In: Kraut, A. (eds) *Organisational surveys: Tools for assessment and change.* San Francisco, CA, Jossey-Bass. pp. 67–87.

West, M. (2001) Reforming teachers' pay: Crossing the threshold. In: M. Fielding (ed.) *Taking education really seriously: Four years' hard labour.* London, Routledge. pp. 169–82.

Wertsch, J.V. (1985) *Cultural, communication, and cognition: Vygotskian perspectives.* Cambridge, Cambridge University Press.

Whimster, S. (ed.) (2004) *The essential Weber: a reader.* London, Routledge. p. 269. [This chapter 19, *The vocation of politics*, was itself from P. Lassman & R. Speirs (eds) (1994) *Weber: Political writings.* Cambridge, Cambridge University Press. pp. 352–69.]

Wikipedia (2020) *Online image, no authorship.* Available at: https://en.wikipedia.org/wiki/Six_Sigma Accessed November 6 2020.

Womack, J. (2013) *Gemba walks* (2nd ed.). Boston, MA, Lean Enterprise Institute.

Wray, R. (Thursday 5 June 2003) Telecoms firm returns to roots after Global fiasco, *The Guardian.* p. 17.

Yang, R., Ming, Y., Ma, J. & Huo, R. (2017) How do servant leaders promote engagement ? A bottom-up perspective of job crafting. *Social Behavior and Personality.* 45(11), 1815–27.

Yukl, G. (1971) Toward a behavioral theory of leadership. *Organizational Behavior and Human Performance.* 6(4), 414–40.

Yukl, G. (2006) *Leadership in organizations.* Upper Saddle River, NJ, Prentice-Hall.

Yukl, G. & Van Fleet, D.D. (1992) *Theory and research on leadership in organizations. Handbook of industrial and organizational psychology* Vol. 3 (2nd ed.). Palo Alto, CA, Consulting Psychologists Press. pp. 147–97.

Zaccaro, S. (2007) Trait-based perspectives of leadership. *American Psychologist.* 62(1), 6–16.

Zaccaro, S., Kemp, C. & Bader, P. (2004) *Leader traits and attributes. The nature of leadership.* Thousand Oaks, CA, Sage Publications. pp. 101–24.

INDEX

Page numbers in **bold** indicate tables, page numbers in *italic* indicate figures and page numbers followed by n indicate notes.

Printed in Great Britain
by Amazon

43613286R00163